ISLANDS OF
DESTINY

OTHER BOOKS BY JOHN PRADOS:

In Country: Remembering the Vietnam War (written and edited)

Normandy Crucible: The Decisive Battle That Shaped World War II in Europe

How the Cold War Ended: Debating and Doing History

William Colby and the CIA: The Secret Wars of a Controversial Spymaster

Vietnam: The History of an Unwinnable War, 1945–1975

Safe for Democracy: The Secret Wars of the CIA

Hoodwinked: The Documents That Reveal How Bush Sold Us a War

Inside the Pentagon Papers (written and edited with Margaret Pratt Porter)

The White House Tapes: Eavesdropping on the President (written and edited)

Lost Crusader: The Secret Wars of CIA Director William Colby

Operation Vulture

America Confronts Terrorism (written and edited)

The Blood Road: The Ho Chi Minh Trail and the Vietnam War

Presidents' Secret Wars: CIA and Pentagon Covert Operations from World War II through the Persian Gulf

Combined Fleet Decoded: The Secret History of U.S. Intelligence and the Japanese Navy in World War II

The Hidden History of the Vietnam War

Valley of Decision: The Siege of Khe Sanh (with Ray W. Stubbe)

Keepers of the Keys: A History of the National Security Council from Truman to Bush

Pentagon Games

The Soviet Estimate: U.S. Intelligence and Soviet Strategic Forces

The Sky Would Fall: Operation Vulture: The Secret U.S. Bombing Mission to Vietnam, 1954

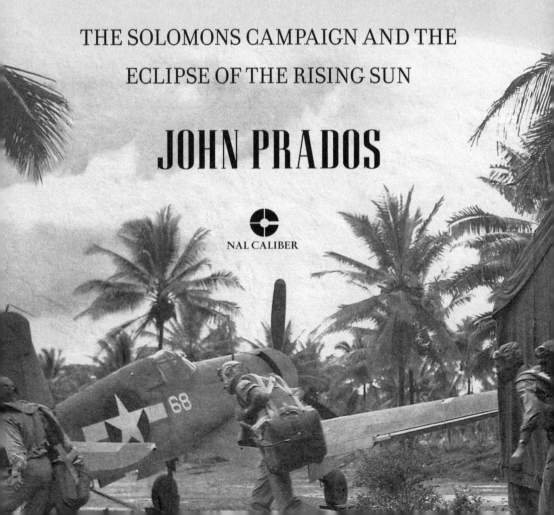

ISLANDS OF DESTINY

THE SOLOMONS CAMPAIGN AND THE
ECLIPSE OF THE RISING SUN

JOHN PRADOS

NAL CALIBER

NAL CALIBER
Published by New American Library, a division of
Penguin Group (USA) Inc., 375 Hudson Street,
New York, New York 10014, USA
Penguin Group (Canada), 90 Eglinton Avenue East, Suite 700, Toronto,
Ontario M4P 2Y3, Canada (a division of Pearson Penguin Canada Inc.)
Penguin Books Ltd., 80 Strand, London WC2R 0RL, England
Penguin Ireland, 25 St. Stephen's Green, Dublin 2,
Ireland (a division of Penguin Books Ltd.)
Penguin Group (Australia), 250 Camberwell Road, Camberwell, Victoria 3124,
Australia (a division of Pearson Australia Group Pty. Ltd.)
Penguin Books India Pvt. Ltd., 11 Community Centre, Panchsheel Park,
New Delhi - 110 017, India
Penguin Group (NZ), 67 Apollo Drive, Rosedale, Auckland 0632,
New Zealand (a division of Pearson New Zealand Ltd.)
Penguin Books (South Africa) (Pty.) Ltd., 24 Sturdee Avenue,
Rosebank, Johannesburg 2196, South Africa

Penguin Books Ltd., Registered Offices:
80 Strand, London WC2R 0RL, England

First published by NAL Caliber, an imprint of New American Library,
a division of Penguin Group (USA) Inc.

First Printing, October 2012
10   9   8   7   6   5   4   3   2   1

Copyright © John Prados, 2012
Maps by Jason Petho

LIBRARY OF CONGRESS CATALOGING-IN-PUBLICATION DATA:

Prados, John.
   Islands of destiny: the Solomons campaign and the eclipse of the rising sun/John Prados.
   p.   cm.
   Includes bibliographical references and index.
   ISBN 978-0-451-23804-7
   1. World War, 1939–1945—Campaigns—Solomon Islands.   2. Guadalcanal, Battle of, Solomon
Islands, 1942–1943. I. Title.   II. Title: Solomons campaign and the eclipse of the rising sun.
   D767.98.P76 2012
   940.54'26593—dc23   2012011417

Set in Spectrum MT STD
Designed by Alissa Amell

Printed in the United States of America

PUBLISHER'S NOTE
While the author has made every effort to provide accurate telephone numbers, Internet addresses, and
other contact information at the time of publication, neither the publisher nor the author assumes any
responsibility for errors, or for changes that occur after publication. Further, publisher does not have any
control over and does not assume any responsibility for author or third-party Web sites or their content.

For World War II veterans everywhere

CONTENTS

Map Symbol Key

	Allies	Japanese
Light Unit (or destroyer/s)	◐	◓
Light Cruiser	○	○
Heavy Cruiser (or unit)	◎	◎
Battleship (or unit)	●	◉
Transport Force	▲	▲
Aircraft Carrier (or unit)	■	■
Track (Surface unit/Carrier unit)	—— / -------	—— / -------
Maneuver Area	⌐ ¬	⌐ ¬
Naval/Air Base	⚓	⚓
Air Base (on land)	◆	◆
Ship Sunk	⊗ ▣	⊗ ▣

LIST OF MAPS

NOTE TO THE READER

Throughout the text Japanese names are rendered in the Japanese style, with family name first followed by given name. For consistency with the vast body of literature with which the reader will be familiar, however, diacritical marks in the names have been omitted.

There is a fatality, a feeling so irresistible and inevitable that it has the force of doom, which almost invariably compels human beings to linger around and haunt, ghostlike, the spot where some great and marked event has given the color to their lifetime; and still the more irresistibly, the darker the tinge that saddens it.

—Nathaniel Hawthorne,
The Scarlet Letter

INTRODUCTION

This is a book I have wanted to read for a very long time. Long enough, in fact, that I wrote it myself. Raised on a diet of heroic accounts of the Good War, increasingly detailed histories of every campaign and battle, the conflict which began at Pearl Harbor and ended with Japan's surrender became one of my special interests. Several aspects of the Pacific war fascinated or frustrated. One was the "turning point" of World War II in the Pacific. It seemed almost an entrenched interpretation among participants and historians that the Battle of Midway in June 1942 represented that decisive event. Japan might as well have surrendered right then. But for a young enthusiast this did not sit right. It did not take a great deal of exploration of the sources to realize that after Midway the military balance still favored the Japanese. The real turning point had to lie elsewhere, and my reading and research eventually supplied convincing evidence that the moment of decision occurred during the campaign for the Solomon Islands in the South Pacific. In roughly a year and a half, starting with the Allied invasion of Guadalcanal and ending in the Allies' siege of the Japanese bastion of Rabaul, the war situation was transformed. *Islands of Destiny* is my exploration of why and how that happened.

Among the many reasons that the Solomons campaign became the turning point that it did is the stellar performance of Allied intelligence—not just that of the United States but also Australian, New Zealand, and British intelligence officers, who contributed mightily to enabling thin forces to counter the adversary. Japanese intelligence proved much less adept. I discussed these issues some time ago in my book *Combined Fleet Decoded*, but, as a general war history, that work could not attain the depth and richness of what is presented here. More recently I have maintained that the next great challenge for historians of World War II is to take our increasingly deep knowledge of the shadow war and rewrite the battle and campaign histories incorporating the spooky side, showing much more concretely the contributions of the shadow warriors in proper relation to the visible evolution of military and naval combat. I believe that achieving that synthesis has truly become possible. My book *Normandy Crucible* shows the insights permitted by this approach for the Normandy breakout of 1944. In *Islands of Destiny*, I return to the Pacific Theater and apply the method to document what I argue is the real turning point of the war against Japan.

A Pacific history affords special advantage in this endeavor. Naval and air operations proceed by means of discreet, individual missions by fleets and formations. The historian can investigate the intelligence impact on such activities with specificity and present them in detail. This book does exactly that. The Solomons campaign is an especially fruitful illustration because it shows the effects of different kinds of intelligence activity—what I term the "pillars of intelligence"—in cooperation with one another. The impact of these pillars, as the reader will discover in these pages, was literally stunning. The Solomons became the decisive campaign in the Pacific in large part due to the contributions of intelligence.

By no means was intelligence the sole factor in the outcome of this struggle. The wisdom and determination of individuals, the quality of forces on both sides, the training and preparation of armies and navies, all played their roles. Technological developments were quite important too, and put the sharp point on the spear of armed force. *Islands of Destiny* discusses those matters as well. In addition it shines some light on the conflict's impact upon South Pacific islanders.

As a campaign fought among the islands, the war in the Solomons proved to be overwhelmingly about air and naval bases. The building and operating of them, their capture, the relative desirability of sites on different islands drove the fighting and determined its progress. Strategy revolved around obtaining the best combination of bases. In contrast to the war in Europe, where ground forces sought to conquer territory, in the South Pacific soldiers and Marines fought to secure possession of bases or sites for them. As a consequence, although the operations of all kinds of outfits are covered here, the narrative centers on the activities of naval and air forces, which were the arms the ground troops supported.

When I was a boy reading this history, I was repeatedly struck by its one-sidedness. Some authors were better than others, and official histories made a more explicit effort to look at both sides. There were very few works from a Japanese perspective. That grated. In *Combined Fleet Decoded* I noted that the problem for historians of the Pacific war is to explain how the Imperial Navy, so powerful in its day, could have achieved so little in exchange for its utter destruction. One element that sustains my proposition that the Solomons marked the turning point is that during this campaign the Japanese remained capable of giving as good as they got. Deterioration was just setting in. In the Solomons the Imperial Navy inflicted eleven major warship (cruiser and above) losses and endured the sinking of nine of its own big ships. But from the end of this campaign until their surrender, the Japanese managed to sink just two major enemy warships while losing dozens of their own. Examining this question is impossible without sustained attention to the Japanese—and to the intelligence.

Meanwhile, the focus on Allied actors and strategy in existing accounts also cried out for equivalent consideration given to the adversary. Historians have moved somewhat in that direction during recent years, and this book furthers the trend. With the Allied side of the war as familiar as it is, what is truly fresh—and fascinating—is more of the story told from the Japanese point of view. I have provided adequate coverage of the Allies while devoting considerable space to the little-known adversary.

Islands of Destiny is a classic military history. While the memory-versus-history debate continues, and works focused solely on personal experiences have furnished some vivid narratives, I prefer the big picture. This does not mean that individuals are ignored—the reader will find characters in these pages whose stories are quite extraordinary. Rather it means that individual feats are integrated into an overall narrative that explores every element of the story. A primary focus on memory impedes the search for larger truths. Identifying this campaign as a turning point, and presenting my reasons for that conclusion, requires a level of analysis beyond the personal narrative. I have nevertheless gone further into such narratives than elsewhere, as in the Normandy book. Here the reader will find accounts of Japanese sailors and soldiers that illuminate important themes and illustrate the Solomons experience in unprecedented detail. The idea of showing both sides is carried down to the personal level.

It is remarkable that at this remove, with so much having been written on the Pacific war, it is possible to present an account that is not merely derivative. I do indeed owe much to the giants in this field, and knowledgeable readers will recognize my agreement—and occasional differences—with arguments advanced by such historians as Samuel Eliot Morison, E. B. Potter, John Toland, Paul S. Dull, John B. Lundstrom, Richard Frank, Eric Bergerud, Robert Sherrod, Ron Spector, John Winton, and others, along with less well-known authors such as Samuel B. Griffith II, Edwin P. Hoyt, and Henry Sakaida. I have made substantial use of memoirs from both sides, official histories and documents, periodicals, and other material.

A few words are in order regarding Japanese sources, and I also wish to make special acknowledgment of groups and individuals who have labored in this vineyard with great benefit to the historian. I am not fluent in Japanese nor affluent enough to afford the kind of research and translation services required to access the Japanese literature. This led me to search for material that had been translated into English, which I have mined to considerable effect, as the narrative will demonstrate. The focus here on intelligence also opened the door to a huge array of Japanese information that had been translated at the time by Allied personnel, not just codebreakers but Nisei experts of the Allied Translator and Interpreter Section, the South Pacific Command, the Japanese language officers of the U.S. Navy, and other intelligence personnel. Their work afforded access to diaries, ships' logs, after-action reports, command directives, interrogations of captured Japanese, and a wealth of similar material. Let me give special thanks for their service.

Another acknowledgment needs to be made to the people who worked for the United States Strategic Bombing Survey and those who served in intelligence with the Supreme Commander for the Allied Powers in Japan after the war. Their efforts to uncover the Japanese side, including finding Imperial Navy veterans who became key intermediaries and sources, a host of interviews with former Japanese officers, the set of high-command directives, the action and movement records of major Japanese warships, a mountain of technical studies of the Japanese war effort and operations, and the set of monographs commissioned from Imperial Navy (and Army) officers. Together the intelligence records plus the postwar investigations furnished much of the raw material used here.

In addition I want to acknowledge the efforts of certain individuals whose enthusiasm for the subject has made available incomparable resources. The first of these people is the author John Toland. In researching his book *The Rising Sun*, Toland did what I could not—he went to Japan, hired a translator, and interviewed many Japanese veterans. Moreover, he did that in the 1960s, when many more of them were alive than is now the case, and with their memories fresher. Toland's careful notes, available at the Franklin D. Roosevelt Presidential Library and Museum, encompass far more than what he used in his history of Japan's war, and form a vital set of source material. Less ambitious but also drawn from Japanese participants is the work of Haruko and Theodore Cook. Historians Donald M. Goldstein and Katherine V. Dillon, through their association with Gordon W. Prange, developed an interest in the Japanese that led them to produce several collections of documents concerning Pearl Harbor and also, of key importance, a translation of the diary of fleet chief of staff Ugaki Matome. Finally I cannot leave the issue of sources without extending special thanks to historian Anthony Tully, author of important reinvestigations of the battles of Midway and Surigao Strait. On his Web site, www.CombinedFleet.com, Tully has created a priceless collection of material, much of it his own but also in cooperation with like-minded enthusiasts, on virtually every ship in the Imperial Navy as well as numerous related subjects.

Many persons helped in the compilation of the sources I used here. I am indebted to Jane Smith-Hutton, an OSS officer and wife of a senior U.S. naval intelligence expert, who provided important source materials and spent many hours illuminating for me the inner ethos of the Navy's World War II intelligence community. I had similar conversations with Phillip Jacobsen, one of the Navy's intelligence radio monitors actually on Guadalcanal. At a key moment in the writing Ron Spector lent me a vital set of documents. Louis Fisher graciously read a portion of the manuscript and commented on certain issues of international law. For special advice on the project I wish to thank Rena Szabo Masters. I also want to acknowledge John E.

Taylor, Judy Thorne, and Richard von Doenhoff at the National Archives (NARA). At the John F. Kennedy Presidential Library of NARA let me thank Stephen Plotkin and Michael Diamond. At the Naval Operational Archives I am indebted to Michael Walker, in particular, as well as to John Hodges, Kathleen Lloyd, and Gina Akers. At the Roosevelt Library I was assisted by Susan Y. Elter, John C. Ferris and Robert Parks. Elizabeth Mays of the Navy Department Library, Linda O'Doughda of the U.S. Naval Institute, and Edward Finney Jr. of the Naval Historical Center all provided valuable help. Some of these persons have passed away, retired, or gone on to other things since I conducted this research. Jane Smith-Hutton, an elegant and fine lady, passed away in 2002. Phil Jacobsen left us four years later, my last letter to him never answered. I especially regret the passing in 2008 of archivist John Taylor, who merits extra mention as a tower of wisdom, insight, and knowledge of the source material for many generations of researchers. Another figure, John Ferris, has become a noted historian of intelligence. Ellen Pinzur read and edited the manuscript and extended her usual cheerful support. These persons, individually and together, have contributed much to what is good about this book. I alone am responsible for its faults and omissions.

—John Prados
Washington, DC
July 2011

ABBREVIATIONS AND ACRONYMS

AA	Antiaircraft
AIRSOLS	Allied air command for the Solomons (also used for commander, AIRSOLS)
Belconnen	Station name for U.S. Navy codebreakers in Australia, 1942–1945 (aka FRUMEL)
CAG	Carrier Air Group
Cast	Station name for U.S. Navy codebreakers in the Philippines, 1941–1942
C-in-C	Commander in chief (Japanese)
CINCPAC	Commander in chief, Pacific Ocean areas
COMINCH	Commander in chief (U.S.—also the chief of naval operations)
CUB	Navy Base Unit
FRUMEL	Fleet Radio Unit Melbourne
FRUPAC	Fleet Radio Unit Pacific
GC&CS	Government Code & Communications School (British)

GI   Government-issue (common usage for a U.S. soldier)

G-2   U.S. Army Intelligence (also Southwest Pacific
                  Theater Intelligence)

HMS   His Majesty's Ship (in a ship name)

Hypo   Station name for U.S. Navy codebreakers at Pearl
                  Harbor, 1941–1943 (became FRUPAC)

ICPOA   Intelligence Center, Pacific Ocean area

IGHQ   Imperial General Headquarters

JNAF   Japanese Naval Air Force

MAG   Marine Air Group

NEGAT   Station name for OP-20-G codebreaking activities

NGS   Navy General Staff

ONI   Office of Naval Intelligence

OP-20-G   Codebreaking organization of the Office of Naval
                  Communications (aka Station Negat)

SBD   Douglas Dauntless dive-bomber

SEFIC   Seventh Fleet Intelligence Center

SNLF   Special Naval Landing Force

SOPAC   South Pacific Command (also used for commander,
                  South Pacific)

SOWESPAC   Southwest Pacific Theater command

TBF   Grumman Avenger torpedo plane

TBS	Talk Between Ships (low-frequency intership radio net)
USS	United States Ship (in a ship name)
VB	Navy carrier-based dive-bomber squadron
VF	Navy carrier-based fighter squadron
VMF	Marine fighter squadron
VMSB	Marine scout bomber squadron
VSB	Navy carrier-based scout bomber squadron

ISLANDS OF DESTINY

PROLOGUE

THE JAPANESE AFTER MIDWAY

The sky was fair, and aboard the battleship *Yamato*, flagship of the Imperial Japanese Navy's vaunted Combined Fleet, sailors traded winter uniforms for summer ones. The heat could be brutal in the Pacific's middle latitudes where *Yamato* cruised. Rear Admiral Ugaki Matome saw the desirability of lighter clothing, but he remained attired in his old gear. He had other concerns.

As fleet chief of staff, Ugaki struggled to understand what had just happened. Only days before, the Navy, with a huge preponderance of force, had advanced on Midway Island, to be dealt a stinging defeat by Americans inferior in almost every respect. This day, June 10, 1942, offered an opportunity to review the debacle with senior officers of the First Air Fleet, the carrier task force that had suffered stunning losses, also known as the Nagumo Force for its commander, Vice Admiral Nagumo Chuichi, and by its operational nomenclature, the Striking Force, or *Kido Butai*. Light cruiser *Nagara* took advantage of a calm sea to approach the *Yamato*, lowering a boat to carry Nagumo across to the flagship. Officers were unceremoniously bundled into straw mats to be lowered to the waiting launch.

For days since Midway little had gone well. Ugaki's burdens were many. Fleet staff walked around in a daze. While serving the officers, steward Noda Mitsuharu noticed air staff officer Commander Sasaki Akira acting as if he were personally responsible for the Navy's defeat. Sasaki's eyes showed his lack of sleep, and, unshaven, he sat impassive in the operations room. The big boss, Combined Fleet commander in chief (C-in-C) Admiral Yamamoto Isoroku, his own eyes glittering strangely, had disappeared after the final, horrific news. Yamamoto had taken to bed for several days, eating nothing. He'd now been diagnosed with roundworms.

Insult had been added to injury when destroyer *Isonami* ran down another screening ship, *Uranami*, during a routine course change to avoid suspected submarines. At Midway the Imperial Navy had lost a prized heavy cruiser, the *Mikuma*, when she was crippled by collision with another warship and could no longer evade the enemy bombers.

Admiral Yamamoto finally reappeared on the *Yamato*'s compass bridge sipping rice gruel. Ugaki professed joy, for Yamamoto was the soul of the fleet, acknowledged as its most brilliant leader. *Isonami*'s collision brought back sour thoughts of the *Mikuma*, but both men knew the really disastrous result was the destruction of *Kido Butai*'s main strength—all four fleet carriers committed to Midway. Now they would review the battle with Nagumo's officers.

Among those who boarded the *Yamato* were *Kido Butai*'s chief of staff, Rear Admiral Kusaka Ryunosuke, air staff officer Commander Genda Minoru, operations chief Captain Oishi Tamotsu, and the flag secretary. Their transfer had been simplified, ironically, because Nagumo and his staff had evacuated to the *Nagara* when their own flagship, the aircraft carrier *Akagi*, had had to be abandoned. Kusaka suffered minor leg wounds. But Genda was the one officer Admiral Yamamoto worried about. The power of *Kido Butai* air strikes, with which Yamamoto had struck Pearl Harbor and virtually swept the Pacific, derived precisely from Commander Genda's championing of concentrated carrier forces and his innovating tactics to employ the airpower. Now the crucial question was whether Midway called those tactics into question. The Imperial Navy did not know at the time that Allied codebreakers had divined the Japanese plan, enabling Admiral Chester W. Nimitz, the American Pacific commander, to position his fleet in ambush.

Nagumo's officers arrived early in the morning, and the staff conference dragged into the afternoon. Admiral Ugaki started on a conciliatory note, saying, "As the Combined Fleet headquarters, we realize our own fault, for which we extend our regrets." Specialists on both staffs then broke off to discuss their respective areas of concern. Combined Fleet and First Air Fleet seniors mulled over the vagaries of underway refueling, dangers of radio emissions under precombat conditions, and the shortcomings of *Kido Butai*'s dawn airborne search pattern. Mistakes had been made in arming the waves of strike aircraft, delays waiting to recover planes rather than launch fresh ones, and there were problems inherent in the overconcentration that had been built into the plan. Ugaki remarked that it would be good to have some carriers for fleet air defense entirely equipped with fighters. The chief of staff could see Admiral Kusaka afflicted by guilt and tried to buck him up, pressing yen and other gifts into his hands and extending assurances. Yamamoto, who had told his own staff at the height of the catastrophe, "I am the only one who must apologize to His Majesty," rejected proffered apologies from Nagumo's officers. "This present setback has not made us at all pessimistic," Ugaki told Kusaka. "We still intend to try the Midway operation again and also to carry out the southern operation."

Admiral Ugaki understood the war situation in the wake of Midway perfectly. "Above all," he told Kusaka, "to rehabilitate the fleet air force is imperative." That was the main reason for the *Yamato* confab, as well as why Yamamoto ordered Genda to go ahead to Japan in a seaplane as soon as his ship reached flying range of the Empire. The commander would manage the reorganization of carrier air groups. The Japanese officers correctly marked Midway as a serious defeat, but they were also right not to regard it as a crippling one. And the Navy already had another plan, the "southern operation," on the drawing board.

Captain Tomioka Sadatoshi later told friends of the dour atmosphere at the Navy General Staff as the news arrived dispatch upon dispatch. But the horror among his colleagues—Baron Tomioka was operations chief—flowed as much from dawning realization of Midway's implications for the South Pacific scheme as it did from the sheer tragedy. Whatever the concrete effects, the Navy General Staff (NGS) treated Midway as an embarrassment. The high command began by delays informing Emperor Hirohito of events. Hirohito received his first news only when the *Kido Butai*'s power had been broken, half its carriers sunk, the others floating derelicts soon to founder or be scuttled. It is not clear that NGS fully admitted the losses. Lord Privy Seal Marquis Kido, possibly the emperor's closest associate, heard from a naval aide twenty-four hours later. Hirohito spent almost a day closeted with Navy officers, and Kido met with Japanese aeronautical experts and industrial leaders. The emperor saw Marquis Kido only on June 8. Hirohito strove to minimize the crisis, indicating to Kido the losses were serious—deplorable—but the Navy must carry on. Speaking to Admiral Nagano

Osami, chief of the General Staff, the emperor demanded he continue boldly and work to prevent falling morale.

The Navy followed the emperor's lead, minimizing the public face it put on the disaster, but it is equally probable the naval authorities did this for their own reasons. Everything about Midway was held in the strictest secrecy. Sailors on returning ships were restricted on shore leave and ordered to say nothing. Yamamoto's battleship force, the Main Body, reached its anchorage at Hashirajima on June 14. More than six hundred wounded and injured crewmen brought home aboard the hospital ships *Mikawa Maru* and *Takasago Maru* were taken by night and kept incommunicado in hospitals at the Sasebo and Kure naval bases. Other injured seamen were treated at Yokosuka naval hospital under identical protocols. On June 10 the Navy released an official communiqué on Midway, describing it as a victory, admitting to the loss of a single flattop as against two American ones. The true situation was that the Imperial Navy had lost four fleet carriers and a heavy cruiser and the Americans a single equivalent, the *Yorktown.** Emperor Hirohito discussed issuing an imperial rescript that would honor participants—and naturally add to the misinformation—but courtiers dissuaded him.

The Navy's dissimulation crossed the line when it avoided telling the Japanese Army the true state of affairs. In Tokyo's system the Navy and Army were equal partners in an Imperial General Headquarters (IGHQ), and policy was not so much coordinated as carried out in parallel, with each service contributing as necessary to achieve the jointly agreed aims. The services negotiated "central agreements" on operations and were then to furnish requisite forces. By not providing accurate information, the Navy left Army planners under the impression that Japan possessed more capability than it did. There is conflicting evidence on whether Japanese prime minister Tojo Hideki, an Army general, knew the real score, but that knowledge did not extend very far within the Army. At an IGHQ liaison conference coincident with release of the Navy communiqué, the NGS

---

*   This obfuscation may have resulted partly from confusion over U.S. losses. The Imperial Navy left the Midway battle area under the impression that one American carrier had succumbed to air attacks and another to submarine torpedoes. Actually the *Yorktown* had been the target in all the successful air strikes but had remained afloat to be finished off by submarine *I-168*. The Navy may have thought it had reported American losses accurately, but the key point is that it was suppressing Japanese ones.

briefed its sister service. The presentation hardly went beyond the public information. Judging from subsequent IGHQ decisions it seems likely the Japanese Army for a time remained ignorant. This set the ball rolling down a path of myopic strategic planning which led to fresh disasters.

Aboard the *Yamato* other meetings took place that held the key to post-Midway operations. The day after his arrival in port, Yamamoto convened those most heavily involved on his flagship. This brought back Kusaka Ryunosuke as well as Nagumo Chuichi—who had visited briefly when the task force anchored to present his own apology. Also there were destroyer commanders; the leader of the seaplane unit; and the commander of the Second Fleet, Vice Admiral Kondo Nobutake, with staff chief Rear Admiral Shiraishi Kazutaka. It was Kondo's force, supposed to execute the actual Midway invasion, that had lost the *Mikuma* and now had *Mogami*, instigator of the collision leading to that loss, in dry dock to replace her bow. Yamamoto and Ugaki assembled the group to discuss future plans.

The most important project on the table was the southern operation, which the Japanese code-named the "FS Operation." The FS plan aimed at isolating Australia by occupying islands enabling Japan to threaten its coast and break the sea-lanes linking the United States to the southern continent. FS, which referred to Fiji and Samoa, was a compromise solution to Tokyo's debate about invading Australia. Midway had been a Yamamoto initiative, carried out over the objections of the General Staff once the Combined Fleet commander threatened to resign. Now Midway was done—with appalling consequences—and the FS Operation was next up.

The FS offensive, in fact conceived by Baron Tomioka, had been enshrined in an IGHQ central agreement. Tomioka was third-generation Imperial Navy, born while his father superintended the naval academy at Etajima. Tomioka himself graduated the academy fifteenth in his class in 1917, and had been top among his cohort at the Navy War College. Later he taught strategy there. Captain Tomioka was brilliant—and one of few noblemen in naval service—but Combined Fleet's opposition to FS mystified him. Yamamoto argued that Japan would be overextended if it occupied the South Pacific islands, but did not apply that logic to his own scheme to take Midway as a preliminary to invading Hawaii. Tomioka was not averse to a Midway-Hawaii offensive *after* the FS Operation, and Combined Fleet ultimately accepted the reverse compromise. The South Pacific offensive would follow Midway. Yamamoto's concession at least brought Fleet plans back into line with the IGHQ concept.

Preparations for the Fiji-Samoa offensive were complete by the end of April. Strategists debated the alternatives. Under an NGS directive of May 18, the "southern operation" was tentatively set for early July. The companion Army document specified that Navy units were to assemble at Truk beginning on June 18. The *Kido Butai* would sail on July 1. It would support invasions of New Caledonia (July 8), Fiji (July 18), and Samoa (July 21). Yamamoto issued orders nominating Admiral Kondo as primary executor, with his Second Fleet backed by land-based aircraft of the Eleventh Air Fleet plus Nagumo's *Kido Butai*. The Japanese Army would provide troops for the invasions. It was immediately clear that this timetable could not be kept. When Admiral Nagano briefed Emperor Hirohito on June 8, he had finished with proposals to modify plans, including a two-month postponement of the FS Operation.

None of the Japanese, neither Yamamoto nor his NGS counterpart, Nagano, had any idea that their concern about southern waters might lead to a clash of arms. Decisions made on the other side of the world, in Washington, were drawing American attention to the same region. Both sides thought their South Pacific plans aimed at a backwater the adversary ignored. No one imagined themselves in a race for strategic position. That universal ignorance meant the actors stumbled blindly into what became the decisive campaign of the Pacific war.

Yamamoto Isoroku had earned his reputation the hard way. Over a long career the admiral had been fearless in advocating his causes, no matter how unpopular; perceptive in recognizing evolving technological and operational dynamics, working to incorporate or overcome them; and pragmatic in difficult circumstances. Yamamoto had been a central figure in the development of Japanese naval aviation, now crucial to the war. Before that he had backed naval arms limitation despite bitter cleavages regarding disarmament within the fleet. At the Navy Ministry during the turbulent 1930s, dismissing threats of assassination, Yamamoto had stood up to the political machinations of the Japanese Army. He was full of insights, some developed during three tours in the United States, one to study, the others as a naval attaché. Yamamoto appreciated the enormous energy and productive capacity of a nation against which the Imperial Navy had planned for decades.

When Tokyo began considering war, Admiral Yamamoto had counseled against initiating conflict. It was Yamamoto again who warned that in such a war Japan might explode for six months or a year—"go wild" was his phrase—but then go down to defeat. His view on an armed struggle, encapsulated in the aphorism that war with America would have to be ended by dictating peace terms in the White House, added up to the idea that Japan, after seizing what it could, would defend it so well an exhausted United States might desist. When a concept came to him for attacking Pearl Harbor, Yamamoto had recognized its possibilities—and he had overridden existing war plans to champion that, threatening the unthinkable—to resign as C-in-C—if his preferred course were not approved. The Midway maneuver had been a repeat performance. An April 1942 profile published in *Harper's* magazine considered Yamamoto "America's Enemy No. 2," right after Adolf Hitler.

In a way the admiral was now hoist on his own petard. The surprise attack at Pearl Harbor on December 7, 1941, so enraged Americans that they were not likely to stop until *they* could dictate terms in Tokyo. Startled by the pinpricks of early U.S. carrier raids in the Central Pacific, goaded by the mid-April Doolittle raid directly on Japan, Yamamoto had demanded the Midway invasion. Following almost exactly six months of struggle, triumphing everywhere, the Imperial Navy suddenly suffered staggering losses in a single fight. Defeat had eliminated two-thirds of Japan's fleet carriers, her most powerful weapons. How Yamamoto responded would determine much that happened in the next phase of the war.

The post-Midway reckoning culminated in a full-dress conference held over the weekend of June 20. Senior officers and planners from the Navy General Staff and the ministry, and officers from the fleet, all participated. It was cloudy with a light rain that Saturday morning at Hashirajima. The brass attended a reception and lunch, with talks in the afternoon. Kusaka

Ryunosuke of the *Kido Butai* presided over this part, where officers from the forces engaged at Midway recounted their experiences, advising changes in tactical procedure that could reduce the danger of fresh tragedy. Debate continued late into the night. Apart from anything else, the exchanges served as an auto-da-fé for the Combined Fleet.

A smaller group, the inner circle, gathered early on Sunday. Now the talk focused on measures to increase Japan's fighting power and compensate for the Midway losses. Among those present were the chiefs of the ministry's aeronautical bureau, its shipbuilding department, budget planners, and NGS staffers for naval administration and aeronautics. The Imperial Navy had already programmed two new classes of fleet carriers, one of them a large vessel with an armored flight deck, the other a more conventional design. *Taiho*, the supercarrier, had been under construction nearly a year. The design for ships of the *Unryu* class, ordered in 1941, was complete and the lead ship about to be laid down. The construction program would be modified, with the *Taiho* class increased to five vessels and the buy of smaller *Unryus* expanded to as many as fifteen. In addition the *Shinano*, a *Yamato*-class battleship already on the way, would be completed as a super-carrier instead. Admiral Ezaki Iwakichi described the ministry's building plans, and ministry officials, the General Staff, and Combined Fleet officers agreed on the figures. Ugaki's observation after the conference sums it up well: "What we need at present is numbers, and no choice remains in this respect."

But it would be two years before the first fruits of these decisions could take to the sea, and much longer until the new warship programs would be completed. Bridging that gap was the problem. There was a war to fight. Admiral Yamamoto was well aware that the massive U.S. building program for a "Two-Ocean Navy," adopted in 1940, would begin to kick in very shortly (indeed, the first vessels of American fleet and light carrier classes were about to be launched). Much anguished deliberation aboard the *Yamato* that day concerned stopgaps to get through the time of danger. For Ugaki the debate over which warships or merchant vessels could be converted into aircraft carriers seemed interminable. His take from Midway was that all the Japanese carriers had been lost due to hangar deck fires and inadequate damage control. The fleet would increase the proportion of fighters in its carrier air groups and work harder at defense. The striking force, *Kido Butai*, would be reorganized around the surviving fleet carriers *Shokaku* and *Zuikaku*, with slower or less capable vessels making up for the lost ones. Even older, slower ships, more vulnerable, would have to be used in a strike role, and must be prepared to make sacrifices. The Nagumo force, less formidable, would still pack a punch. This new Third Fleet was established in mid-July with Admiral Nagumo at its head.

Combined Fleet commander Yamamoto summed up the sense of the meeting. Shipbuilding must proceed. Fighting must proceed. Measures to reduce vulnerability would be taken. There was no time to lavish on conferences, however useful. Ugaki reinforced that message in private.

Beyond the question of platforms—air-capable warships—lay the issue of the planes themselves, along with aircrews and maintenance personnel. The Navy Ministry briefings that day had been based upon discussions within the "Red Bricks"—as officers knew the ministry building in Tokyo—which had considered those questions. This brought new decisions to increase the pace of training for pilots and other personnel. That will be considered later, but for the moment it is worth noting that one of the worst consequences of Midway from the Japanese point of view was the loss of experienced aircraft maintenance personnel on the four destroyed aircraft carriers. The ministry created new training courses for damage control and arranged that officer aspirants received instruction as part of their education. All this might improve the fleet in the future, but the inescapable fact was that the next campaign would be fought by forces in being.

Many histories of the Pacific war take it as an article of faith that Midway crippled the Imperial Navy, according superiority to the Allies. This is really a retrospective judgment, flowing more from how the war ended. Certainly the Ugaki diaries express none of the desperation that might be expected in the private ruminations of a senior commander suddenly faced with complete inferiority. Only after several weeks does the Combined Fleet chief of staff allude to the Midway results, and then he terms them the Americans' "small success." Prominent Japanese officers Fuchida Mitsuo and Okumiya Masatake, who collaborated on the first detailed account to appear in the

West of the Imperial Navy at Midway, similarly display no such fear. Recording the atmosphere at the Navy General Staff, they write, "The Japanese Navy still had more warships of every category than the United States Navy had in the Pacific." They were right.

If Midway did anything it was to affirm the decisive role of the aircraft carrier as the primary bearer of naval offensive power. Despite the grievous losses, on the day the *Yamato* anchored at Hashirajima and officers began their deliberations, the Combined Fleet still possessed eight aircraft carriers, twice as many as the U.S. Pacific Fleet. While it was true the Americans had three heavy carriers in the Pacific to Yamamoto's two, the Imperial Navy vessels had spaces for 382 aircraft, compared to 300 on the U.S. warships. Moreover, the Japanese had another carrier already fitting out to join the fleet and two more in late stages of construction. The American industrial colossus would deliver only small escort carriers during 1942, and more than two-thirds of them went to the Atlantic. The U.S. building program would not hit its stride until the following year. For the moment Japan retained the advantage.

As for aircraft, the Imperial Navy was as strong as it had been at the beginning of the war. Until May and June, which featured the successive carrier battles of the Coral Sea—the first significant action of the Solomons campaign—and Midway, Japanese air losses had been limited. Production kept pace. From the outset of fighting through the end of June, according to Imperial Navy records, Japanese naval air losses totaled 1,641 aircraft. Almost half occurred during the months of Coral Sea and Midway, the bulk in June and many of those at Midway itself. Over the same period aircraft deliveries numbered 1,620. The most significant shortfall was in single-engine attack aircraft—dive-bombers and torpedo planes—where 374 were lost against 240 new warplanes. Commander Okumiya Masatake, an air staff officer and experienced pilot, records that at mid-July 1942 the naval air force order of battle was slightly stronger in fighters than before the war, though it had declined by roughly a quarter in attack aircraft. Land-based medium-bomber strength was actually greater than it had been on December 7, 1941.

Apart from numbers of planes with the forces, the Imperial Navy was also in good shape with respect to new aircraft designs. It is hardly noticed in histories that two of the three fighters that promised significant advances over the Zero were already in advanced development. The J2M Raiden (Jack), already in prototype, had made its maiden flight in March 1942. Another warplane, the N1K1-J Shiden (George) prototype, was under construction. It would fly for the first time in December. The plane the Navy specifically intended to follow the Zero, the A7M Reppu (Sam), to be innovated by the Zero's designer and manufacturer, Horikoshi Jiro and Mitsubishi, had earlier been put on hold, but in April 1942 was dusted off, with specifications issued a month after Midway. A carrier bomber to replace the current standard was already present in small numbers at Midway, though problems forced the Navy to convert it to a scout. The next-generation bomber, also exhibiting problems, had been delayed but would be ready for carrier landing trials by the end of the year, and *its* follow-on existed as a prototype by May 1942. New-model floatplanes were being tested at that same time. Only in the category of heavy bombers were the Japanese significantly behind their adversaries.

As regards pilots, the Japanese were also in relatively good shape. The Navy had begun the war with nearly 2,000 pilots, almost all of them quite expert, and about half of whom were carrier-qualified. Careful studies later showed that most of the initial cadre had more than 600 hours of flying experience, many of them master pilots with thousands of hours in the air. A typical U.S. Army Air Force pilot in the autumn of 1942 went to the front with 300 flight hours. Casualties at Midway were not so bad as advertised. Study there shows that a large majority of *Kido Butai* aircrew returned despite the sinking of their ships. Somewhat more than a hundred crews or pilots perished. Again the worst aspect was that losses were concentrated among the carrier attack squadrons. The Imperial Navy would train about 2,000 new pilots in 1942. That summer, when the Solomons campaign began, it is estimated that over 85 percent of naval pilots still met the expert standard of more than 600 flying hours.

In other categories of naval strength the Combined Fleet was well off. The light carrier *Shoho* had been lost at the Battle of the Coral Sea in May. Until the sinking of cruiser *Mikuma* and the carriers *Akagi*, *Kaga*, *Soryu*, and *Hiryu* at Midway, she had been the biggest Japanese combatant to go down. Only a few other vessels had been sunk, fleet auxiliaries mostly, and no warship larger than a destroyer. Until now Japanese luck had held. They remained powerful. Admiral Yamamoto would need all his strength to meet the test of the Solomons.

Among those who made the pilgrimage to flagship *Yamato* was Rear Admiral Matsuyama Mitsuharu, who visited with Ugaki on June 17. Matsuyama was on his way to Truk in the Central Pacific to assume command of Cruiser Division 18. While it was customary to touch base with top leaders when taking posts under them, Matsuyama was closer to Admiral Ugaki than that. They had graduated together from Etajima in 1912. The three-year course there threw midshipmen into close proximity, playing sports and in classes. Over the years they had risen through the ranks, with the brilliant Ugaki promoted to captain first, but perhaps gazing longingly at the gunner Matsuyama, who had skippered a succession of cruisers and other vessels, where Ugaki advanced mostly through staff and school billets. Ugaki had been master of a cruiser and a battleship but spent only two years at sea. Then he had made admiral and been drawn away to yet more staff assignments. Matsuyama sailed the Pacific. It was a measure of their relationship that ten days before Pearl Harbor, with the press of fleet business so intense, Ugaki took the time to visit Matsuyama at Kure naval base, where his comrade supervised the barracks and guard unit. Matsuyama's return drop-by was a reunion of old associates, marking his first unit command. Admiral Ugaki had once led a cruiser division, but only for a few months. Now Matsuyama would lead a cruiser division too—but into battle. Ugaki wished him good luck.

Cruiser Division 18 was hardly the Imperial Navy's cutting edge. It comprised a pair of the oldest light cruisers on the active list, assigned to the "South Seas" (*nanyo*)—what the Japanese called the islands they had taken from Germany in World War I—and had then been mandated by the League of Nations. But Matsuyama's would be a seagoing command, and he expected, with the FS Operation impending, to play an important role.

It is not clear whether Admiral Ugaki told his friend that that endeavor stood in jeopardy. Less than a week later, two of Combined Fleet's key staff officers went to Tokyo to present fresh objections, including that the *Kido Butai* should not be expected to engage air bases, only warships. Concerned about the weather, Ugaki was relieved that his officers took the train. More important, however, was that the staffers would oppose a fully agreed IGHQ project. An appraisal filed at the end of June by the land-based air command the Eleventh Air Fleet deepened doubts. The air fleet argued that numbers of Zero-type fighter aircraft were insufficient and that Allied strength in New Guinea had to be neutralized. Admiral Tsukahara Nizhizo of the air fleet advocated delaying the invasions to begin with the New Hebrides in late September, New Caledonia and Fiji in October, and landings on Samoa only in November 1942.

There were renewed consultations during the second week of July. It now seemed the FS Operation could not be carried out even with a delayed schedule. The NGS first cut back the Samoa component to provide only strikes against that island; then it proposed indefinite postponement of the entire endeavor. On July 9, Combined Fleet agreed to postponement. On July 11, Emperor Hirohito approved. Combined Fleet also dropped a renewed attempt against Midway. Three days later the Navy General Staff issued Directive No. 112, canceling the South Pacific offensive. The NGS suggested substituting a foray into the Indian Ocean. Combined Fleet studied this idea. Having opposed the NGS Fiji-Samoa plan, Ugaki resisted a new Indian Ocean attack too. A cruiser-destroyer force that had sailed to the west coast of the Malay Peninsula to prepare for that mission had just reached the area when recalled.

With the demise of the FS Operation, strengthening the "Outer South Seas" (*soto nanyo*), as the Japanese called the South Pacific, became critical. The Eighth Fleet had been intended to besiege Australia once the FS maneuver created blockade lines. Now it was activated for defense instead. Unknown to the Japanese—and a harbinger of what was to come—the Americans were immediately aware of this. On July 12—the eleventh at Pearl Harbor—the daily intelligence summary issued by the U.S. Pacific Fleet recorded activation of the Imperial Navy's new Outer South Seas unit.

Vice Admiral Mikawa Gunichi was selected to lead it. Mikawa, who had shepherded the battleships of the Nagumo force, here enjoyed his first fleet command. He met his newly assigned operations officer, Commander Ohmae Toshikazu, at home in the Setagaya district of Tokyo on July 14.

That day the heavy cruiser *Chokai* was designated fleet flagship—again a Japanese action that appeared in U.S. intelligence summaries the same day. Escorted by two destroyers, Mikawa left Kure in the *Chokai* on the nineteenth. That had to be gratifying, since Mikawa himself had skippered this vessel less than a decade earlier. As Mikawa departed, Ugaki was in Tokyo conferring with ministry and NGS officials on aircraft production and the Indian Ocean plan. Mikawa headed for Truk, the big base in the Mandates where the Fourth Fleet controlled the sea, a place of mysteries that U.S. intelligence had sought to penetrate for years.

So the first mission entrusted to Rear Admiral Matsuyama would not, after all, be an opening move in the FS Operation. Instead his cruisers sailed from Truk to convoy the 11th and 13th Naval Construction Units to an island in the lower Solomons called Guadalcanal. The builders were to prepare an airfield at Lunga Point along its north coast. This installation would be vital, for the Japanese intended to fly planes hundreds of miles to the south and east. Guadalcanal was to be the springboard, projecting an air umbrella over Combined Fleet task forces if they ever advanced toward FS objectives. A seaplane installation already on nearby Tulagi would fly scouts, while strike aircraft from Guadalcanal provided the hard punch. The Eighth Fleet would operate in tandem with the 17th Army.

Of course, plans hardly survive contact with reality, and so it would be here. The construction units sent to Guadalcanal had little heavy equipment—just four tractors, half a dozen hand-pulled earth compactors, and materials for a mine railway. The Korean laborers were not enthusiastic. The site also turned out to be more difficult than expected.

Meanwhile Allied intentions were becoming a factor. Why the Japanese should have missed this remains a mystery. After all, the Allies had tried to mount a carrier attack on the main Solomons base, Rabaul, as early as February 1942. In May, when the Imperial Navy set up its seaplane installation on Tulagi, that too had been struck by American carriers even as the ships unloaded. The bombing became an opening chord in the Battle of the Coral Sea, in which American and Australian forces repulsed a Japanese attempt to conquer New Guinea. The salient points were that the Allies were very sensitive to activity in the Solomons–New Guinea area, and that they often struck Imperial Navy bases. Preoccupied with fresh maneuvers in the Indian Ocean, belittling the South Seas as Tokyo had been wont to do, or discounting the potential for an Allied offensive, the Combined Fleet paid little heed to the other side of the hill.

Hard realities needed to be recognized. Admiral Mikawa sent Commander Ohmae to investigate conditions. At Truk the operations expert found Fourth Fleet staff had no indications of any American attack in the Solomons. Ohmae went on to the new fleet's base, Rabaul, arriving at noon on the twentieth. A half-sunken wreck in Rabaul's Simpson Harbor demonstrated the Allies' interest in this target. Light smoke plumed from the crater of a nearby volcano. Ohmae found Imperial Navy officers suspicious of the new Outer South Seas command, and air officers anxious to leave. Base personnel laughed when Ohmae wanted a building to house fleet headquarters—a naval commander should be afloat. He countered that Admiral Mikawa wished to minimize risks to valuable warships. Captain Kanazawa Masao of the 8th Base Force reluctantly set aside a dilapidated wood-frame shack. Situated near Rabaul's cricket field, Eighth Fleet headquarters did not even have a toilet.

Japan might be powerful, but defending the *soto nanyo* would pose challenges. Another was revealed when Ohmae reunited with Mikawa at Truk. The *Chokai* reached there on July 24. At Truk there was a banquet hosted by Fourth Fleet commander Vice Admiral Inouye Shigeyoshi in honor of both Admiral Mikawa and his Army counterpart, General Hyakutake Haruyoshi. The 17th Army, it turned out, had been formed with a strength of just nine battalions—the equivalent of a single infantry division. That thin strength Hyakutake intended to concentrate against New Guinea. The Solomons might as well be on another planet. Meanwhile Inouye, concerned with his responsibilities in the Central Pacific, wanted no part of the Solomons either. At midnight on July 26, his Fourth Fleet ceded authority for the Outer South Seas to Mikawa's Eighth. After a couple of days listening to Inouye's briefs, Mikawa departed for Rabaul in his cruiser. The *Chokai* steamed into Simpson Harbor on July 31. After depositing Mikawa, Ohmae, and others at their new home, the warship left for Kavieng, a nearby port on New Ireland.

Vice Admiral Mikawa barely had time to get used to Rabaul's intense tropical climate. By early August the Japanese had almost completed the Guadalcanal airstrip. Then, one day at dawn, the waters offshore were filled with Allied vessels. Cruisers and destroyers bombarded Japanese positions on both Guadalcanal and Tulagi. Transports began to lower landing craft and fill them with troops. The campaign had begun.

I.

ALL ALONG THE WATCHTOWER

Every ship in the invasion armada was filled with men keyed to action. Aboard the command ship, USS *McCawley*, general quarters sounded at 3:00 a.m. Many were already awake. This was true for Colonel Clifton Cates, leading a regiment slated to land in the second wave, as well as for Lieutenant Herbert C. Merillat of the division intelligence staff. Aboard attack transport *American Legion*, war correspondent Richard Tregaskis awoke an hour later to find excited Marines already lining his ship's railings. All the vessels were darkened, smoking lamps out for fear of alerting the enemy. The dank fastness of Guadalcanal appeared a little after 1:30. About the time the fleet went to battle stations it split, one section headed to the big island, Guadalcanal, another for Tulagi across the water. On the *McCawley*, Major General Alexander Archer Vandegrift, leader of the 1st Marine Division, and Rear Admiral Richmond Kelly Turner, fleet commander, were full of hope. The weather closed in as they approached. Low cloud ceilings had kept Japanese search planes away. They might achieve surprise in this, the first major Allied offensive of the war.

With dawn a carefully choreographed sequence began with the order— the first of many times it would be issued—"Land the landing force." Soon afterward, aircraft from American carriers one hundred miles away swept in to strafe the invasion beaches. At about 6:15 a.m., cruisers and destroyers added their gunfire to the din. The Japanese were discombobulated enough that more than half an hour passed before their base at Tulagi alerted the 25th Air Flotilla at Rabaul that a bombardment was under way and invasion preparations visible.

Events thereafter moved quickly. The attack transports glided to their assigned anchorages off Lunga Point and lowered Higgins boats and other craft. Most were worked by U.S. Coast Guard coxswains. Marines began climbing down into the assault craft. Lieutenant Merillat descended a cargo net to his boat at about 9:00 a.m. By then two battalions of Colonel LeRoy P. Hunt's 5th Marines were nearing Red Beach on Guadalcanal. On the Tulagi side the landing had already begun. Hunt's last battalion, along with the 1st Marine Raider Battalion and the 1st Marine Parachute Battalion, had engaged the Japanese. Coast Guardsman Douglas Munro waded ashore there to supply Turner with field reports. Boats grounded at Red Beach at 9:10. Colonel Cates's command group landed at 9:38, the initial echelon of division headquarters about twenty minutes later, among them Lieutenant Merillat, with reporters Richard Tregaskis and Jack Crane. Marines quickly seized the airfield and fanned out to establish a perimeter.

General Vandegrift wasted no time. He immediately ordered in Cates's 1st Marines, and behind that the divisional artillery, the 11th Marines of Colonel Pedro del Valle. He even widened Red Beach to hasten the landing. Glenn D. Maxon, a young lieutenant, led a platoon of the 1st Marines aboard the transport *Alchiba*. They hit the beach at 10:45. Corporal James R. Garrett was an ammunition handler with I Battery of the 11th Marines. He too reached the shore around this time. Coast Guard Lieutenant Commander Dwight H. Dexter brought in two dozen guardsmen early in the afternoon to implant a small boat unit, Naval Operating Base Guadalcanal. They set up shop at the manager's house of a Lever Brothers coconut plantation east of Lunga Point. Marine commander Vandegrift landed at 4:00 p.m. *Alchiba*'s skipper later observed that the physical effort of getting troops into assault boats and moving them to the beach taxed his sailors. Ensign Jack Clark would have agreed. Aboard the transport *Fuller*, he worked one of the boats landing the 1st Marines. Clark went ashore as "beachmaster" for Red Beach, managing the circulation of landing boats and the arrival of supplies, getting them off the shore. Clark's job became vital to the entire Allied enterprise in a way he could never have imagined. What supplies he landed would be all the Marines had.

The Japanese on Guadalcanal fled at the first sight of the invasion. That was probably understandable. The defense force consisted of only about 500 naval infantry. These Special Naval Landing Forces (SNLF) were tough troops, but they had no chance against more than 12,000 U.S. Marines. Captain Monzen Kanae's 1,700 construction workers, who made up the bulk of the Imperial Navy complement, hardly figured in the equation. In fact, the SNLF were responsible for their safety.

The t day ended with American control unchallenged save for some tough fighting on Tulagi and the adjacent islet of Tanambogo, where the SNLF fought hard. The most important enemy resistance was an air attack on the ships offshore—and there the Allies had a remarkable advantage—advance notice from "coastwatchers," Australian and indigenous patriots who stayed behind Japanese lines and radioed warnings of enemy activities. The coastwatchers became a pillar of Allied intelligence in the Solomons.

BETWIXT PILLAR AND POST

Coastwatchers were able to hold on in the Solomons and New Guinea because of how the Japanese had occupied the islands. The Outer South Seas had never been Tokyo's major priority. Reserving most of its combat strength for the war in China, the Japanese Army viewed the "strike south," or Pacific war, primarily as an Imperial Navy venture. There is a backstory to Japanese interest in Australia that is rooted in the vagaries of national politics and the intense competition between Army and Navy for dominance in the government, but details are not necessary. It is sufficient to note that the Japanese Army sought to conduct its Pacific war as a sideshow, allocating just ten divisions to do everything—conquer Malaya, the Philippines, Burma, and the Dutch East Indies; garrison those places; and wage battle across the full range of Pacific islands. Thus the South Seas Detachment the Army set aside for the Bismarcks region—New Guinea and the Solomons—consisted of just 5,500 troops built around the three battalions of a single infantry regiment.

The Imperial Navy focused on the Mandates, or South Seas proper, and its prewar plans had not envisioned a Solomons campaign. Once it happened, forces were sufficient to garrison only a few posts. Except for small islands like Tulagi or big bases like Rabaul, the Japanese could do little more than patrol from their enclaves. Australian coastwatchers went on living on the same islands. Knowing the land better, and with the help of Melanesian friends, they evaded Japanese patrols with impunity. The Japanese selected their posts through staff studies. Vice Admiral Inouye Shigeyoshi of the Fourth Fleet had held war games at Truk a couple of months before Pearl Harbor. The *nanyo* commander realized that unless Japan held some positions in the Bismarcks, he would have a long open flank exposed to Americans or Australians. His war games showed the need for protection by air bases at key points. Inouye selected Rabaul and Gasmata on New Britain, Lae and Salamaua on New Guinea, and Tulagi in the lower Solomons as the most desirable positions. When IGHQ agreed to this aspect of the war plan, on November 10, 1941, the port of Kavieng on New Ireland was added. A few days later the Army's South Seas Detachment issued a pamphlet to familiarize its soldiers with the Bismarck Archipelago. The detachment's initial operation, immediately after Pearl Harbor, had been to capture the island of Guam in the Mandates. On December 9, as that battle ended, Australian coastwatcher Cornelius Page reported Japanese scout planes flying toward Rabaul, the first confirmed report from the Bismarcks. Rabaul, defended by just a pair of Australian antiaircraft guns, was bombed by big Japanese flying boats at the end of December.

On January 4, 1942, the Combined Fleet ordered Admiral Inouye to execute the Bismarcks offensive, code-named the "R Operation." A Japanese Army companion order alerted the South Seas Detachment. The same day twenty-two medium bombers attacked Rabaul. Australian planes there, ten Wirraway fighters and four Hudson bombers, did not catch them. Inouye issued his operations order on the fifth. An Australian plane that managed to reconnoiter Truk four days later discovered preparations in full swing, with a dozen cruisers and destroyers plus another large vessel at anchor. Land-based bombers continued to raid Rabaul, losing only one plane. The Army troop commander, anxious for better intelligence, got one of his staff attached to the Fourth Fleet and sent that man on a pair of Rabaul missions to photograph defenses. Army troops were supplemented by three battalion-size units of the SNLF, the Japanese Marines.

The Australians suffered no illusions. For weeks authorities had been gathering the small numbers of citizens who lived in the villages and plantations dotting the islands, moving them to Rabaul, where at least there was a garrison, in the form of Lieutenant Colonel John J. Scanlan's Lark Force, about 1,400 troops built around the 2nd Battalion, 22nd Infantry, Australian Imperial Forces. There were some militia from the New Guinea

Volunteer Rifles, plus a true oddity, a battalion band recruited entirely from members of the Salvation Army. Small detachments had been posted to the Solomons, including at Gasmata and on Tulagi. Bougainville also had an independent infantry company. As civilians regrouped, a few planters, managers, and missionaries stayed behind, marking the beginning of the coastwatcher network.

Before the war there had been roughly a thousand Australian civilians at Rabaul. Now there were several times that many. By mid-January most women and children had been evacuated, along with some men. The rest, plus twelve hundred Chinese residents, a handful of Japanese, and the native population numbering more than ten thousand, stayed where they were. The Japanese were coming. The only question was when.

Meanwhile the Imperial Navy detailed its formidable striking force to help the invaders. Admiral Nagumo sailed on January 5 with four *Kido Butai* carriers. After a stop at Iwakuni to take on aircraft, he cruised on to Truk, arriving on January 14. Seaman Kuramoto Iki, a lookout aboard carrier *Kaga*, had dreamed of the *nanyo* since he was a boy, imagining naked natives dancing under palm trees. But the blazing sun broiled the inside of the ship and shattered those fantasies. Suddenly Iki longed for home. At Truk the crews changed to tropical uniform, a welcome relief. Kuramoto had never imagined he would look forward to rain—squalls and wind dissipated some of the heat. Evening breezes also brought respite. The *Akagi* installed armored shields on its AA guns to protect the gunners. After replenishing, the fleet left Truk on the seventeenth. Seaman Kuramoto gazed at the night sky and marveled at the brilliant stars of the Southern Cross constellation—it is remarkable how often South Pacific veterans from both sides invoke the Southern Cross as somehow defining their experiences. Kuramoto, for one, lay on his back on the upper deck, among the machine guns, and never closed his eyes. On the flag bridge Vice Admiral Nagumo likely had similar thoughts.

Kido Butai took position northeast of New Ireland, steaming back and forth across the equator, heading north in the daytime to avoid possible Australian air action, and south at night to attain attack position. At dawn on January 20, it flung ninety planes at Rabaul. Commander Fuchida Mitsuo, master of the Pearl Harbor attack, led the air groups. They launched from 200 miles away. There was little resistance. The base had two airfields then. The Japanese encountered a pair of Australian aircraft attempting to flee, and Zeroes quickly destroyed them. (Australian sources maintain that eight of Squadron Leader John Lerew's No. 24 Squadron fighters intercepted the strike, and that six of Lerew's planes were lost, including the two mentioned by Fuchida.) Dive-bombers blew up the only ship in the harbor, a merchantman. Fuchida led the level bomber unit himself, and they demolished the only target they could find, the single coast defense gun emplacement at the entrance to Simpson Harbor. "If ever a sledge hammer had been used to crack an egg," Fuchida later reflected, "this was the time."

Admiral Nagumo divided his force the following day, with deckload strikes from one carrier division against Kavieng, and from the other on Lae and Salamaua in New Guinea. Once again there were no targets worth speaking of. On January 22 the planes smashed Rabaul all over. Fuchida felt the operations misguided, exposing the striking force to possible enemy attack, plus aircraft wastage, for few results. As for Seaman Kuramoto, he felt crestfallen that *Kido Butai* had never seen an enemy.

The sailors and troops aboard the invasion flotilla bound for Rabaul were no doubt grateful for carrier air support. Their path was smoothed, for example, by destruction of the Australian coast defense battery. Carrier fighters shot down the Australian patrol plane that sighted the heavy cruiser unit slated to support the landings. A coastwatcher also reported the flotilla as it negotiated the strait between New Britain and New Ireland on January 22. The Lark Force commander, a veteran of Gallipoli and the Western Front in 1917, knew the dangers of artillery bombardment and accurately surmised that Japanese strength was several times his own. Not willing to see his men slaughtered by naval gunfire, Jack Scanlan ordered them to new positions at the edge of Rabaul and the southern point of Blanche Bay. Later that day, following the second round of carrier air strikes, Scanlan realized his most vital installations were gone. With the remnants of the Australian air unit withdrawn, he gave orders to blow up remaining positions and concentrate to the west and south.

Shortly after midnight Japanese soldiers began landing in Simpson Harbor, near the town, and in Keravia Bay, under the lip of Vulcan volcano, aiming at Vunakanau airfield. The landings went without incident, illuminated by parachute flares. An Australian first saw the Japanese onshore at about 2:30 a.m. A brief firefight occurred at Keravia Bay, but the Australians could not stop the invaders. Japanese troops quickly moved off the beaches, and with dawn their transports entered the harbor and began to disgorge equipment. JNAF aircraft swept over to strafe anything that moved. Close air support cost the *Kido Butai* one level bomber and one dive-bomber.

Colonel Scanlan's units were out of touch with one another except by messenger. Rumors of large Japanese forces were rife, and truck convoys were actually spotted. Bit by bit the Australians retired until Scanlan ordered a withdrawal. By midafternoon the company holding Vunakanau airfield had been driven back. Japanese reported the capture of 6,000 bombs and sixty drums of aviation gas. Rabaul town and Lakunai airfield had already fallen. Japanese losses were sixteen dead and twenty-five wounded. A desultory war of patrols took place across New Britain, until Japanese troops massacred roughly 160 Australian soldiers at Tol Plantation on February 4. Hearing of the atrocity, his supplies dwindling, Scanlan donned dress uniform and emerged from the bush to surrender his men.

One Australian company got away in good order, and scattered bands of others did too. Coastwatchers organized secret evacuations. Roughly 400 soldiers and civilians escaped New Britain. Approximately 1,050 Australian troops were taken captive and held in a camp at Rabaul through summer, when most were sent to Japan. Sadly a great many were aboard the steamer *Montevideo Maru* when the American submarine *Sturgeon* torpedoed her on July 1, 1942. Jack Scanlan survived the war, becoming a prison warden in Hobart.

Rabaul would be the big base of the *soto nanyo*. At Truk, Admiral Inouye ordered JNAF units there, including the Yokohama Air Corps of patrol bombers, plus a formation of medium bombers and fighters. The fleet created a special base force for the Outer South Seas with 8,800 seamen, engineers, stevedores, maintenance and repair specialists, plus SNLF troops. Rear Admiral Goto Aritomo brought the four heavy ships of his Cruiser Division 6 to Simpson Harbor, where they dropped anchor on January 30. A unit of Zero fighters reached Vunakanau airfield that very day. Starting the day after Rabaul fell, the Australians bombed it every other night through early February.

Simultaneous with the Rabaul attack, another Japanese flotilla captured Kavieng. There the invasion began shortly after midnight. The assault unit was the 2nd Maizuru SNLF. The town fell at about the time Japanese troops started landing at Rabaul. Kavieng had been held by only part of a single infantry company, which withdrew except for a few men who stayed to destroy supplies. The rest moved into the interior, circled back to the coast, and made a heroic attempt to escape to Port Moresby aboard a patched-up island steamer, the *Induna Star*. Their harrowing voyage deserves more attention than we can give it. Almost caught by a Japanese destroyer, they were bombed in early February while crossing the Solomon Sea some ninety miles south of Rabaul. The ship actually surrendered to aircraft, which watched them for hours until a destroyer arrived to take off the men and tow the captive vessel.

Other enclaves followed Rabaul and Kavieng. On New Ireland, the latter functioned as a satellite port. Little time had passed by January 29, when the Navy General Staff ordered the occupation of Tulagi, Lae, and Salamaua. The NGS directive instructed Fourth Fleet "to invade strategic points in the Solomon Islands and the eastern part of New Guinea in order to cut communications between these areas and the Australian mainland and to neutralize the waters north of Eastern Australia."

The next Japanese enclave became Gasmata on the southern coast of New Britain. A coastwatcher there, P. Daymond, had alerted Port Moresby to the first air raid against it from Rabaul. The Japanese discovered him when Australian commercial radio broadcast news that the strike had been seen over Gasmata. The Japanese promptly bombed and strafed. Daymond got away before the enemy invasion ships arrived on February 9. SNLF troops landed with the 4th Engineer Unit, which began that indispensable element of warfare in the South Pacific, an airstrip.

Japan's outposts were soon disturbed. The Allies struck at the Outer South Seas bases. On February 20, an American carrier unit, Vice Admiral Wilson E. Brown's Task Force 11 with the *Lexington*, attempted a carrier raid on Rabaul. The fleet was nearing its intended launch position that morning when a JNAF plane appeared on radar just thirty-five miles away. The *Lexington* launched fighters and caught that snooper, then another, but a third search plane escaped. That afternoon two bomber formations led by Lieutenant Commander Ito Takuzo streaked toward Brown's task force, which dispatched combat air patrols to intercept them. With most of the ship's fighters engaging the first wave, a second was detected, and just two fighters were positioned to oppose it. Pilot Edward H. ("Butch") O'Hare became the sole interceptor when his wingman's guns jammed. Butch O'Hare pressed his attacks and shot down two Japanese aircraft, damaging a third so badly it crashed. O'Hare had also been in on the fight that morning, making his score five planes. Butch O'Hare became America's first Pacific war ace. In all, thirteen of seventeen JNAF bombers and three flying boats were destroyed (by Japanese sources), against the loss of two U.S. planes. Lieutenant Noel Gayler, a future U.S. Pacific commander and head of the National Security Agency, was saved when a Japanese bullet failed to penetrate his windshield. Admiral Brown, surprise lost, broke off. Starting a few days later, B-17 bombers hit Rabaul in the first strike of what became a sporadic aerial campaign.

Still the Americans were not done. Brown recommended fresh efforts. At Pearl Harbor, U.S. Pacific commander Admiral Chester W. Nimitz agreed and sent Task Force 17, led by Rear Admiral Frank J. Fletcher, to join Brown, with orders to attack in the Solomons–New Guinea region. The combined force was headed there when the Japanese executed their next landing, on the north coast of New Guinea, capturing Lae and Salamaua from weak Australian units on March 8. These towns became the American targets, with a strike of 104 aircraft against them. The warplanes had difficulty climbing high enough to cross the Owen Stanley mountain range, but managed that feat and found the Imperial Navy in their sights. A fierce battle ensued. U.S. intelligence initially exaggerated the results, including two heavy cruisers among assorted other victims. But Japanese losses were serious enough: four merchant vessels blasted, plus damage to light cruiser *Yubari*, the seaplane tender *Kiyokawa Maru*, and light damage to three destroyers and other merchantmen. Pilot Nemoto Kumesaka of the *Kiyokawa Maru* recorded this as "our biggest loss since the beginning of the war." Captain Ban Masami's *Yubari* had to repair at Truk, out of action for a month.

Japan's landings on New Guinea completed the agreed Outer South Seas offensive so far as the Japanese Army was concerned. Despite U.S. air attacks, General Horii Tomitaro's South Seas Detachment regrouped at Rabaul, replaced on New Guinea by naval troops. But the Imperial Navy continued eyeing the Solomons, and began raids on Port Moresby. By mid-March it had moved a detachment of Zero fighters forward to Lae, where they flew counterair missions against Moresby. A unit of Type 1, or "Betty," bombers followed. Lae also functioned as a recovery station for bombers damaged in the Moresby raids. On April 1 there were nearly a dozen Japanese aircraft at Lae—but ten more under repair. That day there were only twenty-four planes at Rabaul, all of them at Vunakanau field. JNAF aircraft photographed Port Moresby and, in the Solomons, the island of Bougainville.

Allied air reconnaissance detected construction at Rabaul as early as March 9. At the end of that month the headquarters of Rear Admiral Yamada Sadatoshi's 25th Air Flotilla arrived to take closer control of the several JNAF air groups now flying from Rabaul. Conditions were primitive. Only improvised officers' clubs served the Japanese cadres. One of the several volcanoes surrounding the town had erupted in 1937, and others were semiactive. Rabaul was subject to debilitating vapors and rains of volcanic dust, especially in summer. Ash from Vulcan volcano mountain eroded aircraft fuselages at Vunakanau, and fumes from Tavurvur ate away at fabric wing surfaces at Lakunai, major headaches. Vunakanau had fifteen fighters and nine medium bombers. At Lakunai field on April 10 there were six Zero fighters but twenty-four under repair. A couple of days later an equal number landed from the aviation ship *Kasuga Maru*. They had to be modified for tropical service. Yamada also lacked crews, especially after the one-sided fight with the *Lexington*. The JNAF often maintained only a one-to-one ratio of crews to aircraft, low by the standards of many air forces, and tropical diseases took a toll as great as enemy action. More than a dozen fresh crews were called up from Japan and the East Indies to make up shortages. One section of the flotilla's bomber group was still training in Japan and had to be called to the front.

The fifty-year-old Admiral Yamada had never faced anything like this. He had been a flier for half his life and had skippered two aircraft carriers. In fact, Yamada was the only aviator of flag rank in the Imperial Navy. Not just the aviation headaches, but the South Pacific climate and New Britain volcanoes posed challenges. If not on the bridge of a flattop, Yamada would have been more comfortable on the streets of Paris, where he had been a naval attaché, or Tokyo, where he had served with NGS. A resourceful officer, Yamada devised ways to protect aircraft from the elements. The admiral began pressing for new fields farther from the volcanoes. Unfortunately surveyors did a poor job selecting the first site, Kerevat, where construction began in June. When completed, its drainage was so bad the field could not initially be used. Allied air attacks were rated as "probable" by the 25th Air Flotilla war diary for this period. As raids picked up, Yamada ordered revetments camouflaged. He established new patrol patterns for scout planes to warn of task forces, searching 600 miles out on several vectors from Rabaul and two from Lae.

On April 16 the last elements of Yamada's fighter group* arrived aboard the *Komaki Maru*, sunk by an Allied air raid before she could clear the harbor. Master pilot Sakai Saburo arrived on that ship. The tropical heat had Sakai believing *Komaki Maru* a stinking old tub, whereas in reality she had been built in 1933. Sakai had made his reputation as a combat ace over the Philippines and the Dutch East Indies.

"Sea eagles" like Sakai filled the ranks of the air flotilla, for the JNAF pilots of this time, if not numerous, were certainly expert. More planes of the bomber group flew in a week later. The last bombers appeared on the first of May. Also arriving in Rabaul at this time were a number of geisha, as well as Korean "comfort women," whose misery at the front would be enormous. Some accounts put their number at Rabaul in the thousands, but this seems excessive, at least in the spring of 1942, since such a number would nearly have equaled the total of naval and military personnel.

Meanwhile on Bougainville, excepting the few hardy men and women

---

*   To avoid confusion in this text, and because certain forms are more familiar to readers, the narrative will adopt several conventions. In actuality, until late 1942 the JNAF followed a practice of calling its main operating units "air corps" under command of air flotillas, which used that title for administrative purposes but were styled "base air forces" in operational planning and communications. The JNAF used a mixture of numbered and named air corps, but switched to all numbers and restyled the units as "air groups" in November. This text will adopt the air group nomenclature, but the flotilla names, throughout. This avoids confusion between JNAF "base air forces" versus the Imperial Navy's practice of designating "base forces"—units of sailors manning installations. In addition, the Japanese and Allies had different ways of referring to particular aircraft, with JNAF actually possessing two systems, one based on the year of the reign of the emperor when a design was adopted (e.g., "Type 1" bomber), and the other describing aircraft by type and generation of design ("G4M2" for the same aircraft). Allied forces referred to each JNAF type by a name ("Betty" bomber). The narrative will use the Allied nomenclature except for the Zero fighter (A6M2, Zeke), and where variation is useful. An appendix will identify aircraft types by each of their identifiers. Finally, wherever material permits, each side's sources will be regarded as authoritative in recording its losses, and assertions for losses by the opposition will be termed "claims."

who decided to take their chances, white civilians had been evacuated in late December. Coastwatchers kept up their reporting. The Japanese looked for the watchers to neutralize them. Several air searches came from Rabaul. On March 6, two Imperial Navy cruisers stopped at a cove to put a patrol ashore. The SNLF found nothing but the whites at a nearby plantation, whom they put on parole. Naval infantry occupied points on Bougainville at the end of March. On Buka, off the main island, there was a 1,400-foot airstrip guarded by two dozen Australian commandos from the unit that had held Kavieng, under Lieutenant John H. Mackie. With no chance against Japanese Marines backed by their fleet, the Australians withdrew. In residence on Sohana, a tiny island in Buka Passage, was coastwatcher Jack Read, who concerted with Mackie to take to the bush and set up a post for his teleradio, the coastwatcher's most vital equipment.

An official of the civil administration, Read had been hastily commissioned into the Royal Australian Navy. New to Bougainville, he had a dozen years' service on New Guinea. With Sohana even more exposed than Buka itself, Read moved to the mainland with the help of natives and some Australian commandos. He made a brief excursion into Kieta town, where, backed by a few native policemen, Read used his official powers to stop looting and rioting by indigenous people that had erupted after the colonials left. The coastwatcher settled down. The Japanese nearly caught Lieutenant Mackie back on Buka planting demolition charges. Read warned him and sent a Fijian missionary, Usaia Sotutu, to rescue Mackie. Sotutu hid him under palm fronds in a canoe and smuggled him across Buka Passage in the dead of night. That marked the start of a game of hide-and-seek that went on for a full year. Japanese patrols visited villages to ask about the whites. The indigenous would pretend ignorance, give false leads, or, when friendly natives provided the Japanese real information, Read, Mackie, and their "missionary boys" would disappear deeper into the jungle.

As chief on Bougainville, Jack Read assigned Paul Mason to work from Kieta. Mason had been an islander for over two decades and, a radio hobbyist, he joined the coastwatcher organization soon after Australian Navy Lieutenant Commander Eric A. Feldt set it up. Mason prepared his ground carefully, caching supplies widely. In early March, Japanese warships put in at Kieta. A former Japanese resident, now employed by their base force at Rabaul, landed with the troops and threatened the indigenous people. Japan had come to stay, he warned; the whites were through. Afraid of betrayal, Mason moved to one of his hide sites, only to be felled by malaria. He recovered slowly, joined by four Australian commandos who had fled their position at Buin, at the southern tip of Bougainville, when the SNLF arrived there. The Buin-Shortland-Faisi complex featured fine natural harbors and had an airstrip. The Imperial Navy coveted it, and Paul Mason realized that it needed surveillance. Having recovered, Mason asked Commander Feldt for permission to relocate there. Australian aerial reconnaissance had already established that the enemy were setting up installations at this Bougainville complex. Feldt, pleased, readily agreed. Mason set up his teleradio and a lookout post.

From June 7, when the Bougainville coastwatchers received their first supply airdrop from Australia, the network functioned as a pillar of Allied intelligence. This had been envisioned long in advance by the Australian naval staff, which made provisions after World War I for what became the coastwatchers. Eric Feldt, himself a naval reservist and civil official on New Guinea, was recruited by Lieutenant Commander Rupert B. M. Long, the director of Australian naval intelligence, in 1939. More than 800 persons worked in the "Ferdinand" organization, as it was code-named. Commander Feldt set up shop at Townsville on the Australian east coast. When the U.S. Marines were plotting their Guadalcanal invasion, they sent officers to Ferdinand to learn everything the coastwatchers could tell them. In August 1942 there were a hundred teleradios sending to assorted control centers. Some circuits Feldt handled directly. Many reported through a Ferdinand station at Port Moresby. Tulagi was a net control too until it was lost. Once Marines were ensconced on Guadalcanal, station KEN there became a new net control. There were others. When the Allies established a combined command for the Southwest Pacific, an Allied Intelligence Bureau under Colonel C. G. Roberts would be created to manage operations, including the coastwatchers.

Coastwatchers Read, Mason, and Mackie were by no means Ferdinand's only principals. Henry Josselyn and John H. Keenan reported from Vella Lavella; Nick Waddell and Carden W. Seton from Choiseul; Arthur R. Evans from Kolombangara; J. A. Corrigan and Geoffrey Kuper from Santa Isabel;

Dick Horton from Rendova; David S. McFarlan from Florida; Sexton and William S. Marchant from Malaita; F. A. ("Snowy") Rhoades, Hugh Mackenzie, and Martin Clemens from Guadalcanal. Snowy Rhoades, Commander Feldt records, was the only one who truly looked the part, though what a coastwatcher *should* look like he never says. Donald G. Kennedy reported from Santa Isabel and later New Georgia. From time to time replacements or supplementary personnel would be sent to them. Other coastwatchers worked from New Guinea. Their hide-and-seek with the Japanese was more than a game; it was deadly. Thirty-eight coastwatchers perished in their dangerous pursuit.

The coastwatchers effectively spied on the enemy. Submarines and seaplane patrol bombers succored the watchers when necessary, and sometimes picked up aviators Ferdinand's people had rescued—at least 118 by the best count. The American sub *Gato* took in supplies and brought out people. In the summer of 1943 the Japanese made a concerted attempt to wipe out the Read-Mason organization. They captured several, but others were rescued by the *Guardfish*.

Japanese commanders not only made efforts to neutralize coastwatchers; they knew a good thing when they saw one. In his secret order for defense and civil policy in the Tulagi area of April 28, 1942, Captain Kanazawa of the 8th Base Force directed that lookout posts be set up on Guadalcanal and other islands, including Florida, San Cristobal, Malaita, and Santa Isabel. Kanazawa also ordained that all Japanese enclaves be hardened for defense. Florida should be occupied if possible. Tulagi would become the seat of Japanese civil administration in the Solomons. White missionaries and others were to be removed, Germans left alone but watched closely (thus the freedom—after questioning—the Japanese had permitted an Austrian planter on Bougainville—and the suspicion with which the Ferdinand spies then viewed him). Influential persons in the community were to be co-opted and used. Captain Kanazawa envisioned Tulagi, with its floatplane base on adjoining Gavutu-Tanambogo, as a rendezvous point for schemes aimed at Australia, "the farthest advanced base for conducting operations in the Coral Sea and against New Caledonia and the New Hebrides."

PILLARS IN PLACE

As the Imperial Navy looked ahead to second-phase operations, it reconsidered the strategic question of the continent down under. At Combined Fleet headquarters, Admiral Ugaki anticipated completing initial operations by March 1942. As early as the New Year he turned to thoughts of the follow-up. Others did too. Baron Tomioka at NGS thought more and more of Australia and developed a plan to invade the continent. His basic idea was to use the newly seized Dutch East Indies to catapult five Army divisions into western Australia and then springboard along the coast grabbing ports and bases. As Tomioka saw it, Australia was really a facade—half a dozen cities along the coast with desert behind them. Had he consulted the Australian general staff in the spring of 1942 they might have agreed. At the time, their defense forces in toto numbered 12,000 regulars (a little more than eighteen battalions of coast defense and internal security troops) backed by 116,500 citizen militia. Not much to defend an entire continent. The brilliant baron thought his plan a practical one.

The main action took place at Imperial General Headquarters. There, Tomioka's Army counterpart was Colonel Hattori Takushiro. When his operations section of the Army general staff looked at Australia, the planners gagged. They calculated that an invasion would consume as many as ten to fifteen Army divisions and require 1.5 million tons of shipping for the Army alone. That was a larger contingent than the Army had allocated for the entire Pacific war; in fact almost a third of the full force and nearly a quarter of Japan's entire merchant fleet. Hattori could not fathom how the Army could fight in China while invading Australia. It simply could not be done. Apart from anything else, the diversion of merchant shipping would reduce raw material imports, affecting production of all manner of war matériel, most disturbingly aircraft.

Hattori lunched with his naval counterpart at Tokyo's Army-Navy Club. Tomioka pointed out that the Army had a huge force doing nothing in Manchuria. Hattori countered that those men deterred a Soviet invasion. He raised a cup of tea. "The tea in this cup represents our total strength," Hattori said. He inverted the cup and the tea puddled on the floor. Of course the puddle did not cover the entire floor. "You see, it goes just so far," the

Army planner continued. "If your plan is approved I will resign." The Navy would not get its way.

Admiral Ugaki also did not think much of the plan, although, as already recounted, he also had difficulty with the alternatives, the FS Operation or thrusts into the Indian Ocean. Soon enough the Combined Fleet presented its Midway-Hawaii scheme. But IGHQ had still to reach a compromise, which led to the concept of isolating Australia. The FS Operation had been part of this, but there was another element—to complete the conquest of eastern New Guinea by taking Port Moresby. This became the "MO Operation," and both services approved it. On March 13 the Navy and Army chiefs of staff presented their program to the emperor. The MO Operation would solidify the defensive perimeter. Port Moresby would be captured by amphibious landing through the Bismarck Archipelago. The Navy General Staff released its directive on April 16. As in the occupation of Rabaul, the Army's South Seas Detachment provided the main ground forces, and, with Eighth Fleet not yet created, the Navy's Fourth Fleet was the executive authority. Admiral Inouye Shigeyoshi would come down from Truk to direct the maneuver. He would have part of the *Kido Butai* to neutralize the Allied carriers that had revealed themselves. Admiral Inouye issued his fleet secret order number thirteen, which provided for the MO Operation a week later. Inouye's forces began to gather at Truk and Rabaul.

As Japan coiled to strike, a new factor entered the equation. For many years the United States, Great Britain, and Australia had all had intelligence organizations intercepting the radio communications of other nations, breaking their codes, including the Japanese. There had been major successes in the 1930s, but as the world moved toward war the Japanese introduced new code and cipher systems. The Imperial Navy changed its codebook. Here is not the place to debate whether the Japanese naval codes were being read before Pearl Harbor—in my view they were not—but by early 1942 the Allies had made much progress.

A brief description of radio intelligence activities is useful. All the Allied communications units listened to Japanese transmissions and recorded their messages to provide the raw material. The British and Australians separated these specialist radio monitors and knew them as the Y Service, with codebreakers in another entity. The United States ran interception operations as part of the same unit of the Office of Naval Communications—called Op-20-G—that was responsible for actual codebreaking. The U.S. Army had its own organization known as the Signals Intelligence Service. In addition to intercepting radio transmissions, the services took bearings on the emitters to ascertain their locations—called radio direction finding—and counted messages from the emitters to maintain traffic profiles.

The radio units produced three types of intelligence. The first consisted of decoded and translated decrypts of actual messages. The second kind of data embodied the results of pattern analysis—radio traffic analysis—wherein emitter locations and traffic volume profiles permitted conclusions on the identity, movements, and sometimes the intentions of forces. During the initial months of the Pacific war, when codebreaking had yet to hit its stride, and later when codes changed, radio traffic analysis would be the most valuable element of communications intelligence. The third type of information consisted of analysis applied to all this material.

The British codebreaking operation formed part of the Government Code and Cipher School (GC&CS), and the Australian one a part of its Directorate of Naval Intelligence. Each had field units. The British, with commonwealth participation, had the Far East Combined Bureau, originally located in Hong Kong, then Singapore until the Japanese threatened that place, then Ceylon and East Africa. The Australians formed a small Signal Intelligence Bureau at Canberra. The Americans had Station Cast in the Philippines at Corregidor, subsequently evacuated to Australia as Station Belconnen, though during the prelude to the Port Moresby battle, that unit functioned in both places. Pearl Harbor had Station Hypo, while in Washington Op-20-G ran its own communications intelligence element, called Station Negat. The U.S. field units would later become Fleet Radio Unit Melbourne (FRUMEL) and Fleet Radio Unit Pacific (FRUPAC), FRUMEL being a joint Australian-American activity. All the stations and home offices had their own private, top-secret communications channel, or "circuit," to exchange information using a machine-encryption device known as Copek. In the Allies' drive to crack the Japanese codes, the first decrypts from JN-25, as the Allies called the Imperial Navy's fleet code, came from messages sent in early March 1942. "Ultra" became the generic term for data derived from communications interception.

Radio intelligence fed its information to high commands and fleet commands. In the U.S. system, Op-20-G reported to COMINCH, the commander in chief of the fleet and chief of naval operations, Admiral Ernest J. King, and through him to the Joint Chiefs of Staff. At Pearl Harbor, Admiral Chester Nimitz, leading the Pacific Command and the Pacific Fleet, received his data through his fleet intelligence officer, Captain Edwin T. Layton. Though this gets a little ahead of our story, Nimitz ordered the creation of "advanced intelligence centers," starting with a Combat Intelligence Unit plus FRUPAC at Pearl Harbor, to meld data from all sources, including radio intelligence. The British Far East Combined Bureau, upon evacuation from Singapore, mainly served the chief of the British Eastern Fleet. In Australia the information came through their own units, which benefited from the findings of all the Allies. General Douglas A. MacArthur, after March 1942 the leader of the theater that included Australia and New Guinea, was served by his intelligence officer (G-2), Major General Charles A. Willoughby. All this apparatus came into play when the Japanese aimed at Port Moresby.

Different codes had different degrees of complexity. Breaking into a code was affected not only by the number of messages sent and intercepted in that system, but also the amount of repetition that occurred. Standard reporting items generated repetition. Thus weather codes, constantly reporting the same basic data, were among the easiest to break. The first Allied indication of enemy interest in Port Moresby came after the fall of Rabaul, when monitors intercepted Japanese high-altitude weather reports for the Moresby area. On March 5, using the Copek circuit, FRUMEL suggested that a Japanese operation against Port Moresby impended. Another repetitive element in codes is employment of standard letter groups or words to designate places. These disguise locations and reduce transmission length, and the Imperial Navy made broad use of them. The tale of the Japanese use of "AF" to refer to Midway—and how verifying that helped Admiral Nimitz win that battle—is well-known. The Imperial Navy simplified Allied difficulties in identifying such indicators by their reliance on a method that utilized the same root to refer to related places. "R" in Japanese messages referred to Rabaul, "RZM" to Lae. Station Hypo recovered a March 25 message from Admiral Yamada instructing units on attacks against "RZP." Two days earlier Station Cast (FRUMEL) had published a list of Japanese location designators that included RZP as Port Moresby. Commander Joseph J. Rochefort, the eccentric genius who ran Hypo, realized that Moresby was the only target Japanese naval air was attacking in the South Pacific, confirming RZP as that place.

More RZP messages appeared over succeeding days, along with mention in JN-25 of an "RZP campaign," as well as ones linking the Japanese aircraft carrier *Kaga* with that operation. On April 9 a JN-25 decrypt revealed the plan's architecture—it would include a striking force of carriers, an attack force, occupation force, and a support force. The existence of occupation forces for other places, one of them Tulagi, also stood revealed. At Pearl Harbor two days later, Captain Layton issued a fleet intelligence summary warning of a South Pacific offensive. On April 13 the Americans circulated a nearly complete decrypt of a message from Rear Admiral Hara Chuichi, commanding Carrier Division 5 with the *Shokaku* and *Zuikaku*, advising Vice Admiral Inouye of his expected arrival at Truk in two weeks. Already shown by an earlier intercept was that the *Kaga* had been damaged running aground. Hara's ships replaced her. The British contributed a report on April 14 noting the withdrawal of the Nagumo force from the Indian Ocean, speculating that part or all of it might attack Port Moresby. Later data indicated that light carrier *Shoho* would participate, as well as the four heavy ships of Cruiser Division 6. Traffic analysis followed the movements of many Japanese fleet units as they gathered. Australian intelligence noted increased air patrols over Moresby, the Coral Sea, the waters bounded by New Guinea, the island chains, and the Australian mainland. Intelligence then discovered the actual code name "MO Operation." On May 1, Commander Rochefort was able to report that MO had begun.

Admiral Nimitz responded to the threat even before he had a complete picture. At Pearl Harbor on April 17, while the famous Doolittle raid was being launched against Japan, Nimitz brought together his experts to examine the existing reports. Fleet intelligence officer Layton predicted the Japanese would divide into an assortment of forces and conduct parallel activities. With a few more days' intelligence, Nimitz confirmed his decision, more confident that two U.S. aircraft carriers plus Australia-based airplanes could face down the Imperial Navy. The Pacific fleet commander had kept the *Lexington* task force in the South Pacific; now he ordered it to rendezvous with another built around carrier *Yorktown*. The Royal Australian Navy also participated, with an Allied cruiser-destroyer group led by British admiral John G. Crace. The united force would inhabit waters the Japanese had to pass. Nimitz made a quick trip to the continental U.S. to brief Admiral Ernest J. King, who met him in San Francisco. Upon returning to Pearl, Nimitz formalized his instructions in an April 28 directive. He foresaw a battle in the Coral Sea focusing on countering the Japanese.

The Imperial Navy's first move came on April 28, when an aviation tender advanced to Shortland islet off Bougainville to act as a forward base for air patrols. Then Rear Admiral Shima Kiyohide steamed toward Tulagi, where he appeared on May 3. There the Japanese intended to install a major seaplane facility. At the moment Shima began landing SNLF infantry and aviation specialists, Admiral Inouye's invasion armada still rode at anchor in Rabaul. Carriers *Shokaku* and *Zuikaku*, with Rear Admiral Takagi Takeo's striking force, were en route. Covering and support forces sailed west of the Solomons, about a day from Tulagi. Also west of the Solomons were Rear Admiral Frank J. Fletcher's U.S. carriers, which joined on the first of May. It was Fletcher who opened the battle, with an air strike against the Japanese at Tulagi. The Americans did little damage, but they stunned the enemy.

In Imperial Navy practice, in which the battleship held sway even though the aircraft carrier proved itself more and more the decisive weapon, heavy ship leaders exercised command over carriers when they acted together, except where special provisions were made—as in the creation of the First Air Fleet, the *Kido Butai*. Thus the Japanese carrier group sailed under Admiral Takagi, the cruiser leader, not Hara Chuichi, the carrier boss. Until Coral Sea there had never been a naval battle in which aircraft carriers duked it out with aircraft, and surface ships never fired their guns except at planes. Takagi had no basis for judgment. He himself was a veteran of the Dutch East Indies fighting—and victor of the Battle of the Java Sea—but Japanese forces there had not been seriously threatened by aircraft. To complicate matters, no current Imperial Navy carrier formation leader was a pilot—not Hara, not Nagumo, not anyone else. This reflected the gradual acceptance of carriers in the Japanese Navy.

Slightly ameliorating this situation was the fact that Takagi and Hara were academy classmates and friends, disposed to cooperate, and that their senior staff officers had somewhat more knowledge of airpower, one a former manager of aircraft development, the other a torpedo specialist whose staff work in armaments production had included monitoring aircraft manufacture. At Truk before this sortie, the staff men Yamaoka Mineo and Nagasawa Ko had speculated on the possibility of an aeronaval battle. Though Japanese intelligence knew of no U.S. carriers in the Coral Sea, they expected to find them. Once Fletcher hit Tulagi, Yamaoka and Nagasawa knew they were right.

Preparations cost the Japanese a full day. Because of losses among Yamada's land-based groups, Rabaul needed more Zero fighters to cover the Port Moresby invasion force. A canceled ferry mission led to the need for Admiral Hara's carrier pilots to fly replacements into Rabaul, returning aboard aircraft sent to retrieve them. Meanwhile the American task force took position, and the intelligence network produced critical decrypts. On May 3, Station Hypo relayed details of Fourth Fleet's orders to Takagi, plus a Rabaul status report. Allied codebreakers continued to stream position, heading, and intentions data for the Moresby invasion flotilla.

Nimitz sent Fletcher two dispatches on May 5. The first outlined the Japanese strike force plan; the second specified the probable date for Japan's invasion and alerted the admiral that it would open with a carrier strike on Moresby likely to be launched from the Coral Sea. Fletcher had admirable intelligence if he chose to use it. A set of air searches predicated on this data might have revealed Hara's carriers. Fletcher does not seem to have laid on any such scouting pattern. He relied upon standard searches.

Admiral Fletcher also had the blessing of a mobile radio unit, a communications intercept detachment embarked on the *Yorktown*. Led by Lieutenant Forrest R. "Tex" Baird, this small unit, complemented by another under Lieutenant Ransom Fullinwider in the *Lexington*, afforded real-time ability to listen in on Japanese transmissions. Tex Baird is truly scathing on the subject of Frank Fletcher, whom he saw as having squandered this advantage through indecisive leadership, mistrust, and poor coordination. Baird and Fullinwider were among a small cadre of "language officers" the U.S. Navy had trained in the tongue and customs of the adversary as well as codebreaking techniques. Where the math and cipher experts were masters on Japanese codes, the language officers formed the core of U.S. ability to interpret the results, as well as the interface between codebreakers and line officers.

Station Hypo created these detachments to accompany task forces on their missions. One day Commander Rochefort summoned Tex Baird and another language officer, Lieutenant Gilven R. Slonim, to his office and flipped a coin, asking Baird to choose heads or tails. He lost the toss. This led to his assignment to Fletcher (Slonim went with "Bull" Halsey aboard *Enterprise*). Baird served Fletcher as conduit for secrets and supplied the results of his own monitoring. Before the battle Tex Baird aroused Fletcher's ire by refusing to describe the top-secret U.S. codebreaking to the admiral's entire assembled staff. They had another run-in when Rear Admiral Alva Fitch told Fletcher his *Lexington* had intercepted a sighting report from an enemy submarine—Baird found it not credible. Fletcher and Fullinwider had previously served together, which inclined the admiral to believe the *Lexington*'s claim. At Coral Sea, Tex Baird's unit recorded a message revealing Hara's position. Fletcher preferred Fullinwider's erroneous interpretation, preventing a U.S. attack. On the first day of battle, when Fletcher had already ceded tactical control to Admiral Fitch—here Baird disputes Fletcher's after-action report, which he views as falsified—the task force commander refused to act on the intelligence.

At Coral Sea both sides experienced what U.S. officers would later term "makee learnee," educating themselves by trial and error. Fletcher sent his carriers in succession to refuel, removing them from the battle area. Hara's ships abandoned their communications security with first contact, enabling the U.S. mobile radio units to intercept uncoded messages. The Americans struck at Japanese light carrier *Shoho* with all their aircraft very early one morning. Though Fletcher and Fitch knew a large Japanese task force was somewhere nearby, they held nothing back in case it was sighted. Aircraft continued hitting *Shoho* once she was visibly sinking, forgoing the chance to cripple other warships. The Japanese misidentified an American oiler and destroyer as a carrier and cruiser—corrected as a transport and cruiser, and wrong both times—then waited too long to recall attack groups, leading to a wasted strike. They then misidentified Admiral Crace's force, detached to block the final passage to Port Moresby, as a unit of battleships and cruisers. Japanese planes returning from their attack—with no bombs or torpedoes—saw the U.S. carriers late in the day. A desperate attempt at an evening attack led to Japanese planes in the air after nightfall. Some of them even tried to land on the U.S. ships.

On May 8 came the climactic day. Hara's carriers resumed radio discipline and changed their call signs, confusing U.S. monitors at a key moment. Each side sighted the enemy's carriers within moments of the other. Both sent out the biggest strikes they could muster. The Japanese scored many hits on the *Lexington*, and one crucial bomb fell on *Yorktown*, until then lucky and skillful at evading many torpedoes. The bomb missed Baird's radio room by just thirty feet. When the Americans hit the Japanese, carrier *Zuikaku* happened to be hidden beneath a squall and the attack went against *Shokaku*, disabling her flight deck. The Imperial Navy retreated. Admiral Inouye had already recalled the Moresby invasion force. On the American side, it seemed at first that the *Lexington* might survive, but a terrific internal explosion rocked the ship, fires spread, and she had to be abandoned.

The Battle of the Coral Sea is usually accounted a draw. Its most important impact lay in educating the warfighters in aeronaval tactics, though to judge from Nagumo's performance at Midway, the Americans learned better. But it also confirmed the value of codebreaking, especially in conjunction with aerial reconnaissance, as pillars of intelligence. Though Tex Baird left the *Yorktown*—to be replaced by Ransom Fullinwider—mobile radio units became firmly established as elements of American admirals' staffs. Midway, of course, prized communications intelligence in unmistakable fashion. The codebreakers and the aerial photographers, along with the coastwatchers, would watch intently as the Japanese continued their war.

Around the time of Coral Sea, Japanese naval commentator Ito Masanori wrote a series of articles for a Nagoya newspaper. He warned against overextending Japan's perimeter. Ito had covered naval affairs for years, and even with Japan's tightly restricted public debate he got the sense the high command was advancing mindlessly. Now Ito advocated a halt, a terminal point for the offensive. Later a friend, an Army officer, warned him against publicizing such views—they might lead military hotheads to act against him. Nothing would dissuade the Imperial Navy.

The next stage began innocently enough. Japanese naval troops from Tulagi crossed to Guadalcanal, where they shot a half dozen cows, carrying them off for food. Coastwatchers on the big island reported that. A scout plane spotted a JNAF aircraft photographing Guadalcanal. Almost a month later a Japanese survey party came from Tulagi and began examining a site at Lunga Point. They stayed. Several barges of men arrived on Guadalcanal after June 19. On June 25, Army G-2 reported the SNLF soldiers burning off grass, putting up tents, and starting work on a boat dock. Two water tanks were erected. Japanese patrols sought the coastwatchers, asking around the villages about whites. In early July the two vessels of Admiral Matsuyama's Cruiser Division 18 dropped anchor off Lunga and landed construction troops and naval infantry. The Japanese soldiers dug trenches and set up machine guns. Several days later Matsuyama returned to deliver the balance of the 11th and 13th Construction Units and more soldiers of the 81st and 84th Naval Guard Units. Captain Monzen of the engineer force became island commander. Most of these developments appeared in one or another Allied intelligence report. On July 5 the codebreakers identified the construction units and inferred their purpose—building an airfield.

By this time the Allies also knew of Captain Kanazawa's 8th Base Force at Rabaul, the 14th Base Force at Kavieng, the 1st Base Force at Buin, and the 7th Base Force at Lae, all from radio traffic. Photo reconnaissance permitted strength estimates: 21,000 around Rabaul, 1,500 at Kavieng, some 13,000 on Bougainville, and 2,000 at Lae. At Emirau, a small island off Kavieng, a Japanese patrol captured coastwatcher Cornelius L. Page. He was held for a couple of weeks, then executed as a spy. General MacArthur sent Admiral Nimitz a dispatch on June 27 that evaluated Japanese air strength at Rabaul as having returned to pre–Coral Sea levels, except in fighter aircraft, of which only about two dozen were estimated. MacArthur noted shipping activity exceeding normal requirements, plus signs of new shore installations and airfields.

The Allies had also caught wind of Japan's FS Operation: a CINCPAC intelligence report the same day observed that the Japanese Second Fleet—which had acted as the Midway occupation force—had a new, important mission. For a time intelligence debated a move on the Aleutians or New Guinea, but CINCPAC finally predicted action in the New Guinea–Solomons area. An American B-24 spotted several JNAF long-range patrol bombers between Fiji and New Caledonia. In a fleet intelligence summary on July 10, Captain Layton confidently asserted that the Japanese were assembling troops at Truk, naming Kavieng, Guadalcanal, and New Guinea as destinations. Pearl Harbor also observed the creation of the Eighth Fleet. In mid-July CINCPAC confirmed that the construction on Guadalcanal aimed to create an airfield.

The Japanese indeed intended fresh operations. Fleet units screened Army troops landing at Gona on the New Guinea coast. They would try to march over the Owen Stanley mountains, doing by land what had failed by sea. Imperial Headquarters promulgated a new central agreement on New Guinea. Troops of the South Seas Detachment reached Kokoda by early August. Imperial Navy planners anticipated an amphibious move against Moresby once the Army threatened from the landward side. Some naval officers viewed the Kokoda Trail march as an Army stunt, not to be taken seriously, others as a waste of strength. When Commander Ohmae came to Rabaul as advance man for activation of the Eighth Fleet, he found Admiral Yamada doubtful, because of the engagements on New Guinea, that there were sufficient planes to put some at the new Guadalcanal airfield.

In any event, the Japanese were in motion and the Allies knew it. The Allies also understood it would be only a matter of time before Japan consolidated its positions. This was the moment to strike. The Allies had a plan to do that. On August 5 the Owada Communications Group, the Imperial Navy's radio intelligence organization, alerted all commands that Allied units were at sea. On the sixth, Guadalcanal informed Eighth Fleet that natives helping prepare the airfield had run away. But search planes saw nothing to the south. The next morning Rabaul and Truk received the frantic messages from Tulagi reporting invasion. Guadalcanal was silent. At Truk, where the Combined Fleet flagship was now moored, Ugaki Matome wrote, "This enemy employed a huge force, intending to capture that area once and for all. That we failed to discover it until attacked deserves censure as extremely careless."

THE CARTWHEEL FORMULA

Allied invasion forces materialized with the dawn. This resulted from one of the most gigantic improvisations imaginable, makee learnee on a grand scale—none of the careful preparation that preceded D-Day at Normandy. Rather the 'Canal—or "Operation Watchtower," to give it its proper code name—became the first major American amphibious landing of the war, an application of doctrines hitherto extant only on paper, practiced in small-scale exercises with rudimentary techniques and novel, unproven equipment. The landing boats, cross-shipping, and fire-support arrange- ments, plus much more that would be routine by D-Day, was mostly ex- perimental at Guadalcanal. Moreover, Watchtower would be carried out by an untried area command, viewed with some suspicion by another theater boss quite zealous in protecting his own prerogatives. All of this amounted to something far less than a formula for success.

The command structure and strategy that led to Watchtower began with the Allied Powers wrestling with the quandaries of warfare over the vast Pacific and Indian oceans. Japanese conquests rendered obsolete the initial arrangements that had distinguished between the United States in the Pacific, working out of Pearl Harbor, and a combined Allied command leading the fighting in East and South Asia. Reorganization of the theaters became essential. The broad oceanic expanse was the easy part. The United States designated the Pacific Ocean Area as a theater command early in April 1942 and made Admiral Chester W. Nimitz its commander in chief (CINCPOA) on April 20, in addition to his role in charge of the U.S. Pacific Fleet (CINCPAC). The Pacific Ocean Area, in turn, was subdivided into re- gions for the North, Central, and South.

The choices made in regard to the South Pacific and Australia, on the one hand, and the Indian Ocean, on the other, were most difficult. Much as special efforts rescued American codebreakers in the Philippines, an- other had been mounted to extract Philippine C-in-C General Douglas A. MacArthur, who reached Australia in March 1942. MacArthur's future employment in a position commensurate with his stature became a con- cern. He appeared on the scene at a crucial moment, when the Allies had come to the final stages of their division of Pacific operational areas. The new Southwest Pacific Command (SOWESPAC), to be responsible for Australia, New Guinea, and the islands surrounding those places, was established on April 18, a couple of weeks after recognition of the area as a military theater of operations. Although Washington planners had envisioned a different officer heading SOWESPAC, MacArthur's selection emerged as an easy solution, and he was duly appointed.

General MacArthur organized the defense of Australia with alacrity and began building SOWESPAC forces into the juggernaut they became. Profiting from the presence of a body of U.S. troops and airmen, on their way to the Philippines when the war began, MacArthur created a maneuver force in Australia that soon intervened in the New Guinea campaign. MacArthur's bombers quickly overshadowed Australian planes in aerial attacks on Rabaul, and SOWESPAC aircraft played a role in the Battle of the Coral Sea. But his command focused on checking the Japanese advance, which at this time meant halting Tokyo's army in New Guinea.

As a result of early agreements between the major Allies—the United States and Great Britain—the powers had adopted a "Europe first" strategy. Operations and forces would be concentrated to stop Hitler's Germany and defeat the Nazis. The strategy provided for a defensive stance in the Pacific. Given that approach, the allocation of forces and of the stream of new tanks, trucks, and planes rolling off the production lines favored the Atlantic. The Pacific would be accorded only a fraction of the troops and equipment. This raised the concomitant question of where they should be sent. During the very first months, shipments were funneled to Australia because of its weakness, its undeniable importance as a base for an Allied counteroffensive, and the fact that a supply flow to the continent down under was already under way when hostilities began.

As General MacArthur stocked his training camps, organized troops, and packed the air bases with planes, the SOWESPAC situation seemed less critical. But there remained the matter of defending the sea-lanes to Australia. Allied intelligence had found several indications of Japanese interest in a South Pacific offensive. There were a few New Zealand troops scattered among the islands, and the Australians had extended a defense umbrella over the Vichy French colony of New Caledonia in late 1940, placing a small garrison at Nouméa. American Marines held Johnston Island. The New Hebrides, Fiji, Samoa, Canton, Palmyra, Tonga, Bora Bora, and other places appeared vulnerable. Planners in Washington and Canberra devoted great energy to debating how to divide meager equipment among the many vulnerable, strategic places that required defense. More than 50,000 troops would eventually be deployed there.

The first major dispute arose over these arrangements. The U.S. Army viewed the South Pacific islands as part of the SOWESPAC domain. Maintaining that the island bases were integral to preserving the sea-lanes, and that defense of sea frontiers was inherently a maritime mission, the Navy argued that the islands belonged under CINCPAC. Eventually the Army conceded. As a result the South Pacific command (SOPAC) emerged as one of CINCPAC's operational sectors. Admirals King and Nimitz conferred at San Francisco on April 23, 1942, and there delineated SOPAC's role. King had by then selected Vice Admiral Robert L. Ghormley, recently returned from London, where he had headed the U.S. naval mission to Great Britain, as the new head of SOPAC.

Beyond means and command there were inevitable practical questions. It was one thing for presidents and prime ministers to agree on a "Europe first" approach with their Combined Chiefs of Staff, quite another to decide what the available forces should actually do. The United States had spent decades tinkering with its blueprint for fighting Japan, "War Plan Orange," but that contingency assumed a focus on the Pacific, and some of the important forces for executing it had been wiped out at Pearl Harbor. The U.S. Asiatic Fleet and many Allied forces, including the British capital ships that formed the backbone of the Royal Navy's Eastern Fleet, had then been destroyed in the futile effort to hold the Malay Barrier. There needed to be a new design to use existing Allied strength.

Admiral Ernest J. King, the COMINCH or commander in chief of the U.S. Navy, took the lead in Pacific strategy debates. King won his point when arguing at the Arcadia conference for defense of the South Pacific islands. As early as February, a planning paper written by King's staff suggested that an island in the Solomons be taken and held to link the Allied bases. Admiral King did not stop there. Not willing to countenance a passive posture, King prodded CINCPAC to engage in offensive action to the extent possible, mentioning the Bismarcks-Solomons area in this specific context. The carrier raids Nimitz initiated in February and March 1942, including the abortive mission to Rabaul, and the raid actually carried out on New Guinea, accorded with King's concept. Even before interservice agreement on a Solomons operation, King instructed Nimitz to prepare a major amphibious attack to be carried out between the areas of SOPAC and SOWESPAC. The King-Nimitz meeting at San Francisco in April—the same one where the CINCPAC explained his determination to fight in the Coral Sea—confirmed the offensive. Days after that confab Admiral King ordered the creation of a South Pacific Amphibious Force built around the 1st Marine Division. In a sense SOPAC was established for the specific purpose of carrying out a Solomons offensive.

British prime minister Winston Churchill also encouraged a U.S. Pacific offensive to prevent the Japanese from concentrating on Burma and India. As the British discovered obstacles to early action in Europe or North Africa, they agitated even more for an offensive simply in order that the Allies be seen as combating the enemy. Not long before the Battle of Midway, Admiral King capitalized on these attitudes, pointing out that the Japanese were focusing on the front that arced from Australia around to Hawaii and Alaska in the eastern Pacific. Offensive action would be the appropriate counter. Toward the end of June, flush with the enthusiasm from victory at Midway, Admiral King directed CINCPAC to prepare to invade the lower Solomons with U.S. Marines. King and Nimitz met again at San Francisco in early July. As they conferred, Station Hypo codebreakers supplied a decrypt revealing Japanese troops and construction units on Guadalcanal. The admirals instantly zeroed in on that area. The enemy base at Tulagi, which COMINCH wanted taken before the Imperial Navy could consolidate, became a specific objective. King's formal directive made this a priority.

Meanwhile, after the Coral Sea, General MacArthur also weighed in. The SOWESPAC chieftain proposed to concentrate almost all Allied resources under himself to strike past New Guinea to the Philippines, then on to Japan. While this grandiose scheme was not feasible, it put MacArthur, too, on record favoring an offensive. When departing the Philippines he had promised to return. But a straight-up northerly advance, leaving Rabaul untouched on his right flank, would be extremely hazardous. SOWESPAC foresaw capturing the Japanese base outright using a single amphibious division. That did not seem doable either. MacArthur and Nimitz worked with Washington to refine concepts, and "Operation Cartwheel" emerged, intended to capture or isolate Rabaul as an adjunct to the SOWESPAC battle on New Guinea. The disputes between SOWESPAC and CINCPAC need not

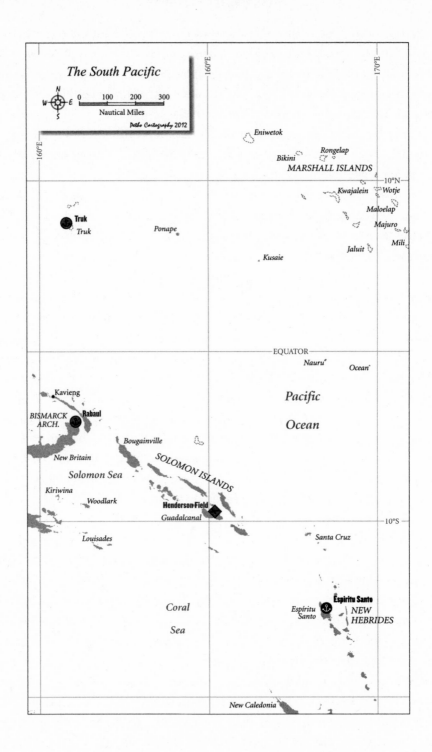

The South Pacific

0   100   200   300
Nautical Miles

Patho Cartography 2012

160°E

170°E

160°E

Eniwetok

Bikini   Rongelap

MARSHALL ISLANDS

10°N

Kwajalein   Wotje

Maloelap

Truk   Ponape   Majuro

Truk   Mili

Jaluit

Kusaie

EQUATOR

Nauru   Ocean

Pacific

Ocean

Kavieng

BISMARCK   Rabaul
ARCH.

Bougainville

New Britain   SOLOMON ISLANDS

Solomon Sea

Kiriwina

Woodlark   Henderson Field

Guadalcanal   10°S

Louisades   Santa Cruz

Coral   Espíritu Santo

Espíritu   NEW
Sea   Santo   HEBRIDES

New Caledonia

detain us except to note that relations between General MacArthur and his colleagues remained touchy throughout. But due to the amount of naval activity required to attack the lower Solomons, MacArthur agreed to cede a portion of his theater to give SOPAC authority over the waters in which a Solomons operation would occur. That became "Task One" of Cartwheel, to proceed to later phases—culminating in the direct attack on Rabaul— over which SOWESPAC would again hold sway.

Fredericksburg, Texas, is not quite a two-horse town, but it is a place where Main Street still means something. There are just a couple of major inter- sections and a population of less than seven thousand people, many of them, like Chester W. Nimitz himself, of German immigrant stock. It was much smaller—just a few streets—when Nimitz was born in a white frame house there in February 1885. Nearly 200 miles from water, above all this town could be considered unlikely to produce an admiral of the ocean seas. But that would be to ignore the determination of the man, his hard-boiled common sense, and the influence of his grandfather—a former German merchant seaman. In fact, the practical Nimitz sought a college education and saw the service academies as the way to obtain his degree. Nimitz chose the Army and applied to West Point, only to discover no appointment was available. So he entered and won a competition sponsored by his congress- man for an appointment to the U.S. Naval Academy. Nimitz graduated from Annapolis seventh in the class of 1905, initially serving aboard the battleship *Ohio*. He was commissioned two years later.

Nimitz was perceptive, resourceful, and smart as a whip. As a young en- sign in the Philippines he skippered the gunboat *Panay*, and got a destroyer command when his contemporaries were mostly still division officers. Nimitz remained unaffected by the court-martial required when he ran his destroyer aground at Batangas. That kind of incident could finish a less talented officer. But his admiral downgraded the proceeding to a board of inquiry, which issued a reprimand, and then rejected any public upbraiding, confining the reprimand simply to its statement in the board report. With submarines in their infancy in the U.S. fleet, Nimitz became a submariner—under protest, it is true (he had wanted a battleship billet), but a key career development. Barely four years out of Annapolis, Nimitz led a submarine flotilla as a lieutenant. His evident ability and ease at making friends served Nimitz well.

He was also intrepid and resourceful, as shown when Nimitz rescued a sailor fallen overboard. On a different occasion he saved another seaman from drowning. An engineering specialist, Nimitz championed diesel power to replace gasoline engines in the submarine fleet. Later he survived a potentially fatal accident with a diesel engine, losing part of a finger but saved by his Academy class ring, which jammed the works and prevented the machine from sucking in his arm. Nimitz participated in the first underway refueling ever conducted by the Navy, was an aide to top admirals commanding the entire U.S. fleet, and established the Navy's first reserve officer training corps unit. He captained a cruiser with the Asiatic Fleet; submarine, cruiser, and battleship divisions; and made rear admiral in 1938. Admiral Chester W. Nimitz was in charge of the Navy's personnel department when, ten days after the Pearl Harbor attack, he was suddenly ordered to the stricken base to breathe life into the still-stunned Pacific Fleet. In a highly unusual tribute to his qualities, Chester Nimitz was promoted from rear directly to full admiral as he took up the Pacific Fleet command.

The wrecks of the warships devastated by the Japanese still smoldered as Nimitz arrived at Pearl. He raised eyebrows, holding his change-of-command ceremony on the deck of a submarine—the first time a fleet command had ever transferred on an undersea boat—and more by refusing to relieve officers on the Pacific Fleet staff. Already the dispute over who was "responsible" for Pearl Harbor had ignited a witch-hunt for scapegoats. Admiral Nimitz proved equally loyal to subordinates and superiors—a crucial element in restoring the fleet's confidence. He did fire a few men, most important some of those responsible for the fiasco during an attempt to reinforce Wake Island, but only after careful consideration.

Admiral Nimitz coupled this consideration with smarts and a tactically aggressive stance. His carrier attacks materially annoyed the Japanese. Nimitz had no problem with the improvised scheme to fly land-based B-25 bombers off an aircraft carrier for the Doolittle raid. He appreciated the information from Captain Layton, his fleet intelligence officer, and Commander Rochefort of Station Hypo. The admiral's response laid the basis for the Coral Sea and Midway actions. While higher-ups were still disputing theaters and commanders, it was Nimitz, in the spring of 1942, who first suggested taking a Marine Raider battalion and using it against the Japanese at Tulagi. Then, four days after the Battle of the Coral Sea, Admiral Nimitz issued guidance to Vice Admiral Ghormley at SOPAC. The orders instructed Ghormley to prepare a major amphibious offensive against Japanese-held positions. Guadalcanal had yet to become the target.

Thus Chester Nimitz set the stage. In the South Pacific, Vice Admiral Ghormley spent a month familiarizing himself with the area and visiting the key players, from General MacArthur to Australian government officials and French colonials in Nouméa, where SOPAC headquarters would be located. Ghormley assumed command of SOPAC on June 19. He planned to drive the Japanese off Tulagi and occupy a suitable airfield site on adjacent Guadalcanal. In mid-July Ghormley was joined by Rear Admiral Richmond Kelly Turner, who left his post as a Washington planner to take over the South Pacific Amphibious Force. Together they would mount the actual landing on Guadalcanal. By then there were just two weeks left before the invasion's target date.

Alexander Archer Vandegrift was a fighting Marine. The Guadalcanal landing force would be his own 1st Marine Division plus some extra units, but less a regiment in Samoa. When called into Ghormley's office and told to arrange for an assault landing on August 1, Vandegrift did not even know where Guadalcanal was, much less have the detailed knowledge to plan an invasion. But Major General Vandegrift set out to obtain it. The push to nail down the facts on Guadalcanal helped enshrine the last two pillars of intelligence, overhead photography and combat intelligence—the kind of data provided by willing private citizens or prisoner interrogation.

Division intelligence officer Lieutenant Colonel Frank B. Goettge did much of this work from Australia. It was Goettge who sent officers to visit Ferdinand and find out what the coastwatchers knew. Commander Feldt forwarded current reporting to Goettge. Yearbooks and standard reference sources were culled for data. The Australian government quietly spread the word among its citizenry, yielding a stream of postcard pictures, letters to and from people who had lived on Guadalcanal, and recollections of civil administrators. Goettge looked for the most informative contacts and had officers interview missionaries, nuns, traders, island clipper sailors, government officials, and planters. Eight former employees of Lever Brothers or Burns-Philp South Sea Traders were given reserve commissions in the Australian Navy and assigned to the 1st Marine Division, where they assembled a sketch map of the Lunga Point area. The cartography was poor—mislocated hills, misplaced and misnamed rivers—but it was all the Marines would have. Their most recent nautical chart dated from 1910. Goettge pressed for a scout mission. A sub could carry him with a team of experts to the 'Canal. Ghormley thought that too dangerous and nixed the idea.

Two Marine officers flew on a SOWESPAC air mission over Guadalcanal. But their B-17, attacked by Japanese Zeroes, left quickly. SOWESPAC's overhead photography was converted into a photo mosaic of Lunga Point. Then MacArthur's air intelligence people sent the mosaic to the wrong address. General Vandegrift's planners never got the take. Admiral Ghormley has generally received short shrift from historians, and this account will not differ. But on the matter of overhead photography he deserves high marks. In England, Ghormley had seen the miracles the British were accomplishing with aerial spies. He took steps to replicate these skills in the United States. The Navy set up a photographic interpretation school in Washington headed by Lieutenant Commander Robert S. Quackenbush, familiarly known as "Q-bush." Once he arrived at SOPAC, Ghormley demanded a field unit with Q-bush in charge. The fiasco with the SOWESPAC aerial mosaic confirmed the admiral's sense that South Pacific Command needed its own photographic interpretation capability.

Beginning with the Guadalcanal landing, SOPAC would be well served by its photo interpreters. Admiral Ghormley's estimate of Japanese strength in the Guadalcanal-Tulagi area would be nearly exact. Vandegrift's headquarters wildly overestimated enemy strength, putting it at 8,400, about two and a half times the actual, while Admiral Turner also produced a huge overestimate (7,100). JNAF aircraft strength was similarly overestimated. But Captain Frederick C. Sherman of the carrier *Wasp*, which helped support the invasion, later commented that he had received everything he needed from an August 2 photo mission and from radio intelligence.

Accurate or not, General Vandegrift's staff took what data they had and incorporated it into the plan. Much as the intelligence was improvised, so was everything else. The last elements of the division were not even scheduled into New Zealand until July 11, and every ship would need to be "combat loaded," which necessitated docking all their cargo and then reloading it in the order in which it would be used in battle. Not only was this an enormous job; it consumed more space in vessels' cargo holds. The Marines left behind as much baggage as they could, but it was not enough. Vandegrift made the hard decisions to forfeit some of his artillery and vehicles, then to cut back the scale of supply to sixty days of fuel and food and just ten to fifteen days' worth of ammunition. Even with that, reloading continued on Aotea Quay until virtually the moment the invasion armada left Wellington.

Summoned to Ghormley's headquarters on July 18, General Vandegrift sat down for the first time with amphibious commander Admiral Turner. The Marine general had known Turner as a naval planner in Washington and the two got on well, though Kelly Turner's abrasive manner rubbed some the wrong way. In any case Vandegrift felt relief, since Turner, just arrived, had no time to craft a plan and perforce had to rely upon the Marine one. The senior officers agreed the schedule just could not be met and applied for a delay until August 7. Higher command accepted that. Ghormley informed the others that he was giving tactical command to Frank Fletcher, absent during all these preparations.

The morning of July 22—a perfect South Pacific day of bright sun and spotless sky—the fleet sortied from Wellington. They were headed for Fiji, where an invasion rehearsal had been laid on. Arriving on July 26, the force rendezvoused with Fletcher's carriers, plus flotillas carrying other invasion units. Admiral Fletcher summoned the senior officers to flagship *Saratoga* for a face-to-face meeting. The destroyer *Hull* had just arrived, carrying Ghormley's chief of staff, Rear Admiral Daniel J. Callaghan; SOPAC land-based air chief Rear Admiral John S. McCain; and other officers. Turner and Vandegrift joined them for the ride to the *Saratoga*. Protocol dictated that the senior officer, in this case "Slew" McCain, board first. Just as the admiral climbed the Jacob's ladder, some fellow opened a garbage chute and dumped a stream of milk, drenching McCain. He was furious. Worse was to come.

Admiral Fletcher received the visitors in the *Saratoga*'s wardroom. Last to arrive was Rear Admiral Thomas C. Kinkaid, who led the *Enterprise* battle group in Fletcher's Task Force 61. With the brass seated, Fletcher opened the meeting. After preliminary remarks he advised his counterparts that Task Force 61 would cover the invasion for seventy-two hours and then withdraw. The others were aghast. Kelly Turner warned that he needed at least four days after the invasion (five in all)—not the three Fletcher offered—to unload his cargomen. General Vandegrift seconded Turner, observing that the era of small landing forces quickly put ashore was over. Even with five days, the 1st Marine Division would have difficulties. Admiral Callaghan of SOPAC also warned against premature withdrawal of air support, adding that land-based aircraft lacked the range to help. Participants differ on whether the conversation amounted to a bitter dispute or simply spirited debate, but the central points are that Frank Jack Fletcher knew that his carriers were critical to the invasion, that the project was critical to the U.S. high command, and that he had been put on notice that his own idea of leaving after three days was deemed dangerous by the key executive commanders.

There is no gainsaying the importance of this episode. Fletcher's defenders and Kelly Turner's biographer try to shift blame onto Admiral Ghormley's shoulders, and some measure of that is justified. But the evidence conflicts. As theater commander, Ghormley ought to have been present at the only exchange that would take place among his key subordinates, rather than simply sending a representative, however senior. But his general instructions were to run SOPAC and leave fighting to the combat commanders. On the other hand, specific messages from both admirals King and Nimitz instructed Ghormley to "exercise strategic command in person." One can debate the meaning of "strategic" in the phrase "strategic command" and dispute whether this meant operational control, but it remains clear that Ghormley was to do that personally. His passivity augured against overruling Fletcher's peremptory dictum. Yet, whatever Robert Ghormley's sins, they were of omission; Frank Fletcher's were a different matter. The task force commander brazenly told colleagues he would pull the rug out from under them, and held to that in the face of fair warning.

The most powerful argument in Fletcher's favor goes to the question of who held the advantage in the Pacific. Task Force 61 included every flattop the Americans had. Lose those flight decks and Japan might take Midway after all, not to say Pearl Harbor. Fletcher's caution might preserve those precious warships. At Midway, Nimitz had set a policy of calculated risk, which he interpreted to mean carriers should be put in harm's way only for results that justified the risk. Nimitz had not rescinded that, and he was aware of Fletcher's intention to withdraw early. Excusing Fletcher on this basis, however, requires a judgment that CINCPAC's general operational policy overrode his own specific orders—and those of Washington—to afford this invasion all the support it needed. Moreover, as will be seen, Admiral Fletcher ultimately did not meet his own promises.

Meanwhile the invasion drill at Fiji turned into a fiasco. On the first day some landings were canceled despite calm seas due to worries over damage to the small craft. Coral offshore threatened the boats. Defective boat engines were discovered. Marines reached two planned beaches before the recall. The best aspect would be having the men practice climbing down onto the boats. It also became apparent that ships bearing key units for the Tulagi landing would arrive too late to exercise. About a third of the Marines succeeded in boarding their landing craft. The gunfire support ships and the aircraft from Fletcher's carriers also rehearsed coordination. Refueling the fleet went slowly, and critically needed tankers failed to arrive. Some destroyers were not full when the Guadalcanal voyage began. During the cruise the amphibious group actually fueled destroyers from invasion transports. Fortunately enemy defenses were nothing like what Marines had predicted.

Under Marine procedures the division intelligence section was in charge of the care and feeding of the news media. Lieutenant Merillat encountered many of these war correspondents while the 1st Marines were in New Zealand, from Tillman Durdin of the *New York Times* to Francis McCarthy of the United Press and Douglas Gardner of the *Sydney Morning Herald*. The press was fed a stylized version of events. On the day of the invasion the *New York Times* reported on *Japanese* offensive action in the Solomons, although the paper made the important point that the enemy was bypassing many islands in their quest for victory, leaving these entirely unoccupied. On August 9 in New York—with Marines now ashore for three days—the *Times* headline read, "Japanese Occupy 3 Island Groups." It took time for the news to reach home. Americans first learned of Operation Watchtower and the Guadal-canal invasion from a CINCPAC communiqué on August 8, which informed readers that "Forces of the United States Pacific Fleet and Pacific Ocean Areas, assisted by units of the Southwest Pacific Area, launched offensive operations in the Tulagi area of the Solomons Islands on August 7th." The notice added that "operations are progressing favorably." That news had already been overtaken by events.

II.

UNDER THE SOUTHERN CROSS

When Marines invaded Guadalcanal, the Japanese responded instantly. Certainly the enemy needed to do something, but what they did astonished everyone. It began at Rabaul early that morning. Staff officer Ohmae knocked on Admiral Mikawa's door with Tulagi's first radio message. Mikawa answered quickly. The admiral immediately ordered forces assembled. He then dressed and walked the single block to fleet headquarters. In the time it took to do that, the news had been confirmed: Americans were landing at both Tulagi and Guadalcanal. Emergency!

What happened next had much to do with Captain Kami Shigenori, Mikawa's senior staff officer. In the Imperial Navy, Kami had a justified reputation as a hothead. It was rumored he had once done a handstand from a sixteen-inch gun on the battleship *Mutsu* with her main battery inclined to maximum elevation. Forty years old, Kami expressed himself very emotionally and was a fitness devotee who used off-hours for sumo wrestling and the sword-fighting style known as kendo. After graduating top of his class from the War College, and service at the ministry, Kami had been posted to Germany as assistant naval attaché. Impressed with Hitler's dynamism, he dallied with fascism, emerging as an important member of the Navy's pro-German faction. Kami returned to the Navy Ministry, then the War College as tactics instructor, and he promoted the Tripartite Pact aligning Japan with Nazi Germany and Fascist Italy. His extreme views and forceful style made Kami a dangerous man. Even some friends felt he should not have been seconded to sea commands. At NGS, where he had worked for Baron Tomioka, colleagues recalled Kami as holding the strongest opinions, with Tomioka having a tendency to bend to him. Promoted captain shortly before Pearl Harbor, Kami had been the biggest proponent of an attack on the Panama Canal. When news of Guadalcanal reached Rabaul, Captain Kami immediately demanded the Eighth Fleet make an all-out assault.

Admiral Mikawa responded without knowing whether the Allies had come to stay. Fortuitously, plans for New Guinea now played in favor of action at Guadalcanal. The 25th Air Flotilla had been slated to bomb Buna. Its mission was redirected. Mikawa then planned a night surface attack on the Allied fleet with everything he could scrape together. He summoned flagship *Chokai* from Kavieng. Rear Admiral Goto Aritomo's Cruiser Division 6, its four heavy ships also there, would have escorted a Buna convoy. Goto participated along with Admiral Matsuyama's light cruisers and the single available destroyer. About 400 naval troops were herded aboard a transport and sent to the 'Canal as an emergency reinforcement. Admiral Mikawa with his staff boarded the heavy cruiser *Chokai* at 4:30 p.m. Captain Kami reunited with an Etajima classmate who was the ship's executive officer. Kami had never been in a naval battle. This would be a wild one.

Mikawa put his intentions into a dispatch to Combined Fleet and the Navy General Staff. At the NGS, Admiral Nagano Osami thought Mikawa rash and wanted to countermand his plan. But staffers convinced Nagano to subside. At Combined Fleet there was concern too, but, anxious to fight the enemy promptly, lest the Allies establish themselves and attack Rabaul, neither Yamamoto nor Ugaki voiced any objection.

Meanwhile, the pillars of Allied intelligence were hard at work. The Combat Intelligence Unit at Pearl Harbor had reported steadily on the Japanese cruisers in the Solomons, seen by air searches at least twice in the days before Watchtower. Radio traffic analysis placed *Chokai*, Mikawa's flagship, the heavy ships of Cruiser Division 6, and the light ones of Cruiser Division 18 all in the Solomons. This formula was repeated several times. A wartime history of Ultra in the Pacific is worth quoting here: "[I]t is evident that [Allied] operational authorities were aware of the presence in the Solomons of the enemy cruisers." Further, the codebreakers intercepted messages formatted as operational orders, directed to Yamada's 25th Air Flotilla and Rear Admiral Kono Chimaki's Submarine Squadron 3, plus to SNLF commanders demanding troop reinforcements. Traffic analysis confirmed Admiral Mikawa aboard a flagship, not positively identified, but he had already been associated with the *Chokai*. A message *from* Rabaul *to* Mikawa's chief of staff gave the tip-off that the fleet boss was at sea, and the reply gave direction finders the geographic coordinates. A partially decrypted Ultra message contained Yamada's tabulation of available aircraft, while others ordered aerial reinforcement of Rabaul. Admiral Richmond Kelly Turner had refused to bring along one of the fleet's mobile radio detachments and now paid dearly for that. But Frank Fletcher certainly had one—Ransom Fullinwider's unit.

On the night of August 7, as Mikawa's warships rendezvoused outside Rabaul to run down The Slot—as the waters between the Solomon Islands became known—they were sighted and reported by American submarine *S-38*. The radio intelligence on Mikawa should not be overplayed; since some dispatches took longer to decrypt, all were partial breaks subject to interpretation, and they failed to reveal concrete intentions. But the submarine contact alone was enough to warn Allied admirals, and the radio items related the Japanese fleet commander to it. Admiral Turner called for extra air searches of The Slot, but these do not seem to have been carried out. Mikawa's cruiser group was, however, sighted and followed by an Australian search plane on the morning of the eighth. Its valiant efforts to deliver the information were frustrated, and the report reached Turner too late. There are also questions about the searches carried out by Admiral Fletcher's task force.* Beyond that, Ultra finally did intercept a Mikawa message containing details of his plan, but the new version of JN-25 the Imperial Navy was using still resisted penetration. This key dispatch would be recovered—more than two weeks after the disaster about to occur.

The Guadalcanal invaders also helped. Australian vice admiral Victor Crutchley was in tactical command. The necessity of blocking two possible approaches perplexed him—Savo Island split The Slot above Guadalcanal. The Japanese could reach the anchorage either way. Crutchley's solution was to post groups of cruisers and destroyers on either side of Savo, with a couple more within the anchorage. Crutchley himself had been in the southern group on the *Australia*, but left to attend a meeting Admiral Turner had called. Each of the forward units had three cruisers and a pair of tin

---

* There are important discrepancies over both whether Turner's "extra" search was carried out, and the scope of the Task Force 61 afternoon scouting pattern. The accounts of Bruce Loxton with Chris Coulthard-Clark, on the one hand, and John B. Lundstrom, on the other, investigate these in the greatest depth. Lundstrom, in particular, maintains that Fletcher's afternoon search reached to within thirty miles of Mikawa's position, though he presents no direct evidence for that.

cans. *Australia*'s departure left two cruisers with the southern group. The disposition looked good on paper but invited piecemeal destruction.

Imperial Navy night battle tactics were very good. Indeed, the Battle of Savo Island confirmed their reputation. Admiral Mikawa's vessels saw the Allies first, approached the southern cruiser group in line-ahead formation, and launched torpedoes before firing. The U.S. destroyer that had the picket duty remained oblivious. Within minutes the American heavy cruiser *Chicago* and the Australian light *Canberra* were both crippled. The latter sank. No warning reached the other Allied cruiser group before Mikawa was upon them. Heavy cruisers *Astoria*, *Vincennes*, and *Quincy* were all blown apart within fifteen minutes. Admiral Mikawa obtained a decisive victory.

The Japanese could have pressed on into the anchorage to smash the Allied transports. Commander Ohmae was with Mikawa when he chose not to. The admiral based himself on several factors. First, his ships had expended much ammunition (roughly a fourth to a third of main battery shells and half the available torpedoes), making a shipping attack more problematic. Battle maneuvers had put the Japanese on a heading away from Guadalcanal. The time required to regroup and enter the anchorage would put a fight just before dawn. Mikawa knew that daylight would leave him open to air attack no matter what, and it seemed desirable to be moving away from the danger area at speed when that happened. Imperial Navy radio intelligence had intercepted transmissions characteristic of U.S. aircraft carriers, so Mikawa knew a task force lay within about a hundred miles of him. Finally, the Japanese Army had told the Navy that wiping out the Americans would be a simple thing. At this moment when an aggressive attitude could have served his Navy the most, Kami Shigenori's posture remains unknown. Admiral Mikawa ordered the withdrawal at 2:23 a.m. on August 9. That marked the beginning of a long and bloody campaign in which victory in the Pacific hung in the balance.

IRONBOTTOM SOUND

The other prong of Admiral Mikawa's immediate counterattack had been an air strike the day of the invasion. Yamada assembled twenty-seven Betty bombers escorted by eighteen Zero fighters and sent them toward Guadalcanal. Coastwatcher Paul Mason saw them over Bougainville and warned of the raid. Australian cruiser *Canberra* piped its crew to lunch early so they would be ready. When the Japanese arrived, Fletcher's carrier fighters quickly engaged them. An *Enterprise* flight met the enemy over Santa Isabel Island. They splashed a Betty but lost several F-4F Wildcats to the escort. More *Enterprise* interceptors battled over Florida Island. They downed another Betty and claimed four more probables. Armed to strike New Guinea, the JNAF bombers could do no better than a level bombing attack. They made no hits.

The JNAF escort fighters, led by Lieutenant Commander Nakajima Tadashi, flew in small "squadrons" of six Zeroes each, because of Rabaul's shortage of planes. But the Tainan Air Group was among the Imperial Navy's best, containing several leading aces. One unit preceded the bombers to disrupt interceptors. The others flew close escort. Petty Officer Sakai Saburo encountered the Wildcat fighter here for the first time and was amazed at the plane's durability. Closing to point-blank range, Sakai managed to shoot one down. Its American pilot, "Pug" Southerland of the *Saratoga*, incredibly, endured cannon fire right into his cockpit, bailed out, and survived. Sakai's comrade Nishizawa Hiroyoshi claimed six U.S. planes. According to Sakai, none of the other Zero pilots scored that day. Historian John B. Lundstrom, however, records an array of JNAF claims totaling more than forty aircraft, and finds that nine Wildcats plus a Dauntless dive-bomber were actually blasted. The redoubtable coastwatchers rescued several pilots. Four JNAF bombers were lost, two so badly damaged they were written off, and excepting two others the rest were hit to some degree. Among the fighters, two Zeroes failed to return, and Sakai's plane was an effective loss. Half a dozen were damaged enough or so low on fuel they landed at the base the JNAF had now opened at Buka on Bougainville.

Sakai Saburo's survival story is epic. Sakai closed in on a group of planes in tight formation, not realizing they were Dauntless SBDs, featuring paired, rear-firing machine guns. When Sakai discovered the error it was too late to abort his attack run. The eight SBDs laced Sakai's Zero with bullets, one of which grazed his head while others shattered its windshield. The airman briefly blacked out but recovered his plane from a dive and flew instinctively, bleeding, hardly able to see, for several hours until landing at Lakunai. Petty Officer Sakai's plight well illustrates JNAF's difficulties fighting at Guadalcanal. Damaged airplanes had far to go for anywhere to land.

Quite often they never returned. The lack of air bases in the lower Solomons became a major Japanese strategic headache.

Meanwhile a second wave of JNAF planes approached the 'Canal. This was a squadron of nine "Val" dive-bombers. Anxious to hit the enemy, Admiral Yamada had sent these planes knowing they lacked the range to return. Crews were told to make for Shortland and ditch where the aircraft tender *Akitsushima* had a floatplane base. Only three reached that place—and one crew perished in the water landing. The rest were destroyed by U.S. fighters or flak. The strike inflicted slight damage on destroyer *Mugford*. Japanese land-based dive-bombers were typically armed with 120-pound bombs that lacked the punch to seriously affect a warship. Yamada's second wave had been a desperate mission.

Rabaul might not have scored much on D-Day, but so long as the JNAF could keep up its attacks, it was merely a matter of time until they did. Thus, neutralizing Rabaul was a key element in Watchtower. That mission went to MacArthur and SOWESPAC, where General George C. Kenney had just taken the reins of what became the Fifth Air Force. MacArthur and he discussed a Rabaul attack, and, following his inspections, Kenney decided SOWESPAC could put eighteen to twenty B-17s over Rabaul on invasion day. He later wrote that the flight had run into an equal number of Japanese interceptors, had had to fight its way in, and had scored "a real bull's eye," wrecking at least half the 150 enemy planes "lined up wingtip to wingtip along both sides of the runway" at Vunakanau—results supposedly verified by poststrike photography. The commander was awarded a Distinguished Flying Cross, and one pilot—captured and executed—received the Congressional Medal of Honor.

General Kenney's claims are not accurate. Not only were there not 150 Japanese flying machines at Rabaul—nor, for that matter, the additional hundred Kenney says were observed arriving days before Watchtower—but nearly half of Admiral Yamada's aircraft were off attacking Guadalcanal when the B-17s struck. In addition, the runway damage proved insufficient to prevent returning planes from landing a few hours later. A squadron of twin-engine Bettys came from Tinian that afternoon and had no difficulty either. Nor did Vice Admiral Tsukahara Nizhizo, Yamada's boss as C-in-C of the Eleventh Air Fleet, who arrived to lead the countercharge. At 7:30 the next morning the JNAF began launching the first of twenty-six Bettys with fifteen more Zeroes for escort. They too had no trouble taking off. Rabaul had not been neutralized.

Lieutenant Kotani Shigeru led the formation, this time torpedo-armed. Kotani hoped to hit the American carriers but, lacking word of them, went for Guadalcanal. Remarkably a Japanese scout plane passed close to Fletcher's force that morning without seeing it. Kotani's planes passed coastwatcher Jack Read, who promptly alerted the 'Canal. Read had problems with his connection, but another radio finally picked up his message and relayed it in time. Admiral Turner ordered the flotilla to weigh anchor so they could maneuver under attack. Marine Herbert Merillat watched from the beach and recorded the action this way:

> Someone told me that an air raid was due in about ten minutes. This was the first I had heard of it. I rushed up to the beach to watch the show. And what a show it was. I didn't see the Jap planes at first, but a sky full of flak from our transports told me they were there. Then I saw them. They swooped in from the east, unbelievably low, and swept along the lanes of transports. Antiaircraft fire from the ships was terrific. Jap planes plunged in flames—one, two, three, so many I lost count. One ran the gauntlet and started out to sea, toward the west. A fighter dived on him and sent him flaming into the sea. There was so much smoke and flame in the transport area that I thought surely many of our ships must have been hit.

Despite early warning, the patrolling Wildcats were out of position. They engaged only after the raiders' torpedo runs. The Japanese attacked ferociously, some planes only a few tens of feet above the sea, but their determination went unrewarded. Transport *George F. Elliott*, struck by a crashing Betty, and destroyer *Jarvis*, hit by a torpedo, were the only vessels harmed. The *Jarvis* limped away to be finished off by airplanes the following day. The *Elliott* burned down to the waterline and finally sank. But flak and fighters savaged the raiders. Only five bombers returned to Rabaul, a couple too badly damaged to fly. The 125 disappeared crewmen represented the biggest single loss of JNAF land-based aircrews of the entire campaign.

Exhausted survivors of Lieutenant Kotani's mission made fantastic claims of success, but their real impact was on the mind of Frank Jack Fletcher. It was significant to the admiral that the Japanese had hit with torpedoes. Fletcher knew that one strike the previous day had utilized dive-bombers of the type borne by Japanese aircraft carriers. Although U.S. intelligence still placed the enemy carriers in Empire waters, the COMINCH intelligence summary of August 8 recorded sighting a carrier-type ship seventy miles northwest of Rabaul. While the report noted the craft as most resembling aircraft tender *Kasuga Maru* (the Japanese were now regularly using such ships to ferry aircraft to Rabaul), in light of the Val attack Fletcher worried about a real Japanese carrier. For a leader anxious about his vulnerable flight decks, who had had carriers shot out under him in two previous battles, fear galvanized action.

At midafternoon, having learned details of the torpedo attack, Admiral Fletcher consulted his tactical commander about withdrawal. Shortly after 4:00 p.m., Task Force 61 turned southwest, then south, then bore southeast, to judge from the track of carrier *Wasp.* These alterations meant Admiral Fletcher was steaming *away* from Guadalcanal. At that instant Mikawa's Japanese cruisers were about 300 miles away, off Choiseul and bearing down The Slot, yet to fight at Savo Island. By the next morning the reverse applied—had Fletcher remained in place or moved toward the enemy, Mikawa's retreating cruiser force would have been exposed to a powerful retaliatory assault. This episode was fraught with consequence. Anxious to defend Fletcher against every criticism, biographer John B. Lundstrom quotes sources indicating the admiral wanted to make a night attack. But Fletcher's heading lengthened the range every minute, his position data on Mikawa was eight hours old, and his own decisions limited his afternoon search. These were not the actions of a leader seeking battle. Though *Wasp* had squadrons qualified in night flying, they were not used. The morning after Savo the American flattops were out of range, when they could easily have been poised to strike.

Lundstrom obfuscates Fletcher's timing by referring only to the last turnaway, shortly before 7:00 p.m. About an hour earlier Fletcher had sent SOPAC a dispatch recommending he withdraw due to loss of fighter air-

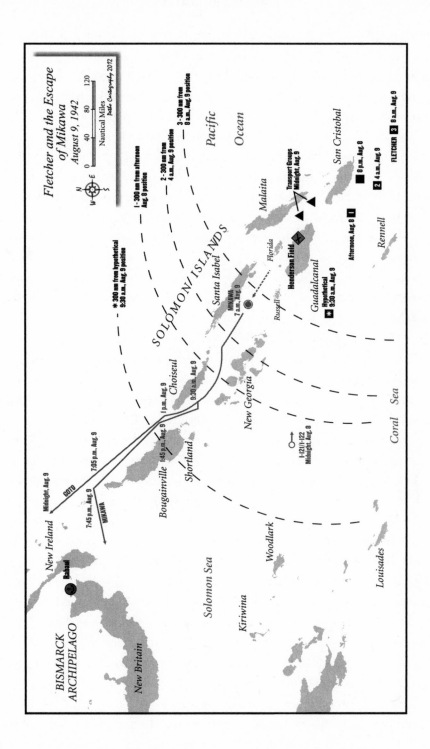

Fletcher and the Escape
of Mikawa
August 9, 1942

Délé Cartography 2012

Nautical Miles

0   40   80   120

N
W   E
S

1 - 300 nm from afternoon
Aug. 8 position

2 - 300 nm from
4 a.m. Aug. 9 position

3 - 300 nm from
8 a.m. Aug. 9 position

* 300 nm from hypothetical
9:30 a.m. Aug. 9 position

Pacific

Ocean

SOLOMON ISLANDS

Santa Isabel

Malaita

San Cristobal

Florida

Russell

Rennell

Transport Groups
Midnight, Aug. 3

Henderson Field

Guadalcanal
hypothetical
9:30 a.m. Aug. 9

MIKAWA
7 a.m. Aug. 9

Afternoon, Aug. 8   ▮ 1

0 p.m. Aug. 8   ▮

2 4 a.m. Aug. 9   ▮

FLETCHER 3 8 a.m. Aug. 9   ▮

* hypothetical
9:30 a.m. Aug. 9

Choiseul

New Georgia

9:30 a.m. Aug. 9

1 p.m. Aug. 9

Coral
Sea

1:45 p.m. Aug. 9

Bougainville

Shortland

I-121/I-122
Midnight, Aug. 8

Woodlark

Kiriwina

Solomon Sea

Louisades

GOTO   Midnight, Aug. 9

7:05 p.m. Aug. 9

7:45 p.m. Aug. 9

MIKAWA

New Ireland

Rabaul

BISMARCK
ARCHIPELAGO

New Britain

craft, Japanese air strength, and low fuel. It is often recorded that Fletcher left without awaiting Admiral Ghormley's reply, but in truth, when he requested permission, Fletcher had *already* been steaming away from Guadalcanal for two hours, albeit within a maneuvering area. He did in fact turn southeast before authorization. Task Force 61 held that course until 1:00 a.m. of August 9, when for several hours Fletcher headed back toward Guadalcanal. Only after 3:00 a.m. did he receive Ghormley's approval, and an hour later he reversed again and left the scene. It is likely that these alterations reflected Fletcher's sense that he should not complete his departure without SOPAC approval. Had the carrier commander pressed ahead, even from his 4:00 a.m. position, Mikawa's retreating fleet would have been in grave danger. (The map on page 63 projects U.S. air ranges from several of Fletcher's positions, including a hypothetical 9:30 a.m. location based on a speed of advance of twenty-six knots.) Fletcher's withdrawal angered many.

The night of Savo, Admiral Crutchley left his own position, depriving the Allied cruisers of their tactical leader at Savo. Crutchley's absence was because Admiral Turner had summoned senior officers, including the cover force commander, to figure out how to proceed in the absence of Fletcher's aircraft. Turner felt he had no choice except to pull out, abandoning Vandegrift's Marines. Thus Fletcher's decision had at least three contingent effects: It removed one of six major warships (and the commanding officer) from the Allied battle line; it discarded the opportunity to blunt Mikawa's attack by means of a carrier air strike (and, additionally, the possibility of catching the retreating Japanese with a strike the next morning); and it isolated the U.S. Marines on Guadalcanal.

Many trees have been slaughtered in debating the merits of Fletcher's withdrawal. It is true that Richmond Kelly Turner's plan for Watchtower foresaw unloading to be completed in two phases—by the second day for troops and the fourth for supplies. Turner had also anticipated leaving sometime during that interval for a secondary landing at Ndeni in the Santa Cruz Islands. In theory, Fletcher's departure merely jeopardized supply off-loading. But supplies would be critical, and whatever his stated rationale, Fletcher did exactly as he had told his horrified colleagues at Fiji. In fact, worse: Timed from when the landing began, Fletcher's pullout occurred thirty-six hours into Watchtower—thirty-four if counted from the instant of his first southwesterly course change. He had promised at least forty-eight hours, seventy-two if counting D-Day itself.

Supply handling at Guadalcanal had been a headache from the outset. Jack Clark, the beachmaster, lacked sufficient men to move crates and boxes quickly off the shore. Matériel piled up. Sailors were drafted to help the shore parties. At one point a hundred landing craft crowded the beach, while fifty circled offshore awaiting space to land. Partway through the first day, Vandegrift had expanded the original beach area, but that had been a mixed blessing, injecting even more confusion. Then Japanese attacks interrupted the unloading. That day the cargo ships at least remained at anchor, but on August 8 they maneuvered and then had to regain the anchorage. The vessel *Betelgeuse* gives a good example. On D-Day she discharged cargo during two periods totaling ten and a half hours. The next day there were three spurts of off-loading totaling just under twelve hours. On August 9, before Turner pulled away, the *Betelgeuse* managed to unload for less than four hours. When she raised anchor the vessel still contained half her freight.

The Marines dug in at Lunga Point, under the stars of the Southern Cross. Disappearance of the invasion armada left the Marines in a sorry state. Alexander Vandegrift had cut back supply levels before Watchtower, and now he could not land what he had. His 10,900 men on Guadalcanal proper had food for just two weeks, ammunition for less than one. General Vandegrift soon put Marines on half rations. Their long-range communications for several weeks depended on captured radio equipment. Medical staff used Japanese instruments. The *George F. Elliott* and the cruisers sunk at Savo Island became the first of many vessels to founder in these seas. So many that the waters off the Point, bordered by the islands of Guadalcanal, Tulagi-Tanambogo, Florida, and Savo, acquired a new name: Ironbottom Sound.

CHRYSANTHEMUM AND CACTUS

Whatever the faults in Watchtower's execution, the initial Japanese response also proved inadequate. Neither Mikawa's cruisers nor Yamada's airplanes had destroyed the invaders, and despite their successes the effort proved costly. Mikawa's cruiser force got away from Savo scot-free, but lost a heavy cruiser nonetheless—American submarine *S-44* put four torpedoes into the *Kako* as she neared Kavieng. Meanwhile the *S-38*, which had been too close to get off a shot at Mikawa before Savo, torpedoed the *Meiyo Maru* the next day. That ship bore the Japanese reinforcements, and her loss meant the Imperial troops on Guadalcanal were beleaguered, exactly like Vandegrift's Marines. The first dispatch from the garrison would be a cry for help.

Due to the few messages received from the front, Rabaul knew little of the real situation on "Cactus," as the Allies code-named the island. In Tokyo, IGHQ believed Marines aimed to raid Guadalcanal, not conquer it. Emperor Hirohito was not so sure. Acording to his naval aide, when told of the landing Hirohito wondered whether it was the beginning of an Allied counteroffensive. The emperor proved nearer the mark than the high command. Intelligence put American strength at just 2,000 men, a gross underestimate. The command decided to match that by sending the Army regiment previously tagged to capture Midway, Colonel Ikki (often rendered as Ichiki) Kiyonao's 28th Infantry, presently camped on Saipan. Japanese Army circuits on August 8 carried traffic between 17th Army (Rabaul) and Saipan, plus Davao, rear base of the South Seas Detachment and camp of Major General Kawaguchi Kiyotake's 35th Brigade, already slated as a later reinforcement. Kawaguchi went immediately to Rabaul for consultations. The landing of Ikki's troops led to another great naval battle.

While preparations were made to transport the Ikki detachment, the Japanese harassed Cactus. That began with submarines. Here too the Imperial fleet was caught flat-footed. Concentrating against shipping off Australia, Rear Admiral Kono Chimaki's Submarine Squadron 3 operated in the Outer South Seas. Kono had a boat of the smaller RO-type off Port Moresby, another cruising near Townsville, Australia, plus fleet boats *I-121* and *I-122* at Rabaul and *I-123* then servicing at Truk. Rear Admiral Tamaki Tomejiro's Submarine Squadron 7 had four I-boats off Australia, one in the New Hebrides, and one at home. Tamaki had just been ordered to Japan, so 7th Squadron simply mustered the boats available in the Mandates and the South Pacific and sent them to the Solomons.

Kono's 3rd Squadron led the attack. They were too late. The I-boats at

Rabaul left on invasion day and reached Cactus on August 9, just after Kelly Turner departed. Lieutenant Commander Kuriyama's *RO-33* arrived from Papua twenty-four hours later. Lieutenant Commander Ueno Toshitake had sortied from Truk in *I-123* on August 7 and approached Ironbottom Sound ninety-six hours later. Admiral Kono recalled *RO-34* (Lieutenant Commander Morinaga Masahiko) from northeastern Australia, and she patrolled off Guadalcanal's southern tip but found nothing. Morinaga made up for his bad luck by relaying messages from Japanese lookouts at Taivu Point.

The Japanese subs owned these waters for weeks. With no way to differentiate individual enemies, Marines called the irritating undersea craft "Oscar." The *I-121* and *I-122* reported shelling Guadalcanal numerous times, and both also communicated with the lookouts. Lieutenant Commander Norita Sadatoshi's *I-122* stayed in Ironbottom Sound until ordered away to support fleet operations. When reporter Richard Tregaskis crossed the sound in a launch bound for Tulagi, to gather accounts of the biggest firefight of the invasion, a sub chased the little flotilla of three motorboats. The next day, August 13, an I-boat surfaced in broad daylight to bombard. At night, subs fired star shells, interrupting Americans' sleep. Lieutenant Jack Clark of the Navy boat unit recorded that Oscar used to surface around midnight and make high-speed runs up and down the sound, creating waves that pushed his boats farther up the beach, making them harder to refloat. Oscar typically shelled at 6:00 a.m. and 3:00 p.m., Clark recalls. Meanwhile, profiting from the subs' dominance, several times Imperial Navy destroyers came to bombard Lunga Point too. Because Vandegrift had no coast artillery, the Marines were powerless against them. A captured Japanese 75mm was wrestled into position on the shore, and Marines used field artillery to fire seaward. On August 14 a gunner rejoiced that his 105mm howitzer of I Battery, 11th Marines, had hit a submarine. Japanese officers simply learned to surface outside gun range, and destroyers stayed there too.

During late August, by Tregaskis's account, submarine shells fell on Guadalcanal about every other night. When SOPAC mounted its first resupply sortie, the fleet used fast destroyer-transports timed to arrive at night, minimizing the submarine threat. Lieutenant Commander Fujimori Yasuo's *I-121* filed a sighting report of Allied cruisers and destroyers approaching Guadalcanal on August 22, which led to the torpedoing of U.S. destroyer *Blue* by a Japanese warship. The next day Commander Morinaga's *RO-34* launched torpedoes at supply ship *Fomalhaut* and was credited with sinking her. The Marine gunners shot back. Both sides missed, and one of *RO-34*'s expended tin fish washed up on the beach, but the *Fomalhaut* hightailed it away, depriving Cactus once more. The *I-121*, *I-122*, and Morinaga's boat all received battle honors for their work off Guadalcanal.

As the Japanese submarines harassed the Americans however they could, Tokyo began to realize this was no raid. Guadalcanal would be a campaign, not a battle. Command was reorganized at Rabaul. Vice Admiral Tsukahara Nizhizo of the Eleventh Air Fleet became the new supremo on August 8. He controlled all Imperial Navy ground, maritime, and aerial operations in the Solomons. Tsukahara summoned fresh air groups, including the 26th Air Flotilla as a reinforcement, not a replacement for Yamada's unit. Admiral Mikawa led Eighth Fleet under Tsukahara's overall command.

At Hashirajima, where the *Yamato* arrived a few days after the invasion, Combined Fleet staff huddled over their charts. Admiral Yamamoto issued some orders even before the Savo Island battle. His measures included the dispatch of Tsukahara, aerial units, a recall of the heavy cruiser force then in the Andaman Sea, preparations for a midget submarine attack on the Ironbottom Sound anchorage, planning for a fleet sortie, and the creation of a Guadalcanal Reinforcement Unit to specialize in pushing troops and supplies onto Cactus. To lead the latter, Yamamoto chose Rear Admiral Tanaka Raizo of the 2nd Destroyer Squadron, then conducting antisubmarine operations off Japan. Yamamoto summoned the Second and Third fleets. The Third Fleet was Nagumo Chuichi's re-formed *Kido Butai*. On the afternoon of August 10, in Yamamoto's cabin on *Yamato*, the staff briefed admirals Nagumo and Kondo Nobutake, of the Second Fleet, on the roles they would play. The fleet would cover arrival of reinforcements on Guadalcanal, while the Japanese Army plus SNLF troops overpowered the enemy. Briefly distracted by an American deception—Nimitz sent a light cruiser toward Japan to mimic a repeat of the Doolittle raid—Yamamoto never wavered.

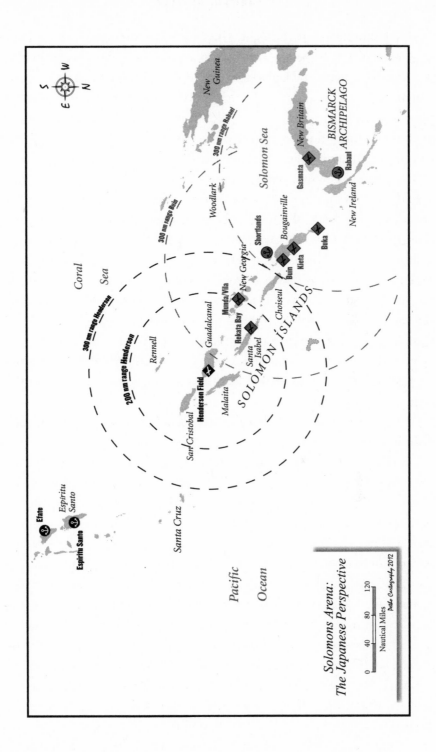

N

W   E

S

New
Guinea

Solomon Sea

BISMARCK
ARCHIPELAGO

300 nm range Rabaul

Gasmata

New Britain

Rabaul

New Ireland

Woodlark

300 nm range Buin

Shortlands

Bougainville

Buka

Kieta

Coral

Sea

New Georgia

Buin

Munda/Vila

Guadalcanal

Rennell

Rekata Bay

Santa
Isabel

Choiseul

SOLOMON ISLANDS

300 nm range Henderson

200 nm range Henderson

Henderson Field

Malaita

San Cristobal

Santa Cruz

Pacific

Ocean

Espiritu
Santo

Efate

Espiritu Santo

Solomons Arena:
The Japanese Perspective

0   40   80   120

Nautical Miles

Pete Cartography 2012

Radio intelligence became the Allies' only instrument to watch this first stage unfold. The Imperial Navy was aware of that. Having recently modified their fleet code, the Japanese changed their radio call signs just before Watchtower, and again at mid-August. Allied codebreakers found indications that the Japanese intended to shift presently to yet another version of JN-25. Yamamoto sent key messages from Kure in a seldom-used personal code that had not been penetrated. The fleet also made efforts at radio deception and utilized special single-use codes. Commander Wilfrid J. Holmes, of Station Hypo, notes that the Allies were now reading codes used by the port director at Truk, plus local ones employed in the Marshalls and Carolines, not JN-25. Despite that, traffic analysis permitted a clear picture.

On August 13 Allied intelligence reported dispatches indicating an imminent movement of *Kido Butai* from Empire waters south. Four days later the fleet implemented its call sign change, always a suggestion of impending operations. Intelligence was aware the cruisers returning from the Andamans were scheduled to join the Second Fleet, Yamamoto's major surface unit, at Truk between the nineteenth and twenty-first. Traffic analysis showed elements of the Second Fleet en route to Rabaul as its main body refueled at Truk.

While the Imperial Navy resorted to radio deception, having other units assume the call signs of their carriers, by August 17 the CINCPAC war diary noted this prospect. Meanwhile movements of destroyers associated with the Third Fleet gave notice that Nagumo was under way. But confusion persisted. That day SOPAC issued an intelligence summary declaring the Japanese carriers, though in Empire waters, were definitely heading south, if they had not already set out. Pearl Harbor felt less certain of the carriers, but confident that a strong effort to recapture Guadalcanal was in the offing. CINCPAC believed a surface fleet might reach Cactus around August 20, but one including flattops could not attack before the twenty-fifth. Captain Layton mentioned potential carrier movements repeatedly, but still located the Nagumo force in Japan on August 20, though he allowed that its tactical exercises could cover a sortie. As late as the twenty-second Layton placed at least Carrier Division 2 at home, despite knowing some messages for its commander were being sent to Truk. Layton's summary that day explicitly drew attention to the possibility that the *Kido Butai* might have departed, undetected, at any point after August 16. The summary for

August 23 affirmatively located Nagumo at sea, bound for Truk. At SOPAC, Admiral Ghormley had no doubt. He signaled Fletcher in the evening on the twenty-second, "INDICATIONS POINT STRONGLY TO ENEMY ATTACK ON CACTUS AREA 23–26 AUGUST." However, even Ghormley was uncertain about Nagumo's fleet, noting in his dispatch, "PRESENCE OF CARRIERS POSSIBLE BUT NOT CONFIRMED."

The Japanese obtained at least tactical surprise. Kondo's force steamed out of Hashirajima at 5:00 p.m. on August 11. Nagumo should have gone too but begged for a few more days to train pilots, sailing on the evening of August 16. Yamamoto departed for Truk with the main body at noon on the seventeenth. Emperor Hirohito sent the fleet a declaration of confidence through the Navy General Staff. Meanwhile, at Guadalcanal on the eighteenth, Admiral Tanaka's destroyers delivered nine hundred troops of Colonel Ikki's Army regiment. Rather than awaiting arrival of the bulk of his troops and equipment, plus the lead echelon of the Kawaguchi brigade, Ikki led his men in a vain frontal assault across a river against entrenched Marines. The Japanese were wiped out. On this news Admiral Nagumo canceled a stop at Truk and made directly for the battle area northeast of the Solomons. Tanaka, with the rest of Ikki's troops plus the 5th Yokosuka SNLF, pressed on. When search planes discovered a U.S. carrier at sea on August 20, the die was cast. A sighting the next day confirmed the presence of a task force—Fletcher's command.

The American game changer would be the "Cactus Air Force." Watchtower's objective had been to obtain the almost-completed Guadalcanal airfield, and General Vandegrift had worked overtime to finish it. The 1st Marine Division lacked construction equipment—this had sailed away with Turner's ships—but the Marines captured a bulldozer, five steamrollers, and the narrow-gauge mining railway. Vandegrift remembers that the two gasoline-powered mine cars were key. There was no other way to move the more than 7,000 cubic yards of earth necessary to finish the runway. There were also cement mixers, thirty tons of high-grade concrete, fifty to sixty tons of steel plate, a few hoisters, and two generators. And the 1st Marine Engineer Battalion benefited from the Japanese work, including most of the runway, several bomber-size revetments, five open-sided hangar workshops, and aircraft dispersal areas cut out of the surrounding coconut palms. Marines declared the runway complete on August 12.

Several days later American destroyer-transports came to Lunga Point to deposit Lieutenant Colonel Charles L. Fike, executive officer of Marine Air Group (MAG) 23; a portion of his staff; sailors of CUB-1, a naval base unit, who substituted for mechanics; ammunition and parts; 400 barrels of aviation gas; and 300 bombs. Captured gasoline had impurities making it unsuitable for U.S. aircraft engines, but here were resources for combat. On August 20 Fike christened the base for Lofton Henderson, a Marine pilot lost defending Midway Island.

That day escort carrier *Long Island* launched the first planes for Henderson Field. They became the Cactus Air Force. This initial group comprised nineteen Wildcat fighters of Major John L. Smith's VMF-223, plus twelve Dauntless dive-bombers of Marine Squadron VMSB-232. Another squadron of each was still in the pipeline. With the *Long Island* then the only U.S. escort carrier in the Pacific, the buildup would be slow. Army Air Force planes appeared on August 22 with Captain Dale Brannon, a flight of five P-400s of the 67th Fighter Squadron. The Cactus Air Force suddenly threatened every enemy ship and unit within its air range.

The new battle began with a convoy carrying the troops who were the focus of the KA Operation. This was Admiral Tanaka's reinforcement unit. Tanaka, his destroyer squadron shorn of its divisions and reassembled with assorted warships, worried they would not cooperate well, but he had Admiral Mikawa's firm decree to move the Ikki and SNLF troops. Tanaka's fast destroyers had delivered Ikki's advance guard in good order, though the Army wasted that success with its stupid attack. One destroyer that stayed at the landing point was damaged by a B-17, forcing her return to Truk in company with a second; then a third was hit by U.S. carrier aircraft, clinching suspicions of the presence of Fletcher's task force. Tanaka turned his slow convoy around to mark time, ignoring conflicting orders from Mikawa and area commander Tsukahara. Then he learned U.S. aircraft had arrived at Henderson Field, strengthening his foreboding. Tanaka drew blood when destroyer *Kawakaze*, detached for a futile mission, torpedoed U.S. destroyer *Blue*. Meanwhile Mikawa radioed that the Japanese surface and carrier forces would be in place on August 23, giving Tanaka a position for that day, plus instructions to prepare the troop arrival for the twenty-fourth. But on the twenty-third, about two hundred miles from Cactus, Tanaka again received conflicting orders, with Mikawa directing him to head north, requiring a one-day postponement, while Tsukahara charged him to proceed as planned. Atmospheric disturbances played havoc with radio transmission, preventing Tanaka from resolving this dilemma.

A PBY Catalina found Tanaka's convoy that morning, but lost it in squalls. Fletcher launched an afternoon strike anyway, with planes led by *Saratoga* air group boss Commander Harry D. Felt, another future CINCPAC. Major Richard C. Mangrum's VMSB-232 dive-bombers took off from Cactus too. Along the storm front neither unit found the convoy. Both flew to Henderson, since Tanaka's reported position put Commander Felt's planes too far afield to return to the ship.

Under pressure to neutralize Henderson so troops could land, Yamamoto ordered *Kido Butai* to detach a carrier to rush ahead and smash it. He knew American flattops were present. There had been carrier air attacks and sightings, and submarine *I-122* had reported attack by carrier aircraft off the Santa Cruz islands on August 20 (U.S. carrier aircraft claimed a record number of attacks on submarines during this period). But weather aborted strikes from Rabaul for two days running. In the predawn hours of August 24, Nagumo sent Hara Chuichi forward with light carrier *Ryujo*. Lookouts on Tanaka's flagship *Jintsu* actually spotted the *Ryujo* with heavy cruiser *Tone*, wearing Admiral Hara's flag, passing along the eastern horizon. That was before the main action, for daylight brought what has since been known as the Battle of the Eastern Solomons.

Both sides worked at a disadvantage. The Imperial Navy lost its surprise when U.S. air scouts spotted Vice Admiral Kondo's Advance Force, as well as Hara's detachment speeding to its attack position at twenty-six knots. So far the Japanese had no direct information. But Admiral Fletcher had his own disadvantages. The previous evening he had detached the *Wasp*'s unit to refuel (!), reducing Task Force 61 to *Saratoga* and *Enterprise*—and now part of *Saratoga*'s air group was at Henderson Field. These planes needed to return and rearm before Fletcher could strike. Their departure from Cactus was duly observed by Japanese troops at 9:30 a.m. Tanaka received that report and prepared for a mass assault, but really the Americans were merely regrouping aircraft.

The *Ryujo* launched her Cactus bombing, which led to a swirling dogfight over Guadalcanal so fierce that the JNAF barely touched Henderson. Aboard escort destroyer *Amatsukaze*, skipper Hara Tameichi watched the *Ryujo* with increasing apprehension. Her flight activity appeared sluggish, seeming to confirm Navy scuttlebutt that the best aviators were never assigned to these older carriers. Everyone knew *Ryujo* had been spotted. Commander Hara (no relation to the admiral) had just wolfed down lunch when a half-dozen B-17s appeared. They missed. Meanwhile Fletcher had launched Harry Felt's air group against *Ryujo* at 1:45 p.m. On the Japanese side, fighters were preparing to launch when Felt's *Saratoga* planes appeared from the southeast. *Ryujo* stood little chance. Quickly hit by four bombs and a torpedo, the carrier's starboard engine room flooded. The vessel leaned to expose her waterline. Though fires were extinguished, she had no power. The inclination increased until *Ryujo* heeled over and sank. No Allied aircraft witnessed this, so the Americans launched a repeat strike, finding nothing. Only a month later, in late September, did U.S. intelligence report the *Ryujo* as sunk. They never knew for sure until intercepting an early 1943 notice striking the vessel from the Imperial Navy list.

With *Saratoga*'s strike in progress, *Enterprise* scouts discovered the Nagumo force an hour later. Some of "Big E's" scout bombers dived on cruiser *Maya*. Two others, about to attack lesser warships, suddenly saw carriers in the distance. They shifted to Captain Arima Masafumi's *Shokaku*. Lieutenant Ray Davis and Ensign Robert C. Shaw piloted the Dauntless aircraft that went after Arima at 3:15 p.m. The *Shokaku*, newly equipped with radar, actually detected the planes, but ignored the warning until lookouts also spotted them. At the last minute Captain Arima turned his vessel, and the American bombs were near misses, one barely a dozen yards away. It had been an awfully close call.

The Japanese made frantic efforts to locate Fletcher's carriers. That morning two JNAF scouts got close to Task Force 61, but its radar-directed fighters blasted them before they could report. The Nagumo force dispatched a morning search of nineteen "Kates" and seven "Jakes" while readying an attack wave. Japan's carrier admiral had learned some things from Midway. But the snoopers found nothing. A later floatplane from cruiser *Chikuma* finally discovered Task Force 61. It too was shot down—in the middle of transmitting, before sending the position. Sharp staff work by

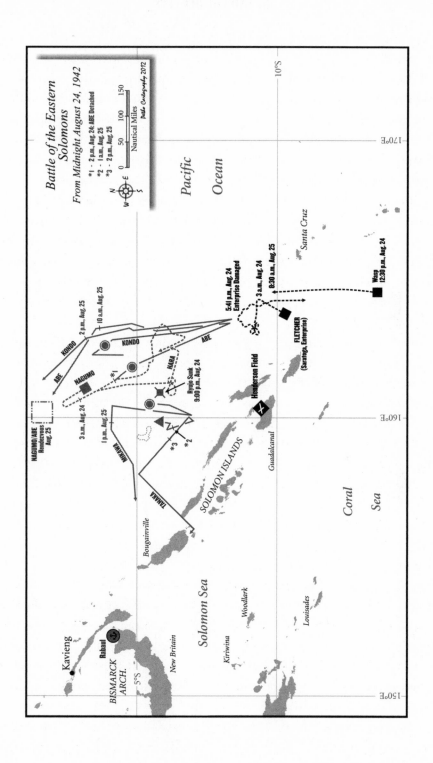

Battle of the Eastern Solomons
From Midnight August 24, 1942

*1 - 2 p.m., Aug. 24: ABE Detached
*2 - 1 a.m., Aug. 25
*3 - 2 p.m., Aug. 25

Nautical Miles
0   50   100   150

Pelle Cartography 2012

Pacific Ocean

Santa Cruz

Wasp
12:30 p.m., Aug. 24

8:30 a.m., Aug. 25

3 a.m., Aug. 24

5:41 p.m., Aug. 24
Enterprise Damaged

FLETCHER
(Saratoga, Enterprise)

Henderson Field

KONDO
2 p.m., Aug. 25

10 a.m., Aug. 25

KONDO

ABE

ABE

NAGUMO

HARA

Ryujo Sunk
9:00 p.m., Aug. 24

NAGUMO/ABE
Rendezvous
Aug 25

3 a.m., Aug. 24

1 p.m., Aug. 25

NAGUMO

TANAKA

*1

*3

*2

Guadalcanal

SOLOMON ISLANDS

Solomon Sea

Bougainville

Coral Sea

Kavieng

Rabaul

BISMARCK ARCH.

New Britain

Kiriwina

Woodlark

Louisades

10°S

5°S

150°E

160°E

170°E

Nagumo's air officer and navigation specialist estimated Fletcher's location by computing where the scout must have been along its allotted course. The *Kido Butai* immediately began launching—this rapidity was another Midway lesson. Indeed, *Shokaku* was doing that when the Americans bombed her. She sent up eighteen Vals and nine Zeroes led by Commander Seki Mamoru. The *Zuikaku* contributed six more Zeroes and nine Vals. Nagumo hastened a second strike, led by Lieutenant Takahashi Sadamu, totaling twenty-seven Vals and nine Zeroes from both aircraft carriers.

Reports of Nagumo's carriers reached Fletcher with *Saratoga*'s air group away for its attack on *Ryujo*, and half of *Enterprise*'s bombers still completing searches. The *Saratoga* managed to field a small group of seven bombers and torpedo planes, and another unit of twelve TBF "Avenger" torpedo planes for the repeat attack on *Ryujo*. They never found Nagumo, but attacked Vice Admiral Kondo's group instead, inflicting some damage on the seaplane tender *Chitose*.

At 3:36 p.m. Admiral Fletcher approved Admiral Thomas Kinkaid's recommendation to catapult the available *Enterprise* planes. She put up thirteen Dauntlesses to attack *Ryujo*. But the carriers needed more Wildcats for combat air patrol. The task force was completing its fighter launch when Commander Seki's strike wave appeared on *Enterprise* radar. Defense went to the fore. The aerial melee failed to prevent Japanese pilots from pressing home their attack. *Shokaku* planes concentrated on *Enterprise*, while *Zuikaku*'s bombers went after the *Saratoga*. Interceptors followed the JNAF planes right into the hail of the American AA fire. Lieutenant Elias B. Mott, an *Enterprise* gunnery officer, recalled, "We were completely unable to see the planes, due to the fact that they were so high and so small, and that it was late in the afternoon and the sky was considerably bluer than it would have been earlier." At 4:44 p.m., one of the Japanese dive-bombers connected, putting a 550-pound bomb through the "Big E's" number three elevator. Two minutes later another bomb holed her flight deck. More dive-bombers scored near misses, one so close it dented the side of the carrier. The planes headed for *Saratoga*—obscured in a squall—attacked battleship *North Carolina* instead. Only thirteen Japanese planes returned, but *Enterprise* was out of commission. She could not attack.

Lieutenant Takahashi's second wave missed the Americans. Pursuit into the night by Admiral Kondo's surface ships did not catch Fletcher. The *Sara-*

toga emerged untouched. On the *Enterprise*, skillful damage control restored ship handling. Refugees of "Big *E*'s" Air Group 10, foiled in attacking *Ryujo* because they could not find her, flew to Henderson, where they would fight alongside Marine air. The vessel herself would be *hors de combat* for weeks. *North Carolina* and a destroyer suffered minor damage. The Japanese incurred the loss of light carrier *Ryujo*, and damage to *Shokaku*, *Chitose*, and a few other vessels, but seventy planes were destroyed and precious aircrew killed. American aircraft losses were just twenty-three. Fletcher's task force steamed south to refuel. In his roundup to Admiral King, Nimitz reported, "INTERCEPTS INDICATE TWO CARRIER GROUPS GENERALLY NORTHEAST OF MALAITA AND LAST NIGHT WITHIN 150 MILES OF THAT PLACE. *RYUJO* IN WESTERN GROUP DAMAGED AND REPORTED BURNING FIERCELY. *SHOKAKU* AND *ZUIKAKU* IN EASTERN GROUP . . . DURING THE NIGHT 7 DDs SHELLED CACTUS."

Meanwhile, at about noontime Admiral Nagumo had detached Rear Admiral Abe Hiroaki's Vanguard Force with its battleships. Both Abe and Vice Admiral Kondo Nobutake—his Advance Force also with battlewagons—dashed for the reported position of Fletcher's carriers. Late that day they actually reached the place where the *Enterprise* had been damaged, but by then the Americans had retired and there remained no game for the hunters. Kondo and Abe turned back, marking the end of Japanese offensive action at the Eastern Solomons.

The worst happened with Admiral Tanaka's convoy the next day. Lousy weather kept Rabaul-based bombers from Henderson, and a destroyer bombardment (by five ships, not seven) was ineffectual. Now the Cactus Air Force showed its mettle. Major Mangrum's Marines and *Enterprise*'s Navy dive-bombers were up with the dawn. The half dozen floatplane fighters that Captain Takeda Kakuichi sent from his *Sanuki Maru* and the *Sanyo Maru* to patrol over the convoy never saw the Americans. Cactus planes damaged a destroyer searching for *Ryujo* survivors. Five Marine Dauntlesses broke out of the clouds above Tanaka's flagship, the *Jintsu*, and dived on her. Second Lieutenant Lawrence Baldinus put his bomb into the light cruiser's bow, impacting between the two forward guns. Tanaka takes up the story: "A frightful blast which scattered fire and splinters . . . spread havoc throughout the bridge. I was knocked unconscious, but came to happy to find myself uninjured. The smoke was so thick that it was impossible to keep one's eyes open. . . . I stumbled clear . . . and saw that the forecastle was badly damaged and afire." Fortunately sailors flooded the forward magazines before any ammunition cooked off, but twenty-four were killed, and necessary repairs would take five months. Tanaka shifted his flag to destroyer *Kagero.* In the meantime U.S. Navy dive-bombers went after aviation ship *Kinryu Maru,* the biggest transport in the convoy, and holed her too. Destroyers and patrol boats stood alongside. As they worked to rescue the soldiers and crewmen, B-17s arrived overhead and plastered the sea with high explosives, wrecking destroyer *Mutsuki.* Both ships sank. Admiral Tanaka withdrew his battered force to Shortland. Combined Fleet canceled the operation. It would need some new formula.

THE WAY IT WAS

Now came expedients to rush Japanese soldiers to their destination. Before Tanaka even reached Shortland, he got instructions from Tsukahara to send some troops forward on destroyers. Hours after the warships left, Eighth Fleet directed him to recall them. Furious, Tanaka perhaps felt the world was mad. It was the third time his superiors had issued conflicting orders. Tanaka could not understand why Tsukahara and Mikawa, both at Rabaul, could not coordinate. But it turned out more was involved. Confusion also resulted from the advent of General Kawaguchi's 35th Infantry Brigade. Admiral Mikawa had sought to leapfrog part of it while arranging to move the rest. The Cactus Air Force frustrated that initial reinforcement with thirteen Dauntlesses that sank a destroyer and damaged two more. Guadalcanal had begun to cost dearly. Capping these headaches, on August 29, the U.S. minelayer *Gamble* depth-charged Ueno Toshitake's *I-123* and sent her to the bottom.

Kawaguchi paused briefly at Rabaul, then headed for Shortland to huddle with Tanaka. The latter had moved his flag to cruiser *Kinugasa* to utilize its more ample radio room. Aboard Tanaka's flagship, Kawaguchi proposed sending most of his men to New Georgia on transports, proceeding from there aboard barges. Tanaka, with orders to use destroyers, was dumbfounded. Each consulted superiors.

Here, within weeks of the Watchtower landings, were proposals for both methods that would sustain Japan's war in the Solomons. The basic parameters were determined by airpower, at that time the Cactus Air Force. A destroyer that left Shortland before noon and steamed at speed could be off Guadalcanal by midnight and well on her way home by dawn. With its surface ships vulnerable to planes, the Imperial Navy had either to move reinforcements quickly, exiting the Allied air umbrella before daylight— hence the use of destroyers—or stealthily in small packets—thus barges (and in due course, submarines for small supply shipments).

By trial and error the Navy evolved tactics to operate in the face of enemy airplanes. Both methods were used. The destroyer operations were called "rat" (*nezumi*) sorties, the barge voyages "ant" missions. General Vandegrift and his Marines quickly appreciated these Japanese tactics, and began calling warships offshore the "Rat Patrol" or the "Cactus Express." As journalists began using the term, some wag of a censor, anxious to preserve Guadalcanal's code name "Cactus," changed that to "Tokyo Express." Thus was born one of the best-known phrases of the Pacific war.

Destroyers were the mainstay of the Tokyo Express. They typically carried 100 or 150 men on each transport mission. The Japanese came to a technique of having a guard ship fully combat-ready to lead the column, with loaded ships following in trail. If the threat level was low, the force small, or the mission urgent, all the vessels might be loaded. There were many challenges to the Tokyo Express, the Cactus Air Force only the biggest. Allied subs were active in these waters, surface ships could catch the Express, mines could explode beneath them, and, beginning in October, American PT boats became an increasing annoyance. When a destroyer sank, stopping to rescue survivors was dangerous. A damaged ship could be calamitous—endangering others traveling in her company while offering the Allies a ready target. Four destroyers were damaged and two sunk during August, three sunk and six damaged in October, and four sunk and seven damaged in November. The worst month was December 1942, when eight tin cans were damaged, though only two were sunk. Best would be September, when but a single ship succumbed.

But fate remained fickle—Chief Petty Officer Oshita Mitsukuni of the *Hayashi* recalls that his ship made three or four transport missions to Guadalcanal before she was ever attacked. Some ships were never struck at all. Seaman Watanabe Hashio's destroyer made multiple runs to Guadalcanal and was never in a battle. Petty Officer 2nd Class Tokugawa Yoshio in the

Kawakaze remembered twenty-five to thirty Express runs. His ship was bombed in The Slot during September but back off Cactus a month later. Warships with slight damage remained on duty.

Coupled with peril was the sheer oppressiveness of the climate. The heat and humidity of the tropics multiplied exponentially when the ship had to button up for protection. Lieutenant Nakamura Teiji of the *Yudachi*, which first arrived at Rabaul on August 22, found the hot air in the ship terrible, but there were also fatigue and exhaustion plus endless air raids. Nakamura credits the warm personality and open heart of *Yudachi*'s skipper, Commander Kikkawa Kiyoshi, for the destroyer's high morale. On *Yudachi* even supply officers watched for planes. Sharp eyes kept the enemy at bay.

Meanwhile, at Shortland, the dispute over reinforcement methods continued. Admiral Mikawa affirmed his instructions to deliver troops by destroyer. General Kawaguchi finally acceded, though some subordinates never did. The general himself with 2,000 men traveled to Cactus aboard destroyers on the last two nights of August and the first of September. A big mission the night of September 4–5 deposited another 1,000 men and covered a barge convoy. Their intent to bombard Henderson was vitiated when they discovered a couple of U.S. ships in Ironbottom Sound. Rear Admiral Hashimoto Sentaro's tin cans sank the destroyer-transports *Little* and *Gregory* instead. The barge unit encountered various delays and had not beached by dawn. The Cactus Air Force found them at sea—now for the third time—and strafed them mercilessly. The convoy disintegrated. About a hundred of the 1,000 passengers died, but the rest were scattered, including almost half marooned on Savo Island. The survivors regrouped over a period of days, starting with shuttles by the next night's Tokyo Express, which also landed another 375 men on Guadalcanal. The survivors would not be in position for Kawaguchi's planned offensive—he wanted to attack from Taivu Point, east of the Marine position (they had landed at the west end of the island)—nor would they be in time. At this point, after numerous transport missions, the Japanese had roughly 5,400 troops on Cactus, and about half that many had perished in the effort to get there.

Among those who stumbled onto Guadalcanal's shore was Colonel Tsuji Masanobu, a notorious operative of the Japanese Army. The forty-year-old Tsuji, a mainstay of Army cabals through the 1930s, enjoyed the benevolence of imperial family members and had access to the office of the Army's chief of staff. Tsuji had played his part in Japan's machinations in Manchuria and China. He led the unit that gathered intelligence for the Malayan invasion and participated in the last stage of the Philippine conquest. Tsuji was ubiquitous in Japan's war, and the Solomons were no exception. Now he headed the operations section of the General Staff, and traveled to the Outer South Seas on a personal inspection. Tsuji passed through Truk in late July, just ahead of Admiral Mikawa. At Rabaul he found Hyakutake's 17th Army headquarters located in a nice concrete building, but almost everything else in the fleet way. With typical Army disdain for things Imperial Navy, Tsuji remarked on the music concerts and sake joints that entertained the sailors, not to mention the geisha houses that had sprouted at Rabaul.

When the Americans landed at Guadalcanal, Tsuji immediately suspected the intel on their strength was bogus—such a large invasion flotilla would not have landed the paltry force estimated. After a few weeks' frustration, Tsuji secured Hyakutake's permission and set out to see for himself. He went with the barge convoy, mesmerized by luminescent waters at night that made him forget about the war. The convoy faced aerial strafing by Major Mangrum's Dauntlesses on September 2, then storms. The compass on his barge was knocked out, and the crew steered using a handheld compass. Their barge shipped so much water its occupants jettisoned provisions and half their ammunition. Then came the Cactus Air Force's last-minute attack. Soldiers staggered ashore—some jumping into neck-deep water—but that was just the beginning. Colonel Oka Akinosuke, who led the regiment with which Tsuji had deployed, spent five days just gathering the survivors. American planes looked for them too—and had such plentiful munitions, it seemed to Tsuji, that they could drop bombs like rocks. The Japanese hid under palm fronds. Colonel Oka finally began marching toward Mount Austen, the assigned destination, hacking through jungle. Food was almost gone. A mission house they encountered was a godsend—shelter—and the men slept like pigs, but once they began cooking rice the smoke betrayed them, and Marine artillery pounded their position. Oka's group finally found Colonel Ikki and some Navy construction troops. They were practically naked and had nothing to eat. Oka shared his men's sparse rice. Their ordeal continued.

The other way to get to Guadalcanal was to eliminate the Cactus Air Force. Then the Imperial Navy could steam anywhere, in daylight if it liked. The Eleventh Air Fleet did its best to accomplish that. An interdiction campaign began in late August and continued unabated for four months, with almost daily raids on Henderson. Sometimes the missions failed due to weather over Cactus or at the launch points, occasionally because of operational factors. Usually the raids were conducted by two to three squadrons (twenty to thirty bombers) covered by roughly equal numbers of fighters. The JNAF altered routine by mounting fighter sweeps or else sending a few bombers with substantial fighter escorts.

The Japanese also used their seaplanes offensively, creating the R Area Force, a unified command for floatplanes and patrol bombers under Rear Admiral Joshima Takatsugu. Admiral Joshima anchored seaplane carrier *Chitose* at Shortland for his main base. He rotated aviation ships *Sanuki Maru*, *Sanyo Maru*, and *Kamikawa Maru* through Rekata Bay on Santa Isabel, 140 miles from Henderson, as a forward refueling and control point. It was *Sanuki Maru* and *Sanyo Maru* that failed in covering the Tanaka convoy. Aviation ships not at Rekata shuttled new aircraft up from Truk or performed antisubmarine patrols around Rabaul. *Chitose* herself sailed with Admiral Kondo on the KA Operation, providing air cover until damaged. Captain Sasaki Seigo would return to Japan for repair and *Chitose's* conversion to a light aircraft carrier, but Sasaki sent his floatplanes to the R Area Force.

On July 1 the *Chitose* had had fifteen active and twenty-one reserve aircraft. Two months later her air group would have ten aircraft with no reserves. The aviation ships usually contributed six to eight aircraft, and the air fleet's complement of four-engine flying boat patrol planes ranged from none to about a dozen. Most nights the R Area Force put a floatplane over Guadalcanal, dropping flares and occasional bombs just to shake up the Marines, who began calling these aircraft "Louie the Louse" to distinguish them from twin-engine night intruders, known as "Washing Machine Charlie." Closer to Cactus, the R Force also made small attacks on Henderson Field at odd hours.

Vice Admiral Tsukahara, the Imperial Navy's senior air admiral, was the man for the job, most experienced at conducting a long-range air campaign. It was he who had masterminded the long-distance interdiction of Clark Field during the Philippine invasion, and before that Tsukahara had led JNAF formations in the first extended bombing of the China Incident. But Guadalcanal was different and more complex. In the Philippines, a months-long air campaign had been unnecessary. In China the operations had not been over water, so it was easier for crews to survive aircraft damage, and there had been plentiful emergency airstrips. Neither campaign had featured an adversary able to sustain its defense, and this time the enemy maintained its strength. Tsukahara's Eleventh Air Fleet, though powerful, had to fly from primitive airfields in a challenging climate. He also faced competing needs for his component air flotillas and was unable to mass them to overpower the Cactus Air Force. But the Japanese were serious about this effort—just how serious became evident when the high command sent Tsukahara a new air staff officer, Captain Genda Minoru.

The admiral, originally a gunner, had been associated with naval aviation in Japan since the early 1920s. He had been executive officer of Japan's first carrier, the *Hosho*, and skipper of *Akagi*, and he had led the JNAF development command. As a captain, Tsukahara had participated in naval arms limitation talks at Geneva, where the powers' aircraft carrier tonnage had been a major issue, and he had visited the United States too—at a time when the young Yamamoto was assigned there. Tsukahara was the senior aviation officer in the Imperial Navy. If anyone could overcome the difficulties of flying in the Solomons, it would be he.

In addition to the climate, the enemy, and the campaign's duration, at least four factors hampered the Japanese Naval Air Force in the Solomons. First, lack of an effective bombsight decreased precision. In combination with Tsukahara's inability to mount true mass attacks (bomb raids in the European war already comprised hundreds of aircraft and would grow larger), inaccurate bombing severely limited the possibility of neutralizing Henderson Field. Second, U.S. defenses forced the Japanese to higher altitudes, further diminishing accuracy. Third, the relatively small JNAF bombs (the heaviest at 550 pounds, compared to 2,000 pounds for the Allies) reduced damage potential. And finally, the small payloads of JNAF aircraft (1,750 pounds on the "Nell" or 2,200 pounds on the Betty; even an early American model, the B-25, carried 4,000 pounds) curtailed the overall weight of force loadings. The JNAF had long oriented itself toward tactical naval warfare. Both the Nell and the Betty had been developed as land-based long-range torpedo planes.

Japan paid dearly for its failure to produce a true heavy bomber. Only in February 1943 did the Japanese Navy ask industry to work on a multiengine bomber, and JNAF specifications were not forthcoming until that fall. The resulting aircraft had reached only the prototype stage by the end of the war, much too late for the Solomons arena.

Zero fighters had an early advantage in being armed with cannon in addition to machine guns, whereas the F-4F Wildcat had only the latter, meaning the JNAF could hit opponents with explosive projectiles. But the Americans had both armor and self-sealing tanks, and they could dive faster. In the very first dogfight over Cactus, U.S. pilots learned that even when damaged their planes could often reach home. And while the .50-caliber machine gun might not be so powerful as the Zero's 20mm cannon, Cactus pilots bragged that their Wildcats could stand up to fifteen minutes or more of Zero fire, while the Japanese planes often flamed within seconds of taking hits. Pilots even claimed their .50-calibers had sunk a couple of Jap destroyers. Nevertheless, from the F-6F on, subsequent American fighters had increased armament, providing additional firepower.

The other side of the coin lay in aircraft vulnerability. Japanese aircraft design emphasized speed and maneuverability in preference to armor and armament. This contributed to attrition, since planes, once hit, frequently caught fire or were crippled even if not destroyed. Damaged aircraft had little chance. It was 560 nautical miles from Henderson to Rabaul, more than 400 to Buka, and more than 300 to the Buin-Ballale-Faisi complex. A major reason the Japanese later installed an air base at Munda on New Georgia was to recover aircraft damaged over the lower Solomons. In the meantime there was no alternative except the long return at great hazard—as Sakai Saburo's experience illustrates so vividly. The attrition was appalling. After the Eastern Solomons, to take one example, the *Shokaku* and *Zuikaku* sent thirty planes to fly from the new Buka base on Bougainville, which the carriers' expert pilots did for two weeks. Only half the aircraft survived that assignment.

Cynics nicknamed the twin-engine Betty, known to the JNAF as the Type 1 bomber, the "Type 1 Lighter," referring to a cigarette lighter. The lack of self-sealing tanks added to aircraft fire hazards (JNAF would introduce armored tanks and automatic fire extinguishers rather than self-sealing tanks, but later), while the absence of fuselage armor and bullet-proof glass increased the danger to crews. Just as losses forced Tokyo to spur aircraft production, shipping allocations required Japan to cut raw material imports, resulting in the need to *reduce* the weight of metal in airplanes, further limiting survivability improvements. At the same time, climactic factors—like Rabaul's volcanic ash—increased wear just as battle damage boosted the proportion of aircraft not flyable upon landing.

During August the JNAF would lose 214 planes in combat and 138 more in accidents, malfunctions, weather, crashes on landing or takeoff, and the like. The figures for September were 113 combat against 123 operational losses. The vast majority of this attrition took place in the Solomons, and the September figures, when incidental losses first exceeded combat ones, indicate the difficulty of flying there. They also suggest the declining experience levels of JNAF crews, and the growing shortage of mechanics. That December operational losses again exceeded the combat toll—and began a trend that continued throughout the war.

By August 26, Admiral Tsukahara's serviceable aircraft had declined to twenty-nine bombers and nineteen Zeroes. That was the reason for the temporary detachment of fighters from Nagumo's carriers to Buka, as well as plans for a more comprehensive solution. By the end of the month strength had increased to thirty-eight Bettys, forty-one fighters, six dive-bombers, and three patrol bombers, plus more than a dozen floatplanes. With the addition of the 26th Air Flotilla, on September 20, Tsukahara would have 131 fighters, eighty-one bombers, four reconnaissance planes, fourteen patrol bombers, and the floatplanes. He also ordered construction of a new airfield near Buin. Tsukahara soon found it preferable to bring replacement aircraft to the Solomons rather than maintain existing planes, so serviceability rates often stood at half or less.

At Henderson Field the stalwarts of the Cactus Air Force had problems too, including many of the same ones. The tropics often turned Henderson into a mudflat or a dustbowl, sometimes simultaneously. Rabaul had volcanic ash, Cactus black dust. The planes' hard rubber tail wheels, designed for carrier landings, rutted the field. Planes of MAG-23, brand-new when they arrived, needed little more than gas and oil—a good thing, since most sailors of CUB-1 could not do much more than pump gas. And that was by hand, just like rearming the aircraft, which took hours. Of course, there were enemy bombs and naval bombardments to contend with, along with the Zeroes. Within a few weeks the planes were flying wrecks. On the day of the Battle of the Eastern Solomons, the thirty-one aircraft of MAG-23 had been reduced to twenty. Possibly the low point came on October 12, when Cactus had just five flyable fighters.

Its fluctuating strength betokened Henderson Field's importance, the pace of operations from Cactus, and strenuous Japanese neutralization efforts. Henderson Field posed a lethal threat to any Japanese force within about 300 nautical miles. That remained the standard engagement range for several reasons: Radio beacons and air navigation restricted long-distance flight; the longest-legged Allied aircraft were based back in the New Hebrides or on New Guinea and could not operate from Guadalcanal; aircraft actually at Cactus had limited ranges. So long as Henderson functioned, it inevitably dominated Japanese calculations. Conversely, the struggle to maintain its effectiveness became a major focus of all Allied activities. Airpower was the hammer that would smite the enemy.

The SOPAC effort went to a new level beginning in September. The missing fighter and dive-bomber squadrons of MAG-23 arrived with thirty-one fresh planes and its commander. Transport *William Ward Burrows* brought MAG-23's maintenance men to take over from the sailors. Japanese aircraft sank the ship, but only after the mechanics and critical equipment were unloaded. The liaison flight from Efate on the evening of September 4 carried Brigadier General Roy S. Geiger, who took charge of the air effort. A couple of transports also delivered the Seabees of the 6th Naval Construction Battalion. Geiger put the Seabees to work on a new airstrip, Fighter 1. One thing Seabees did excellently was build and repair, and that became central to the Cactus Air Force. Marston matting—perforated aluminum plates (named for a town in North Carolina where they were first manufactured)—helped solve the mud problem. The Seabees pre-loaded dump trucks with earth to fill a typical crater, and precut Marston matting to replace runway panels, discovering they could fix the damage from a Japanese 550-pound bomb in about forty minutes. Repairing the runway was vital.

The Cactus Air Force developed its own routines. Air raids typically arrived within a couple of hours either side of noon, due to the required flying time from Tsukahara's bases, plus the need for the JNAF planes to roost before dark. Coastwatchers usually warned of the raids, giving Geiger's pilots an hour or more notice. The *Burrows* delivered radar, enabling Henderson to pick up incoming aircraft and update the interceptors. Unlike carrier combat air controllers, who vectored fighters to their prey, the Marines developed "vertical interception." This was also necessary because base radio, which worked poorly amid tropical humidity, could hardly be heard more than about twenty miles away. Scrambling fighters clawed for altitude, listened to the chatter until they could see the Japanese beneath them, dived in pairs to loose a burst of fire, then climbed to repeat the exercise. Machine guns had to be wiped clean of lubricants before fighters took off or the guns froze at altitude and jammed when fired. Pilots made no effort to maneuver against agile Zeroes, relying instead on their diving speed.

Offensive operations developed their particular rhythm too. The natural counter to nightly Japanese naval activity was to put up experienced pilots to try to get in some licks. At dawn enemy task groups would be retreating, and at dusk approaching, so scout bombing became axiomatic for morning and afternoon searches. And the days would be punctuated by the noontime Japanese bombing and the nighttime shelling. Some of the most dangerous episodes occurred when the JNAF broke pattern, such as in late-afternoon or early-morning strikes. Pilots got whatever sleep they could. When the JNAF bombed—despite the difficulties noted earlier—there was always the possibility they would succeed in laying a tight pattern, cratering the airfield and wrecking parked planes. Thus the bombers and the Army Air Force P-400s, useful mainly for close air support, would scramble just to be safe. On August 28, for example, the Cactus Air Force might have been smashed save that its bombers took to the air. Harold L. Buell was one of the pilots of VB-10, the *Enterprise* Dauntless unit temporarily at Henderson. "Like a broken record," he recalled, "the routine of noon bombings, morning and afternoon searches, night shellings, and harassment missions went on day after day with little variance."

The Allied analog to the unavoidable dribbling of reinforcements that hampered Japanese efforts was undoubtedly the flow of aircraft and crews to the Cactus Air Force. Of the twenty-one pilots who arrived with the original Marine Fighter Squadron 223, only nine left with it in October. Of the others four men were wounded or invalided off the island, seven were killed, and the fate of the last pilot is not clear. Leaders considered that pilots and crews could last a month at Cactus. General Geiger asked the high command for eighteen F-4Fs and another eighteen SBDs *every ten days.* The pressure was tremendous. Pilot Buell, injured in a nighttime crash landing, was sent up again after one day's rest.

In early September, Cactus had eighty-six pilots and sixty-four planes. By the tenth only eleven of the thirty-eight F-4Fs that had been delivered were operational; one day alone eight fighters crashed on takeoff. "At this rate we can whip ourselves without any assistance from the Japs," a pilot groused. On October 14, Henderson had seven flyable Dauntlesses plus a number of Wildcats, with more than seventy aircraft in need of repair after a major Imperial Navy bombardment. During that interval Cactus had been reinforced by replacement aircraft, flights of Army warplanes, a Marine dive-bomber squadron and one of fighters, plus Navy fighter, torpedo, and dive-bomber squadrons from the carriers *Wasp* and *Saratoga.* The redoubtable Marine Fighter Squadron 212, many of whose pilots had already fought at Cactus under VMF-223, entered the fray with its own banner. Eventually eight fighter, twelve dive-bomber, and two torpedo squadrons would fight from Henderson. Guadalcanal was a meat grinder for aircraft.

It was a constant struggle to keep the planes flying—when they had gasoline and ordnance. At one point in October fuel was in such short supply that liaison planes were airlifting gas to Cactus. An index of the significance of this is that a C-47-type plane could carry a dozen barrels of aviation gas, each sufficient to fuel one Wildcat for one hour. Oxygen bottles for the Wildcats ran out within days of arrival and, along with critical spare parts, became a staple on the transport planes from Efate. One time the Japanese plastered the "Pagoda," Henderson's control tower, another its main ammunition dump. Shelling destroyed the food dump in October, scattering cans of SPAM everywhere. They would be found at odd moments for a long time afterwards.

Japanese airmen may have been able to relax with geishas at Rabaul, but there was no such luxury for the Cactus Air Force. The men were on half rations until mid-September, and that was made possible by captured provisions. Even later they existed on dehydrated potatoes and SPAM or cold hash. When carrier *Wasp* embarked a flight of Marine planes for delivery, the pilots were enchanted by its quality food and accommodations, only to be subjected to the reality of Guadalcanal. The tentage, bedding, and blankets were all captured from the Japanese. On Cactus there was no way even to wash laundry except take it to a stream and do it yourself. Ensign Buell was washing his one day in the knee-deep Lunga River when the bombers came. He and everyone else streaked for cover buck naked.

The pilots' experience would be of a piece with that of ordinary Marines. Herb Merillat is a good example. Lieutenant Merillat held an anomalous position in the 1st Marines' hierarchy. A lawyer by trade, he had been recruited to a Marine information office, then assigned to Vandegrift's division, which seconded him to its intelligence staff, but as a historian. Merillat was in a good position to observe the inner workings of Vandegrift's staff, kept careful notes and a diary, and used them to produce a wartime account of Guadalcanal he titled *The Island.* That book takes the campaign as a simple matter of units and battles and says little of the trials and tribulations the Marines faced. But Merillat's later reflections, which include many entries from his diary, tell another story. Soon after the landing Colonel Randolph Pate, Vandegrift's supply officer, informed the general they had food for five days. A more careful review on August 15, after the Marines had already gone on half rations, found field rations for seventeen days, C rations for three, and captured food sufficient to extend that another ten.

That day Marines grabbed some wicker baskets that had been airdropped to the Japanese in the bush. They contained mimeographed leaflets— unwelcome to the Americans—designed to boost morale with news of the Imperial Navy's victory at Savo Island. But what the men really wanted from the baskets was their canned goulash. Some units were subsisting on rice and fish heads. Captain Nikolai Stevenson, commanding the 1st Company, 1st Marine Regiment, recalled the meager diet. Almost everyone got dysentery. On August 12, Corporal James R. Garrett of I Battery, 11th Marines, enjoyed his first hot food in days. A few days after that, Glenn D. Maxon, a lieutenant in the 1st Marines, noted a big food shortage. The men exploded grenades in the Lunga River to catch fish. Like many others,

Maxon later contracted malaria. It was common to lose dozens of pounds of body weight on Guadalcanal. When Marines launched a raid into the Japanese rear area early in September, every man loaded himself down with tins of crab and beef taken from enemy stocks before destroying the rest. The raiders also brought back twenty-one cases of beer and seventeen half-gallon bottles of sake. The admirals had code names, but Marines called their invasion "Operation Shoestring."

War correspondent Richard Tragaskis went out with a Marine patrol. When they halted, instead of resting the men scavenged for good coconuts. When they found a dead Japanese, one needled their cook, attributing the enemy's demise to Marine chow. Dinner was a candy bar. When Tregaskis left Cactus late in September, one of the reasons, he records, was that he had worn out his last pair of shoes. On September 18 the food problem was finally solved with a large shipment of supplies—so big it included post exchange materials. Suddenly Marines had tins of white shoe polish no-body wanted or could use. Typically, the cargo ships were able to unload less than two-thirds of their freight before they pulled out, but even so, arriving Marines ate beef stew that night.

Marines suffered a big setback soon after the Watchtower landing. Van-degrift's intelligence chief, Lieutenant Colonel Frank Goettge, learning from a prisoner that a group of the enemy wanted to surrender, insisted on leading the twenty-six-man patrol sent to find them. Lieutenant Jack Clark of the naval operating base provided the Higgins boat that carried the patrol to its doom. He never forgot joking with the Marines before they left, and since this was a routine mission, the landing craft returned after dropping them off. The Marines were ambushed. Goettge sent a runner for help, but the man had to swim more than four miles through shark-infested waters, and by then it was too late. Scuttlebutt had it that one Marine's tongue was cut out and another's hands cut off. Only three men returned, including the runner. Frank Goettge was not among them. Goettge's disappear-ance was a potential disaster far greater than the simple loss of an intelli-gence officer, bad as that was, because he knew about Ultra. It is fortunate the bloodthirsty Japanese killed these men rather than interrogating them.

Goettge's loss was offset to a degree by the appearance of Martin Clem-ens, the coastwatcher, who joined the Marines and worked closely with Vandegrift's intelligence people, setting up a radio post that gave Cactus direct contact with Mason, Read, and other key observers. Clemens, joking with staff officers, admitted that he too had had just a few tins of food left when he appeared. The dangers were starkly demonstrated less than two weeks later. Clemens sent his trusted indigenous aide, Sergeant Major Jacob Vouza, to scout a suspected Japanese lookout post. The enemy caught Vouza with a small American flag he carried to identify himself. The Japanese tied Vouza to a tree and tortured him but got no information. Then they bayoneted Vouza and left him to die. The coastwatcher managed to free himself and regain U.S. lines. Vouza distinguished himself again later as a guide for the Marine Raider Battalion.

Vandegrift soon got his own Ultra radio section. Lieutenant Sanford B. Hunt ran the (captured Japanese) radio that kept Vandegrift in touch with SOPAC. He delivered what intel the theater command sent. A radio intelligence element arrived in mid-September with the convoy that brought the 7th Marine Regiment. This was a tiny two-man direction-finding unit that helped generate target information for the Cactus Air Force. A couple of weeks later they were augmented by a full mobile radio detachment led by Lieutenant Commander Daniel J. McCallum. The "cryppies" knew their unit as Station AL. Marines like Herb Merillat knew them more informally as the "Cactus Crystal Ball." McCallum flew up from Espíritu Santo with four sailors on one of the daily flights. The C-47 could not carry all their gear, so they took half and left the rest to arrive a month later by ship. McCallum brought two special-keyboard typewriters that could print Japanese characters, several Hallicrafters radio receivers, and a Copek—the encryption device that provided secure communications within the Allied radio intelligence net. As a Japanese-language officer, McCallum could translate decrypted enemy messages. Naturally there were teething troubles. Chief Radioman James J. Perkins, who arrived with the direction-finding team, lost a receiver in the confusion of unloading the convoy under Japanese bombardment. Months later he found its shell on the beach—Marines had been using the thing as an oven.

With just one, later two, receivers or "posts," the mobile radio unit had limited capacity, but it put Cactus on the circuit for traffic analysis and decrypts obtained elsewhere. Some cryppies groused that McCallum was not a technician and wondered why he was there. His shortcomings put much of the weight on Lieutenant Charles "Homer" Kisner. Commander

McCallum could use JN-25 codebooks, and, coached by Kisner, did his best. The commander passed his data to Marine Lieutenant Hunt, who continued to be Vandegrift's Ultra liaison. Among their most important information was a daily list of radio fixes on Japanese ships, used to target air strikes. The Cactus Crystal Ball established itself in a tunnel dug into a hillock below Henderson Field.

Though the JNAF concentrated on Henderson Field, their bombing affected everyone. On August 16, bombs wounded five Marines of Corporal Garrett's I Battery. On the twenty-fifth, enemy ordnance missed the air base but struck near Vandegrift's nearby headquarters. One bomb left a fifteen-by-twenty-five-foot crater, sprayed the command post with shrapnel, and sent shards into the general's own tent. Lieutenant Merillat, who had taken up residence under a coral outcropping, traded that for a slit trench when bombs showered him with bits of broken coral. As another 1st Division Marine said of a later U.S. invasion, coral comes high.

Beyond enemy action were the dangers of tropical disease, which were only magnified for men losing weight on half rations. In September, when the 1st Marine Division had incurred only about a thousand casualties, twice that many were laid up with malaria or dysentery. And that was *before* the rainy season brought tons more mosquitoes and widespread disease. Vandegrift's whole command went on a preventive course of antimalarials (quinine, but mostly atabrine) that month. A rumor quickly arose that atabrine caused impotence, and Marines resisted taking it. Even having medics stand in chow lines to make Marines quaff the pills before receiving food proved none too successful, judging from medical casualties. More than 8,500 of Vandegrift's Marines were felled by malaria, some more than once, nearly three-quarters of them in the period from mid-September to December. When the 7th Marines arrived, it had the only battalions anywhere near full strength.

During their voyage to the Solomons, General Kawaguchi marveled to a Japanese journalist that, unlike themselves, forced to sneak into Guadalcanal, the Americans had everything. That image of plenty belied the shoestring experience of Marines, but it was a lurid fantasy for Japanese. In mid-August, Japanese naval infantrymen were approaching Marine lines at night to search for food. Others surrendered just for something to eat. Japanese soldiers had the same problems on Guadalcanal, magnified. They had no antimalarials. They called the 'Canal "Starvation Island." It was a wonder Japan's soldiers could fight. But they did. For many men of both sides, Guadalcanal was an emotion not an island, a trial rather than a battle.

BLOODY RIDGE AND AFTER

General Vandegrift was desperate for troops. Reinforcements seemed remote—in fact, Ghormley and MacArthur were just then fighting over the destination of the 7th Marine Regiment—yet to be given to SOPAC and sent to the 'Canal. Vandegrift could not defend a full perimeter plus his long beachfront, much less provide reserves. The only men he could draw upon were on Tulagi. Early in September he did that, ordering the 1st Marine Raider Battalion and 1st Parachute Battalion over to the big island. Colonel Merritt A. "Red Mike" Edson, commanding the Raiders, was ready. A pioneer in Marine special warfare, Red Mike had teamed up with another legendary Marine, Evans Carlson, to create the Raiders. Now Edson led the 1st Battalion and it seemed marooned on Tulagi, where fighting had been savage during the invasion, but nothing had happened since.

Itching for action, Colonel Edson sent two companies to Savo Island to look for Japanese but found none. That had a sad postscript, because destroyer-transports *Little* and *Gregory*, which carried the Raiders, were trapped by a returning Tokyo Express and blown to bits in the early morning of September 5. Commander Kikkawa Kiyoshi of the *Yudachi* impressed his cohorts: landing fresh troops, bombarding Henderson, *and* sinking the American vessels. More metal to line the seabed of Ironbottom Sound. It could have been worse—the original idea had been to keep the Raiders on board that night.

Meanwhile Edson suggested that on their way to Cactus, his Raiders should strike the Japanese rear. Vandegrift's staff readily agreed. The landing took place at Tasimboko on September 8, and it hit General Kawaguchi's depot. Coincidentally, just as the four-ship Raider flotilla approached, an American convoy appeared in the distance, a pair of cargo vessels with a strong escort of a cruiser and four destroyers. The Japanese feared an invasion and fled. Furious, Kawaguchi ordered them back. He could not help, because his main force was deep into the jungle on its way to assault Henderson. There was a sharp firefight at Tasimboko, ending with the Japanese

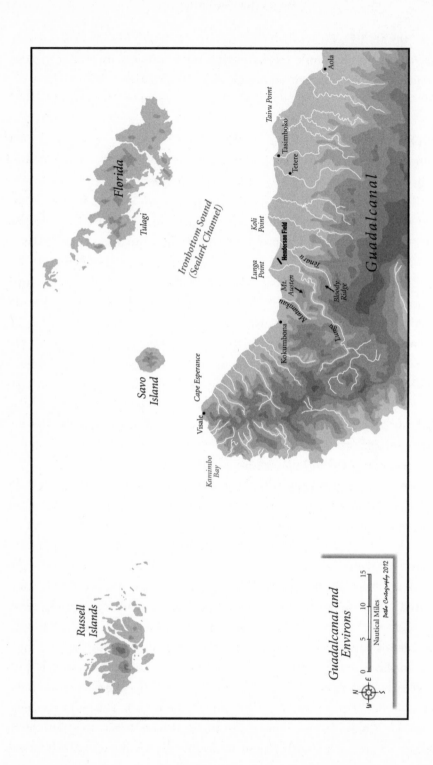

Russell
Islands

Florida

Tulagi

Ironbottom Sound
(Sealark Channel)

Savo
Island

Cape Esperance

Visale

Kamimbo
Bay

Kokumbona

Matanikau

Mt.
Austen

Lunga
Point

Henderson Field

Koli
Point

Tenaru

Bloody
Ridge

Lunga

Tasimboko

Tetere

Taivu Point

Aola

Guadalcanal

Guadalcanal and
Environs

N
W   E
S

0   5   10   15
Nautical Miles

Pate Cartography 2012

driven into the bush again. Marines disabled the artillery they found, destroyed supplies, appropriated more, and returned with a haul of maps and documents that convinced Vandegrift a major attack impended.

At the time General Vandegrift was moving division headquarters to a location he thought safer, overlooked by a ridge. Colonel Edson brought in the captured maps and, together with Colonel Gerald C. Thomas, the 1st Marines operations officer, announced they had figured out where the Japanese would strike. Vandegrift thought Red Mike respectfully disapproving when he came to the punch line: "The ridge you insist on putting your new CP behind." But the general quickly bought that analysis and arranged counters. Edson would take an amalgam of his 1st Raiders plus the 1st Parachute Battalion to defend the ridge. Marine artillery zeroed in on the position. Del Valle moved a battalion to beef up the fire support. Vandegrift deployed his reserves to interpose between the ridge and Henderson Field and alerted another battalion to intervene if necessary. The Marines waited.

The Tokyo Express hit again that night. Admiral Ghormley, alert to the enemy, recalled the latest convoy before it had emptied. Japanese bombing continued also. Seabees were putting finishing touches to Fighter 1, but it was yet to become active. The Cactus Air Force lost twelve-plane ace Captain Marion Carl on September 10. SOPAC warned that day of an Imperial Navy task force that might reach the area in a couple of days. Henderson was like a pot of honey attracting bees. Surveying the damage, Vandegrift called in Jerry Thomas and asked him, without telling anyone else, to craft a plan for last-ditch guerrilla resistance from the interior. If it came to that, the Marine leader wanted to be ready.

General Kawaguchi had his own problems. With the uncertain supply line up The Slot, Kawaguchi had to reduce the rice ration for his soldiers by two-thirds. The Tasimboko raid cut his radio relay to Rabaul. Hacking through the jungle, progress remained slow, unpredictable. Captain Inui Genjirou led the 8th Antitank Company, originally part of the Ikki Detachment. Inui's men had already learned to slice open coconuts, supplementing meager rations with their milk and meat. So far, at least, the men did not seem to have weakened from the harsh regimen. Partway to his assembly area, General Kawaguchi dropped off the remaining Ikki Detachment troops for one prong of his attack. But Japanese knowledge of the battlefield remained so sketchy that Kawaguchi did not even know that his planned line of advance went right over a ridge. And he had no contact with Colonel Oka. The general sent a search party ahead to contact the 124th Regiment commander and tell Oka of his plans. Those men, practically emaciated, found the colonel only the very morning of the attack. It had not been a good start.

The outcome matched the run-up. Shouting their battle cries of "Banzai!" the Japanese assaulted the ridge, and the other prongs of Kawaguchi's offensive hit as well. It was raining. A cruiser and three destroyers, for once, shot at targets other than Henderson Field. In another departure from custom, the Imperial Navy warships used searchlights to illuminate the beach. Louie the Louse lit the night with parachute flares. All for naught. Red Mike had prepared his men well. Sergeant Frank Guidone of the Raiders' C Company on the right flank, saw almost no Japanese reach the crest, though some broke past where his unit tied in with A Company. Marines lost a little ground, but slowly and exacting a great price. The Oka and Ikki prongs were complete failures. Admirals Richmond Kelly Turner, the amphibious boss, and John S. McCain, Commander Air Solomons, who both happened to be visiting Cactus, stayed through the night, witnessing this delicate moment. At the new headquarters, Herb Merillat ran out of his tent and hit the ground amid the downpour.

Kawaguchi repeated his attack the next night. The battlefield became known as "Bloody Ridge." Some called it "Edson's Ridge." The fighting was much like World War I, with the difference that the Japanese, great infiltrators, managed to insert little packets of soldiers inside Marine lines. By daylight Edson used Raiders and parachutists to roust out the enemy, and in darkness Kawaguchi sent them back. On the second night, fighting raged barely a quarter mile from Vandegrift's headquarters. A couple of Marine artillery rounds, falling short, plastered the command post. Edson sent back word that many Japanese were filtering through. Vandegrift committed his reserve battalion, but Red Mike, increasingly confident he could hold, did. His troops sustained 263 casualties, including 49 dead and 10 missing. From prisoners and documents the Marines calculated that the Japanese had employed 6,230 troops and suffered more than 700 killed and missing and more than 500 wounded.

As the various Imperial Navy sea and air activities suggest, Combined Fleet had coordinated closely on the Kawaguchi offensive. The Fleet had made a specific agreement on operations with 17th Army a week ahead of time, and chief of staff Ugaki had flown to Rabaul on September 10 to supervise. But Tokyo's major effort collapsed. The *Kido Butai* left Truk to cruise east of the Solomons. The morning after Kawaguchi struck, scout planes flew to check Henderson Field and one tried to land. Finding forty American fighters on the ground there, the pilot gave up. Later, information that Cactus fighters intercepted Japanese bombers made it certain. In the face of conflicting reports, Ugaki had hoped for Henderson's fall. Now he felt dejected. The Eleventh Air Fleet morning search on September 13 discovered a U.S. task force, but *Kido Butai* was 600 miles away. Nagumo wanted to attack. The Americans stayed beyond striking distance. By the fourteenth Admiral Ugaki concluded that the Kawaguchi offensive had miscarried. In almost two weeks at sea, Nagumo accomplished nothing.

The ultimate embarrassment came in the afternoon on September 14, when ammunition at a Rabaul dump ignited, driving everyone into bomb shelters for more than two hours. Munitions continued to brew up all night. Eighth Fleet headquarters sustained damage. A splinter struck next to the armchair where Ugaki had been sitting hours before. Finally a message from Kawaguchi admitted failure. The admiral drew several conclusions from the Imperial Navy point of view. There had been a critical lapse in naval communications when the radio on Guadalcanal tried to move prematurely to the area thought captured. Such movements had to be more cautious. The Navy had also erred by not having someone directly positioned on the battlefield, who could report independently of the Japanese Army. Ugaki could not understand why officers of the various commands at Rabaul—this applied to Tsukahara and Mikawa, exactly reprising Tanaka's complaint, as well as to Navy and Army—could not simply walk down the street and visit one another. Time together meant better liaison. At air fleet headquarters Ugaki instructed staff to prepare a new plan, negotiating with General Hyakutake for modifications to their local cooperation agreement. Both had underestimated the Americans and overvalued their own strength. A serious effort needed to be made. Ugaki sent a dispatch to Yamamoto at Truk asking him to take the matter up with IGHQ and secure agreement on a plan for a real offensive.

One thing Admiral Ugaki did *not* do in his week at Rabaul was spend much time with Tsukahara Nizhizo. The air fleet leader was in bed with fever and intestinal problems. At first this seemed uncomplicated; then Tsukahara was diagnosed with dengue fever and malaria. He would have to be sent home. The Solomons consumed men as much as airplanes. In an allusion to the Russo-Japanese War of 1904–1905, naval writer Ito Masanori decided that Guadalcanal had become the Port Arthur of the Pacific war. As for the emperor, when told of the failed attacks, Hirohito encouraged his commanders, assuring them he remained confident the island could be held. He coupled that generality with a more pointed question to Army chief General Sugiyama as to whether the eastern tip of New Guinea could be seized. The emperor's underlying purpose was to galvanize his military and naval leaders to greater action. On September 16 Hirohito told Lord Kido of the failure.

Colonel Tsuji now returned after weeks on Starvation Island. He was astonished at Rabaul's transformation. Suddenly there were signs of battle everywhere. It was not just the burned-out houses. When Tsuji walked outside town he found munitions and tins of food scattered about that must have blown clear in the depot explosions. This was a base at war.

Search planes discovered the convoy carrying the 7th Marines on September 15. The U.S. task force, in fact, was steaming east of the Solomons precisely to protect this movement. That day Henderson Field was spared because the air fleet sent its bombers after the convoy. Bad weather turned them back. The sighting, however, led to the greatest Japanese submarine success of World War II.

Much as men had nicknamed the waters off Guadalcanal Ironbottom Sound, Allied seamen called those south and east of the Solomons, the waters separating SOPAC's bases from its combat zone, "Torpedo Junction." These seas were a regular hunting ground for I-boats and quite dangerous. On August 31, Lieutenant Commander Yokota Minoru's *I-26* had put a torpedo into the carrier *Saratoga* that left her out of action for three months. A week later Commander Shichiji Tsuneo's *I-11* took a shot at the *Hornet*, saved by an alert patrol plane that deflected the torpedo by dropping bombs in front of it.

Then came September 15. Lieutenant Commander Kinashi Takaichi, on station in the *I-19*, detected sound on the hydrophones powerful enough for a fleet. Kinashi's boat had survived an air attack during the Eastern Solomons battle, diving quickly to escape the scout bombers. Now he sought revenge. The adversary was a task force with the *Wasp* and *Hornet*. The I-boat gave chase but, submerged, had no chance of catching up, except that the Americans zigzagged across his course. Then *Wasp* turned into the wind to launch aircraft, putting her right in front of Kinashi. The *I-19* emptied all six bow tubes and the torpedoes ran true. In an incredible act of fate, three hit the *Wasp*. Another ran past her stern and on to the other carrier group, passing under the keels of two destroyers to hit the battleship *North Carolina*. One torpedo hit the destroyer *O'Brien*, also part of the *Hornet* task group. Kinashi's single spread sank a 15,000-ton aircraft carrier, damaging two more warships of 36,500 tons.

Chance and circumstance saved the mobile radio unit that might have been aboard the *Wasp*. Lieutenant Gilven Slonim led this group of five sailors, previously aboard the *Enterprise* and *Saratoga*, and they had been driven from pillar to post. Petty Officer Kenneth E. Carmichael had been standing in a chow line at Pearl Harbor when asked if he'd like sea duty. Carmichael was told to be on board in an hour, and sailed with Slonim in the *Enterprise*. The unit transferred to the *Saratoga* when "Big E" suffered damage at the Eastern Solomons, and they had barely found their bunks when *Saratoga* got hit in Torpedo Junction. Slonim's unit went ashore at Tonga, were shuffled among ships and planes to reach SOPAC, and were on a destroyer preparing to transfer to the *Wasp* when Kinashi's torpedoes sank her.

With the damage to *Enterprise* and that to *Saratoga*, suddenly the *Hornet* became the only American aircraft carrier in the South Pacific. Dockyard workers at Pearl Harbor, where the *Enterprise* was by now under repair, raced more desperately than ever to return her to sea. The entire campaign could depend on it.

Admiral Ugaki reappeared at Truk on September 18. He huddled with communications specialists over plans to improve radio transmission in the southeast area, notoriously bad, and the procedures for which would be changed at the end of the month, and puzzled over how to improve the fleet's fuel situation. The Navy burned oil at a rate of 10,000 tons a month, and this had become a problem. At Rabaul the scarcity of tankers limited deliveries. The Army did not help with its antics to avoid drawing down troop strength in China, culling reinforcements for the South Seas by the regiment, battalion, even company, from places all over Southeast Asia. Finding escorts for these units bedeviled the Combined Fleet, and transporting them burned even more oil. In late September, when Rabaul begged for *Kido Butai*'s intervention because it feared the Americans were about to strike Shortland, there was a fuel shortage at Truk too. The Nagumo force stayed at anchor, because the *Zuikaku* had not quite attained combat readiness, but fuel played a role in that calculation.

Nevertheless the die was cast for a fresh operation on September 28, when a raft of staff officers flew up from Rabaul to confer with Combined Fleet. Its own operations chief, Commander Watanabe Yasuji, returned with them, as did Colonel Tsuji, representing the Army General Staff. Commander Ohmae Toshikazu attended for the Eighth Fleet, and Major Hayashi Tadahiko for the 17th Army.

Colonel Tsuji's reactions visiting Truk were much like his first impressions of the Imperial Navy base at Rabaul. Warships filled the lagoon, though he was surprised to see only two aircraft carriers. Nearing flagship *Yamato* in a launch seemed like a fly approaching an elephant. Of course, Tsuji knew the Navy nicknamed her the "*Yamato* hotel" because the battleship never seemed to go into combat. Except for the hatches and the pipes that ran everywhere, *Yamato* might actually have been a hotel. But an organic one—a broken pipe, like a blood vessel, might drain its lifeblood. Anyone visiting the huge ship would fear getting lost, so Tsuji's fantasy was not unusual. But when it came to dinner he was overwhelmed. The staff ate on nice china—fish made into sushi and also broiled, washed down with ice-cold beer. The Army man thought of Guadalcanal, where soldiers were "thinner than Gandhi himself."

The key conversations took place in flag country, the area of *Yamato* reserved for fleet staff. The officers went there immediately upon boarding the huge battleship. Principals on the Combined Fleet side of the table were Admiral Ugaki and Captain Kuroshima Kameto, senior staff officer. Tsuji presented plans for a major offensive. The Army insisted on a high-speed convoy down The Slot to deliver a full division of troops with their heavy equipment. The 2nd Infantry Division would come from Java for this purpose, while the 38th, training on Borneo (today Sulawesi), could reinforce if necessary. General Hyakutake would lead in person. Army heavy artillery would fire directly on Henderson Field. Kuroshima told the Army men of the Imperial Navy's losses, pressing for agreement on moving by fast destroyers. Tsuji demanded transports—the only way to deliver big guns. The Navy did not agree. Seaplane carriers with their heavy-duty cranes were better suited for big artillery pieces. Kuroshima also emphasized that, once they were in motion, fuel would limit the Navy to a fortnight at sea. It is not clear that Tsuji appreciated the significance of that remark.

To break the impasse, Ugaki took Tsuji to Yamamoto's cabin. The colonel found the admiral drawing Japanese characters in a letter. Tsuji described the plight of the men on Starvation Island. The Navy and Army united at last, in tears, according to Tsuji. Both Yamamoto and he cried. "If army men have been starving through lack of supplies," Tsuji quotes Yamamoto, "then the navy should be ashamed of itself." The admiral promised, "I'll give you cover even if I have to bring the *Yamato* alongside Guadalcanal." Here came his decision on the fleet staff's earlier ruminations about battleship bombardments of Henderson Field. Yamamoto insisted on one thing—that General Hyakutake himself travel by fast destroyer, not vulnerable transport. The Navy would extend an air umbrella using the *Kido Butai*, and bombard Henderson Field this time with battleships—fulfilling Yamamoto's promise.

Admiral Yamamoto had set in motion initiatives that led to the climax of the campaign. At Cactus, General Vandegrift and his colleagues were winding down, congratulating themselves on defeating a big enemy attack. At SOPAC the staffs were grasping at every straw to cobble together viable carrier forces. No Allied commander, whether on Guadalcanal, at SOPAC, or at Pearl Harbor, had any inkling of what was about to engulf them.

III.

A CRIMSON TIDE

Chester Nimitz had had a bellyful. There were the day-to-day frustrations of managing war across the far-flung Pacific and the pressures of finding ships and planes to sustain his line commanders. His Washington masters demanded answers Nimitz did not have, and forced him to defend subordinates in whom he had his own doubts. Both King and Nimitz had lost faith in Frank Fletcher as Pacific carrier chief. King was very critical of Admiral Ghormley in the South Pacific. Early in September the COMINCH and CINCPAC held another of their periodic get-togethers at San Francisco, joined by Navy secretary James Forrestal, just returned from the South Pacific. Ernie King wanted assurances on Ghormley. Forrestal backed the SOPAC, which pleased Nimitz, but returning to Pearl Harbor the CINCPAC found a letter from Ghormley that revived his concerns. Between diatribes on British colonials, dark expressions of suspicion about Ernest J. King, and fears of diminished carrier strength (at a time the *Wasp* had yet to be sunk), Ghormley defended his cautious tactics and suggested he needed no greater authority—where many agreed operational command was precisely what SOPAC lacked.

Admiral Nimitz decided to visit the South Pacific himself. The seaplane carrying his party alighted on the water at Nouméa on September 28. The CINCPAC boarded flagship *Argonne*. Also there were General Henry H. ("Hap") Arnold, leader of the Army Air Force, returning from an inspection of MacArthur's command, and General George Kenney, who had come with Arnold for the conference. Nimitz got an earful. Bob Ghormley had worked in his little office on the *Argonne* for months. He had not left the ship, not to visit Marines on Guadalcanal, not even to coordinate with MacArthur. When Hap Arnold chided Ghormley for his sedentary manner, the

SOPAC commander, his back up, told off the Army air boss in no uncertain terms. No one could question Ghormley on how he exercised command.

Nimitz and Ghormley both knew they had been pleading with the Army for planes. The CINCPAC also knew, even if Ghormley did not, that as an informal member of the Joint Chiefs, Arnold had resisted additional aircraft for the Pacific, even torpedoing already approved programs in favor of sending more to Europe. Only recently had Arnold agreed to provide some of the new, higher-performance P-38 fighters to the South Pacific. Antagonizing Hap Arnold was not smart, even less where Hap had a point. The SOPAC's exhaustion was obvious even to George Kenney. "I liked Ghormley," Kenney recorded, "but he looked tired and really was tired. I don't believe his health was any too good and I thought, while we were talking, that it wouldn't be long before he was relieved."

There was more. Admiral Nimitz had discovered that the *Washington*, a new fast battleship assigned to SOPAC, had been left behind at Tongatabu, far from the battle zone. Ghormley pleaded fuel shortages. SOPAC *was* deficient on tankers, but the harbor was full of merchantmen awaiting cargo transshipment—theater logistics were a nightmare. *And* the admiral still resisted running warships up to contest the nightly Japanese dominance of Ironbottom Sound. Ghormley had been defensive on this when writing CINCPAC, and Nimitz nudged him now, suggesting he had been holding too tightly on to his cruiser-destroyer strike force.

Twice during the conference aides entered with action messages for the SOPAC, and both times the admiral seemed to have no clue what to do. Then came an eye-opening exchange between Ghormley and Kenney. SOPAC officers naturally appealed to the SOWESPAC air commander for mass strikes on Rabaul. Kenney replied that his airmen wanted to knock out Rabaul's airfields, even burn down the town, but that several requirements of the New Guinea fight had to be met first. Kenney refused to say when Rabaul might be attacked. Admiral Ghormley responded that he appreciated what SOWESPAC was doing and wished them luck over Rabaul when they got there. Nimitz bristled at such flaccidity.

Next day Admiral Nimitz hopped a B-17 flight to Cactus. Even now Ghormley failed to seize the moment to visit the front. The aircraft went off course in stormy weather and found Guadalcanal almost by chance—CINCPAC's air staff officer had to use a *National Geographic* map. They were an hour late, landing in rain, taxiing through mud, then disgorging Nimitz, disappointing Marines who hoped the plane carried nurses or chocolate. General Vandegrift, who wished Nimitz to see the real conditions under which his men fought, was privately pleased.

Vandegrift met the plane and squired the admiral around Henderson, then to see Bloody Ridge and some of the perimeter. Later they joined Roy Geiger for a nuts-and-bolts talk on flying planes from Cactus. The two boss men talked long into the night on everything from naval regulations to Vandegrift's mission of defending Henderson, which he felt was threatened by Kelly Turner's latest brainstorm—creating a new air base elsewhere on Cactus. It must have gratified Nimitz when the Marine, thinking about aggressive ship handling in Ironbottom Sound, advocated changing Navy regs to make skippers more venturesome, less anxious about running their ships aground. That was exactly what a young Lieutenant Nimitz had been charged with so many years before.

In the morning Admiral Nimitz awarded a number of medals, including the Navy Cross to Alexander Vandegrift. A dozen recipients were Cactus fliers. Then Vandegrift bundled the admiral into his B-17, wanting to get him out before rain turned Henderson into mud or the Japanese noontime raid hit. The aircraft failed on its first try and had to wait for a break in the weather. Back in Nouméa, Chester Nimitz ordered Ghormley to upgrade the facilities on Cactus, providing Quonset huts for the airmen, Marston mats for the entire runway, better fuel and ordnance storage, plus reinforcements. He overrode SOPAC's objections about garrisoning islands far from the combat zone. Returning to Pearl Harbor, Nimitz professed himself satisfied with the situation in the South Pacific, though in truth he was far from happy. Admiral Nimitz told *Time* magazine the men on the spot "will hold what they have and eventually start rolling northward."

TWO WALKS IN THE SUN

The advent of the 7th Marines afforded Alexander Vandegrift fresh opportunities. The Marine general was not content on the defensive. As a young officer he had served in China at the outset of its civil war and knew the costs of passivity, shown by the Chinese nationalists there. Happy to make an incursion with the Marine Raiders when he brought them over from

Tulagi, Vandegrift did the same with his reinforcements now. He probed Japanese positions. Aerial photography showed the main body of Japanese stood west of a river called the Matanikau. The Marines knew little more than that. A probe would reveal the situation. It would also invigorate Marines who had sat far too long in their foxholes.

Vandegrift nominated Red Mike Edson to lead and told him to use any troops he wanted. Elevated to command the 5th Marine Regiment, Edson selected one of its battalions, included his old 1st Raider Battalion, and called on the fresh 7th Regiment for a unit too. The latter choice fell on Lieutenant Colonel Lewis B. "Chesty" Puller's 1st Battalion, 7th Marines (1/7), a solid unit led by a famous Marine. The Raiders and the 1/7 were to swing to the south, skirting Mount Austen and crossing the river to establish precisely where the enemy might be. The 2nd Battalion, 5th Marines, would be at the Matanikau's mouth in reserve.

Nothing went according to Edson's plan. The overland trek across foothills, through jungle and elephant grass, slowed to a crawl. Chesty Puller's 1/7 tarried. The Marine Raiders got into a fierce firefight, climbed a hill to obtain better positions, and ended up defending themselves. Lieutenant Colonel Samuel B. Griffith, who had succeeded Edson in charge, was badly wounded and his deputy killed. Puller's men followed the Matanikau to the sea, unaware the Raiders were trapped behind them. Chesty had sent a reinforced company back to base as bearers and guards for wounded, and these men were commandeered for a rescue mission to the Raiders. As a result of bombs that wrecked Vandegrift's radio center, a message from Griffith had been misunderstood to mean the Raiders were on the far side of the Matanikau. So division called on Jack Clark of the naval support unit, who sent Higgins boats to carry the 1/7 Marines to save the Raiders. But there was no one to rescue, and the relief party was itself surrounded just inland from the beach. Puller and Edson were standing together at the river mouth when the Higgins boats chugged past, ignoring their frantic efforts to wave off the craft. Finally Puller boarded destroyer *Ballard* offshore and signaled his trapped men to move off in another direction. They were extracted, but not before Coast Guardsman Douglas A. Munro, diverting the enemy with some of the Higgins boats, fell dead. The fiasco cost 140 men.

September gave way to October, with General Vandegrift deciding to extend his perimeter to the Matanikau. He planned a new operation using six full battalions, almost half his troops, under direct command. This time most of Edson's 5th Marines advanced along the coast; the 2/7 would cross the Matanikau and take up blocking positions, while Puller's battalion and the reinforced 3/2 Marines made a right hook inland and marched to the sea. Puller would capture Point Cruz. The Japanese might be pocketed. In that case Edson should continue over the river, pass Point Cruz, and make for the enemy base at Kokumbona.

The operation began early on October 7. Red Mike quickly ran into trouble and asked for help. Vandegrift sent the 1st Raiders. All stalled. Blissfully ignorant of American plans and intent on reaching good jump-off positions for their own offensive, General Maruyama of the Sendai Division had ordered his Aoba Detachment to advance also. The result was fighting on both banks of the Matanikau. Rain delayed movement late into the next afternoon. Some Marines in the enveloping force wavered, and neither 3/2 nor 1/7 could complete the encirclement. That afternoon Vandegrift received a vexing dispatch from Ghormley. SOPAC intelligence believed a large Imperial Navy task force was on the way. Though by then he had three battalions across the river, Vandegrift decided to pull back and defend the Matanikau line. On October 9 Marines began laying out new defenses.

Japanese troops were indeed marshaling for a big push, though intelligence was wrong about timing. On their side everything depended upon the buildup. Arrival of the 2nd Sendai Division would be the leading edge, dribbling in from the Tokyo Express. Lieutenant General Maruyama Masao arrived between the first and second Matanikau battles. Maruyama's October 1 order of the day—captured by the Americans—was highly suggestive. "This is the decisive battle," Maruyama had said, "a battle in which the rise or fall of the Japanese Empire will be decided. If we do not succeed in the occupation of these islands, no one should expect . . . to return alive." Lieutenant General Hyakutake landed on Guadalcanal on October 9 with his Seventeenth Army forward headquarters. His own plan echoed Maruyama's, stating, "The operation to surround and recapture Guadalcanal will truly decide the fate of the control of the entire Pacific area."

Hyakutake left his chief of staff, Major General Miyazaki Shuichi, at Rabaul as a relay between the battlefront and IGHQ. Lieutenant General Sado Tadayoshi's 38th Division had begun moving up from Borneo, and liaison officers were already at Rabaul. Special provisions were made for the 150mm heavy guns of the Army's 4th Artillery Regiment, supposed to help neutralize Henderson. A Navy delegation visited Guadalcanal to survey conditions and reported that for effective bombardment the guns would need to be on the west bank of the Matanikau—one reason the Japanese contested this ground so fiercely and ordered that Aoba Detachment attack.

The Tokyo Express had gone into high gear. Some troops would complete their voyage to Starvation Island by ant runs—the Japanese employed enough barges to deliver half a dozen loads every day. There were four rat missions during the last week of September, and the Navy ran the Tokyo Express almost nightly during the first half of October. The Army's heavy equipment, in particular tanks and the 150mm guns, would arrive on a pair of missions by seaplane carriers *Nisshin* and *Chitose.* The long-ballyhooed "high-speed convoy" would deliver the balance of the Army troops. Hyakutake had scheduled his offensive for October 21. The Imperial Navy bent every effort to make that possible.

POTENT FORCES

In the South Pacific, Allied fleets deployed thin resources to meet vast demands. Destroyers were especially hard-pressed in SOPAC. Not only were they vital for convoy protection and to cross Torpedo Junction, but they had to sweep harbor entrances during the entry or exit of fleet units, screen the task forces, conduct antisubmarine patrols, protect oilers refueling the fleet at sea, bombard enemy shores, and engage the Japanese fleet. American ships maintained one of several levels of alert. The highest form of readiness, battle stations, was called Condition 1. In Condition 2 half the guns were manned and the ship prepared to maneuver. Condition 3 was for normal cruising. Vessels in these waters almost never set Condition 3. Battle stations were the norm every day at dawn, whenever approaching Guadalcanal, often in its anchorage, and anytime action impended. Mostly skippers set Condition 2. This cycle of constant medium to high readiness played havoc with men's lives—sailors had to eat on the run or at their action stations, grab sleep when possible, and perform at peak despite their constant demanding work. Guadalcanal convoys were timed to enter the eastern approach, the Lengo Channel, before dawn, arriving early at the anchorage. Escort commanders decided whether to up-anchor and ske-daddle when things got too hot. The importance of unloading usually had them standing in Ironbottom Sound when the JNAF came, though ships might get under way to avoid damage.

Task Force 64, the SOPAC cruiser-destroyer flotilla, had been reconsti-tuted since Savo Island. Still, with SOPAC's meager forces and the available warships constantly called upon for anything and everything, it was diffi-cult to prepare for surface combat. Rear Admiral Norman Scott led the unit. Scott had skippered one of the light cruisers that escaped Savo because she had been in the anchorage to protect the transports. He had no inten-tion of allowing that tragedy to repeat. The Imperial Navy had had better night tactics. Scott made his ships practice night maneuvers whenever they could be spared. Gunnery exercises were numerous. At least twice in late September, Admiral Scott held night maneuvers with his complete force.

The Americans had one key advantage with their radar, then a new-fangled gizmo, and a word constructed of an acronym that stood for "radio detection and ranging." The technical development of radar had gained momentum quickly. An SC-type radar used longer-wavelength pulses, well suited to detecting targets at altitude, hence its utility for discovering enemy aircraft. The innovation of powered revolving antennae increased coverage to a full 360 degrees, and that of the "planned position indicator" enabled radarmen to "see" targets in a spatial relationship to the emitter. This became the basis for the aircraft carrier's practice of positive control over intercepting fighters, vectoring them to engage specific targets. The SC radar was becoming widely distributed and now equipped all battleships and aircraft carriers, many cruisers, and late-model destroyers. But with its long radio wavelength (150 centimeters), the SC equipment had poor target discrimination closer to the surface, where signals were absorbed by land-masses and vegetation or broke up amid wave action. A new machine, the SG-type radar, had a micro waveform (10 centimeters) that promised excel-lent performance close to the surface, discriminating ships from land, even vessels of different sizes, and this became the basis for radar-directed gunnery. So far only the newest vessels had that equipment. The Japanese were far behind, their first, primitive radars installed in the summer of 1942.

By October a number of Norman Scott's warships featured SC radars, and a couple had the SG-type also. Integrating technology into seamanship posed the next great challenge. The use of radar data in gun laying was one headache—could it be translated directly into direction and azimuth instructions or should it be fed to gun directors? Another problem was the effect of gunnery on radar. In a number of ships, when main batteries fired, the radars were knocked off-line and had to be repaired. These problems would eventually be worked out, and the first practical solutions came at Guadalcanal.

When SOPAC knew the Tokyo Express was coming, Task Force 62, Kelly Turner's amphibious force, might strengthen convoy escorts with cruisers, or Scott could bring his surface action group up to engage them. In October, the operating tempos of the two sides meshed to produce the first round of what became a crucial passage. Initial contenders were the JNAF and Tokyo Express versus the Cactus Air Force. Anxious to prepare the way for the Japanese Army, the Navy sent bombers by day, the Tokyo Express at night. With Nimitz still returning to Pearl Harbor, the South Pacific erupted.

The Eleventh Air Fleet opened with a fighter sweep on October 2. Bombers, included as decoys, turned back short of Cactus, and most of the Zeroes went on. Japanese airmen downed six Wildcats, including those of two pilots Nimitz had just decorated, damaging several more. Tsukahara's fliers repeated the formula the next day, but Cactus air was prepared, dispatching nine JNAF fighters and badly hitting another. That was a critical day at sea also. Seaplane carrier *Nisshin* steamed down The Slot carrying nine of the Japanese guns, their gunners, and General Maruyama. Scout bombers found her late in the afternoon but were driven off by Zeroes. The SBDs jumped *Nisshin* that night while unloading. The ship sprang a leak from a near miss, and Captain Komazawa Katsumi cut short the mission with two artillery pieces still aboard. The Cactus Air Force struck twice again, missed, and B-17s tried their luck too, but were put off their aim by a *Chitose* floatplane crashing into a bomber, shearing off a wing. The responsible airman, Warrant Officer Katsuki Kiyomi, actually survived the collision and parachuted to safety.

The Americans attempted to come back the next day. Commander Air Solomons (AIRSOLS) arranged for *Hornet* planes to hit Shortland while Army B-17s struck the Buin complex. Amid cloud cover the attackers could not find their targets. That night the Express ran, as it did on October 5, when Cactus fliers pounded the destroyer sortie, damaging two ships. Mikawa assigned light cruiser *Tatsuta* and seaplane carrier *Chitose* to augment the Reinforcement Unit, now facing a backlog of matériel to land, including eight of the 150mm howitzers plus a number of other artillery pieces.

Coastwatchers and aerial reconnaissance assumed primary importance. Radio intelligence had temporarily been blinded. On September 30, the Imperial Navy modified its entire system of communications, copying some U.S. methods, changing call signs, and introducing a revised D Code (the Japanese name for JN-25). At that moment the most recent CINCPAC monthly estimate had a good understanding of Mikawa's fleet strength. Weekly reports on Japanese fleet dispositions issued in Washington by the F-22 section of the Office of Naval Intelligence, based primarily on radio direction finding, agreed with CINCPAC's accounting in dispatches sent on September 29 and October 6.

Pearl Harbor credited the JNAF with twelve to eighteen floatplanes and two patrol bombers at Shortland, and twenty-seven medium bombers, forty-five Zeroes, forty-eight floatplanes (half scouts, half the Zero seaplane version), and a dozen patrol bombers in the Rabaul area. Intelligence assessed that forty-five Zeroes and fifty-four Bettys were in the pipeline to the front.

Officers commented on Japanese intentions in their appreciation of October 1: "For the past six or seven weeks the Japs have been assembling planes, troops and ships in the general Rabaul area. There are no indications whatever of a move in any other direction." But Pearl Harbor was complacent: "While the Japs may want to start such an [offensive] effort in the near future," they had suffered heavy losses already, with Allied planes and submarines taking a steady toll, so that "all this has definitely slowed up their preparations." CINCPAC tabulated Japanese losses and damage during September at several aircraft carriers, an equal number of cruisers, a battleship, plus lesser vessels, a distinct overestimate. In reality Yamamoto's fleet was at its greatest strength since the invasion.

Disturbing indications mounted. The CINCPAC bulletin on October 6 mentioned Army and SNLF troops in the Solomons and predicted an impending attempt to overcome the Marines. Two days later the bulletin expected constant Tokyo Express runs, and the fleet intelligence summary noted the flow of aircraft to Rabaul, located the Sendai Division's chief of staff on Guadalcanal, and commented that the Japanese Seventeenth Army was "increasingly associated" with the island. Next day Admiral Mikawa was thought to have gone to Buin. Then, on October 10, the CINCPAC summary mentioned the Nagumo and Kondo forces in relation to the Solomons, again associated the Seventeenth Army with Cactus, located the Sendai Division as possibly on the island with the Kawaguchi Brigade, listed several SNLF units as "implicated" in the islands, and ominously led with this: "The impression is gained that the enemy may be getting ready for larger-scale operations in the Guadalcanal area." According to codebreaker Edward Van Der Rhoer, Op-20-G—hence Washington and presumably Pearl Harbor—knew the Japanese would lead off with a cruiser bombardment of Henderson.

The fat was in the fire. At SOPAC, Admiral Ghormley finally agreed to send U.S. Army troops to Cactus, and the 164th Infantry Regiment began loading out on October 8. Their move would be covered by the *Hornet* task force. The Japanese were intent on completing their transport schedule. Early on October 11 they put in motion the latest heavy reinforcement, employing both the seaplane carriers *Chitose* and *Nisshin* bearing artillery, and half a dozen destroyers in escort, most bearing troops. A daytime JNAF fighter sweep followed by a bomber raid tried to cripple the Cactus Air Force, which had just opened Fighter 1 to supplement Henderson Field. Weather and interceptors rendered the strikes ineffectual. But there was a third arrow in the Japanese quiver, a cruiser group sent to administer a naval bombardment. The enemy was bearing down at that very moment.

Norman Scott's surface action group left Espíritu Santo on October 7. With just three cruisers and three destroyers, Task Force 64 was on the weak side, and at the last moment other warships in the area, light cruiser *Helena* and a pair of destroyers, joined Scott. *Helena* sported one of the new SG radars. Admiral Scott wanted to hunt. He had a healthy awareness of Tokyo Express activity and a desire to avenge Savo. From west of the Solomons, Scott closed The Slot, timed to arrive off Savo near midnight, then steamed back to his holding position. For two nights Task Force 64 encountered nothing. On the third, the night of October 11–12, Scott found game. On Guadalcanal, Cape Esperance happened to be the closest point, and the battle took that name.

Rear Admiral Goto Aritomo led the Japanese flotilla, composed of three ships of his own Cruiser Division 6 plus two destroyers. A thirty-two-year Imperial Navy veteran, Goto was a torpedoman and had led the Navy's premier night-fighting unit before taking up these heavy cruisers, which had fought at Guam, Wake Island, and the Coral Sea before their stupendous Savo victory. Goto missed at least two chances for warning: Commander Yokota Minoru's *I-26* had seen a U.S. cruiser but radioed the information too late, while the Japanese reinforcement group unloading at Guadalcanal, which Scott's force must have passed, apparently saw nothing. The Japanese had no radar, but they had honed their night skills, with specially trained lookouts and excellent equipment, including low-light, high-magnification glasses.

Admiral Scott's Americans, on the other hand, only beginning to experience the use of radar, nearly squandered that advantage. Light cruiser *Helena* detected Goto first, at almost fourteen nautical miles, closing at thirty-five knots. *Helena*, which had never operated with Task Force 64, did not report her sighting. Heavy cruiser *Salt Lake City* also detected the Japanese with her less advanced SC radar, but remained silent. So did light cruiser *Boise*, with an SG radar, which assumed Admiral Scott had the information. *Helena* finally passed along her sighting at 11:42 p.m., and a couple minutes later *Boise* did too, but ambiguities in language and navigation terms left confusion as to the Japanese position and even whether there were different groups of them. By that time the range had shrunk to less than 5,000 yards, and Goto's vessels were plainly visible. Aboard the *Helena* an officer grumbled, "What are we going to do, board them?"

Lookouts on the Japanese flagship, heavy cruiser *Aoba*, finally saw three U.S. vessels at 11:43. Admiral Goto tentatively reduced speed to 26 knots,

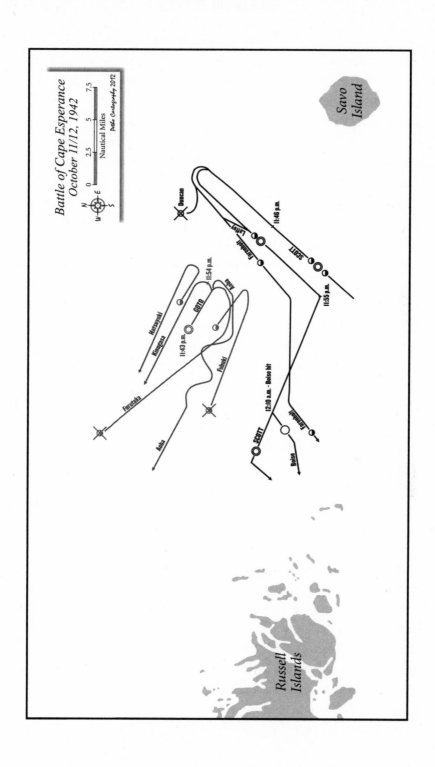

Battle of Cape Esperance
October 11/12, 1942

N
W E
S

0   2.5   5   7.5
Nautical Miles
Peter Cartography 2012

Savo
Island

Duncan

Laffey

Farenholt

SCOTT

11:46 p.m.

11:55 p.m.

Matsuyuki

Kinugasa

GOTO

11:54 p.m.

Aoba

11:43 p.m.

Furutaka

Aoba

Fubuki

SCOTT

12:10 a.m. - Boise hit

Farenholt

Boise

Russell
Islands

but just a moment later the *Helena* opened fire followed by the rest of Scott's ships. Goto had been steaming directly at the Americans, disposed in a line across his course, creating the sailors' dream of "crossing the T" of an adversary, where all guns could shoot at the enemy, who could reply only with weapons on the bow or stern. The *Aoba*, leading the Japanese line, was quickly reduced to a wreck, both forward eight-inch gun turrets smashed, her bridge hit by heavy-caliber shells. The *Boise* landed a salvo, including a dud shell on the flag bridge that mortally wounded Goto and killed two of his staff. Rear Admiral Scott, worried his ships were shooting at one another, ordered a halt, resuming fire once he felt more confident.

The Japanese force disintegrated. *Aoba* veered to port to bring her broadside to bear, only to offer the Americans a bigger target. She staggered off, struck more than forty times, but lived to fight another day. Saima Haruyoshi, a petty officer with the damage control detail, was sleeping at his battle station in the stern when the shells began to fall. He did not feel the first hit, but after that, destruction came quickly. One shell wrecked the number three turret, in the compartment immediately forward. When Saima tried to open the hatch, flames drove him back. There were dead, wounded, and fires everywhere. They had to pile up the bodies to get at the fires.

Destroyer *Fubuki*, haplessly caught as Scott steamed across her course, was blasted to pieces. Captain Araki Tsutau of the *Furutaka*, second in the Japanese line, turned to starboard, followed by the *Kinugasa*. The *Furutaka* came around to support her flagship, sustaining more than ninety hits, but she scored twice on the *Boise*, once against a forward magazine. The shell, of a type the Imperial Navy had designed to hit water and travel beneath the surface to impact a ship hull, actually functioned as advertised, recording the only known wartime success for this munition. The magazine hit would have blown *Boise* up save that seawater pouring into her from the hole extinguished the fire. *Furutaka* finally succumbed. The *Kinugasa* was slammed four times but punched back at the USS *Salt Lake City* with eight hits. *Aoba* was badly damaged. The Imperial Navy vessels survived the huge numbers of hits due only to high-quality design, brave seamen, and the proportion of duds among the American shells.

The *Boise* would be out of action for six months, the *Salt Lake City* for a full year. And Admiral Scott had not been entirely wrong about friendly fire—

destroyers *Farenholt* and *Duncan* were both hit by U.S. shells, the latter mortally.

Goto Aritomo's death sent shudders through the Imperial Navy. Goto was the first Japanese admiral to die on his bridge in a surface battle. Yamaguchi Tamon had gone down with flagship *Hiryu* at Midway, but he had elected to stay behind when sailors were abandoning ship. Worse, Navy gossip had it that Goto died believing the *Aoba* a victim of friendly fire, not enemy action. After Aoki Taijiro, captain of the carrier *Akagi* at Midway, Goto became the second member of Etajima's class of 1910 to succumb in the war. That was important to a lot of Imperial Navy officers who, at that very moment, were leading the fleet against the Americans on Cactus. Among Etajima classmates on the scene were Goto's boss, Mikawa Gunichi of the Eighth Fleet; Kusaka Ryunosuke, chief of staff of the *Kido Butai*; and Kurita Takeo, leading a force of battlewagons. His close friends included destroyer master Tanaka Raizo, now heading *Kido Butai*'s screen, and battleship commander Abe Hiroaki, both of whom had been a class behind Goto; as had Hara Chuichi, driving a cruiser division in Abe's Vanguard Force. The Japanese officers redoubled their determination.

"WHERE IS THE MIGHTY POWER OF THE IMPERIAL NAVY?"

Marines had standing orders to examine the dead enemy for documents that might help divine intentions and movements. Many Japanese defied orders not to keep diaries. These were fodder for the Americans, part of the pillar of combat intelligence. Some documents Vandegrift's staff exploited immediately. The bulk went to Nouméa, where SOPAC translated and examined them. During the second Matanikau battle a captured diary, translated at SOPAC, yielded a soldier's plaintive cry, "Where is the mighty power of the Imperial Navy?"

The complaint hardly needed to be heard. Admiral Yamamoto issued preparatory orders for his fleet sortie on October 4. The Tokyo Express chugged, and the Eleventh Air Fleet roared into Cactus, but it was a race with the Americans. The morning after Cape Esperance, the U.S. convoy bearing the 164th Infantry arrived. Destroyer *Sterett*, among its escorts, dropped anchor. Unloading had barely begun when the air raid sirens sounded and the ships weighed again. On the bridge, Lieutenant Herbert May grabbed the skipper and pointed to planes breaking through the clouds. "Christ, Captain—look, there's a million of 'em." Lieutenant C. Raymond Calhoun, *Sterett*'s gunnery boss, fired the main battery at maximum elevation to disrupt the Japanese V-of-Vs formation; then they were past. Calhoun watched. "The pilots exhibited excellent discipline. They kept tight formation and never wavered. . . . Their aim was excellent and we watched a perfect pattern fall smack on Henderson Field." Several hours later the JNAF repeated the performance in every detail save direction of the attack.

The Cactus Air Force got in its own licks. They helped track down Cape Esperance survivors, and they attacked destroyers that had been detached from the Japanese artillery convoy to rescue them. One enemy warship, crippled, had to be scuttled. Meanwhile, sharp as they had looked from the *Sterett*, Japanese bombardiers did not actually crater Henderson, so U.S. missions continued into the afternoon, blasting another destroyer to the bottom. Undeterred, Rear Admiral Joshima, the R Area Force commander leading the mission, immediately sailed on another artillery run in the *Nisshin*.

Yamamoto's operation gathered momentum. Combined Fleet planned to wallop Henderson in conjunction with the sailing of the high-speed convoy. This would open with a battleship bombardment—the C-in-Cs notion of putting the *Yamato* alongside Guadalcanal—followed by heavy cruiser shellings on succeeding nights. In a way Yamamoto's flagship *would* be at Guadalcanal—*Yamato* had sent expert lookout Lieutenant Funashi Masatomi to the island as an observer and installed him atop Mount Austen with radio gear.

The morning after Cape Esperance, Vice Admiral Kurita Takeo and his bombardment force, led by battleships *Kongo* and *Haruna*, left the main body. Suffering from fevers a few days earlier, Kurita was back on his mark. Rear Admiral Tanaka escorted. Battleship *Kongo* carried incendiary AA shells of a new type, tested at Truk in early October, which promised to be very effective. *Haruna* had older shells that could still be destructive. Theirs became the first opportunity to avenge Goto's death.

For a prelude, Admiral Kusaka Jinichi sent his Rabaul bombers to hit Henderson, flying a course like the *Sterett* had seen—out to sea, avoiding

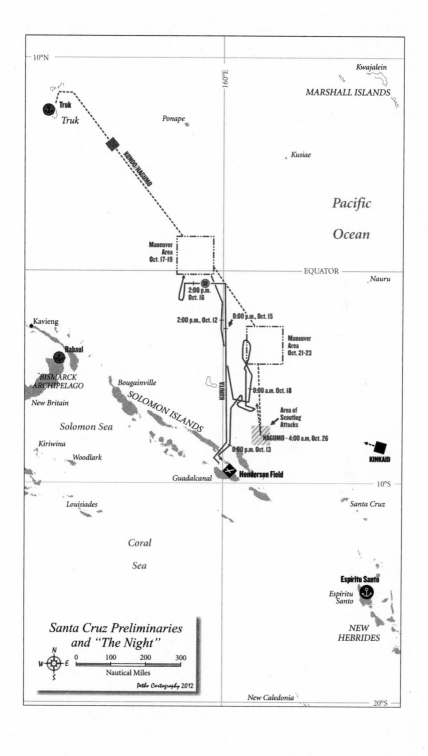

10°N

Kwajalein

MARSHALL ISLANDS

Truk

Truk

Ponape

160°E

Kusiae

Pacific

Ocean

KONDO/NAGUMO

Maneuver
Area
Oct. 17-19

EQUATOR

Nauru

2:00 p.m.
Oct. 16

2:00 p.m., Oct. 12   8:00 p.m., Oct. 15

Maneuver
Area
Oct. 21-23

Kavieng

Rabaul

BISMARCK
ARCHIPELAGO

New Britain

Bougainville

SOLOMON ISLANDS

KURITA

8:00 a.m. Oct. 18

Solomon Sea

Kiriwina

Woodlark

Area of
Scouting
Attacks

NAGUMO - 4:00 a.m, Oct. 26

KINKAID

8:00 p.m. Oct. 13

Guadalcanal

Henderson Field

10°S

Louisiades

Santa Cruz

Coral

Sea

Espíritu Santo

Espíritu
Santo

NEW
HEBRIDES

Santa Cruz Preliminaries
and "The Night"

N
W   E
S

0   100   200   300

Nautical Miles

Petho Cartography 2012

New Caledonia

20°S

coastwatchers and approaching from the south. This time the runway *was* damaged. Then the Japanese Army chimed in with the first shells from its 150mm howitzers, quickly christened "Pistol Pete," impeding American efforts to repair the Marston matting. Kusaka followed with several night intruders that arrived at intervals, twin-engine Nells the Marines knew as Washing Machine Charlie.

Kurita arrived off Guadalcanal late in the evening of October 13. He made a high-speed circuit of Savo, set an easterly course past Lunga Point, then swung onto the reciprocal track, with the two battleships' fourteen-inch guns pummeling Henderson and the U.S. positions for ninety minutes. Kurita launched floatplanes to illuminate the scene. The warships pumped out 918 shells, mixing their time-fused incendiaries with armor-piercing shells, both to destroy aircraft in the revetments and to dig under the runways. Captain Koyanagi Tomiji had his *Kongo* space her salvos at one-minute intervals. The pace allowed Lieutenant Commander Ukita Nobue, gunnery officer, to ensure accurate gun laying. Marine shore batteries that replied—they were beyond range anyway—were engaged by the battleships' secondary armament, and searchlights were used to blind the Marine gunners.

Those on Guadalcanal remember this simply as "The Night." General Vandegrift, who records that he used to go to sleep every evening about 7:00, after listening to the shortwave broadcast from San Francisco, refrains from commenting on The Night, though he surely must have awoken. In the same passage Vandegrift notes his first act every morning was to inspect the previous night's damage. Marine Bud DeVere, a control tower operator at Henderson's "Pagoda," recalls a continuous ordeal of Pistol Pete shooting them up, Washing Machine Charlie harassing them, then the battleships. At Cactus Crystal Ball, radioman Phil Jacobsen was trying to relax in a bunker the Seabees had built to protect their intercept gear when he saw a star shell burst almost directly overhead. He had barely sought cover when all hell broke loose. After The Night, whenever it rained, their receivers went on the blink.

Lieutenant Bill Coggins, with 2/1 rifle battalion, located a full mile from Henderson, remembers the Marines had become inured to naval bombardments, but that, from the beginning, everyone realized this was different— star shells, tight six-gun salvos, heavy blast concussion. Far away though they were, the baseplate of a fourteen-inch shell landed awfully near the E Company cookhouse. When greenies of the Army's 164th Regiment arrived to replace Coggins's men the next day, wily Marines frightened them with promises of greater horrors to come. Captain Nikolai Stevenson, whose C Company of the regiment's 1st Battalion was relieved that night by Army newbies, pulled into reserve near Henderson. He was playing poker when the fireworks started. "All at once the murmuring night exploded into ghastly daylight. . . . The concussion knocked me halfway over as I dived headlong for the puny cover of the ditch, where I lay shaking among the fallen palm fronds." Japanese shells roared and screeched, like subway cars tearing through a thousand bolts of cloth strung together. Warren Maxson, also of the 1st Marines, counted five air raids that night. Lieutenant Merillat of Vandegrift's staff remembered the alarming series of "Condition Red" alerts—always announced by siren for incoming air raids—followed by the bombardment: "The shelter shook as if it were set in jelly. Bombs, artillery, big naval shells made it sheer hell."

From an American point of view the one good aspect of The Night was that it marked the appearance of a new piece on the board, the Patrol Torpedo (PT) boat. These high-speed seventy-foot craft, each armed with .50-caliber machine guns, a 20mm cannon, and torpedoes, would contest Ironbottom Sound full-time. The convoy that brought Army troops had also deposited the first elements of PT Squadron 3. They based at Tulagi. Four PTs came out to fight Kurita's fleet, attacking shortly before the bombardment ended. Commander Ukita on the *Kongo* recalled the PT boats' intervention, but stoutly insisted Kurita's worst fear was of running aground on the treacherous shoals and reefs in the channels. Destroyer *Naganami* contemptuously brushed off the PTs, but those gnats would be back, gnawing painfully at the Imperial Navy.

By morning Cactus had descended into crisis—Henderson Field holed, Fighter 1 damaged. Only seven SBDs and thirty-five fighters could fly; forty-one men were dead, including two more of those Admiral Nimitz had decorated so recently. The Pagoda was demolished. Roy Geiger ordered it bulldozed. Aviation gas was mostly destroyed, enough left for just one mission. Mechanics worked desperately on crippled planes. This was the day of the high-speed convoy, which had left on the thirteenth with six transports and eight destroyers. Scout bombers found both it and a fresh Japanese surface force—Admiral Mikawa with cruisers *Chokai* and *Kinugasa*—the latter bouncing right back to seek vengeance for Cape Esperance. Naturally, Japanese bombers struck at midday. Only late that afternoon did Cactus scrape together a flight of four SBDs and seven Army fighter-bombers to fling at the convoy. Draining the gas out of a couple of B-17s permitted a second wave of nine SBDs before dark. They achieved nothing save the loss of one plane and the crash of another.

Now the night cast Mikawa Gunichi as avenging angel. His cruisers lashed Henderson with 752 eight-inch shells. U.S. radio intelligence reported Mikawa at sea, probably in *Chokai*, that very day, but Cactus had had to choose between cruisers and convoy. While nowhere as destructive as Kurita's battleship bombardment, Mikawa's shells inflicted more damage on planes and renewed the craters that pockmarked airfields.

To complete their mastery of Ironbottom, the Japanese may have sent a midget submarine sortie into the anchorage. Orders for the mission exist. It was to have been launched from seaplane carrier *Chiyoda*, which had shuttled eight of the craft to the Solomons. These small two-man subs, notably used at Pearl Harbor and at Sydney, Australia, were to invade the sound around midnight. But there is no evidence of their actual presence. Some American small craft, escorted by a pair of the new PTs, crossed undisturbed from Guadalcanal to Tulagi that night. Admiral Ugaki complained that plans for the midgets' employment were incomplete, and notes that he ordered a study, puzzling since Combined Fleet staff had discussed using the subs in the very first days of Watchtower. Ugaki recommended putting the boats at Kamimbo and loosing them when there were suitable targets. It is not clear whether Yamamoto overruled him. The Japanese *did* set up a midget sub base at the designated place, and other sorties did run from there. Months later the American salvage ship *Ortolan* found a midget and raised her long enough to recover this day's attack order and other documents, but a storm broke her grip and the submersible was lost.

At dawn on the fifteenth, Marines were outraged to see Japanese transports unloading in broad daylight across the sound. But Cactus air was in disarray. Roy Geiger demanded his men find gas, and they did—an officer remembered fuel barrels had been cached in swamps and groves, and several hundred were found and laboriously hauled to the strips. That brought two days' supply. Guadalcanal called upon SOPAC to fly gasoline aboard its daily flights and even bring a load on submarine *Amberjack*. Mechanics rushed repairs. Starting early, scratch flights of SBDs and Army planes took off to hit the transports at Tassafaronga Point. Fighters engaged R Area Force floatplanes and Japanese interceptors—ominously, from *Kido Butai's* Carrier Division 2—to open the way, strafing ships when they had the chance.

Mitsukuni Oshita, a chief petty officer on destroyer *Hayashi*, was impressed at the way the Americans pressed their attacks in the face of murderous flak. Half the Japanese transports, damaged, withdrew. The others, also damaged, were beached—hopefully to be emptied later. The *Nankai Maru* and *Sasago Maru* were hit by the first U.S. wave, *Azumasan Maru* in the second attack, the *Kyushu Maru* later. An American bomb wrecked the *Kyushu Maru's* wheelhouse, killing her captain and all the bridge crew. Ignorant of this, the ship's engineers kept her at full speed until she ran up on the beach. The ammunition aboard another ship cooked off and she blew up. The *Nankai Maru*, the only cargoman not to catch fire—and the only damaged ship that tarried to unload—would be the only vessel of this group to escape. Men of the Independent Ship Engineering Regiment struggled to unload the supplies. The Japanese estimated the ships were 80 percent emptied. They would be furious in turn when U.S. warships appeared to shell the stacked supplies, destroying many. Beach crews were heavily hit too, with the regimental commander killed and one of his companies wiped out but for eight men.

Yet the Army troops had landed. They could not be stopped. With a Tokyo Express on October 17 the program was fulfilled. Captain Inui Genjirou brought his 8th Antitank Company, now without any guns, to help move the supplies. The men were so exhausted he had to rest them for a day, and they could do little to combat the fire that broke out in a nearby dump. But one of Inui's companies, thrilled to get cigarettes, labored to move the rice sacks away. Inui himself enjoyed the first coffee he had had since leaving Java.

General Geiger so focused on the supply battle that the day's Japanese air raid went virtually uncontested. Come night the Imperial Navy returned. This time it was Rear Admiral Omori Sentaro with heavy cruisers *Myoko* and *Maya*. Commander Nagasawa Ko, whose home prefecture of Fukushima would be devastated by tsunami and the nuclear meltdowns of

2011, was Omori's senior staff officer and recalled later that the Japanese had expected to be sunk. On the *Myoko* the crew were given rifles and instructed to get to shore and fight as naval infantry. Instead they faced no opposition. The warships pounded Henderson Field with 1,500 more eight-inch shells (some sources report 926). Yet next morning the Cactus Air Force could still fly ten dive-bombers and seven Army fighter-bombers. Geiger's maintenance crews plus the Seabees literally saved Guadalcanal.

American commanders recognized the crisis even if the Japanese did not. And they spoke up. Vandegrift cabled SOPAC and demanded every ounce of backing. Slew McCain, the AIRSOLS commander, did the same. Ghormley repeated the essence of their appeals in a dispatch to Nimitz. And the SOPAC had Rear Admiral George D. Murray's *Hornet* task force mount a carrier raid on the R Area Force floatplane base at Rekata Bay. Results were indeterminate.

At Pearl Harbor, Admiral Nimitz decided he had had enough. Ghormley's dispatch struck him as more weak-kneed passing of the buck. Aircraft carrier *Enterprise*, having completed repairs, was rushing to the South Pacific to increase the Allies' paper-thin strength. Vice Admiral William F. Halsey, whom CINCPAC had appointed to lead the "Big E's" task force, had gone ahead to get a feel for the situation. Nimitz huddled with his inner circle late into the night discussing the SOPAC command situation. On October 16, Admiral Nimitz asked Admiral King for authority to substitute Halsey for Ghormley. The COMINCH approved. Just as "Bull" Halsey reached Nouméa, Nimitz sent him a message: The Bull would supplant Bob Ghormley as theater commander. The aggressive Halsey led the next battle, the most important yet. Allied leaders already knew it was upon them.

BLOOD UPON THE SEA

Despite the Imperial Navy's changed codes and communications, Allied intelligence assembled an increasingly alarming picture of its activities. Indications piled up from radio traffic analysis, from the coastwatchers, from combat intelligence, from observation and aerial reconnaissance, even a few from Ultra proper. After Cape Esperance—itself an intelligence windfall, because the Allies captured 113 survivors of the warships *Furutaka* and *Fubuki*, whom they plied for information—the picture darkened further. Starting the next morning, the Allies observed a rapid increase in the volume of messages sent on the Japanese radio nets, especially those used to report radio fixes on Allied ships. Meanwhile a snooper discovered *Kido Butai*, reporting carriers, battleships, cruisers, and destroyers 400 miles northeast of Cactus. Intelligence also detected the enemy intercept of that scout's message, plus Imperial Navy sighting reports, an increasing number of them from I-boats. The fighting around Cactus certainly indicated the Japanese were not giving in.

The captured seamen revealed to Allied intelligence the actual Imperial Navy vessels engaged at both Cape Esperance and Savo, furnishing information that was accurate, if not at first believed, because it did not accord with the claims of U.S. commanders. Richmond Kelly Turner circulated this data on October 21. The prisoners knew nothing of Yamamoto's current plans, but they possessed a wealth of knowledge of Japanese procedures, equipment, and operational methods.

On October 15, codebreakers reported that the pattern of radio traffic showed Yamamoto had taken direct command of operations. Combined Fleet became a heavy originator of messages. Ultra also provided radio bearings for a fleet unit containing at least two aircraft carriers, and reported an unidentified radio emitter on Guadalcanal—likely Lieutenant Funashi's Navy observation post—that had begun providing fairly accurate tabulations of Cactus air strength. The next day Ultra confirmed the traffic flow from Combined Fleet and reported that the Japanese appeared to have focused all their attention on the Solomons. Pearl Harbor was on edge. The CINCPAC war diary for October 17 read, "It now appears that we are unable to control the sea . . . in the Guadalcanal area . . . our supply of the position will only be done at great expense." Nimitz did not believe the situation hopeless, but it had become critical: "There is no doubt now that Japs are making an all-out effort in the Solomons, employing the greater part of their Navy." Ultra noted quiet, or an unchanged Japanese situation, over several succeeding days. Starting on October 19, Ultra tabulated a *reduction* in high-level, high-priority message volume, ominously suggesting Yamamoto's offensive was under way. The next day it furnished a new location for the *Kido Butai* and associated carrier commander Nagumo with surface fleet boss Kondo.

But Allied intelligence was not omniscient. As had happened before the

Battle of the Eastern Solomons, there were doubts about the Japanese air-craft carriers. The Combined Fleet had five of these ships, with the large carriers *Shokaku* and *Zuikaku*, plus the light carrier *Zuiho* in Carrier Division 1, and the slower fleet carriers *Hiyo* and *Junyo* in Carrier Division 2. At the end of September, Washington's weekly estimates located Carrier Division 1 not far from Rabaul, when it rode at anchor at Truk, except possibly the *Zuikaku*, which intelligence believed en route to Yokosuka. A week later it put the *Zuiho* also in Japan—and continued to believe the *Zuiho* in Empire waters right through the estimate of October 20, the last to appear before the bat-tle. The *Zuikaku* the Allies estimated back in Truk on October 13, and they continued to place Carrier Division 1 there a week later, even though Japa-nese carriers had already been seen at sea, with locations for them repeat-edly remarked in Ultra.

The record for Carrier Division 2 was worse. It was continuously placed in Empire waters right through the estimate of October 27, the day *after* the impending battle. The combat intelligence unit at Pearl Harbor wavered on locating these carriers, indicating they were in Japan on October 6, report-ing a "slight" possibility of the Philippines on October 11, and a possibility the two ships might be in Empire waters a week later. In reality, Rear Ad-miral Kakuta Kakuji's Carrier Division 2 had sailed from Japan for Truk on October 2 and sortied for the operation with the rest of the fleet nine days later. At least Pearl Harbor consistently believed that two big carriers were involved, and held them to be *Shokaku* and *Zuikaku*. On October 23, Pearl Har-bor intelligence shifted to declare that "at least" two carriers must be among the enemy fleet.

Estimates for surface gunnery ships were skewed because Admiral Nor-man Scott reported inflicting much greater losses at Cape Esperance than was true. There was also another complication, according to Commander Bruce McCandless: ONI mistakenly believed all four *Aoba*-class cruisers lay at the bottom of the sea. When Scott claimed on October 18 to have sunk three heavy cruisers and four destroyers and possibly dispatched another tin can and a light cruiser (actual losses had been one heavy cruiser and one destroyer), these were scored to units other than the Imperial Navy's Cruiser Division 6, which had the *Aobas*. This effectively minimized Japa-nese heavy cruiser strength. When the *Myoko* and *Maya* bombarded Cactus, ONI believed the former was anchored at Yokosuka and the latter at Palau.

As for battleships, the October 20 estimate carried as "possibly damaged" one of Admiral Kurita's vessels that had smashed Cactus on The Night, placed the *Yamato* and *Mutsu* as possibly at Rabaul, and credited the fleet in the Solomons—again "possibly"—with the *Ise*, then in Empire waters.

Fortunately other pillars of intelligence clarified. The combination continued to furnish a clearer picture. Rabaul would be covered by aerial photography at least a half dozen times during the last ten days before the battle. Estimated aggregate tonnage there ranged between 170,000 and 250,000 tons. At the high point, Simpson Harbor contained two oilers and forty-one merchant ships, with a light cruiser, a minelayer, three destroyers, and several aviation tenders. General Kenney's SOWESPAC B-17s finally kicked off their Rabaul bombing on October 22, claiming to have blasted a cruiser, a destroyer, and eight merchantmen for 50,000 tons, and, two nights later, to have left the *Nisshin* wreathed in flames from a direct hit amidships, claiming her utterly destroyed. The *Nisshin* was at Shortland that night and no ship of her type lay at Rabaul.

As for Admiral Kakuta's carriers, the first to intervene at Guadalcanal when he sent fighters to help screen the high-speed convoy while it unloaded, a scout plane signaled a carrier northwest of Kavieng on October 16, which put new light on the arguments over Carrier Division 2's location.

The Japanese center of gravity had to be the Shortland-Buin complex, and there Allied intelligence benefited from coastwatchers as well as aerial spies. Reports covered that area virtually every day. Interestingly, the several separate forces counted here on October 15 totaled two aircraft carriers, four battleships, seven heavy and an equal number of light cruisers, twenty destroyers, and three aviation ships. An oiler and seventeen cargomen were reported the next day. If the intelligence estimates on Imperial Navy disposition were to be believed, those figures could not be accurate. But Kurita's battleships stopped here briefly after The Night, Kondo's fleet with Kakuta's carriers were in the area, and Shortland was the center of Mikawa's Eighth Fleet operations, with his typical tally some cruisers, aviation ships, and a dozen or so tin cans. The net impression, perfectly correct, was of Japanese might assembled for a big blow.

American air reconnaissance on October 17 recorded two cruisers and seven destroyers, and noontime aerial photography on October 20 revealed a heavy cruiser, four light cruisers, and seventeen destroyers. The other vessels were gone. Additional overhead imagery the next day disclosed the presence of five additional warships, with a different mixture of the cruiser types. On October 24 there was nothing at Shortland but a few tin cans. Over subsequent days sightings of all kinds showed Mikawa's base reverting to its usual strength. The specifics could have been mistaken. What was inescapable was the sense of a mission force assembled, then launched.

Chester Nimitz did not need a weatherman to know which way the wind blew. SOPAC's forces were divided among its cruiser-destroyer group, a unit with new battleships *Washington* and *South Dakota*, now titled Task Force 64, and the *Hornet*'s carrier group. The *Enterprise* group, steaming as fast as possible, promised to reach the theater in time. By October 17, Nimitz knew the Japanese had seen Task Force 64. CINCPAC remained in doubt regarding locations of enemy fleet units, but he knew they were out there, and Ultra had provided some carrier positions and even radio call signs. On October 20, via COMINCH, Nimitz appealed to the British Admiralty for an Indian Ocean offensive to distract the Japanese from the Solomons.

The next day, in conjunction with new SOPAC chief Bull Halsey, the plans were set. The *Enterprise* (Task Force 16) and the *Hornet* (Task Force 17) would join on the twenty-fourth as Task Force 61 under Rear Admiral Thomas C. Kinkaid, and sweep north of the Santa Cruz islands, on the flank of any approaching Japanese fleet. At first CINCPAC foresaw the task force as being unable to act until the following day, but later it seemed they might be ready shortly after uniting. The battleships were sent on a midnight romp through Ironbottom Sound. No Japanese were found, so they moved to strengthen the carriers' defenses. On the twenty-second a snooper saw the *Kido Butai*. Nimitz foresaw that for at least several weeks the Japanese would be able to throw more troops, planes, and ships into a battle than SOPAC. That could not be avoided. CINCPAC would apply calculated risk. "From all indications," Nimitz's war diary recorded on October 22, "the enemy seems about ready to start his long expected all out attack on Guadalcanal. The next three or four days are critical."

In Truk lagoon on the morning of October 11, Yamamoto and Ugaki witnessed a momentous event from the fantail of the *Yamato*. Admiral Nagumo's ships raised anchor and gingerly began their egress. Dark gray warships disappeared beyond the coral reefs of Truk's north channel. After lunch the towering battleships of Admiral Kondo's fleet, with Kakuta's Carrier Division 2, departed south-side. Yamamoto, so sensitive of late, had begun micromanaging, questioning details. One big one was that the operations plan did not cover what to do in case of failure. Ugaki justified that with the comment that the fleet could not afford to fail. Everything had been done to ensure victory. Now was the time. The determined reinforcement program had put major Army units on Guadalcanal, and Navy efforts were near to suppressing Henderson Field. The day after the fleet sailed, Seventeenth Army chief of staff General Miyazaki and Navy staff officers Genda and Ohmae came up from Rabaul to plead for a battleship bombardment of Cactus. They were startled to learn one had already been laid on and was about to occur. Victory—that had a nice ring, rolled off the tongue easily, and it seemed close.

But Imperial Navy doctrine could be an obstacle. Under Yamamoto's plan, Nagumo's Striking Force of carriers would sail alongside Kondo's battleships and cruisers of the Advance Force. Japanese doctrine accorded primacy to battleships, making Vice Admiral Kondo the overall commander. There were many aspects of carrier employment that would seem peculiar to a surface warfare specialist, and Kondo Nobutake had no experience of aeronaval operations. This might prevent success.

The fleet command was aware of the problem. Admiral Hara Chuichi had encountered it at Coral Sea and Eastern Solomons. After the second action Ugaki had Hara in for a long talk. Distilling his experiences, Hara sensitized Ugaki to the dangers in traditional doctrine. Though Hara sailed now as a cruiser commander, his contribution had been helpful. In the course of planning this operation, Ugaki brought Kondo and Nagumo together several times. The two were Etajima classmates and friends, so they were inclined to cooperate. But the reticent Nagumo was not the man to educate Kondo, gracious as he was, in carrier operations. That role fell to Third Fleet chief of staff Kusaka Ryunosuke, who had known Kondo since they had been boys in middle school together. Before leaving Truk, Kusaka coached Kondo on the finer points of aircraft use, and he induced the force commander to agree that in matters involving carriers, Nagumo would exercise control.

So the fleet went to sea. Vice Admiral Kondo maneuvered in the waters northeast of the Solomons. By night they steamed south to attain favorable dawn launch positions. During the day they would turn north and head toward Truk—if battle came, the Japanese wanted to be headed for safety, not destruction. This cautious approach disgusted many. In the screen, Commander Hara Tameichi on his destroyer *Amatsukazi* was among those discomfited by the seeming reluctance to close with the enemy. It bothered Yamamoto too. He had imagined an aggressive sortie beyond the Solomons into the Coral Sea, cutting through Torpedo Junction to isolate Guadalcanal. That would have forced the Allies into the open to restore communications. As Combined Fleet saw *Kido Butai* diverge, Ugaki nudged Kondo and Nagumo to adopt a forward-leaning posture. But neither Ugaki nor Yamamoto made this a direct order.

Rear Admiral Kusaka counseled caution. Kusaka could not escape feeling the American carriers, as at Midway, would appear on Nagumo's flank. A sortie into the Coral Sea invited that. Kusaka was determined not to take the risk until the enemy carriers were accounted for. In the Imperial Navy, chiefs of staff had great power, and Kusaka used his to shield Nagumo from the complaints of inaction. When a new staffer aboard flagship *Shokaku* asked why the fleet did not stop this indecisive to-ing and fro-ing, Kusaka told him off, saying he was still an amateur at battle. The staff chief used the example of the sumo wrestler, who repeatedly left the fight to get salt to improve his grip, an act known as *shikari*. The fleet was doing *shikari*.

Kusaka fended off Ugaki as well. But as the days passed without action, morale suffered. The surface fleet was engaging the enemy. The Army, supposedly, was fighting. The *Kido Butai* did nothing. There were two key questions: the Army's attack and the location of Allied fleets. Actually Hyakutake's troops were still cutting their way through the jungle, struggling to reach assault positions. They literally hacked the "Maruyama Trail," named for the leader of the Sendai Division, through the harsh land. The date of the Seventeenth Army attack was postponed once, then again. General Hyakutake pleaded insuperable difficulties. At Truk, Admiral Ugaki complained that the Army did not understand that postponements of a day here and there, of little consequence to a soldier, were serious for a fleet burning oil and wearing its ships. Delay pressed against operational limits. Had the Army kept its promises, the naval battle would have occurred before the arrival of U.S. carrier *Enterprise*, affording the Japanese overwhelming superiority. Aboard *Amatsukaze*, Commander Hara recalled "waiting impatiently," a Navy that "stamped its feet in disgust."

Intelligence on the Allied fleet posed the other big headache. The Imperial Navy had an inkling of new Allied forces. The Owada Communications Group had reported a task force leaving Pearl Harbor in mid-October. Ready to inform the Japanese was a low-grade aviation codebook captured from a U.S. torpedo bomber downed at Shortland on October 3. The first concrete information came ten days later, when a *Chitose* floatplane spotted a carrier and a battleship through a hole in the clouds. Also that day, Lieutenant Commander Nagai Takeo's *I-7* sent a floatplane over the harbor at Espíritu Santo at dawn, determining that there were no U.S. carriers there. Traffic on Japanese direction finding and intelligence radio nets spiked, especially on Rabaul circuits, something Allied codebreakers noticed. On the fourteenth Nagumo's combat air patrol shot down an Allied scout. The *Kido Butai* (the text will use this term for all the Kondo-Nagumo forces for the moment) went looking for American carriers on its run south next day and found nothing but a tug towing a fuel barge toward Cactus. There had been an Allied convoy, but SOPAC had recalled it.

Continuing this shadow sumo bout, Japanese codebreakers recorded a high volume of *Allied* operational traffic, and on October 16, Rabaul added at least a dozen radio fixes on Allied ships. Aerial searches revealed a battleship group and a carrier force. With Nagumo out of position, the Eleventh Air Fleet sent out two attack units that encountered nothing but a tanker, which they hit but could not sink. Submarines supplied numerous sighting reports, establishing that Allied battleships were steaming south of Cactus. A few days later, Lieutenant Commander Tanabe Yahachi of the *I-176* got close enough to attack, and his torpedoes put the U.S. cruiser *Chester* out of action for more than a year.

At the initiative of Kusaka Ryunosuke, the fleet tried another ploy to locate the American carriers. Kusaka imagined them lurking at the edge of Torpedo Junction. He convinced Nagumo to conduct a special search using the heavy cruisers *Tone* and *Chikuma* of Rear Admiral Hara's Cruiser

Division 8. These had been designed specifically as scout vessels. Carrying five floatplanes and capable of supporting more, they were ideal for work with the *Kido Butai*. Indeed, these cruisers had been sailing with Nagumo since Pearl Harbor. Hara had commanded carriers and knew their habits and workday cycles. For this operation his cruisers were with Abe Hiroaki's Vanguard Force, still part of Nagumo's command. On October 19, the Japanese carrier boss set Hara on a dash forward to the Santa Cruz islands. The *Tone*, screened by a single destroyer, sent aerial scouts to search. They found nothing. Admiral Abe recalled Hara when an Emily patrol bomber from Jaluit sighted a U.S. carrier near Nouméa. A few days later the *Chikuma* repeated the exercise in an easterly direction. Again no result.

Meanwhile the Japanese scouted Nouméa on October 19 with a floatplane from Lieutenant Commander Kobayashi Hajime's *I-19*. No American carriers there. I-boats and air searches sighted battleships and cruisers but not carriers. Japanese intelligence circuits went wild, according to Allied monitors. By October 22, the Allies knew the Japanese were recording and tracking their radio call signs, and a couple of days later reported that the Imperial Navy had installed and was operating a radio direction finder on Guadalcanal itself.

The South Pacific cruise took its toll on the Imperial fleet. By October 17, Admiral Ugaki worried that the *Kido Butai*, running short of fuel, would be unable to maneuver. As an emergency measure one of Kondo's tankers, emptied by the fleet, took half the oil from each of battleships *Yamato* and *Mutsu* at Truk and, after topping off from another vessel, went back out. The Japanese suffered their first important loss that day, in Kakuta's Carrier Division 2, when a fire broke out in the generator room of his flagship, Captain Beppu Akitomo's aircraft carrier *Hiyo*. Damage control extinguished the blaze, but Commander Matoba Shigehiro, *Hiyo*'s chief engineer, thereafter could not produce more than sixteen knots, hardly enough for a fleet engagement. *Hiyo* stayed in formation for the moment, but with growing strain on Matoba's engines, on October 22 she blew out a condenser, cutting steam to some boilers. Admiral Kakuta shifted his flag to Captain Okada Tametsugu's *Junyo*. Lieutenant Kaneko Tadashi led half of *Hiyo*'s planes to Buin, while the rest crowded onto *Junyo*. Escorted by destroyers, Beppu sailed *Hiyo* to Truk at her best speed, six knots. This loss reduced Japanese strength even before the battle.

The quandary continued. On October 22, an I-boat surfaced off Espíritu Santo before dawn and treated the SOPAC base to a rare harassing bombardment. Part of the *Kido Butai* refueled on October 24. In his cabin on the *Shokaku*, even Nagumo Chuichi chaffed. Hara Tameichi relates this scene: Puzzling over the assorted sighting reports and an American news story that mentioned expectations for imminent battle in the South Pacific, Nagumo spoke to his senior staff officer, Commander Takada Toshitane. What to do? Takada mentioned the high level of radio emissions from Allied submarines and aircraft. Nagumo asked for his chief of staff. Kusaka reported on the progress of refueling. Nagumo ordered him, once the oilers had finished, to inform the fleet that major battle impended.

A similar conversation took place on Kakuta's flagship. Commander Okumiya Masatake, the admiral's senior staff officer, drew attention to the date October 27—Navy Day in the United States (today annual naval festivities are part of Armed Forces Day, at that time Navy Day, dreamed up by active officers but enshrined in 1922 by the Navy League of the United States), which was celebrated on the birthday of Theodore Roosevelt, the father of the "Great White Fleet." In conjunction with the expectations expressed in the American press, it seemed SOPAC might engage that day.

Back on the *Shokaku*, Commander Takada, no doubt aware of Admiral Kusaka's views, suggested consulting Combined Fleet. Kusaka assented, but, after a few moments' thought, turned the idea on its head, sending a dispatch that warned of a trap and recommended halting the fleet until the Army captured Henderson Field. He mentioned the idea of rescheduling to October 27. Ugaki's return message was direct: "STRIKING FORCE WILL PROCEED QUICKLY TO THE ENEMY DIRECTION. THE OPERATION ORDERS STAND, WITHOUT CHANGE."

Admiral Ugaki's version of this story appears in his diary. Kusaka's dispatch reached *Yamato* in the evening. Though sent before noon, it was delayed in retransmission by a relay vessel. Ugaki acknowledged that October 27 might be a better moment for battle, but the *Kido Butai*'s failure to attain assigned positions could endanger the entire plan. Combined Fleet sent the Army a different message declaring that if the offensive did not begin immediately, lack of fuel would require the Navy's withdrawal. But Ugaki felt

Kusaka's eleventh-hour démarche outrageous and arbitrary. His urgent reply: "THIS COMMAND HAS THE WHOLE RESPONSIBILITY. DO NOT
HESITATE OR WAVER!"

Everything hinged on the Japanese Army. Admiral Yamamoto recognized
that. As they stood together on *Yamato*'s upper deck, he told Ugaki that the
Army chief of staff must be more anxious for victory than anyone. Only the
Army could actually capture Henderson Field. American bombardments
and air attacks had robbed Seventeenth Army of about a third of the supplies from the high-speed convoy, and the remainder, those to sustain the
fight, had to be carried by the men themselves. General Hyakutake split
the Army into two detachments under his overall control. To attack along
the coast, around the Matanikau, would be Major General Sumiyoshi Tadashi, the Army's artillery commander, with two infantry regiments plus
the tanks and guns. Inland, under tactical command of Sendai Division
boss Lieutenant General Maruyama, the other group would make the direct attack toward Henderson Field.

The difficulties of the land slowed preparations. Except for Sumiyoshi's
men along the Matanikau, in increasingly well-known terrain, the Japanese
were largely navigating by compass bearing through thick jungle. No one
had surveyed Guadalcanal or produced accurate maps. And the soldiers
starved. Hungry men had trouble hacking their way through the under-
growth. Rough country plus rudimentary navigation meant errors in reckoning positions. Thus Hyakutake's postponements. To divert the Americans
and keep to some semblance of the schedule, General Sumiyoshi ordered
one regiment across the Matanikau to probe the Marine defenses. The un-
fortunate Colonel Oka led this maneuver, never intended as the main assault. On October 23 his troops tried to attack but bogged down in the
jungle. At Truk, Admiral Ugaki, learning of Oka's failure, reflected on the
dishonor the colonel heaped on his regiment's flag. Sumiyoshi's other regiment, with the tanks, was to attack across the river as part of the main offensive, most recently scheduled that very day. But General Sumiyoshi was
prostrated with malaria, and his staff never circulated the postponement
notice. The attack along the Matanikau went ahead on the original schedule. It gained little—though Marine General Vandegrift indeed turned

his eyes there. The Marines crushed the developing attack with 6,000 rounds of artillery fire.

Hyakutake's main attack by Maruyama's force had been set for nighttime. But the tactical commander found himself short of the assembly area. Chronic neuralgia also impaired Maruyama's faculties. He pleaded for another postponement. The troops finally swung into action on October 24. This operational group divided into two wings plus a reserve. Each wing, one of them led by General Kawaguchi, comprised a reinforced regiment. Maruyama kept another regiment in reserve. They would attack up Bloody Ridge and to its right.

In U.S. Marine lore, that night through the next went down as "Dugout Sunday." Vandegrift had made preparations too, and his forces were well fortified. With the addition of the U.S. Army 164th Infantry, Vandegrift was slightly superior in men, considerably advantaged in artillery, and now better supplied. One Japanese officer ruefully told comrades that for every shell loosed against the Americans, they answered with a hundred.

The redoubtable Chesty Puller and his battalion had redeployed to the sector Maruyama attacked. Vandegrift sent them a battalion of the green 164th Infantry, making up for a Marine unit hastily pulled away to the Matanikau. The Japanese went in. Unlike in the Matanikau sector, Maruyama had but a single mortar battalion to support him. Kawaguchi's column wandered into the jungle and hardly participated. A fulminating Maruyama relieved Kawaguchi. Colonel Nakaguma Nomasu's regiment bore the brunt of the fight. Their only chance lay in the fact that Puller had had to extend his line to take over the front vacated by the absent Marine battalion, and that Marine artillery had expended most of its ammunition in the Matanikau action. A spirited attack began after midnight on October 25. Puller slowly fed the 164th Infantry reinforcements into his 1/7 Marine line as the fighting progressed. Nakaguma made only a few shallow penetrations. The Japanese left almost 1,000 bodies in the barbed wire.

Following Maruyama's attack, the Army notified the Navy that Henderson Field had been captured. Carrier planes were sent to verify this. Soon afterward, Lieutenant Funashi reported from his observation post that battle raged in Henderson's vicinity. The situation remained obscure. Based on General Hyakutake's instructions and the original capture claims, Admiral Mikawa initiated what was to have been the coup de grâce of the offensive—a variety of actions by several units. One was the landing of a unit called the Koli Detachment to complete the conquest of the airfields from the beach side. A group of three destroyers would also deliver fuel and bombs to the newly captured Henderson Field to enable Japanese planes to fly from it immediately. A formation of tin cans led by a light cruiser would interdict Guadalcanal waters from the west, while another did so to the east. Mikawa recalled them when aerial observers determined that the Americans still held Henderson.

But the Army begged for a naval bombardment, and Mikawa sent back three destroyers, hoping a sudden shelling might stun the Americans into relinquishing their hold. Combined Fleet ordered Rear Admiral Takama Tamotsu's group, with light cruiser *Yura* and five destroyers, to back this sally, unnecessary since the Destroyer Squadron 4 leader had already reversed course for that very purpose. After daybreak, the Navy observation post reported a U.S. light cruiser in the anchorage. Two World War I–vintage tin cans, not a cruiser, actually lay off Tulagi, where they had delivered fuel and torpedoes for the PT boats and towed in four new craft. They cleared harbor once they saw the first Japanese destroyers, which gave chase and inflicted some damage. The Japanese then nearly ran down a pair of U.S. naval auxiliaries before returning to their bombardment mission. At that point shore batteries and the Cactus Air Force intervened, driving off the destroyers.

Cactus airplanes caught up to *Yura.* When the first bomb hit, Lieutenant Kamimura Arashi was at the engineering control station, his body vibrating as the engines strained into a high-speed turn. Kamimura staggered with a direct hit on *Yura*'s number three boiler room. Men in the other two were wounded by fragments. The *Yura* lost power, fires broke out; then more hits followed. Captain Sato Shiro ordered, "Abandon ship." He signaled other vessels to fight to the end. Sato refused to leave, tying himself to *Yura*'s bridge. The sailors evacuated to destroyers. While standard accounts state the *Yura* had to be scuttled, Lieutenant Kamimura believed the cruiser was breaking up as her crew left.

Through the afternoon the Cactus Air Force beat off renewed JNAF attacks with more losses on both sides. But that was only a prelude for the ground battle, when General Maruyama again hit Vandegrift's perimeter, this time with a better-prepared night attack. Chesty Puller's Marines and the U.S. Army infantry had by now taken separate sectors, with Puller on Bloody Ridge. Maruyama hit both and committed his reserve, whose commander, as well as Maruyama's tactical leader, Major General Nasu Yumio, were killed. The weight of the Japanese attack fell on the newly blooded 3/164, which acquitted itself well. Meanwhile, the wing formerly led by General Kawaguchi again failed to engage. On the Matanikau front, Colonel Oka launched his troops against the 2/7 Marines and succeeded in taking one hill, but they were ejected by Marine counterattacks. Although General Maruyama claimed he had penetrated the U.S. perimeter, that was an illusory result. Staff officers, including Colonel Tsuji, told Seventeenth Army the attack had failed. General Hyakutake ordered a stand-down on the morning of October 26. The Army offensive had collapsed. Navy observers reconfirmed the American hold on Henderson at 5:15 a.m. But by that time the Imperial Navy was embroiled in its own battle.

Rear Admiral Kusaka discounted Combined Fleet's peremptory orders. In his view Ugaki was a blowhard with no battle experience, a neophyte not worth listening to. The fleet held to its routine, making the usual run south on the night of October 24. Frustration increased. In the morning Nagumo detached Rear Admiral Abe Hiroaki's Vanguard Force to take station ahead of the carriers. Abe had battleships *Hiei* and *Kirishima*, Cruiser Divisions 7 and 8, and a destroyer squadron. Shortly after 10:00 a.m., a U.S. scout discovered the *Kido Butai* in position roughly 230 miles northeast of Henderson. Kusaka heard that a snooper had been downed by patrol fighters. Nagumo turned north. Carrier planes, then the Navy observation post, advised that the Americans were still at Henderson, affirmed by the bombing that cost the *Yura*. Unknown to Nagumo, Kinkaid had actually sent an *Enterprise* strike wave against him that afternoon, but with *Kido Butai*'s turnaway, and no tracking data, the planes found empty sea. They returned in the dark. A Wildcat plus seven TBFs and SBDs, out of gas, had to ditch.

There was no escaping Combined Fleet's constant prodding, however. Late that afternoon, alone in the flag plot on the *Shokaku*, Nagumo had another heated exchange with his chief of staff. *Kido Butai*'s commander was ready to fight. Kusaka still advised caution. The same conversation had occurred repeatedly before staff. Admiral Nagumo had had enough of that unpleasantness. The time had come to attack without remorse. Ugaki's latest dispatch could not be ignored. The carriers would advance. Nagumo wanted his chief of staff to decide to head south.

"I admit I've objected to your suggestions," Kusaka replied, "but you are the commander and must make the final decisions." Then the chief of staff repeated his litany: The American fleet had yet to be found; now that they themselves had been discovered, the B-17s from Espíritu Santo would surely reacquire them. If they went south they must expect things to happen. Besides, Kusaka continued, as chief of staff his place was merely to assist. Only the two men were present, staring each other down, and Nagumo Chuichi did not survive the war. Kusaka attests that Nagumo insisted. The chief of staff gave in: "It's your battle. If you really want to head south, I'll go along with your verdict."

In the gathering dusk of October 25, the *Kido Butai* came about and set a southerly course at twenty knots. It was one of those enchanting South Pacific evenings, the night warm and the moon shining. At 9:18 p.m. the fleet received Yamamoto's latest operations order, noting the Army's plan to storm Henderson Field, forecasting a high probability that Allied naval forces would appear northeast of the Solomons, directing that the enemy be destroyed.

Japanese forces assumed battle dispositions (from this point the text will refer to forces individually). A hundred miles west of Nagumo, Vice Admiral Kondo steamed with his Advance Force, built around battleships *Kongo* and *Haruna*, with heavy cruisers and destroyers. Rear Admiral Kakuta maneuvered the *Junyo*, screened by a couple of destroyers, a few miles beyond Kondo. Rear Admiral Abe Hiroaki's Vanguard Force, after briefly rejoining Nagumo, was posted sixty miles ahead. Abe assumed a line-abreast formation, his ships eight to ten miles apart in search mode. Sweating on the *Shokaku*'s flag bridge, Kusaka worked to prevent a Midway-like surprise. He arranged for morning scouts to depart Abe's ships at 4:15 a.m., reaching the ends of their search legs at dawn. A second search wave—which *Kido Butai* had not bothered with at Midway—would follow. The carriers armed strike planes in momentary readiness for launch. One more advantage: Nagumo would have the weather gauge at the start, steaming directly into the wind and able to launch immediately, whereas his opponents would have to alter course in order to throw their warbirds into the air.

Like the Americans, the Imperial Navy posted mobile radio detachments aboard key fleet units. During the night, monitors informed Kondo
and Nagumo of strong transmissions. Signal strength indicated proximity,
so while the Japanese could not read the intercepts, they knew the emitters
had to be nearby snoopers. In fact, this was a PBY piloted by Lieutenant
(Junior Grade) George Clute of Patrol Squadron 11. Soon after midnight
Clute's radar-equipped Catalina found Abe's Vanguard, which he reported
and tracked for a time before attacking it. Clute launched two torpedoes at
the destroyer *Isokaze*. In the darkness Clute imagined her a cruiser. Commander Toyoshima Shunichi, the destroyer skipper, saw the PBY six miles
away, waited until it had committed to its drop, then went into a tight turn.
Clute's torpedoes missed. No score.

The PBY attack disturbed Nagumo, but he could draw a little comfort from the fact that it was the Vanguard, not *Kido Butai*, that had been
sighted, though radio emissions could still be heard. Complacency disappeared at 2:50 a.m., when another snooper, Lieutenant Glen E. Hoffman's
Catalina, appeared directly over the carriers and tried her luck with four
bombs. Alarm bells sounded only as the munitions fell. They missed
close to starboard, spraying water on the superstructure of Captain Nomoto Tameteru's carrier *Zuikaku*. On the flagship, consternation. Staff officer
Takada almost fell down the ladder racing to Nagumo's cabin to tell him
the *Zuikaku* was safe. Nagumo and Kusaka were sitting together. Kusaka's
stomach tied up in knots. He was indignant. Nagumo looked at his chief of
staff. "What you said before was true," the admiral conceded. "Reverse
course, full speed." The *Kido Butai* turned through 180 degrees, increasing to
twenty-four knots. The moon disappeared behind clouds, ominous, since
increased darkness would make it harder to see the enemy. For an hour *Kido
Butai* rushed defensive preparations, disarming and draining gas from the
ready strike aircraft. Having carrier decks crammed with armed planes was
another Midway error the Japanese were determined to avoid. But no
Americans came; there would be no attack this night.

Aboard the *Junyo*, which received immediate notice of Nagumo's maneuver, air officer Okumiya had the staff duty watch, and forwarded the order
to Kondo's flagship, cruiser *Atago*. Kondo's and Kakuta's forces followed
suit about half an hour after the *Kido Butai*. Abe's Vanguard turned north
after that. The Japanese launched their dawn search as planned. The

second-wave scouts left Nagumo's carriers at 4:45 a.m., an hour before dawn. Nagumo then prepared a combat air patrol of twenty-two fighters and a strike wave of seventy planes. At that point Nagumo, Kondo, and Kakuta, plus Abe, were headed north, with the latter between *Kido Butai* and Admiral Thomas C. Kinkaid's Task Force 61. The Japanese were primed for battle.

At Nouméa another admiral huddled over his charts. Vice Admiral William F. Halsey, newly minted SOPAC commander, knew little about the theater and had had less than a week to learn. Halsey understood that a huge Japanese offensive impended, and he had the advantage of intelligence—which had accurately informed him that "Y-day," the moment the enemy had picked to set off their fireworks, would be October 23. The top officers— Kelly Turner, Vandegrift, and new AIRSOLS chief Rear Admiral Aubrey Fitch—had briefed Halsey on the overall situation. He recognized Guadalcanal's crucial importance. The Allied fleet already plied Torpedo Junction. Bull Halsey did know about aircraft carriers—he reckoned their combat power increased with the square of the number—so two carriers were as strong as four single ships, and he hastened the rendezvous of the *Hornet* and *Enterprise* forces into Task Force 61 under Kinkaid. Halsey recalled, "The crescendo of the fighting ashore made it plain that the climax was rushing toward us. I thought that the twenty-fifth would precipitate it." For a brief moment that seemed so. The *Kido Butai* was spotted once and that abortive air strike sent after it. But the enemy proved elusive. Halsey sent Norman Scott's surface flotilla on a night sweep through Ironbottom Sound. Again nothing. The Bull felt in his bones that battle must be just hours away. He ordered to all his commands: "ATTACK—REPEAT—ATTACK."

Admiral Kinkaid had already put his task force in motion toward the seas where the enemy had been sighted. He too was certain of battle. Kinkaid assigned flagship *Enterprise* to conduct the morning search and put up antisubmarine patrols, while the *Hornet* readied a strike. On the *Enterprise*, Air Group 10 skipper Commander John Crommelin gave his pilots a pep talk, telling them they were all that stood in the way of Japanese victory in the

Pacific. He would work them to the bone, Crommelin warned; they could not afford to waste a single bomb. The crews manned their planes. Amid final aircraft checks, Kinkaid received a retransmission of Glen Hoffman's sighting. Recalling the fiasco of the previous afternoon, he elected to await precise information before striking. The *Enterprise* turned into the wind, and sixteen Dauntlesses began their takeoff rolls. They were scout bombers armed with 500-pound munitions. It was 6:00 a.m. The sun was just peeking over the horizon. The SBDs struggled for altitude. They would fly in eight pairs on preselected search vectors.

Lieutenant Commander James R. ("Bucky") Lee, boss of Scouting 10 (VS-10), gave himself the most promising sector. But first honors went to lieutenants Vivian Welch and Bruce McGraw of Bombing 10. Barely an hour from the *Enterprise*, both planes saw a Japanese scout pass in the opposite direction. Figuring that bird had to have a nearby roost, they pressed on. Just twenty minutes later they glimpsed warships ahead. It was Abe's Vanguard Force. The two crews counted ships, checked, and compiled a careful contact report, tabulating two battleships, a heavy cruiser, and seven destroyers steaming north at twenty knots. They did not spot Hara's two cruisers, which had become slightly separated from the main formation. There were no carriers. Welch and McGraw flew to the limit of their range, hoping to find Nagumo. They did not. Turning back, they overflew Abe again. Admiral Abe now ordered a northwest course and went to battle speed, thirty knots. About 6:45 a.m., two more search bombers came up and attacked, diving on Captain Kobe Yuji's cruiser *Tone*. Flak from the heavy ship and her consorts threw off the SBDs' aim, and both missed. The defenders thought they had shot the planes down. Abe's flotilla went to battle stations. On destroyer *Akigumo*, Lieutenant Yamamoto Masahide noticed that the sea that morning was quiet and the sky quite beautiful.

Bucky Lee was as good as he had hoped. He and wingman Ensign William Johnson at that very moment encountered *Kido Butai*. Lee saw a carrier, then two—clouds covered *Zuikaku*—and reported them headed north-northwest at fifteen knots. Lee eventually glimpsed the third ship, but Japanese lookouts spotted him too, and fighters intercepted. If he found the carriers, Commander Lee planned to summon his scouts and attack. Instead he had to limp away, damaged, though the Dauntlesses claimed three Zeroes. But others heard Lee's report and closed in. One pair was driven off, damaging several more Zeroes.

Another flight was the Dauntlesses piloted by Lieutenant Stockton Strong and wingman Ensign Charles Irvine. At Eastern Solomons it had been Strong who first spotted the *Ryujo*, and now he had John Crommelin's words echoing in his head—no bombs to waste! He had refrained from attacking *Ryujo*, an act of omission that now obsessed Strong. He was a hundred miles from Bucky Lee. But the SBDs reached the position, emerging through a cloud right above light carrier *Zuiho*. The Americans were in the sun for *Zuiho*'s lookouts. Captain Obayashi Sueo's sailors hardly saw them, and the covering Zeroes were nowhere around. Strong and Irvine dived. The flak began as they dropped through 1,500 feet; then the Zeroes came and the next minutes were hot indeed. Both planes made it to *Enterprise* with gas for just one landing approach. Commander Crommelin put Strong in for the Medal of Honor. He got the Navy Cross. *Enterprise*'s after-action report recorded the attack on a *Shokaku*-class carrier.

Captain Obayashi thought his gunners had gotten one of the American planes. They got him instead. Two 500-pound bombs hit *Zuiho*'s flight deck aft, holing it, wrecking the flak guns and the arresting gear needed to land planes. At an estimated sixteen yards in diameter, the hole was nearly as wide as her flight deck, rendering *Zuiho* useless as a floating airfield. This was a tremendous disappointment for Obayashi's sailors, who had spent almost the entire war training fliers in the Inland Sea. A brief sortie with battleships, an aircraft ferry cruise to the Philippines, and the Midway operation, in which *Zuiho* had seen no combat, made up her entire war record. Now, in the first minutes of her first real battle, *Zuiho* was out of action. It was 8:30 a.m.

Admiral Kinkaid did not await his scouts' return. His staff plotted the Japanese carriers to the west-northwest between 185 and 200 miles distant. Kinkaid increased speed to twenty-seven knots at 7:08 a.m. and altered course to close on the enemy. The first-wave strike from *Hornet* was halfway through its launch within a half hour, twenty bombers and torpedo planes in the formation. The *Enterprise*, operating independently, launched twelve strike aircraft at 7:50. Both units had Wildcats for fighter escort. The *Hornet* launched another wave of twenty planes, also with an escort, and evenly divided between dive-bombers and torpedo planes, about 8:15. At the moment of the *Zuiho* attack, these waves were already winging for Nagumo.

The Japanese were actually ahead of this curve. A *Kido Butai* scout filed the first sighting report at 6:50 a.m. Admiral Kusaka insisted—and Nagumo agreed—on immediate attack with overwhelming force. Nagumo ordered his strike unit aloft at 7:10 a.m. The carriers began launching immediately and had finished inside twenty minutes. *Zuiho* planes were in this group, as well as on patrol duty, so her damage did not prevent her contributing to the battle. Lieutenant Commander Murata Shigeharu led the whole unit, its knife edge twenty *Shokaku* torpedo planes and twenty-one *Zuikaku* dive-bombers. Zeroes from all three ships escorted them. The carriers immediately began cycling a second wave, which departed more raggedly. Lieutenant Commander Seki Mamoru led nineteen *Shokaku* dive-bombers off at 8:10, and Lieutenant Imajuku Jiichiro followed with sixteen *Zuikaku* torpedo bombers at 8:40. In addition, at 8:05 Nagumo directed Abe's van to engage the Americans with guns.

Far to the west, Rear Admiral Kakuta ordered out his initial strike wave at 9:05. It consisted of seventeen Val dive-bombers and twelve Zero fighters under Lieutenant Shiga Yoshio.

Japanese and American strike waves passed within sight of one another as they sped toward their targets. Both sides warned their carriers of incoming aircraft. The *Zuiho*'s Zeroes peeled off to destroy two *Enterprise* TBF Avengers and shot up a couple more torpedo bombers so badly that they had to abort. *Enterprise* Wildcats claimed two enemy and the TBFs three more, but the strike lost its fighter escort. The *Hornet* wave droned on, scattered but unblooded.

Captain Charles P. Mason's *Hornet* had just finished returning seven Wildcats to combat air patrol when, within minutes, Commander Murata's planes swept in. It was 8:55. The *Enterprise* was luckily concealed beneath a squall. Murata went for the enemy he could see. Kinkaid's fleet had the protection of an extremely strong combat air patrol of thirty-seven F-4F Wildcats from both carriers. They engaged as quickly as they could. Unfortunately radar operators were confused. The blip of the incoming Japanese aircraft merged on their screens with that of the outgoing U.S. strike. Radarmen remained uncertain until the enemy were only forty-five miles out—fifteen minutes at a typical cruise speed, less at battle speeds. Air controllers on the "Big E," which had the duty, positioned interceptors low to conserve fuel. The Japanese closed from above, and very fast.

Flak was tremendous. A cruiser on every quarter ringed the *Hornet*, and beyond them lay a second ring of six destroyers. One light cruiser was the new antiaircraft ship *Juneau*. But Commander Murata, the Imperial Navy's torpedo ace, calm and calculating, kept his pilots' shoulders to the wheel. Captain Mason threw *Hornet* into a series of frantic gyrations at twenty-eight knots, putting his rudder hard over, port then starboard, hoping to throw off the enemy. The first two attackers got only near misses and were both flamed. Japanese planes kept coming. Murata's force was nearly anni-hilated, losing seventeen of twenty-one Vals, sixteen of twenty Kates, and five of twelve Zeroes. But in just three minutes beginning at 9:12, the *Hornet* suffered several crippling bomb hits, damage from a pair of planes that crashed aboard, and two torpedo impacts to starboard. By 9:25 Mason's ship was dead in the water, her forward engine room flooding, and fires raged on the signal bridge, the flight deck, the hangar deck, the mess, and the petty officers' quarters. Moreover, the water mains were disabled. More than a thousand *Hornet* sailors formed bucket brigades, combating the flames with water, literally pail by pail.

Kinkaid's strike formations were still winging toward the enemy. They struck within minutes of *Hornet*'s fight for life. *Hornet*'s airmen had been split up when the Japanese intervened against the strike planes. Her torpedo unit never found the enemy. Lieutenant Commander William J. ("Gus") Widhelm's dive-bombers came up behind the Nagumo force, which was speeding north. *Shokaku*'s radar actually detected them almost a hundred miles away, enabling fourteen of twenty-six patrolling fighters to intercept. But only two Dauntlesses were knocked out. Gus Widhelm also did not make it, forced to ditch when his engine gave out during the approach.

Communications experts of the Japanese mobile radio units, having identified the U.S. frequencies, came on the air to mimic American pilots, inserting false information. This was a tactic the U.S. radio units eschewed, probably because Japanese naval slang was even more difficult than the language itself—and few enough Americans were fluent in that. Santa Cruz may have been the first time the Japanese practiced this form of de-ception. Some American pilots were angry at colleagues for providing bo-gus information, until they worked out that none of them had talked the talk. Nevertheless the enemy's radio deception had only marginal impact.

Eleven *Hornet* SBDs reached the carriers, and the key punches were thrown by Lieutenant James E. Vose Jr.'s flight. Five planes pushed over above *Shokaku* about 9:27 a.m. Captain Arima Masafumi evaded some bombs, but three struck her flight deck from midships aft, smashing guns and damaging the hangar deck. In the flattop's wake was Hara Tameichi's *Amatsukaze*, which had stopped briefly to rescue two ditched airmen. Hara, who had been with *Ryujo* when she was crippled at Eastern Solomons, was horrified. He felt the *Ryujo* had been a second-string warship, but *Shokaku* was strictly first-team, with expert crew and a crack air group. How she could succumb so easily mystified him.

Twenty minutes later Admiral Nagumo sent a dispatch bearing the grim news but also some hope. *Kido Butai* was headed northwest, with *Zuiho* on fire and both she and *Shokaku* unable to handle aircraft. On the other hand, the task force leader added, an American carrier was also on fire. Not long afterward, with *Shokaku*'s communications failing, destroyer *Arashi*, then carrier *Zuikaku* took over as focal points for task force message traffic.

Meanwhile the *Enterprise* attack force also sought big game. Reduced to five Avengers and three Dauntlesses, plus escort, by the midcourse firefight, Commander Richard K. Gaines winged past Admiral Hara's small *Tone* group, then eyed the Vanguard Force in the distance. Hoping it contained carriers, Gaines continued, found it did not, and flew beyond that. Short of fuel, Gaines turned back to hit the Vanguard. Abe's ships had formidable defenses, in all seventy-six heavy flak guns, ninety light weapons, and the main batteries of the big ships. Destroyer *Isokaze*, then battleship *Kirishima*, were the first to sight the enemy. Abe had gone to flank speed, making thirty-three knots.

Avenger torpedo bombers assaulted heavy cruiser *Suzuya*, identifying her as a *Kirishima*-class battleship. Captain Kimura Masatomi ordered his main battery into action. Big guns split the sky with two dozen eight-inch rounds. Kimura began to weave his ship. All his AA guns spoke, firing ninety-seven five-inch shells and 921 25mm bullets during the fight, over in just seven minutes. The *Suzuya* ceased fire at 9:38. The American torpedoes missed, though Ensign Evan K. Williams would be awarded the Navy Cross for his bravery in the attack.

A second *Hornet* strike group followed a few minutes behind the *Enterprise* planes. This comprised nine SBD Dauntlesses and ten TBF Avengers under Commander Walter F. Rodee. The torpedo bombers attacked cruiser *Tone*, wearing Admiral Hara's flag. Captain Kobe fought hard, claiming two Avengers. The Japanese saw only half the TBFs launch their torpedoes, and all were avoided. Two sailors were slightly wounded. Against this attack the *Tone* expended 112 eight-inch and 220 five-inch shells, plus 4,075 25mm rounds.

In the most sustained American air attack of the day, between 9:26 and 9:51 Dauntlesses plastered Captain Komura Keizo's *Chikuma* in two matches. Lookouts began spotting U.S. planes shortly after 9:00 a.m. Komura engaged with his main battery. First in were nine *Hornet* SBDs led by lieutenants John Lynch and Edgar Stebbins. Americans hit with a 1,000-pound bomb on the port wing of the bridge, wrecking the main battery director at 9:26. The ship immediately began to list. Standing next to the compass, Captain Komura fell backward at the sudden incline. A young ensign, Ogawa, stood behind him. As Komura fell, Ensign Ogawa was hit by a shell splinter. Had he not been there the captain would have been killed. Komura was wounded nonetheless. Ogawa died from his wounds late that night. The executive officer was killed too. Komura ordered torpedoes jettisoned just before another bomb struck *Chikuma*'s starboard torpedo room. Next came several *Enterprise* SBDs under Lieutenant (Junior Grade) George Estes. They made near misses, one of which destroyed a Jake floatplane on its catapult. Frantically defending themselves, *Chikuma* sailors counted twenty-one attack planes, while observers elsewhere in the Vanguard recorded as many as forty or fifty. Some 190 sailors were killed and 154 wounded. *Chikuma* expended seventy-seven eight-inch and 353 five-inch shells. Her light flak spit out 1,805 25mm rounds.

From the *Tone*, Admiral Hara could see considerable damage to *Chikuma*'s foremast and afterdeck. The ship reported boiler room trouble, and the damage itself hindered communications. At 10:25 Hara sent a flag signal reporting what he knew about the *Chikuma* to Abe, recommending she withdraw to Truk under escort. Twenty-five minutes later the Vanguard commander approved *Chikuma*'s departure and instructed destroyers *Tanikaze* and *Urakaze* to accompany her. She left at twenty-three knots, now her best speed, at 11:08 a.m.

For the Japanese this was the time of decision. Over the next hours a series of choices set a new phase of the Battle of Santa Cruz. At 11:00 a.m., Admiral Kondo returned Kakuta's carrier *Junyo* to *Kido Butai*'s tactical control. Both Kakuta and Kondo were proceeding generally northeast now, toward the carrier task force. By 10:55 the Japanese knew of two U.S. carriers, in separate groups, and that one was crippled. They had yet to confuse themselves with a "third" flattop—actually the stricken *Hornet. Shokaku* and *Zuiho* were leaving the battle zone. Admiral Nagumo was out of the picture. The *Zuikaku* remained undamaged and at 11:15 took over as communications ship for *Kido Butai.* The Japanese fleet retained two effective aircraft carriers against one American, and *Junyo* was prepared to launch a second attack unit. Abe's Vanguard steamed east at twenty-six knots in a surface foray. The outcome now hung on the most minute factors: on split-second timing and sudden opportunity.

On the flag bridge of the *Enterprise,* Tom Kinkaid faced important decisions of his own. The "Big *E*'s" task group, a dozen miles from *Hornet's,* could only watch. When the other flattop got hit, Admiral Kinkaid lost direct communication. He could see the towering plume of smoke—obvious and ominous—but knew not what it meant. At 9:41 he called the *Hornet* group's escort boss, Rear Admiral Howard H. Good, to ask whether *Enterprise* needed to land the other carrier's aircraft. That was when Kinkaid learned that Task Force 61 was in dire straits. The immediate question became whether to continue to close with the enemy. Every minute counted, and half his offensive firepower was dead in the water, burning. At this point Kinkaid thought that the Japanese were down one *Shokaku*-class carrier (the mistakenly identified *Zuiho*), but U.S. strike aircraft had yet to inform him of their other results. Intelligence had repeatedly referred to two big Jap carriers, and morning searches had found two, plus a light carrier. The Japanese *Junyo* had not been seen by any Allied search nor identified in intelligence. On the other hand, the Imperial Navy had powerful surface forces, which the admiral understood were headed north but that could bear down on him at any moment.

Kinkaid chose to play a waiting game. He swung the *Enterprise* group to a southeast course at twenty-seven knots. He then altered to the southwest so as not to open the range too much for returning aircraft—and from the distressed *Hornet.* For a time he would be nearby, and she might recover. The picture would also clarify once he learned more of the strike results. At 9:49

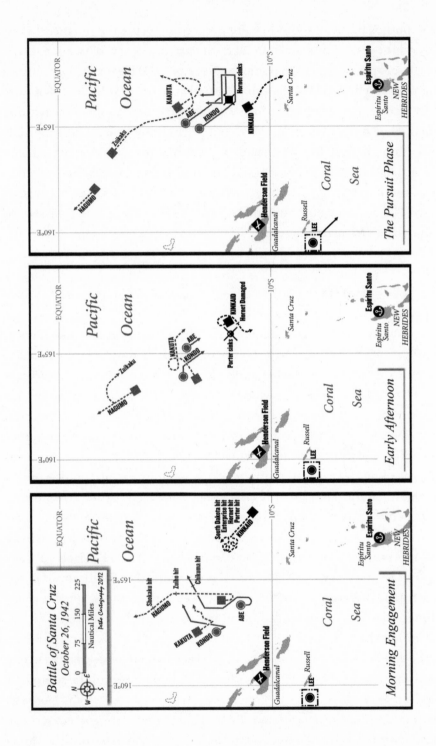

Battle of Santa Cruz
October 26, 1942

Nautical Miles
0   75   150   225

Dale Cartography, 2012

Morning Engagement

Early Afternoon

The Pursuit Phase

he informed SOPAC of the damaged *Hornet*. Bull Halsey's reply was immediate: "OPERATE FROM AND IN POSITIONS FROM WHICH YOU CAN STRIKE QUICKLY AND EFFECTIVELY. WE MUST USE EVERYTHING WE HAVE TO THE LIMIT."

That was the intention. Captain Osborne B. Hardison, the "Big *E*'s" skipper, advised sending an unescorted strike, launched whenever possible with everything available—at that time just ten Dauntlesses. But the *Enterprise* faced huge challenges. There were not just *Hornet*'s planes to land, and returning aircraft to recover; there were also the combat air patrol fighters to be landed, refueled, and returned to the air. Even before radioing Halsey, Kinkaid had twice been warned of new attackers approaching. The carrier's mobile radio unit under Marine Major Bankston T. Holcomb told him of Japanese radio chatter. The enemy duly appeared on radar at 9:53 about forty-five miles away. Based on more of Holcomb's information, Admiral Kinkaid ordered a west-southwest course. Throughout the day radio intelligence continued intercepting messages, some heard as far away as FRUMEL, others at FRUPAC. These were the JNAF contact reports.

The warnings were of Lieutenant Commander Seki Mamoru's group of nineteen Val dive-bombers from the *Shokaku*. Seki immediately saw the *Hornet*, but the *Kido Butai* had already broadcast notices of two American carriers, so he lingered, to be rewarded at 10:00 a.m. with sight of the *Enterprise*. Commander Seki ordered his attack eight minutes later. Of the twenty-one Wildcats then on patrol, only eight were at medium altitude; the others circled low, probably to catch torpedo bombers. While Seki had no aircraft of that sort, there *was* a torpedo incident—a fish broke free of an Avenger forced to ditch, and the torpedo went active, circled, and hit the destroyer *Porter*, which had stopped to rescue the aircrew. Just two fighters managed to engage the Vals before they attacked, and only one Japanese was lost before diving. Wildcats desperately stuck to some of the bombers as they dropped, and got more of them, but could not disrupt the attack.

Enterprise had her own ring of protective warships. They included the fast battleship *South Dakota*, the new AA cruiser *San Juan*, heavy cruiser *Portland*, and seven destroyers in addition to the *Porter*. Seki positioned his aircraft to attack from up-sun and led the charge. His plane, smashed to pieces by intense flak, crashed into the water, Seki's bomb a near miss. Under the lash of the dive-bombers, Captain Hardison maneuvered expertly, and the next half dozen all missed. Then came a glancing hit, a 250-pound bomb that punched through the "Big E's" flight deck forward and exploded in front of the bow. A second bomb impacted less than a dozen feet behind the number one elevator, triggering an explosion and fires on the hangar deck and exploding on the second deck, where it wiped out a damage control party and started a blaze in the elevator shaft. Finally, a near miss shook the *Enterprise* and opened some of her plates, leaking seawater into the ship. Lieutenant Arima Keiichi, a flight leader in Seki's squadron, led his planes into the dive, releasing bombs a minute after pushing over, at about 550 feet. Arima was not certain the carrier they attacked was the *Enterprise*, but he could see her wake churning. *Hornet*, dead in the water, could not have been Arima's target. With Seki, Arima had been in the strike that damaged the *Enterprise* at Eastern Solomons. This time too, at great cost, that goal was achieved. Commander Seki and nine crews were lost, but by 10:20 a.m., "Big E" was afire, with an elevator damaged.

Only fifteen minutes later, *Enterprise* radar detected another enemy wave, sixteen *Zuikaku* Kates under Lieutenant Imajuku. They approached a weakened combat air patrol, some of which was nearly out of ammunition. Controllers divined that Imajuku's were torpedo planes and positioned the interceptors accordingly. Captain Hardison's adroit ship handling prevented the attacks, fiercely driven home, from connecting. Two Japanese planes went for battleship *South Dakota* without success, and Seaman Kiyomi Takei crash-dived the destroyer *Smith*, wrecking her bow and igniting a fearsome blaze. Eight Kates including Imajuku's were torched without touching the carrier, although toward the end of her violent maneuvers the *Enterprise*'s radar antenna seized up. The only real damage was to destroyer *Smith*, and that would have an importance we will return to later. It was 10:52 a.m.

Despite defensive success, the "Big E" had been damaged. The status of the number one elevator was uncertain and the air gang dared not use it. The number two elevator jammed in the down position for some moments, sending shivers through the crew. The *Enterprise* resumed limited flight operations at 11:35. By that time the combat air patrol was virtually nil and the radar only just coming back online. When it did, the scope registered a blip just twenty miles away. It was Lieutenant Shingo's seventeen-plane strike from the *Junyo*. More wild gyrations, intense flak, more desperate fighter engagements. Six dive-bombers dropped on the *Enterprise*, scoring one very near miss (ten feet from her side) that sprang new leaks. Listening to the radio feed on the *Junyo*, an officer shouted with joy. Admiral Kakuta turned to staff officer Okumiya and smiled. "Our men have become quite proficient," Kakuta enthused. "The ship functions as a team. Perhaps we shall compensate for Midway."

Several *Junyo* bombers dived on Captain Thomas L. Gatch's battleship *South Dakota*. Though she was struck with only 250-pound bombs, a direct hit on her number one turret shook its roller-bearing track, wounded Gatch, and momentarily disrupted steering, sending the warship careening through the flotilla. While this hit is recorded as having caused little damage, in actuality it put three sixteen-inch guns out of action. A month later, at a crucial naval battle, the *South Dakota* could not use this turret. The *San Juan*, also bombed, leaked from near misses and briefly lost steering control.

The after-action reports of *Enterprise* and *Hornet* attest to the incredible bravery and skill of sailors on both ships. Crews fought potentially fatal fires and made imaginative repairs. The *Enterprise* managed to resume air activity—crucial, since no fewer than seventy-two airplanes were orbiting her, hoping to land. She recovered planes until the entire flight deck filled up, then cleared them before resuming. At 12:25 handlers started pumping gas again; at 12:51 they sent off fresh patrol fighters. But refugee aircraft were waiting to land as late as 12:40, and some had to ditch. Later the "Big *E*" sent thirteen SBDs to Espíritu Santo just to get them off the ship. By the end *Enterprise* had aboard some forty-one F-4Fs, thirty-three SBDs, and ten TBFs, a number unflyable. Loss of the elevator inevitably slowed down flight operations.

Despite some success, Admiral Kinkaid could not escape the realization that the *Enterprise* had become the only American aircraft carrier in the Pacific. She could no longer be risked. At 11:35 Kinkaid ordered a southwest course toward safety. An hour later Task Force 61 shifted course and increased to twenty-seven knots. The "Big *E*" secured from general quarters at 5:37 p.m. Damage was more serious than thought. Two near misses had sprung rivets or deflected plates—in places as much as two and a half feet inward—opening fuel tanks to the sea over almost a hundred feet of hull. In one area all the frames, floors, and bulkheads had buckled. Leaks threatened to become serious. Her stem was laced with fragment holes, a few up to a foot wide, and she was taking water, down four feet by the bow. On the hangar deck the floor of a fifty-foot section near the number one elevator was heavily damaged and the decks below blown out. Two bomb hoists were questionable. The bridge gyroscope had failed. Several radios and a direction-finding loop were out. Some of these repairs could be done only in port. Although she was launching and recovering aircraft, the carrier was not battleworthy. In a renewed engagement *Enterprise* would have been gravely disadvantaged. Even high waves might threaten her seaworthiness. Kinkaid's message offering a fuller description of the damage went out almost simultaneously with SOPAC orders where Halsey instructed him to retire.

The Bull sent another dispatch, "MOST SECRET," to Admiral Chester Nimitz. Kinkaid's task force had yet to reach Nouméa. In his message Halsey asked for help—one or more *British* aircraft carriers to be sent to the South Pacific. At Pearl Harbor, Nimitz agreed. The CINCPAC forwarded Halsey's appeal to COMINCH, to Ernie King, on an urgent basis. The United States should beg Great Britain for the loan of Royal Navy aircraft carriers. A second Nimitz dispatch went to Bull Halsey: SOPAC should prepare a coordinated defense plan for its rear bases. At Pearl Harbor they appreciated the severity of the South Pacific situation.

Bull Halsey might send messages, but so too could Yamamoto Isoroku. The portents were good at Truk, where the weather was fair and Combined Fleet staff woke up to initial reports of the Americans spotted. Admiral Ugaki considered that most factors favored his side and expected a daylong battle. With confusing search reports plus the *Hornet*'s success at putting out her fires, staff soon thought the Americans had three carriers, but then believed two disabled, leaving just one, against two Japanese. Later, staff settled on the illusion that there were four U.S. carriers and would eventually report that number as sunk. That fantasy would not be dispelled until battle commanders returned and their accounts were compared. But the notional third American carrier unduly influenced Japanese decisions.

Meanwhile, on its northerly heading the *Kido Butai* would soon be more than 300 miles from the Americans. A staffer's comment that this distance should favor Japanese aircraft, which had longer ranges, provoked Ugaki, who wanted to shout at him, "Damn fool!" Instead the chief of staff demanded a strictly worded attack order. At 1:00 p.m. Combined Fleet cabled, no doubt on the basis of radio fixes, that the enemy was retiring southwest, seriously damaged. Yamamoto ordered Kondo to take the Abe force too and pursue the enemy.

Kondo's Advance Force was already headed in that direction, having shifted to east of south, then to the southeast. At that point Kondo was about 260 miles from Kinkaid's noontime position. Admiral Abe's Vanguard Force was closer. Abe put up a pair of floatplanes to report on the Americans at 1:18 p.m. Twelve minutes later Kondo instructed Abe to shift east-southeast and advance, using his planes to discover and track the Americans. The Imperial Navy's gunnery ships were hard on Kinkaid's trail.

The Japanese flattops were also on the move. Captain Nomoto Tameteru led the rump of *Kido Butai* around to the southeast at 1:30. Nomoto had his *Zuikaku*, the heavy cruiser *Kumano*, and four destroyers. He was running on sheer adrenaline, having been continuously on the bridge of his carrier for more than two days. At 1:11 *Zuikaku* put another strike into the air with seven Kates, two Vals, and five Zeroes. Like the "Big E," *Zuikaku* had to land aircraft from all the departed flattops. Once the planes landed it became a question of which were still usable. Many returning aircraft were badly shot up. Lieutenant Arima, for example, landed aboard with his *Shokaku*-based dive-bomber. It was damaged, but Arima felt he could have flown again if necessary. Pressures mounted on Captain Nomoto, a twenty-six-year Navy veteran, and his air officer, Commander Matsumoto Makoto. *Zuikaku* was the only operational carrier left from Nagumo's original force. In the end Nomoto's midafternoon strike would be *Zuikaku*'s last. Admiral Nagumo had been unable to transfer off the *Shokaku* due to the need to get that wounded ship out of the danger zone as quickly as possible. She could not stop to put off Nagumo until at least out of Cactus air range.

Similar scenes took place on carrier *Junyo*. Shortly after 1:00 p.m., Rear Admiral Kakuta reported launching a strike wave of seven torpedo planes and eight fighters. Soon afterward the survivors of her own first strike began returning, lurching above the waves, so low *Junyo*'s radar never detected them. Only the Zeroes flew formation. Just a half dozen dive-bombers appeared. Other planes, again like the Americans, had to ditch. Japanese destroyers did a brisk business in rescues. The *Akigumo* stopped to take on board a man who waved very energetically. He turned out to be an Etajima classmate of her chief engineer, Lieutenant Yamamoto Masahide.

As on Nomoto's flattop, the planes were shot up, but Admiral Kakuta wanted another attack. He sent Commander Okumiya to the flight deck to see which could fly. Okumiya found six Vals and nine Zeroes in reasonable shape, whereupon Captain Okada, *Junyo's* skipper, ordered them armed. Beyond the question of aircraft came the matter of pilots. In the *Junyo's* ready room a scene occurred that must have figured in the dreams of many World War II pilots. Lieutenant (Junior Grade) Kato Shunko, a big, jovial fellow who was among the best-liked men in the air group, wanted no more part of the hellish American defenses. Kato jumped from his seat, exclaiming, "Again? Am I to fly *again* today?" Commander Okumiya felt embarrassed. As senior staff officer he would stay behind, safe. Group leader Shiga Yoshio intervened. "This is war! There can be no rest in our fight against the enemy." Lieutenant Shiga added, "We cannot afford to give them a chance when their ships are crippled. Otherwise we will face the same ships again. We have no choice." Kato relented. Both pilots would return safely, and Kato's bomber flight scored another hit on the *Hornet.*

Meanwhile the *Hornet* restored some power, hoping to get under way—crucial, since an attempt to tow her failed. Her bucket brigades had prevented the fires from getting out of control, and chemical foam began to contain them. Destroyers *Morris* and *Russell* hove alongside and strung fire hoses, and then *Hornet* sailors really quelled the blazes. Commander Edward P. Crehan, chief engineer, decided several boilers could be relit and, by re-routing steam, might work the turbine of at least one shaft. Cruiser *Northampton* got a towline across and began to pull. The line parted but the *Hornet* moved, at least for a time. Combined with the disappearance of fires, this confused the next shift of Japanese scouts, who began reporting a *third* U.S. carrier. However, there could be no doubt the flattop had been stricken. Rear Admiral George D. Murray, the force commander, shifted his flag to heavy cruiser *Pensacola* at noon. A couple of hours later Captain Mason reluctantly decided *Hornet* was endangered, ordering all but essential sailors off the ship. Almost 900 seamen decamped to destroyers. Gradual flooding continued, and *Hornet* began to list. Mason warned his remaining men to prepare to leave.

Coxwain Richard J. Nowatzki was among the damage control party, his battle station as a sight setter on the aftermost starboard-side five-inch antiaircraft mount. Once the initial evacuation had been completed, shortly before 3:00 p.m., Nowatzki was among the team struggling to save the ship. A new towline rigged, the carrier slowly began moving. Thus the *Hornet's* brave crew fooled Japanese pilots that afternoon. Their next onslaught came soon after. The Americans had been so successful at fighting *Hornet's* wounds the JNAF crews thought they were socking a fresh U.S. flattop. Gathering clouds contributed to their confusion. Coxwain Nowatzki could see the Japanese planes line up to attack. The *Zuikaku* fliers, according to Nowatzki, and confirmed by the log of the light cruiser *San Diego*, obtained two further torpedo strikes, a solid heavy bomb hit, and another near miss; the *Junyo's* two attacks scored additional bomb hits. The torpedoes were decisive. The ship righted momentarily, then listed even more extremely to starboard. *Hornet* began to flood more rapidly. The new blitz forced Admiral Murray to abandon his latest attempt at a tow. With the extreme list the blood of dead and injured sailors pooled on the deck, coursed through the gun tubs, and poured into the sea. Coxwain Nowatzki could see sharks circling below. The sailor and his mates agreed that if they had to go overboard it would not be on that side. Remaining crew began to abandon ship shortly after 4:30. Captain Mason finally left the bridge. By dark all surviving crew were taken off. Some 111 sailors died.

Meanwhile Admiral Kakuta's Carrier Division 2 united with Captain Nomoto's *Zuikaku*, and Kakuta assumed command. At midafternoon the Imperial Navy again had a functional carrier task force. After recovery of the last planes that night, the strength available to Kakuta's *Kido Butai* would be twenty-five torpedo planes, twenty-two dive-bombers, and fifty fighters. Kakuta's two carriers were untouched. Their only opposition, the *Enterprise*, was in a damaged condition that impaired her fighting ability. For all practical purposes, by the late afternoon of October 26, 1942, the Imperial Navy had the only effective carrier force in the South Pacific.

It could have been worse. Commentators, if not veterans, have long belittled the Imperial Navy's proclivity for dividing its forces into many detachments. The intense Japanese focus on surface warfare in the face of the growing primacy of airpower has also been derided. And impediments to the Imperial Navy's performance due to its traditionalist doctrine have been noted. But the detachments had specific tactical roles. That of the Advance Force was to dash ahead and crush the enemy with guns. At Eastern Solomons that maneuver had been carried out, but fizzled because the Americans had left. At Santa Cruz the traditionalist Japanese might have succeeded—they had this one glittering opportunity—in putting U.S. carriers under battleship guns. The pursuit phase of Santa Cruz bears instructive lessons. The main actors, as at Eastern Solomons, were Kondo Nobutake and his Advance Force, along with Abe Hiroaki and the Vanguard. Both had battleships, cruisers, and destroyers.

Japanese sailors missed their first opening early. Until afternoon Admiral Abe had been under Nagumo's command, and he had ordered Abe forward for a surface attack at 8:05 a.m. At that time Kinkaid's staff placed the *Kido Butai* 185 to 200 miles from Kinkaid, and the Allied fleet was headed for the Japanese at twenty-seven knots. Kinkaid did not withdraw until 11:35. With Kinkaid's turn into the wind to launch, plus various defensive maneuvers, however, the fleet essentially halted its forward movement at or about 8:30, without being too precise, and continued in the general area. The air attacks on several of his heavy ships delayed Abe, yet he might have gained about fifty miles before Kinkaid's retreat. By 11:30 the Vanguard could have been within about a hundred miles of Task Force 61. Abe's tardiness wasted that opportunity.

Naturally the carrier action tended to absorb admirals' attention, so perhaps not too much should be made of this, but at 1:00 p.m. Yamamoto reinvigorated the pursuit, putting Admiral Kondo in charge and Abe under command. Kondo's original operations order had directed him to attain striking distance of the Allies so as to "apprehend and annihilate any powerful forces in the Solomons area as well as any reinforcements." Kondo had not done much about this so far. What he would do once Yamamoto spurred him remained to be seen. By now Kinkaid had gained some running room, being roughly 240 miles distant from Kondo's Advance Force and less than 200 from Abe. But the Japanese had ships capable of thirty-four knots, and anything that slowed Kinkaid could have been fatal. His headlong retreat, apart from anything else, would increase the *Enterprise*'s seaworthiness difficulties. Kinkaid might not have been able to sustain flank speed without endangering the "Big *E*." As it was, the Japanese gained twenty to forty miles by late afternoon.

Allied intelligence potentially contributed to the problem with its estimates of just two Japanese carriers. Kinkaid believed from scouts and intercepts that both were crippled. A belief that the enemy air threat had been eliminated suggested Kinkaid could take his time nursing damaged warships, favoring a determined Japanese pursuit. Bull Halsey's order summoning Kinkaid home to base helped the admiral escape such a temptation.

At this point Japanese confusion over the "third carrier"—still *Hornet*—reveals its true importance. Scouts kept touch with the *Hornet* rather than flying the full search legs that would have disclosed Task Force 61's presence. The *Kido Butai* afternoon strikes went for the third carrier instead of Kinkaid. No doubt Admiral Kondo also found distasteful the idea of a long stern chase taking him constantly nearer to SOPAC's Espíritu Santo–based aircraft. On the other hand, Kondo and Abe had both been frustrated by their fruitless surface attack missions at Eastern Solomons, and this time they might have been expected to display more dash. Kondo Nobutake kept his silence, but he is recorded as saying of Santa Cruz, "I got the impression that . . . when two different fleets were combined, the commanding officer of the main task force should be assigned to take the responsibility [for] both." Use of the term "task force," which for the Japanese always denoted an aircraft carrier group, suggests that Kondo felt Nagumo should have had command. But Nagumo was absent. There was no one but the Advance Force leader. From his perspective, Hara Tameichi writes that Kondo "made only a halfhearted advance" and that Abe proved "too cautious." Just so.

In the end there *was* a pursuit—focused on the third carrier. The Vanguard Force took the lead. At 2:00 p.m., aware there could be no immediate surface action, Abe had his crews secure from battle stations. Nevertheless, at 2:30 the Vanguard cruisers were making thirty knots and on twenty minutes' notice for flank speed. At 2:41 Kondo ordered night action preparations. Little more than a half hour later a scout reported an enemy flattop minimally under way—more grist for the third-carrier fantasy. Light cruiser *Nagara* put up a floatplane at 4:30 intended as a spotter for night combat. The scout proceeded to *Hornet*'s position. Only then—more than two hours later—did it begin searching to the south. Meanwhile, at 5:00 p.m., the Kondo and Abe forces rendezvoused, with the Vanguard taking station a dozen miles from the Advance Force. The two units began assuming night battle formation ten minutes later. Vice Admiral Kondo had now assembled a powerful surface fleet of four battleships, six heavy and two light cruisers, plus fifteen destroyers. By sunset Kondo had closed to within sixty miles of the "third carrier."

There were some misgivings at Truk. Chief of staff Ugaki ruminated that prewar exercises established that unless the adversary was nearby and close contact cemented before dark, a night action against an enemy retiring at high speed always failed. In this instance Yamamoto apparently overruled Ugaki. His dispatch to the fleet at 7:05 noted that the "largest part" of the Americans near the Santa Cruz islands had been destroyed. Allied ships—including "capital ships"—might well be in the area rescuing survivors. "THE COMBINED FLEET WILL ATTEMPT TO DESTROY THESE FORCES." Kondo should conduct a night battle or, if circumstances required, a dawn engagement.

In actuality the enemy was the derelict *Hornet*. By this time tin cans *Mustin* and *Anderson* were frantically trying to sink the flattop themselves. Captain Mason of the carrier stood on the *Mustin*'s bridge next to her skipper, Commander Wallis F. Petersen. First they tried torpedoes, launching an incredible sixteen fish at the carrier. More than half hit. *Hornet* still floated. Then came gunfire, 130 five-inch shells into the ship. When that did not work, the destroyers shot everything they had, 300 rounds of main battery and even flak guns. The *Hornet* blazed from stem to stern but would not go under. That was when Petersen saw pagoda masts and realized Japanese warships were upon them. He retreated posthaste. Commander Petersen was given the Navy Cross for keeping his ships in harm's way to perform this hazardous task.

The heavy cruiser *Suzuya*, wearing Rear Admiral Nishimura Shoji's Cruiser Division 7 flag, was the first to spot smoke on the horizon. By 9:30 p.m. the *Suzuya* could actually see the burning American carrier. Also on the scene was Vice Admiral Kurita Takeo, leading Kondo's battlewagons from the *Kongo*. Both Kurita and the ship's gunnery officer, Lieutenant Commander Ukita, remembered watching the blazing flattop. Not far away, Rear Admiral Kakuta's *Kido Butai* saw the horizon lit by *Hornet*'s flames. Japanese commanders briefly debated how they might get a towline on the carrier and pull her to Japan, but they dared not approach to rig one. Instead, after midnight, destroyers *Makigumo* and *Akigumo* put four of their own torpedoes into the flattop. The *Hornet* disappeared beneath the waves. She remains the only fleet carrier ever sunk by surface torpedo attack—although, of course, that credit needs to be shared with many JNAF airmen as well as Japanese and American gunners and torpedomen. Aboard the *Akigumo*, Lieutenant Yamamoto recalled the crew's dismay when the fleet was recalled instead of continuing the pursuit.

This episode marked the end of the Battle of Santa Cruz. The destroyers of Abe's van, it might be noted, were down to 30 percent fuel at this moment. Yet he and Kondo remained in the area through the next afternoon, searching for downed fliers or enemy ships. A few American aircrew were among those rescued. Meanwhile Vice Admiral Nagumo finally managed to transfer to the destroyer *Arashi* at 7:30 that night, and resumed command of *Kido Butai* when he reached the *Zuikaku* at 3:30 p.m. on October 27, America's Navy Day. Early that morning Combined Fleet C-in-C Yamamoto issued orders that, if searches proved negative, the Kondo fleet should return to Truk at its convenience. On the Allied side there were a few final ignominies. The destroyer *Mahan* and the battleship *South Dakota* collided while evading a supposed I-boat. A real submarine, Commander Ishikawa Nobuo's *I-15*, got in a potshot at the Allies' other battleship, the *Washington*, but the torpedo did not touch her.

Hirohito's imperial rescript after the battle read, "The Combined Fleet is at present striking heavy blows at the enemy Fleet in the South Pacific Ocean. We are deeply gratified. I charge each of you to exert yourselves to the utmost in all things toward this critical turning point in the war." Hirohito added that he believed the situation critical, and regretted the loss of fliers, seamen, and soldiers.

Admiral Kinkaid joined a lengthening list of those on both sides who overestimated their battle results. Assembling exaggerated reports from his aviators, Kinkaid forwarded to Pearl Harbor an impressive summary of damage, starting with two *Shokaku*-class fleet carriers (one hit with two bombs, the other four to six). The list continued with two bomb hits on a *Kongo*-class battleship, bomb hits to both *Tone*-class cruisers (four on one, five on the other), three torpedo strikes on a *Nachi*-class heavy cruiser, and a bomb on an unidentified light cruiser. An *Atago*-class heavy cruiser was listed for possible hits by both bombs and torpedoes. For a couple of days after the battle, CINCPAC and COMINCH alike continued reporting the enemy fleet carriers eliminated. Radio traffic analysis soon revealed these results to be illusory. In reality the *Shokaku*, *Zuiho*, and *Chikuma* were the only warships touched in the battle. None sank. *Yura*, the only Japanese warship destroyed, was lost off Guadalcanal and did not even figure in Kinkaid's Santa Cruz tally.

After the war, Americans interrogating Imperial Navy veterans went to some lengths to induce them to concede Santa Cruz a defeat. They were unsuccessful. The instances of American veterans, observers, and historians arguing that the U.S. fleet obtained a victory here—some have even claimed it a strategic victory—is remarkable. Those who advance such arguments base themselves either on the continued Allied hold on Guadalcanal or on the heavy losses among Japanese airmen. Some Japanese, such as submarine commander Orita Zenji, fault the Imperial Navy for not carrying out its offensive in September, when the force balance favored Japan even more. But the naval action aimed to facilitate a land battle, and in the earlier time frame the Japanese Army had yet to prepare their big offensive.

By any reasonable measure the Battle of Santa Cruz marked a Japanese victory—and a strategic one. At its end the Imperial Navy possessed the only operational carrier force in the Pacific. The Japanese had sunk more ships and more combat tonnage, had more aircraft remaining, and were in physical possession of the battle zone. SOPAC was rushing to coordinate defense plans for its New Hebrides bases, desperately trying to repair the only aircraft carrier it had left, and begging for the loan of a British warship of this type. Sinking another U.S. aircraft carrier by surface torpedo attack (German battlecruisers had dispatched the British *Glorious* with guns in 1940) was also a notable achievement. Arguments based on aircrew losses or who owned Guadalcanal are about something else—the campaign, not the battle. Disputes over Santa Cruz are sterile. The more important story of the following days and weeks is of how the Imperial Navy squandered this hard-won victory.

One clue is furnished by an episode at Nouméa. With the ship damaged, *Enterprise*'s air group went to Henderson Field, eventually returning. Thomas Powell was an enlisted seaman and a gunner on an SBD of Scouting 10. At

Nouméa the airmen, now grungy, were issued fresh uniforms, but the only stocks available were officers' khakis, not seamen's blues. So Powell looked like an officer when he got to the pier to go out to "Big E." Admiral Kinkaid's barge, the only boat at the dock, took the sailors aboard. Thinking them officers, Kinkaid invited those in khakis to sit with him in the stern sheets. The admiral proceeded to tell these "officers," including Powell, that they ought not to be so unhappy with the tragic losses, at least those on the destroyer *Smith*. When a Japanese plane crashed aboard her, Kinkaid explained, its impact had thrown clear the bodies of the enemy pilot and his radioman, and one of them bore a copy of the current Japanese aircraft code. Bull Halsey and his cohorts were about to use that codebook to their great advantage.

IV.

EMPIRE IN THE BALANCE

"Japanese Fleet Quits Solomons, U.S. Fliers Damage Enemy Carrier and Hit Battleship or a Cruiser," read the *New York Times* headline. It was Halloween, and perhaps a fitting sequel to President Franklin D. Roosevelt's singular intervention in the Solomons campaign, when, just before Santa Cruz, he told military and naval leaders that he expected more to be done in the South Pacific no matter what their arrangements for Europe. As for the battle, Washington admitted one had taken place, in a communiqué issued a day afterward, but the Navy Department was just then owning up to loss of the carrier *Wasp* a month earlier. The Navy released few concrete details. Three days later, Navy secretary Frank Knox stepped up to the microphone for a news conference where the Solomons framed his conversation with reporters. Secretary Knox said the South Pacific fighting had ground to a virtual halt, a lull but not a victory, for Knox followed that comment by picturing the recent battle as merely the "first round," with Halsey's SOPAC forces "waiting for the second to start." He refused to make predictions. "I have no idea what the next move will be," Knox said.

Oddly enough, Radio Tokyo agreed. The two enemies might as well have coordinated their spin. Referring to "naval quarters" and high circles, the Japanese commented that "the battle is still in progress and the final result therefore cannot be foreseen." There was no doubt as to its importance, however: "It can be said that this is one of the greatest naval battles since the outbreak of the war." The Japanese exaggerated enemy losses just as did Americans, claiming, following the Combined Fleet's initial battle report, to have sunk four American carriers. From Pearl Harbor, Admiral Nimitz wrote his daughter that he wished he had as many aircraft carriers as the

Japanese were saying had been sunk. Tokyo admitted damage to two of its own. The figure for the Japanese side was, in fact, accurate.

The lull was real. CINCPAC's war diary observed a withdrawal of the Imperial Navy forces immediately after Santa Cruz, attributing this to a need to refuel and deal with damage. Halsey reported the next two days as quiet, though SOWESPAC claimed direct hits on a Japanese heavy cruiser at Rabaul on the thirtieth—another George Kenney fantasy. But in Nimitz and Halsey, the Allies now had a team perfectly suited to this complex conflict. Not willing to cavil before danger to SOPAC bases, and rejecting inaction despite the aircraft carrier imbalance, Nimitz cabled Halsey on October 28, "GROUND SITUATION AT CACTUS CAN BE TURNED IN OUR FAVOR ONLY BY OFFENSIVE ACTION." The SOPAC commander immediately signaled his complete agreement.

Halsey had already set up escorts for a convoy. He crafted plans for additional Marine and Army reinforcements to Cactus that ultimately led to doubling the troops there, replacing Alexander Vandegrift's 1st Marine Division with a full corps of the Army and Marines. Within the fortnight several convoys departed for the 'Canal, bearing heavy artillery, fuel, more men, and supplies. Halsey also pulled out all the stops on repairing the *Enterprise*. By dint of putting every available specialist on the project, enough holes were patched and decks pounded flat to restore watertight integrity in just eleven days. The "Big *E*" would sail and fight in a damaged condition—still without that critical number one elevator—but sail she would. *That* was the depth of SOPAC's need—and Halsey answered the call. The enemy's window of unassailable superiority lasted barely two weeks.

On the Japanese side, Admiral Yamamoto's plans had been deficient, not merely in omitting any provision for failure, but in neglecting arrangements to exploit success. Americans were right to worry about their SOPAC bases. Had Combined Fleet been ready to execute the FS Operation at this moment, the Allies might have been imperiled. But the Japanese were not prepared for that. Ditto Guadalcanal. Had Yamamoto been primed to really put *Yamato* off Henderson Field and obliterate it, and the Army's 38th "Nagoya" Division ready to sail, Cactus would truly have been in the shit. The Imperial Navy's unpreparedness put the outcome on a razor-thin edge. In Tokyo the emperor seems to have sensed that nexus more clearly than his

admirals. On November 5, Hirohito made another of his indirect inter-
ventions, probing his commanders as to their intentions. But no changes
were in the offing.

Fleet commanders Kondo and Nagumo, meanwhile, reached Truk on
October 30. Instead of fueling the fleet, setting objectives, and getting it
back out, the admirals held memorial services for the dead. The Combined
Fleet chief of staff thought fighting spirit low despite the recent victory.
Yamamoto and Ugaki had already begun rebuilding morale, visiting damaged warships that had arrived earlier. Not until November 2 did the senior
officers begin their battle review.

Ugaki, just promoted vice admiral, met with Colonel Hattori Takushiro,
chief Army operations planner, who had flown down from Tokyo, plus
Combined Fleet staff posted as observers at Rabaul. He also listened to fleet
staff's ideas for new forays. To be fair to Japanese naval commanders, the
Army played an important role in retarding the follow-up to Santa Cruz.
Hattori told Ugaki his service had finally decided to take the South Pacific
seriously, with creation of an army-size force just to fight in New Guinea,
Hyakutake's existing Seventeenth Army in the Solomons, and an area army
to control both—adding up to delay while the Army marshaled the troops.
Transferring a further formation, the 51st Infantry Division, now slated for
Guadalcanal, deferred a full-scale offensive until December. And when
Hattori passed through Truk again, on his way back from Rabaul, he reported conditions on Starvation Island even worse than supposed. The "of-
fensive" would need to be held until January.

Renewed activity began on November 3, when Rear Admiral Nishimura
took heavy cruisers *Suzuya* and *Maya* with a strong escort group to Shortland
on the first leg of another Cactus bombardment. Upon the fleet's return,
these vessels, together with Rear Admiral Tanaka's Destroyer Squadron 2,
were rearmed quickly so they could reinforce Vice Admiral Mikawa. The
carriers damaged at Santa Cruz departed for Empire waters. The next day,
rather than deploying *Kido Butai*, the fleet sent the undamaged carrier *Zuikaku* to Empire Waters to train new aircrew. That made sense for a December
or January offensive but offered no hope for the moment. Yamamoto's
move left the *Junyo* as the only flattop active in the South Pacific.

Two strong Tokyo Expresses delivered 38th Division troops to the 'Canal. The Express ran often. On November 5, Tanaka's destroyers replaced

Rear Admiral Hashimoto's squadron on reinforcement duty. During the first part of November, Imperial Navy destroyers carried sixty-five loads to Starvation Island and landed two cruiser loads as well. Commander Yamada Takashi, a participant in previous midget submarine attacks off Madagascar, launched one of the tiny boats into Ironbottom Sound from his *I-20*. FRUPAC detected that and signaled a warning all the way from Pearl Harbor. The midget entered the anchorage, found the small cargo vessel *Majaba* there, and put a torpedo in her. Although Yamada claimed a kill for the mission, the vessel actually beached and was recovered.

On November 7, Combined Fleet began to ship the bulk of the 38th Infantry Division. Yamamoto ordered up another Guadalcanal convoy. To support that, Rear Admiral Kakuta sortied with the *Junyo* and an escort. A cover force of three cruisers and seven destroyers sailed as well. The Japanese C-in-C intended to repeat the previously successful battleship bombardment of Henderson Field. The fleet operations order was issued at 6:30 p.m. the next day. Vice Admiral Kondo would take the lead. As accustomed, Admiral Yamamoto stayed at Truk, but he had set the stage for fateful encounters.

NIGHTS OF THE LONG KNIVES

Kondo Nobutake, universally considered one of the Imperial Navy's most brilliant officers, had rocketed to high rank. He might have been the only man to match Yamamoto Isoroku as one of the Navy's "golden boys." At fifty-eight in 1942, Kondo was nearing retirement age, but the war mooted such mundane questions. He had led the Second Fleet since before Pearl Harbor, and in the Imperial Navy, where tours of duty usually lasted about a year, Kondo might have looked forward to a new billet. But Yamamoto believed in this golden boy. It was Admiral Kondo's fleet that had protected the Japanese invasions of Malaya, the Dutch East Indies, and the Philippines in the opening months of the war—profiting from his experience in the China Incident, where Kondo had sparkplugged the 1939 invasion of Hainan. His subordinates had beaten the Allies at the Battle of the Java Sea. Kondo's brilliance showed in the misgivings he expressed about Midway, but he loyally led the invasion flotilla there. The sinking of heavy cruiser *Mikuma* of his command had chagrined the admiral, although he had not been directly involved. The *Mikuma* was the first major surface combatant lost in the war, but this had not been counted against him. Later Kondo had held primacy as seagoing commander at both Eastern Solomons and Santa Cruz.

Admiral Kondo had been active for thirty-five years. He missed the Russo-Japanese War—Yamamoto was ahead of him on that, having fought, and lost two fingers, at the Battle of Tsushima. The young Kondo served on a cruiser and aboard the fleet flagship, battleship *Mikasa*, but after the war. Kondo was commissioned an ensign in 1908, a year after graduating Etajima. His early career had been typical—duty on a destroyer, another cruiser, and the battleship *Kongo*. He spent a year in England as junior naval attaché. Kondo married, made a home in the Setagaya district of Tokyo, not far from his Osaka birthplace, and had two daughters, the first of five children. During World War I he held staff posts, then went to sea as chief gunnery officer on a cruiser. Kondo graduated at the head of his class from the Naval War College in 1919. His career moved to the fast track.

Promoted to lieutenant commander, Kondo was immediately sent to Russia as resident naval officer. Japan was playing power politics in the Russian Civil War, occupying parts of the Russian Far East, and Kondo became a player. Then came a year studying in Germany, plus two more on the commission charged with ensuring the Germans paid requisite war reparations. He returned to a position as aide-de-camp to Crown Prince Hirohito.

That strain of power politics continued to run through Kondo's life, accentuated by frequent staff assignments. Kondo acquired the reputation of a polished and literate, even scholarly officer, gracious in the style of an English gentleman, a consummate insider who had no enemies, popular even with the geisha. He spoke fair German and English, never seemed angered, and acted with practiced moderation and caution.

Commander Kondo went back to sea in 1926 on the staffs of the battleship force and Combined Fleet. His next posting was to the Naval War College as instructor—he would be president of that school a few years later. Sea duty followed as skipper of the heavy cruiser *Kako*, then battleship *Kongo*. In between, Captain Kondo had been selected by now-Emperor Hirohito as aide to a special inspector, and served as operations section chief of the Navy General Staff. He made rear admiral in November 1933, heading the war college, became chief of staff of the Combined Fleet, then NGS operations bureau chief. Colleagues considered his service there excellent. At the operations bureau Kondo approved a General Staff plan for the invasion of Hainan, one he later carried out as a seagoing officer. Kondo feared the Hainan operation might trigger war with Britain and France, which suited him fine except that the United States remained unaccounted for. Promoted to vice admiral in 1937, Kondo served in China during 1938–1939. The affable officer next became vice chief of NGS. He was considered pro-German, friendly to the U.S., and anti-British. In the Navy's pre–Pearl Harbor war games, naturally Kondo had played the British.

Admiral Kondo's technical specialty as a gunner placed him among the Navy's predominant community, in which he was the senior officer afloat, ranking thirteenth on the Navy List. By comparison Mikawa Gunichi ranked forty-first, Kurita Takeo sixty-ninth, and Abe Hiroaki eighty-fifth. Even Ugaki, the Combined Fleet chief of staff—a post Kondo had himself held—stood lower, at eighty-ninth on the list. But Kondo's exposure to active command of big ships had been limited, and he was by nature inclined to passivity. Those factors played into what now happened at Guadalcanal.

As Second Fleet commander, Admiral Kondo led the latest expedition. Wearing his flag in heavy cruiser *Atago*, he guided the main body, including battleships *Kongo* and *Haruna*, heavy cruiser *Tone*, and eight destroyers. In support would be Rear Admiral Kakuta with the *Junyo*. Under Kondo, Admiral Abe Hiroaki led the Advance Force, embodying battleships *Hiei* and *Kirishima*; another heavy cruiser, *Takao*; light cruisers *Sendai* and *Nagara*; and thirteen destroyers. Yamamoto's plan focused on a "Z-Day," when a transport convoy would reach Guadalcanal, discharging the remainder of the 38th Division, plus a month's supplies for all the Japanese. Eleventh Air Fleet would continue its strikes, working up to especially strong attacks on Z-3. On Z-2 Kondo would detach Abe's battleship force to bombard Henderson Field. Kakuta would follow with carrier strikes on Z-1. Then the convoy would arrive on Z-Day, screened by Rear Admiral Tanaka Raizo's Destroyer Squadron 2.

The fighting on Cactus made the Japanese effort especially critical. By now General Vandegrift felt confident on the offensive, and American troops flooded out to assault Japanese positions. These early November battles resulted in the Marines capturing Point Cruz, west of the Matanikau, and Koli Point, east of Vandegrift's hedgehog. Hyakutake's troops were sorely tried. The Tokyo Express runs to Starvation Island were barely making good the losses. Bull Halsey visited on November 8 to see for himself. He got an eyeful—emaciated Marines, thousand-yard stares, the sick and the wounded. The soldiers were delighted to see him but obviously in great need. That night one of Tanaka's destroyers peeled off the Tokyo Express to shell Lunga, putting Halsey in fear for his life, worrying whether he was "yellow," and more determined than ever.

Halsey returned to SOPAC on November 9 to get an earful. Captain Miles Browning, SOPAC's new chief of staff, met the Bull's plane to tell him the Japanese were on the move again. Browning's warning represented the culmination of new Allied intelligence breakthroughs that afforded a peek inside Yamamoto's planning rooms. The JN-25 code was becoming transparent again. Codebreakers were already aware of convoys bringing Japanese 38th Division troops from Palau up to Rabaul. The first inkling of an actual Combined Fleet operation appeared in an intelligence summary on November 5. The Kondo fleet had yet to leave Truk. Indications solidified. Seaplane tender and convoy movements were noted, so that by the sixth, CINCPAC intelligence expected ground and air operations at a minimum. Then codebreakers penetrated the dispatch containing Yamamoto's operations order, sent in a JN-25 code transmission on November 8. Though they did not initially break the entire message, the Allies became aware of "Z-Day" and its connection to Cactus. The "Z-Day" terminology appears in intelligence reports and also the CINCPAC war diary.

At his morning staff meeting on November 9 (the eighth at Pearl Harbor), Admiral Nimitz discussed indications of an impending Japanese offensive "on a grand scale." With Captain Layton and his people, Nimitz considered the maximum strength Yamamoto might employ. The next day was key—building on Browning's warning to Halsey. CINCPAC confidently predicted an "all out attempt upon Guadalcanal soon, using transports to carry Army troops and supported by carriers." Admiral Nimitz authorized a warning dispatch sent out that night—a little after 8:00 a.m. on November 10 in Nouméa:

ULTRA. INDICATIONS THAT MAJOR OPERATION ASSISTED BY CARRIER STRIKING FORCE SLATED TO SUPPORT MOVEMENT ARMY TRANSPORTS TO GUADALCANAL. CinC THIRD (CARRIER STRIKING) NOW PROCEEDING REFUELING RENDEVOUS NEAR [OCEAN POSITION BY SOLOMONS]. CinC ELEVENTH AIR FLEET TO OPERATE AGAINST CACTUS FROM [Z-3] DAYS. EIGHTH FLEET TO ESCORT ARMY CONVOY. LARGE MOVEMENT ENEMY PLANES TO KAHILI BASE NEAR BUIN. STRIKING FORCE TO HIT CACTUS [Z-1] DAY. ARMY AA UNIT TO EMBARK 11 NOVEMBER PROCEED LAND CACTUS. [Z-DAY] NOT KNOWN BUT RESEARCH CONTINUES . . . WHILE THIS LOOKS LIKE A BIG PUNCH I AM CONFIDENT THAT YOU WITH YOUR FORCES WILL TAKE THEIR MEASURE.

Radio fixes placed the *Junyo* at sea near Kavieng and indicated that battleships might be moving toward the southern area. Intelligence tentatively expected operations to begin on the twelfth or thirteenth. By November 11 details were becoming apparent: Z-day involved the arrival of a convoy, preceded by strong air attacks. Coastwatcher Paul Mason confirmed, reporting Japanese naval strength around Shortland as including seventeen merchantmen, at least one troopship, two oilers, plus strong fleet strength of four heavy and two light cruisers and thirty-three destroyers. Once direction finding placed Eighth Fleet commander Mikawa in the area, the circle seemed complete.

Missing was the impending Japanese surface bombardment, but radio fixes definitely put Admiral Kondo in the Solomons, and on the fourteenth he was reported to be in command. That intelligence energized Halsey and SOPAC leaders.

In terms of perceptions of the South Pacific balance, it is significant that by now COMINCH was conducting actual conversations with Royal Navy officers about an aircraft carrier loan. Halsey reiterated and amplified his earlier appeal for the ship, and he and Nimitz conducted a cable dialogue on how quickly the vessel could be reequipped with American gear. At the time the British considered the *Illustrious*, but the ship finally selected would be the HMS *Victorious*.

Rabaul looked calm and beautiful as Lieutenant Ito Haruki's plane approached. He too would fall under the spell of the Southern Cross. Ito was among a new contingent of Japanese fighters in the radio wars. Following a Rabaul visit from the Imperial Navy's communications chief, the number of operators at Rabaul assigned to the 1st Combined Communications Unit, which worked with the Owada Group, had been increased. Known as the "special duty group," radio monitors were the key to Japanese communications intelligence as much as they were to Allied. Lieutenant Ito came from the naval signal intelligence center in September. With sixty other officers and men he augmented Lieutenant Ogimoto's 1st Unit complement.

The intelligence unit, located in a palm grove at the west end of Vunakanau base, had a radio shack with a monitoring room, a pair of direction-finding huts, and a barracks. With two direction finders at Rabaul and another on Guadalcanal, the Japanese now had the means to obtain more accurate radio fixes on Allied ships. Ogimoto was an experienced shadow warrior, involved in signals intelligence since before the war, when he listened in on American transmissions from the Japanese embassy in Washington. Traffic levels on Japanese naval intelligence circuits soared.

Combined Fleet also obtained good scouting information. Submarine-launched aircraft from Captain Uchino Shinji's *I-8* scouted Efate during the night of November 2, and Fujii Akiyoshi's *I-9* put its floatplane over Nouméa on November 4 and Espíritu Santo on the eleventh. Lieutenant Commander Nagai Takeo's *I-7* reconnoitered Fiji on the eleventh as well, while another I-boat checked Nouméa again. By radio and aerial means the Japanese knew of convoys headed for the Solomons from Fiji, Australia, and the New Hebrides, and they had covered the principal SOPAC bases at a critical moment in the run-up to Kondo's operation. The covers of Nouméa would have shown the *Enterprise* in port, since the floatplanes flew at dawn and "Big E" sailed at 10:00 a.m. on the eleventh, but this was set right next day as a JNAF patrol bomber sighted an American carrier at sea south of Guadalcanal. In short, Combined Fleet was aware Allied forces were in play, if not of Halsey's specific plans. By November 12 Admiral Ugaki had concluded that the fleet's concentration at Shortland for Z-Day must be known to the Allies.

Determined to make good his promises to the Marines, Admiral Halsey set his various cruiser-destroyer groups to escort convoys. These delivered heavy artillery, coast defense units, and 6,000 more troops. American superiority grew. Once there the warships formed a task force. Rear Admiral Daniel Callaghan, the erstwhile SOPAC staff boss, took command, though Norman Scott, the victor of Cape Esperance, had his ships in the force too. There is a dispute about which of these two was actually superior in rank, but neither seems to have raised the question himself. Callaghan wore his flag in heavy cruiser *San Francisco*, Scott in the light cruiser *Atlanta*. Heavy cruiser *Portland*, light cruisers *Helena* and *Juneau*, and eight tin cans completed the unit. Halsey had Callaghan patrol Ironbottom Sound the night of November 11—without incident.

Admiral Thomas Kinkaid steamed out of Nouméa that day. All fifty-nine sailors of the "Big E's" damage control division, plus eighty-five specialists from SOPAC's repair ship *Vestal*, continued to labor on the ship even as she cruised the South Pacific. Pearl Harbor estimated the "Big E" at 70 percent effective. The *Enterprise* was accompanied by two cruisers and six destroyers. Also in train was Task Force 64, under Rear Admiral Willis A. "Ching" Lee, now consisting of the battleships *Washington* and *South Dakota*. As Kinkaid and Lee hovered in Torpedo Junction, Cactus reported a force of two Japanese carriers about 150 miles away—some 575 miles from "Big E's" position. Kinkaid began a high-speed chase. Meanwhile SOPAC ordered Callaghan's cruisers back into Ironbottom Sound.

At Truk, based on his intelligence, Admiral Ugaki asked Combined Fleet staff to restudy the plan. Ugaki wanted additional strong air attacks and a preliminary prompt sortie by Mikawa's Eighth Fleet cruisers. Senior staff officer Kuroshima Kameto argued against changing the arrangements. Ugaki did not insist. To the south, Admiral Kondo detached his "raiding unit" with battleships *Hiei* and *Kirishima*.

The Abe force had been awarded a commendation for earlier battles, and Abe himself was rewarded with promotion to vice admiral at the beginning of November. Now they were to repeat the bombardment of "The Night." According to Hara Tameichi, who commanded destroyer *Amatsukaze* in Abe's

screen, the admiral feared his sortie would fail. Rear Admiral Kimura Susumu's Destroyer Squadron 10, including Hara's ship, along with light
cruiser *Nagara* and seven other tin cans, had departed Truk on November 9
separately from Kondo's main body. They joined Abe, under way near
Shortland, before dawn on the twelfth. It was early in the day, as the tropical heat rose, that the Abe Force was first seen by an American B-17.

In addition to Kimura's screen, a contingent of Rear Admiral Takama
Tamotsu's Destroyer Squadron 4 strengthened the raiding unit. Takama's
five warships were also spotted by Allied aircraft. Abe ordered a double-ring
cruising formation, with Takama's tin cans in the lead on the outside perimeter. Takama took position around midafternoon. In all, Admiral Abe
would have two battleships, a light cruiser, and eleven destroyers. The *Hiei*
launched a floatplane scout that reported ten Allied vessels off Lunga Point
about sunset. As evening deepened into night, the flotilla entered a storm
front. Unable to return to its ship, the floatplane flew to Shortland. Abe
neared Guadalcanal amid squalls, alternating with soaking rain and occasional calm. At times *Hiei*'s lookouts found the wakes of nearby vessels practically invisible. The R Area Force reported that weather would preclude
aerial spotting. Abe signaled his final plan around 7:00 p.m. Takama would
sweep Ironbottom Sound ahead of the bombardment unit. The battleships
were to execute a forty-minute shoot beginning shortly before 2:00 a.m.
Admiral Abe, who yearned to avenge the death of his boon companion
Goto Aritomo in these same waters a month before, would have his chance.

"WE WANT THE BIG ONES!"

Dan Callaghan had skippered cruiser *San Francisco* before moving to South
Pacific headquarters. A seasoned sailor and practical fellow, Callaghan
wanted to make his command work despite the awkward presence of two
admirals so close in rank. Not overly proud, Callaghan assigned light
cruiser *Atlanta*, Norman Scott's flagship, to the lead position in his line.
Thus the two American admirals sailed in the first two major vessels in the
battle line. Neither of them had the more sophisticated surface search radars. Callaghan posted his destroyers in front of and behind his cruisers, in
a line-ahead formation that became a standard tactic in the U.S. fleet. The

warships cleared for action and expected battle. Heavy cruiser *Portland*, for example, had sent her floatplanes back to Espíritu Santo to prevent their flammability from becoming an issue.

All day Callaghan's ships had been off Lunga Point shepherding transports and cargo ships of Turner's latest convoy and bombarding Japanese positions. Anticipating the usual noontime air raid, the flotilla had gone to Condition Red but then stood down—Kelly Turner signaled that a flight of U.S. cargo planes would be arriving. When the first showed up, sure enough someone began shooting, and bedlam followed. Admiral Turner angrily demanded to know which ships had *not* fired. Fortunately no friendly aircraft were destroyed. At midafternoon the alert was real. The Japanese mounted a torpedo attack alongside their usual bombing. Amazingly, ships that had not managed to score against a single friendly aircraft virtually obliterated the JNAF strike force, which accomplished little except to get the transports to weigh anchor. One torpedo bomber crashed aboard the *San Francisco*, however, disabling her after the main battery gun director. The warships screened the convoy as it left through Indispensable Strait.

Meanwhile, in shelling Japanese positions they claimed destruction of a midget submarine near Kamimbo. Around sunset U.S. sailors went to general quarters again, and Callaghan's flotilla prepared for the expected battle. In the gun director of destroyer *Sterett*, third in the van, despite his advanced optics Lieutenant Ray Calhoun could barely see the ships ahead of them. Their boiling wakes were the most visible feature. The vessels behind were ghosts, the night very dark with squalls.

The rain and dark especially bothered Vice Admiral Abe. Shortly after midnight he elected to turn away, reducing speed. Then the weather seemed to break and messages from Guadalcanal promised better conditions there. About twenty minutes after turning, Abe changed his mind, ordered a course reversal, and increased to eighteen knots. At 12:48 a.m. of November 13—Friday the thirteenth—Abe instructed Takama to begin his sweep. The battleships started loading the special incendiary AA shells that had been so effective on The Night. Another thing they had learned: This time the battleships would use weaker propellant charges to reduce overshoots. Unfortunately for them, Admiral Abe never did deploy into battle formation, and the two successive course reversals threw his armada

into confusion. Rather than an arrowhead of Vs protecting the core battlewagons, Abe now had small clumps of warships scattered across the sea. It
was almost exactly 1:00 a.m.

Suddenly the Allied and Japanese fleets were closing at a speed of nearly
forty miles an hour. Callaghan's flotilla, under tight control, settled onto a
heading to block entry to Cactus waters. The commander intended to circle Savo Island and reenter Ironbottom Sound. At 1:12 Admiral Abe ordered
his force onto a heading of 130 degrees for his bombardment. Light cruiser
Helena detected the oncoming enemy almost fourteen miles distant at 1:24.
Helena was eighth in line, and warships ahead of her might have been able
to see something, but none did. Admiral Callaghan, pulled between radar
reports and the negative sightings of his van, hesitated. Ray Calhoun, in the
main battery director of the *Sterett*, heard *Helena*'s report over TBS, the "Talk
Between Ships" low-frequency radios the U.S. fleet used for tactical communication. But when he looked in the indicated direction with his optics,
there was nothing. His destroyer's five-inch guns had a maximum effective
range of about 18,000 yards, so Calhoun figured he'd have ten minutes until the action commenced.

The TBS announced two columns of Japanese and two big targets—
battleships were suspected. Still nothing to be seen. Dan Callaghan must
have been surprised at that news, but he was game, and altered course to
due north at 1:37. If he could block the enemy he might repeat Norman
Scott's achievement of crossing their T. That would also afford his smaller
guns their best chance against the enemy's big ships. Callaghan's efforts to
obtain information over TBS from the vessels with the best radars were
frustrated as the U.S. ships all talked at once. Suddenly, at 1:42 destroyer
Cushing announced she could actually see three Japanese tin cans. Lieutenant Calhoun spotted the enemy for the first time with the range down to
4,000 yards. It was now clear there could be no clever maneuver. The fleets
were upon each other. Admiral Callaghan ordered odd-numbered ships to
fire to port and even ones to starboard. Calhoun discerned the silhouette
of a *Kongo*-class battleship. Her towering superstructure overlooked the sea
like the Empire State Building towered over structures in New York.

Ahead of Admiral Abe's fractured formation, destroyer *Yudachi* saw the
Americans nearly simultaneously—within a minute. A U.S. tin can appeared out of the night on a collision course. Commander Kikkawa Kiyoshi

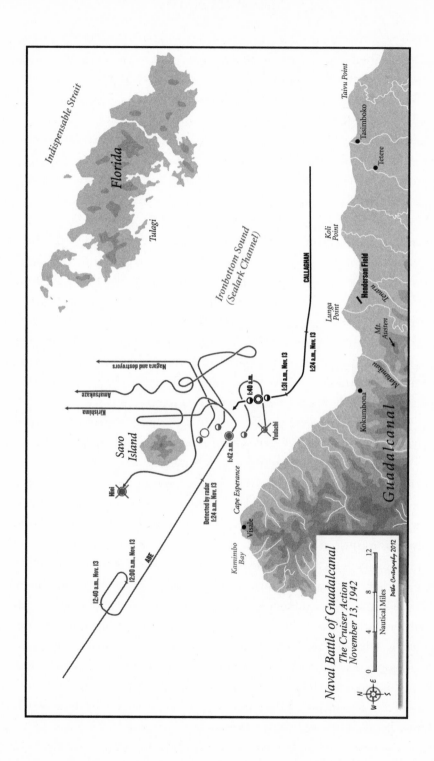

Naval Battle of Guadalcanal
The Cruiser Action
November 13, 1942

0   4   8   12
Nautical Miles

Dale Cartography 2012

N
W   E
S

Indispensable Strait

Florida

Tulagi

Ironbottom Sound
(Sealark Channel)

Savo
Island

Hiei

12:40 a.m. Nov. 13

12:00 a.m. Nov. 13

ABE

Kaminbo
Bay

Visale

Cape Esperance

Detected by radar
1:24 a.m. Nov. 13

Kirishima

Amatsukaze

Nagara and destroyers

1:42 a.m.

1:40 a.m.

Yudachi

1:31 a.m. Nov. 13

1:24 a.m. Nov. 13

CALLAGHAN

Kokumbona

Maravovo

Guadalcanal

Mt.
Austen

Tenaru

Henderson Field

Lunga
Point

Koli
Point

Tasimboko

Tetere

Taivu Point

of the *Yudachi*, flabbergasted, turned hard to starboard, followed by *Harusame*. *Yudachi* flashed a warning but no position, because the dark and the fleet's maneuvers left her without a good reckoning. Early in the war his ship had been taken unawares while Kikkawa concentrated on another target, so he was determined not to repeat that error. Kikkawa launched torpedoes immediately along the length of the U.S. column. Then he retreated momentarily to ready his gun crews. *Yudachi* tried to circle the Americans to come up on the opposite side. The destroyer fired fiercely at ranges down to 1,200 yards—point-blank for a modern warship. The Americans shot back and they had much bigger ships—Kikkawa successively engaged a heavy cruiser, a light cruiser, an antiaircraft cruiser, and two destroyers. *Yudachi*'s luck had run out—a cruiser Kikkawa thought friendly inflicted crippling hits to his engines and boilers. By then there were also fires near the forward magazines. Lieutenant Nakamura Teiji saw crewmen fetching their hammocks and bringing canvas, hoping to rig sails to catch the wind and beach on Starvation Island. But it was not to be. The *Yudachi* drifted until, much later, destroyer *Samidare* came alongside. Commander Kikkawa ordered, "Abandon ship." After evacuating the crew, the *Samidare* fired a torpedo to scuttle her sister, without apparent effect. Kikkawa asked *Samidare*'s skipper to fire a second tin fish, but just then an American cruiser approached and *Samidare* had to flee. The *Yudachi* was finished off after dawn by a crippled U.S. cruiser shelling her at leisure.

Kikkawa's boss, Rear Admiral Takama, was embarked in the *Asagumo*. The fleet's perambulations had left Takama's destroyers behind and to starboard of Abe's force. They were on the disengaged side. They did not come into action until about 2:00 a.m., and retired after a brief firefight.

Hara Tameichi, a good friend of Kikkawa's, was in his *Amatsukaze*, following light cruiser *Nagara*. Commander Hara worried about the closeness of Florida Island, with its dangerous reefs. Abe's battleships were between Hara and the Americans. When U.S. warships engaged them, shells fired long began to fall near *Amatsukaze*. Caught between reefs and shells, Hara ordered a high-speed turn. Suddenly he found himself beside Callaghan's battle line. Commander Hara had literally written the book on Japanese torpedo tactics, having authored the Imperial Navy's torpedo warfare manual. He found himself in a perfect position and at 1:54 launched eight Long Lance torpedoes that crumpled the destroyer *Barton* at the rear of Callaghan's line. Five minutes later, spotting an American cruiser, Hara launched four more tin fish, badly damaging cruiser *Juneau*. At that moment the *Juneau* had been battering *Yudachi*, so Hara's intervention saved her for a time. Later he almost collided with Callaghan's flagship *San Francisco*, initially mistaking her for Japanese, and expended his last four torpedoes on that cruiser. But the *Amatsukaze* blundered into cruiser *Helena*. Firing under radar control, the *Helena* inflicted heavy damage and killed fifty-nine of Hara's shipmates. Hara's vessel limped away and barely reached Truk.

Rear Admiral Kimura's flagship, the light cruiser *Nagara*, was under Captain Tahara Yoshiaki. Like Hara, Captain Tahara broke to the left at the outset. A few minutes later lookouts saw a pair of heavy cruisers and a destroyer. Tahara ordered his gunnery officer, Lieutenant Commander Kuhara Kazutoshi, to illuminate the targets with star shells. Then Kuhara began shooting. Suddenly torpedoes struck the enemy cruiser they were blasting. The ship, identified as a *Portland*-class cruiser, began to sink, though the *Nagara* had so far fired just nine 5.5-inch shells. Captain Tahara credited the torpedoes to *Amatsukaze*. The time recorded does correspond to that destroyer's first Long Lance salvo. Tahara turned the *Nagara* in company with destroyers *Yukikaze* and *Harusame*, and discovered what they identified as a *Cairo*-class antiaircraft cruiser. Admiral Kimura ordered a combined attack. Tahara's 5.5-inch guns fired 127 shells at the warship. At one point the range became so short that Kuhara ordered flak guns into action. The *Nagara* expended 332 rounds from her AA machine guns. Accompanying destroyers were also credited with sinking an American tin can.

If Abe's escort vessels were confused by sudden apparitions from the night, the admiral himself was even more startled. The story from *Hiei's* flag bridge is from Commander Sekino Hideo, communications officer, who related it to Hara Tameichi. Lookouts on the *Hiei* caught their first glimpse of Guadalcanal at the very moment the ship's image appeared on U.S. radar. Admiral Abe expected to execute his shoot on Henderson Field momentarily and had already laid in the course as gunners loaded incendiaries. Observers on the island had informed Abe that the sky was clearing, and he knew JNAF had put up night intruders from Buin. Suddenly came *Yudachi's* contact report.

Agitated, the admiral screamed, "What is the range and bearing? And where is the *Yudachi*?"

Before anyone answered, *Hiei*'s own lookouts piped up. "Four black objects ahead . . . look like warships." *Look like* warships? In those waters, on that night, how could there be any question? "Five degrees to starboard. Eight thousand meters . . . unsure yet. Visibility bad."

Admiral Abe's staff chief, Commander Suzuki Masakane, tried to confirm the range while Abe himself decided what to do. He knew where *Yudachi* was supposed to be, but his course alterations had thrown everything out of kilter. He ordered the battleships to switch their incendiary rounds for armor-piercing shells. Aboard the *Hiei* the main battery gunner, Lieutenant Yunoki Shigeru, hastened to comply. Sekino saw "pandemonium" as turret crews raced to make the substitution and store the flammables. Radiomen spread the warning and yelled for information on every wavelength—so much that U.S. monitors at FRUPAC picked up high-frequency transmissions and began to listen, a vigil that led to a startling end. Had the Americans hit Abe's battleships during those vulnerable moments it would have been like the glorious dive-bomber attack on the Japanese carriers at Midway. But for eight critical minutes no American guns spoke, no shells tumbled from the sky.

Lieutenant Calhoun on the *Sterett* watched the range close with trepidation. His ship awaited firing orders. Four thousand yards, three thousand. Tension grew. Finally Callaghan set the fire distribution, which required *Sterett*, in the van, to fire to the opposite side. As Calhoun turned the gun director the inferno engulfed them. Lieutenant Commander Edward N. Parker skippered the destroyer *Cushing* at the head of the van. Parker turned to bring his broadside to bear. It was his ship that nearly collided with Kikkawa's *Yudachi*. His superior, Commander Thomas M. Stokes, the division commander, requested permission to make a torpedo attack. Admiral Callaghan refused. All his van destroyers were now turning to avoid Japanese warships.

Aboard cruiser *Helena*, Captain Gilbert C. Hoover had his guns trained at zero elevation. The Japanese were *that* close. Suddenly a searchlight split the night, illuminating the *Helena*. That was enough for Hoover, and he opened fire. The searchlight was from Commander Takasuka Osamu's destroyer *Akatsuki*, in company with the *Hiei*. The whole U.S. battle line firing to that side pasted her. *Atlanta* estimated her own range at 600 yards. *Akatsuki* crumpled under the concentrated fire. Fifty years later, at a commemoration of the Guadalcanal campaign, Lieutenant Shinya Michiharu of the *Akatsuki* would meet Lieutenant Stewart Moredock, who had been on the *Atlanta* as Admiral Scott's operations officer. Both men survived the sinking of their ships in this hellish encounter.

Behind *Akatsuki* were destroyers *Inazuma* and *Ikazuchi*. They did not wait for orders to launch torpedoes. The Americans quickly saw Lieutenant Commander Ishi Hagumu's *Ikazuchi* and hit her several times. Ishi led his damaged ship out of the action. Commander Terauchi Masamichi in the *Inazuma* was full of fighting spirit. This was his first sea battle. It was so dark they could see nothing; then the night was lit with flashes and there were big ships. Terauchi loosed his torpedoes at the nearest big enemy vessel, though in his case he received orders first. Ishi's and Terauchi's destroyers proved an inadequate screen for Captain Nishida Masao's *Hiei*. Parker's *Cushing* fired her own torpedoes now, too close to arm properly but impossible to miss. Nishida's ship could not miss either, and even her secondaries were enough to leave *Cushing* dead in the water. But the American torpedoes grievously wounded Admiral Abe's flagship.

Captain Nishida switched on a searchlight, picking out the *Atlanta*. The *Hiei* blasted her. But Lieutenant Yunoki's main battery got off just two salvos before U.S. shells began pitching in on *Hiei*. Meanwhile the *Atlanta* sheared out of line, swerving to avoid the destroyer melee ahead. Lieutenant Commander Bruce McCandless, at that moment officer of the deck on the next vessel, heavy cruiser *San Francisco*, had the conn and wondered whether to follow. He turned to his captain for orders and was told to match her turn. But the bigger ship could not duplicate the tight maneuver; plus the *Atlanta* kept weaving back, causing McCandless to alter slightly in an attempt to clear the bow for his turn. The ships steered shaky parallel courses as a result. Then the *Atlanta* shuddered from the impact of two Long Lances. Torpedoed, battered by the *Hiei*, she was nearly done for. At that moment the *San Francisco*, shooting at Japanese beyond *Atlanta*, dropped one or more shells short. A salvo—probably from *San Francisco*—carried away one of the ship's bridge wings, and with it Rear Admiral Norman Scott. From the flagship Callaghan's talker piped up on the TBS, "Cease firing, own ships!"

But shooting continued unabated. The *Mikazuki*, hit in her number one boiler room, lost a gun and a searchlight. *Akatsuki* simply disappeared. She had gone down with most crewmen, the skipper, and the destroyer division commander. Commander Terauchi on the *Inazuma* was one of the few to see her capsize. The Americans rescued eighteen *Akatsuki* seamen. Captain Hoover of the *Helena* asked whether he could fire if he had targets. The TBS spit back, "Advise type of targets. We want the big ones." This last bit became Callaghan's epitaph, forever marking his determination to prevail.

By this time both Japanese battlewagons were only a few thousand yards away, and Captain Iwabuchi Sanji's *Kirishima* was blasting away too. Iwabuchi had been following *Hiei* in column, but Abe's maneuvers left his vessel on the flagship's starboard quarter. *Kirishima*'s action record claims inflicting four hits on the cruiser illuminated by the *Hiei*, which would have been Callaghan's *San Francisco.* The shells smashed the bridge and conning tower, killing every officer there except Bruce McCandless, who lived to tell the tale. Captain Cassin Young, who had survived Pearl Harbor and, in fact, won the Congressional Medal of Honor there, perished on the cruiser's bridge. Ranges came down to a thousand yards or less. Gunnery Ensign John G. Wallace later recalled that it would have been easy to toss a sweet potato onto some of the Japanese ships. The *Kirishima* claimed to have sunk the enemy cruiser. Lieutenant Tokuno Horishi, the battleship's assistant gunnery officer, recalled that the *Kirishima* received only one hit during the entire battle.

San Francisco got in her licks on the *Hiei.* Lieutenant Commander William W. Wilbourne had only to press the firing key to send six-gun salvos crashing into the battlewagon. The *San Francisco*'s after turret was masked until McCandless swung the ship around. It had to fire under local control, since the after director had been wrecked earlier that day by the Betty crash. *San Francisco* claimed at least eighteen hits. Others fired too. The *Hiei* endured more than eighty hits. Communications were knocked out; fires erupted near the bridge; Admiral Abe was grazed in the head by flying splinters. Nishida's ship mutated into a floating derelict, barely under way, with rudder jammed and flooded compartments barring access. The engines were good but the steering so bad that hours later the battleship still lay only a few miles from Savo Island.

Captain Iwabuchi led his *Kirishima* away from the combat zone. At about 2:00 a.m. Abe canceled the bombardment mission anyway and ordered general withdrawal. The Imperial Navy recorded the end of the battle at 2:34. Iwabuchi radioed a preliminary report about half an hour later, while Rear Admiral Kimura in the *Nagara* reassembled the destroyers, detached ships to attend the *Hiei*, and got the others out of Cactus air range. At 3:44 a.m., Combined Fleet postponed Z-day, leaving Rear Admiral Tanaka to withdraw his convoy up The Slot.

At FRUPAC the radio monitors listened to increasingly frantic messages from Captain Nishida. The *Hiei* was not besting her damage. Dawn meant the Cactus Air Force. Nishida's messages conveniently supplied his position, which U.S. intelligence passed on to Cactus. Meanwhile, Abe wanted to tow the crippled battleship to safety. Some called for beaching her, shelling Guadalcanal until the ammunition ran out, then joining the troops on Starvation Island. Nishida preferred to try to save *Hiei*. But the rudder jam greatly complicated towing. Combined Fleet suggested the jury rig of having the *Hiei* also tow a destroyer behind herself to compensate for the rudder.

Captain Iwabuchi reversed course with *Kirishima* and headed back. His ship would have towed her sister. But U.S. intelligence could have tactical as well as strategic impact. As a result of Ultra, Iwabuchi's *Kirishima* became a U.S. sub's target. Strategic warnings had led to some submarines being sent out from Australia. These included the *Trout*. Lieutenant Commander Lawson P. "Red" Ramage's *Trout* had actually been on the way to repair damage she had suffered patrolling off Truk—where Ramage had succeeded in putting a tin fish into light carrier *Taiyo*. On November 12, sub chief Rear Admiral Ralph W. Christie alerted Red to look out for major warships. Sure enough, in the morning the *Kirishima* appeared. Zigzagging foiled Ramage's first approach, but later he got close enough to launch five torpedoes. Red claimed no hits, but the Japanese felt one—fortunately a dud. Iwabuchi promptly hightailed it north.

Meanwhile Admiral Abe finally gave up on towing the *Hiei* and ordered her beached at Kamimbo instead. He transferred to destroyer *Yukikaze* after dawn. Beginning at 6:15 a.m., relays of Marine and Navy dive-bombers, *En-*

terprise torpedo planes—flying from the carrier to recover at Cactus—and Army B-17s struck the *Hiei* again and again. The JNAF provided some air cover, including from the *Junyo*, but that started out badly—the air force was given the wrong coordinates—and got worse. The first patrol fighters did not reach *Hiei* until nearly noon. At least three American bombs and six or more torpedoes hit the warship. Captain Nishida, preoccupied with the incessant air attacks, did little to beach the ship. Given the mounting danger to the destroyers standing by, Admiral Abe ordered the *Hiei* scuttled and her crew taken off. Yamamoto countermanded that. Abe appealed the decision, twice. By evening the crew had been evacuated and the ship's seacocks opened. Soon afterward arrived Yamamoto's repeat order to keep the *Hiei* afloat. The fleet commander refused to give up on saving the ship, but his dispatch, delayed in transmission, arrived too late. An I-boat received instructions that night to proceed to the *Hiei*'s location and ascertain her status. The following morning Commander Yamada Kaoru signaled from the *I-16* that the *Hiei* was no more.

On the American side, Task Group 67.4 had been virtually annihilated. The *Portland*, hit by *Hiei*, once by *Kirishima*, and aft by a *Yudachi* torpedo, circled helplessly in Ironbottom Sound on a remaining screw with her rudder jammed. She managed to limp into Tulagi harbor. Two destroyers sank where they were. Gil Hoover of the *Helena* regrouped the survivors—his light cruiser and a few tin cans. The *Atlanta*, *San Francisco*, *Juneau*, and *Sterett* joined. The *Atlanta* fell out of formation, too waterlogged to survive, and sank near Cactus. Every ship was damaged. McCandless of the crippled *San Francisco* would be awarded the Medal of Honor. Roughly 1,400 survivors landed on Guadalcanal. Captain Hoover led the battered vessels toward Espíritu Santo. The next day, south of Cactus, they stumbled into Commander Yokota Minoru's *I-26*. Yokota fired torpedoes, which missed the *San Francisco* but hit the *Juneau* instead. She virtually blew up. Besides providing incredible pyrotechnics for the men on Guadalcanal, the first round of this naval battle had been woefully destructive. But there had been no decision. Yamamoto remained determined to have his Z-Day.

Combined Fleet now had a liaison officer on Guadalcanal, Lieutenant Commander Emura Kusao, personally representing the fleet commander.

Emura reported the cripples lying off Lunga Point and various Allied activities in Ironbottom Sound. Air searches discovered Kinkaid's task force with the *Enterprise*, as well as another Allied convoy. The Japanese were racing against time. Yamamoto ordered Admiral Kondo to finish the job. Kondo could cover arrival of the Japanese convoy in person. Now Kondo advised that his fleet, low on fuel, needed to top off. He put back his bombardment a day.

Not willing to leave Henderson Field unmolested, Combined Fleet ordered a cruiser foray. Rear Admiral Nishimura Shoji departed Shortland at 7:30 a.m. with his Cruiser Division 7 ships *Suzuya* and *Maya*, screened by light cruiser *Tenryu* and destroyers. Vice Admiral Mikawa with a cruiser-destroyer group accompanied Nishimura to reinforce him if a surface action eventuated. Combined Fleet undertook this sortie even as the *Hiei* drama unfolded in The Slot. Yamamoto did not intend to let up. It was possible for Mikawa to have taken all of his ships into Ironbottom Sound to put greater weight of shell on the airfields. The admiral, who prided himself on having read Alfred Thayer Mahan's *Influence of Sea Power upon History* four times, surely appreciated the value of contesting the waters off Lunga Point. But he kept to his support role. Nishimura separated from Mikawa's unit about 11:00 p.m. on November 12 and a little over an hour later began his bombardment run. His cruisers shelled Henderson on the outbound leg, and Fighter One on the return. They blasted the fields with nearly a thousand eight-inch shells, destroying a number of aircraft. That night the PT boats intervened. While Nishimura's cruisers blasted away, *PT-47* and *PT-60*, on patrol out of Tulagi, went up against one of the screening destroyers. *PT-47* fired three torpedoes from close range, certain she obtained a hit. This was apparently mistaken.

Chief of Staff Ugaki at Truk disappointedly noted that many of Nishimura's shells had impacted between targets and not on them—there had been communication problems with the *Suzuya* floatplane Nishimura launched to spot for him. But the admiral did not stick around to check. He rejoined Mikawa and exited The Slot past the Russell Islands to escape to the west. In the morning Vice Admiral Mikawa's force experienced the mad hornets. After dawn Lieutenant Commander Glynn R. "Donc" Donaho's sub *Flying Fish*—also cued by Ultra—found Mikawa and sent six torpedoes toward his cruisers. All missed. Submarine attack was followed by air. Marine and

Navy torpedo planes and dive-bombers, from both Henderson and the *Enterprise*, hacked away at Mikawa's ships.

First to run the gauntlet of the Cactus Air Force was heavy cruiser *Kinugasa*. She sustained a direct hit from a 500-pound bomb forward of the bridge, which ignited a gasoline fire, sprang leaks that gave her a list, took out an AA gun, and killed both Captain Sawa Masao and his exec. The ship's torpedo officer took over. The fires were quenched and *Kinugasa*, accompanied by a couple of destroyers, was under way again when several *Enterprise* dive-bombers struck from astern. Their bombs fell close enough to perforate the hull. The cruiser lost both rudder control and engines. Her flooding accelerated. Inside of two hours she capsized, with fifty-one seamen killed, forty-two badly wounded, and thirty-three sailors more lightly injured. Japanese records mention only bomb hits and near misses, though U.S. ones claim three to six torpedo hits.

Next up was Captain Hayakawa Mikio's *Chokai*. She beat off an early torpedo plane attack, but two hours later came dive-bombers. One missed close enough to wound a sailor. In the heat of action a fire broke out in the boiler rooms and reduced speed to twenty-nine knots, but Hayakawa's ship reached safety and required only a short repair from the *Arashi* at Truk. Then came *Maya*. Captain Nabeshima Shunsaku had enough warning to use his main battery, expending nine of those incendiary AA shells that might have been usefully plopped on Henderson Field the previous night. One U.S. plane was damaged so badly it crashed on the high-angle gun deck, igniting ready ammo and starting a fire that spread to the torpedo room. Nabeshima jettisoned his torpedoes. A torpedo tube and two heavy flak guns were wrecked, thirty-seven sailors died, and twenty-seven more were wounded, but the ship survived. Last was light cruiser *Isuzu*, attacked by dive-bombers under the *Enterprise*'s master scout, Bucky Lee. Captain Shinoda Kiyohiko's ship was damaged by near misses that flooded two boiler rooms and left her steering manually, but *Isuzu*, too, lived to fight another day. Given fresh reasons to respect Allied airpower, Mikawa staggered into Shortland late that afternoon.

Rear Admiral Tanaka's Army convoy had to run the gauntlet too. Already repelled once, Tanaka wondered how many ships would survive. Tanaka had a premonition, and he was right to worry. This day might have been a nightmare for Mikawa, but for the convoy it was sheer hell, beginning soon after dawn, when the first scouts—both Cactus dive-bombers and SOWESPAC B-17s—made their instant attacks. At that point the convoy had a combat air patrol. Interceptors claimed several of the scout bombers, which inflicted no damage. An hour later a pair of scout bombers from *Enterprise* also were claimed destroyed. But at 11:50 a major strike arrived—more than forty planes, half of them SBDs, and eight each of Avengers and B-17s. Tanaka's destroyers laid a smoke screen and the transports maneuvered, but the aircraft were upon them. Torpedoes sank two transports, while a third, carrying the Nagoya Division's commander, was hurt and had to turn back.

From Truk the Combined Fleet desperately demanded the Army shell Henderson Field with everything it had. This was the Army convoy, after all. Success depended upon stopping Allied air attacks. The Army blithely replied that it would bombard the American airfields *the next day*! Besides, the soldiers argued, even if they did neutralize Henderson, the Americans still had an aircraft carrier somewhere out there at sea.

More Cactus attacks followed at 12:45 and 2:00 p.m., with three transports sunk. Destroyers rescued survivors. A B-17 strike, another *Enterprise* attack, and a series of mixed raids, ending with a big punch before sunset, sent another transport to the bottom. Tanaka managed to evacuate or pull from the water some 5,000 soldiers and sailors, quite impressive under the circumstances. At SOPAC, clutching the latest situation report, Bull Halsey exulted to his staff, "We've got the bastards licked!"

Only four transports were left. Admiral Tanaka was in a quandary. Though they were not far from Cactus, regrouping the convoy would add delays. Air search had revealed an Allied cruiser-destroyer group (actually Lee's force) racing to intercept, while Mikawa's shot-up cover unit had had to withdraw. Tanaka did not know whether Kondo would come up in support. But Combined Fleet ordered the transports ahead to beach on Guadalcanal. Then a dispatch from Admiral Kondo informed him the Advance Force was, in fact, coming to the rescue. Tanaka pulled into a cove on the New Georgia coast to finish regrouping and await the Kondo fleet. The delays meant he could not make Starvation Island before dawn. There was nothing to be done about that. As Kondo approached, Tanaka put back to sea. Shortly before midnight Tanaka's warships saw Advance Force vessels loom out of the darkness. But the United States was out there too. And the Americans were not cruisers. They were battleships.

The Allied airpower romp was possible because of the latest failure to neutralize newly reprovisioned Henderson Field—and the nearby presence of the *Enterprise*. South Pacific commanders were also blessed with good information in the form of excellent air search results that morning. These revealed not only the Mikawa force and Tanaka convoy, but also the Kondo force and even the Kakuta carrier unit. Radio fixes confirmed the information. Cactus air took advantage, but so did SOPAC. Bull Halsey had ordered Admiral Kinkaid to detach his battleship group the previous day. Rear Admiral Ching Lee and his battleships were to move in on Savo Island, thus covering withdrawal of the Allied cruisers and blocking The Slot. Halsey had been stunned to discover, when Kinkaid radioed back, that Task Force 16's position was such as to preclude the battleships reaching the scene until morning. The detachment was in fact accomplished. Admiral Lee issued a general instruction by signal lamp: "THIS FORCE TO OPERATE SOUTHWARD OF SOLOMONS. OBJECTIVE ENEMY TRANSPORT FORCE OR THOSE ENCOUNTERED. BE ALERT FOR AN ATTACK." By morning Lee had reached a position about fifty miles from Guadalcanal with his battleships *Washington* and *South Dakota* and four destroyers. Avoiding contact with the Japanese enemy then became important, so he maneuvered below Cactus most of the day. At midafternoon Bull Halsey instructed Lee to be in position off Savo at midnight. Here SOPAC hazarded battleships off Guadalcanal.

A SOUTH PACIFIC EVENING

Admiral Kondo, for his part, gathered to push through and sustain the convoy with his battleship bombardment. He summoned Captain Iwabuchi's *Kirishima*. After a brief call at Shortland she left to meet the Advance Force. Kondo joined during the night of November 13–14. The Advance Force commander had been oddly quiescent during the Abe sortie. At this juncture Kondo made a further error of omission that cost him dearly. His

Second Fleet included battleships *Kongo* and *Haruna* in addition to those that had already been in action. These ships were at sea: U.S. snoopers had seen them repeatedly in company with the *Junyo*, at Shortland, or elsewhere. Kondo, in fact, used them to help refuel his destroyers. The Advance Force had an excellent staff, including Captain Yanagizawa Kuranosuke as senior officer, Commander Yamamoto Yuji (no relation to the admiral) as operations staffer, plus Rear Admiral Shiraishi Kazutaka as boss. These were experienced men and, like Kondo, almost professional staff officers. Shiraishi had been with Kondo at the Battle of the Java Sea, where he thought Japanese tactics poor, and surely wanted to avoid those mistakes. Yamamoto looked up to Kondo almost as a father. There *must* have been discussions in the flag plot of *Atago* on whether to include the other heavy ships, but what these were is lost to history.

There is only conjecture as to Kondo's reasoning. He left no account of it. Perhaps his motive was as simple as a desire to shield the *Kongo*, on which Kondo had twice served. Maybe he thought SOPAC's surface forces had been effectively eliminated—yet he knew that battleships had been seen alongside the *Enterprise*. Kondo may have considered that carrier *Junyo* required heavy ships in support. It could have been a question of conserving fuel. The most likely explanation concerns mission. Since he was to bombard Henderson Field, Kondo may have thought the *Kongo* and *Haruna* not well supplied to perform that task. The special incendiary shells considered ideal for this purpose were in short supply. On "The Night," the two participating battleships had taken the entire stock. Now, a month later, only a certain number of the new shells were available, and it is possible that Abe had had all of them. In any case, Admiral Kondo took the *Kirishima* and left the others behind.

The admiral's flotilla also included flagship *Atago*; another heavy cruiser, the *Takao*; light cruisers *Nagara* and *Sendai*; and nine destroyers. He planned to send three tin cans plus the *Sendai* to sweep ahead of the bombardment unit, then screen behind them. Observers of this battle frequently draw attention to the fact that the American destroyers had not served with one another before, came from different divisions, and had no unit commander. The same was largely true of the Japanese. Both of Kondo's destroyer squadrons were composed of different ships than a month earlier. Four of the six vessels of Destroyer Squadron 10 had been in the Abe battle

Z-Day: Cactus Air Attacks and Kondo's Approach

* Nishimura joins Mikawa

0   20   40   60
Nautical Miles

Petho Cartography 2011

Pacific Ocean

Ontong Java

6:00 a.m.

KONDO

12:00 p.m.

Choiseul   SOLOMON ISLANDS

Santa Isabel

Sub Attack
4:35 p.m.

TANAKA

8:30 a.m.

New Georgia

11:50 a.m.

Constant Attacks

9:00 p.m.

Florida

Malaita

MIKAWA

Russell

Savo

8:00 a.m.
First Air Attacks

7:00 a.m.

Guadalcanal

Solomon Sea

San Cristobal

LEE

Rennell

only the previous day. The escort had been thrown together from whatever ships were available. Commander Iwahashi Toru's *Asagumo*, among the last to finish refueling, topped off from the *Haruna* at 5:55 a.m. on November 14.

Kondo's Advance Force headed toward Guadalcanal before dawn. SOPAC airpower, engaging its forces to destroy Tanaka's convoy, paid no heed. Kondo's flagship *Atago*, however, had to evade torpedoes from the U.S. subs *Trout* and *Flying Fish* in the afternoon. Ensign Nakamura Toshio in the *Asagumo* watched as three torpedo tracks came right at him. The tin fish passed underneath the *Asagumo* at 4:35 p.m. The American sub had apparently set torpedo depths to strike the heavy ships. Commander Iwahashi's destroyer counterattacked with depth charges. The American sub escaped.

About a half hour earlier, Red Ramage of the *Trout* had sent a contact report in such haste he did not encode it. Kondo's radio monitors intercepted the message. By late afternoon Kondo knew the enemy would oppose him. The flotilla sent floatplanes for a final daytime probe, but they reported only cruisers and destroyers. So the admiral warned his fleet to expect a few cruisers. He signaled Tanaka at 7:00 p.m. that he would clear away the enemy so the Army convoy could finally reach Cactus.

Kondo received an R Area Force contact report that misidentified Lee's battleships at 8:45 p.m., and later one that mistakenly took the Tanaka convoy for another U.S. cruiser force. Admiral Kondo could have had three battleships to Ching Lee's two, but his decision had reversed the odds. There would be two American battlewagons to one Japanese. In the darkness off Guadalcanal, battleships would meet in surface combat for the first time in the Pacific war.

Willis Lee's behemoths were on the scene. Admiral Lee fully expected to grapple with the enemy. The previous night, still miles away, Ching Lee and Glenn Davis, captain of battleship *Washington*, had had a confab with ships' officers in the wardroom where the leaders went over every aspect of the coming engagement. Captain Davis asked his navigator, a new fellow, whether he was up to the job. At dawn the *Washington* went to general quarters. Davis appeared on the bridge, as did the navigator. In the U.S. Navy it was customary for the navigator to control the helm when the ship went to battle stations. At other times the officer of the deck had the conn. That morning Lieutenant Raymond P. Hunter was officer of the deck, nearing midwatch, and looking forward to action. Hunter was the gun captain of the number two sixteen-inch turret and the man responsible for the main battery gang overall. But Captain Davis asked Hunter to stay on the helm. Lieutenant Hunter would have the conn throughout the day—and the battle—steering the *Washington* for more than twenty-four hours. Other preparations proceeded. Sailors removed paint from ship's surfaces. Every potential flammable substance was being minimized. The other warships did the same.

Bridge lookouts aboard *Washington* first glimpsed Cactus soon after dawn of November 14. Admiral Lee altered course to the west and steered to stay hidden under rain squalls. There were numerous radar contacts with bogeys, and flak fired at one JNAF snooper late that morning. A dispatch from Halsey during the afternoon gave Lee complete freedom of action. Shortly before sunset the force assumed a heading that would take it to Savo Island. The horizon to the northwest was lit by flashes from the last bit of the Tanaka convoy battle. Ching Lee posted his four destroyers in line ahead of the battleships, which steamed with the *Washington* first and *South Dakota* in trail. Admiral Lee suffered from the same weakness as previous U.S. flotillas—and Kondo's: lack of experience working together. His tin cans were simply the four destroyers with Kinkaid that had had the most fuel when Lee detached for his mission. The force steamed due north. Near Savo, Admiral Lee shifted to an easterly course. The sea was dead calm and the sky lit by a bright last-quarter moon.

As he looked for trouble, Lee almost got some. Radiomen heard English-language chatter, uncoded or in codes they did not have. One message reported two battleships, nationality unknown. Ching Lee realized the transmissions were about his own vessels. PT boats were on the prowl and could attack the American fleet at any moment. Lee's nickname, "Ching," came from prewar service in China, where he had been renowned for love of Peking opera and had befriended Marine officer Alex Vandegrift. Admiral Lee now radioed Cactus and got Vandegrift to call off the PT boats. As it happened, this ought not to have been necessary: Several hours earlier Radio Cactus had informed the Tulagi PT base that Task Force 64 could be in the area that evening. Now it was about 9:45 p.m.

Vice Admiral Kondo entered Indispensable Strait at nine o'clock. An hour later, with no sign as yet of Allied warships, Kondo ordered his vessels into tactical array. Expecting cruisers, the admiral provided for his destroyer groups to mass ahead of his main body rather than screen it. With tin cans clearing the way, Kondo would follow and execute his bombardment. Rear Admiral Hashimoto, in the *Sendai*, took three destroyers to make the preliminary sweep past Lunga Point. They would enter east of Savo. Rear Admiral Kimura would skirt the western side of the island with *Nagara* and four destroyers. Kondo kept a pair of tin cans to bring up his rear, and led with his flagship, then *Takao*, followed by *Kirishima*.

On the American side, Rear Admiral Lee had decided to troll for the enemy. He circled Savo, set course toward Lunga, and, at 10:52 p.m., Lee came around to steam along the south side of Savo. To judge from the track charts Imperial Navy officers prepared for U.S. intelligence experts after the war, the Japanese spotted the Americans above Savo while still approaching themselves. At 11:13 the *Sendai* glimpsed ship silhouettes, and she went to battle stations five minutes later. By 11:28 Hashimoto was confident he was looking at two heavy cruisers, and minutes later four tin cans as well. There are claims the *Atago* made visual contact early, but her record is silent on this, and Admiral Kondo took no action. The Japanese chart notes the sighting at 11:17 p.m.

So Rear Admiral Hashimoto's Destroyer Squadron 3 saw the Americans before Lee's radars detected him. The Americans turned west shortly before 11:00. Moments later the *Washington*'s radar detected light cruiser *Sendai* with her destroyers steering past Savo, about nine miles distant. Lee, probably the U.S. Navy's senior expert on electronic systems, elected to await visual contact, which came fifteen minutes later. At 11:16 he signaled his warships to fire when ready. Upon receiving word of the *Sendai* sighting, at 11:15 Kondo changed course to stay north of Savo Island. Kondo clearly intended to keep Savo between his big ships and the U.S. radars until he saw what developed. Captain Morishita Nobue's *Sendai* confirms the Americans opened fire at 11:16. Admiral Hashimoto wasted no time. One minute later he ordered full left rudder, made smoke, and retired to the north. Hashimoto's principal

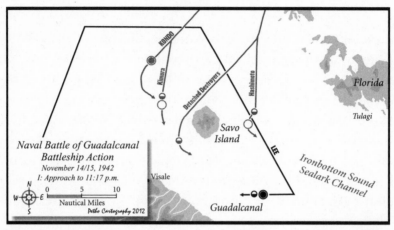

Naval Battle of Guadalcanal
Battleship Action
November 14/15, 1942
I: Approach to 11:17 p.m.

0   5   10
Nautical Miles
Petho Cartography 2012

KONDO
Kimura
Detached Destroyers
Hashimoto
Savo Island
LEE
Florida
Tulagi
Ironbottom Sound
Sealark Channel
Visale
Guadalcanal

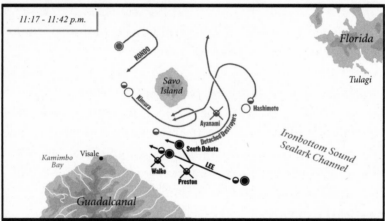

11:17 - 11:42 p.m.

KONDO
Kimura
Savo Island
Hashimoto
Ayanami
Detached Destroyers
South Dakota
Walke
Preston
LEE
Florida
Tulagi
Ironbottom Sound
Sealark Channel
Kamimbo Bay
Visale
Guadalcanal

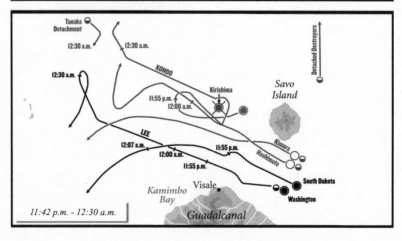

Tanaka Detachment
12:30 a.m.
12:30 a.m.
12:30 a.m.
KONDO
Kirishima
11:55 p.m.
12:00 a.m.
Savo Island
Detached Destroyers
LEE
12:07 a.m.
12:00 a.m.
11:55 p.m.
Kimura
Hashimoto
11:55 p.m.
South Dakota
Washington
Kamimbo Bay
Visale
Guadalcanal
11:42 p.m. - 12:30 a.m.

role became one of keeping Lee's gunners busy. They focused on him until their attention was drawn away. The only ship the Americans touched was Commander Sakuma Eiji's *Ayanami*, engaged by Commander Thomas E. Fraser's *Walke* at 11:22. Lee's battleships checked fire. The *Ayanami* was crippled in less than twenty minutes, though not without launching dreaded Long Lance torpedoes. Destroyer *Uranami* went alongside, took off her crew, and scuttled the *Ayanami* with two tin fish. Sakuma and several dozen men took cutters and went to join the fight on land.

Admiral Kimura's unit did most of the fighting through the first part of the action. Kimura's sailors first launched torpedoes, then opened fire. With the dark fastness of Savo behind the Japanese, Lee's ships at first believed they were engaging shore batteries, but as Kimura maneuvered, the Americans realized the truth. The *Preston* fired on Kimura's flagship until the torpedoes began to strike. At 11:36 Commander Max Stormes of the *Preston* had to abandon ship. The *Gwin* had already been hit in her engine room. In moments Ching Lee's destroyers had fallen to hammer blows. A dozen minutes after Stormes evacuated *Preston,* Lee ordered them to leave. By then only two could respond, and one later sank. Only the damaged *Gwin*, under Lieutenant Commander John B. Fellowes Jr., was to survive.

The battleship action became the main event. By 11:30 Vice Admiral Kondo understood that the U.S. force, if not confronted—he believed, even now, that only cruisers were involved—would pass behind him. Once that happened the Americans would be free to take the approaching Tanaka convoy. A large-scale exchange of gunfire was reported off Savo. Kondo changed to a southwesterly course and ordered battle stations. At 11:35 he received more reports—of a "cruiser" and three destroyers. A few minutes later Kondo altered course to close with the enemy, and at 11:50 he came around to the northwest to parallel them.

At this point the Americans suffered a disaster that was a blessing in disguise. Captain Gatch's *South Dakota* commenced fire at 11:17 on the *Shikinami*, the second ship in Hashimoto's line—and thought her sunk—but after a half dozen salvos the American guns fell silent. *South Dakota*'s chief engineer had tied down the circuit breakers, which put the entire electrical system on a single circuit, instead of many working in parallel. The effect of vibration from firing her own main battery plus the impact of Japanese five-inch shells on *South Dakota*'s superstructure suddenly broke the circuit, and the ship lost all electricity. It was 11:30. Gatch restored power in eight minutes and resumed shooting, while Lee's *Washington* was concealed just behind the tip of Savo when Kondo straightened on his new course. Because she was not firing at that moment, the Japanese did not see her. They had eyes only for the *South Dakota*. Captain Davis's *Washington* would be like a fox loose in a chicken coop.

Kondo received a message sent by the *Ayanami* before her demise. It seemed as if the Long Lance torpedoes were up to their deadly work. The admiral determined to resume his planned bombardment of Henderson Field and led the fleet around to the southeast. Kondo was making between twenty-eight and thirty knots. Within five minutes beginning at 11:52, lookouts on the *Takao*, the *Nagara*, and the flagship all reported U.S. battleships in sight. The *Nagara* accurately observed that there were two. Vice Admiral Kondo professed himself stunned. "The sudden appearance of enemy battleships in that area was utterly beyond my consideration," Kondo later wrote. "Otherwise, I ought to have prepared to launch a systematized night action." As it was, Kondo believed himself overextended. His order for the bombardment had sent Hashimoto's destroyer group ahead on its sweep—the *Sendai* would be off Lunga an hour and a half later—and Kondo's other ships had their hands full with Ching Lee.

Still confused as to the Americans' identity, Vice Admiral Kondo ordered a searchlight lit. Captain Baron Ijuin Matsuji of the *Atago*—another Japanese nobleman in the fleet—opened the shutters of one of his lights a minute after midnight. It focused on the *South Dakota*. The light immediately settled all doubts—but it also brought on the hurricane of Lee's sixteen-inch guns. And Ching Lee had no doubts: he had detected the *Kirishima* in Kondo's line and all the U.S. guns targeted her.

Baron Ijuin's *Atago* and Captain Asakura Bunji's *Takao* both shot at the *South Dakota*, as did Iwabuchi's *Kirishima*. Captain Iwabuchi actually believed his ship had done well, somehow thinking she had hit the *South Dakota* twice on the first salvo and scored at least eight more times, including destroying the target's bridge. *Kirishima*'s gunnery officer even prepared to shift targets after one more salvo. The American battleship was peppered with Japanese shells, but there was only a single fourteen-inch hit on her from Iwabuchi's ship. That would have surprised Lieutenant Commander Tokuno Hiroshi, *Kirishima*'s assistant gunner, who recounted that although his ship had no

gunnery radar—only one of the cruisers present had radar, and that a
primitive search type—she picked out the *South Dakota* and piled on. Tokuno
too thought the American battleship badly hit. But the lighter weapons of
Kondo's cruisers and destroyers could not penetrate *South Dakota*'s armor.
Captain Gatch's vessel suffered all kinds of topside damage yet no critical
hits. Sailors aboard her—like young Ensign R. Sargent Shriver—were astonished at the pounding their ship endured. Wounded by flying shrapnel,
Ensign Shriver earned the Purple Heart. Ten minutes after midnight, Gatch
decided to withdraw and preserve his ship. Meanwhile, Glenn Davis's *Washington* completed the destruction of the *Kirishima*.

Kondo's diffident handling of his fleet became the determining factor. He had Ijuin cease fire after just five minutes—*Atago* expended only
fifty-seven eight-inch shells. Commander Hideshima Narinobu, her gunnery officer, believed that the target (*South Dakota*) was already sinking. The
Takao fired so little she did not bother recording consumption. The fleet
commander's idea was apparently to regain the advantage of darkness to
afford him the chance of a torpedo attack, and beginning at 12:14 a.m. both
cruisers unleashed torpedoes. *Atago* actually fired nineteen of them. Admiral Kimura's *Nagara* plus destroyers were also pursuing the Americans, as
was a division of destroyers that Tanaka sent forward from his convoy. The
long-range torpedo attacks—exactly like the Java Sea battle—achieved
little. Chief of Staff Shiraishi should have been mortified. The *Washington*
turned to evade torpedoes at 12:33. Fearing additional attacks, Ching Lee
left the area, abandoning any further effort to defend Henderson Field.

Kimura's destroyers could still see the *Washington* for more than an hour
after she began her retreat, but Kondo did not order any action. Instead, at
12:32 a.m. he canceled the Henderson bombardment. Fifteen minutes later
the admiral advised Combined Fleet in a dispatch: "GUADALCANAL AT-
TACK FORCE AND THE REINFORCEMENTS ARE ENGAGING WITH
TWO NEW TYPE ENEMY BATTLESHIPS AND SEVERAL CRUISERS AND
DESTROYERS OFF LUNGA . . . TONIGHT'S SHORE BOMBARDMENT
CALLED OFF." At 1:04 Kondo ordered his pursuit ships to execute torpedo
attacks and withdraw. By then the *Washington* had disappeared. An hour afterward the *Sendai* group turned to assist *Kirishima*, but at 2:43 a.m. that effort
was suspended and Rear Admiral Hashimoto headed north.

The final act of this terrible drama was the demise of the *Kirishima*.

Iwabuchi's battleship had been smitten early in the action, her steering spaces so badly damaged she lost rudder control. The battleship turned in circles. Captain Iwabuchi slowed his vessel and attempted to steer with the engines, but that proved futile. Lieutenant Commander Tokuno estimated nine sixteen-inch hits and more than forty from five-inch guns. There were fires everywhere; 90 percent of the engine room gang were dead; leaks aft, though briefly stopped, then disabled all but one screw. Fires approached the forward magazines, which had to be flooded. Eerily, as had happened with *Hiei* in these very waters just two days before, the jammed rudder stymied a perfunctory effort to beach the vessel. Admiral Kimura refused to rig a towline from the *Nagara.* Iwabuchi appealed to higher command to order that the ship be saved, but the progression of flooding mooted that possibility. During the predawn hours *Kirishima* capsized and sank. Iwabuchi and 1,128 seamen were evacuated. Another 300 never came back.

Vice Admiral Kondo's force entered Truk early in the morning of November 18. He estimated nine torpedo hits against U.S. battleships (none were actually made), along with two heavy cruisers and two destroyers sunk, plus another cruiser and a destroyer badly damaged. The Japanese had lost the battleship *Kirishima* and the destroyer *Ayanami.* Actual American losses amounted to three destroyers plus damage to the *South Dakota*, which would return to the United States, out of the war until February 1943. Continuing Japanese confusion as to what had happened—and an implicit claim to heroics—is inherent in the estimate of the Allied force in this battle: Kondo assessed Lee's strength as *four* battleships, two heavy cruisers, and two destroyers. Not only was the estimate considerably larger than Lee's actual force, but the claimed destruction of Allied cruisers included more than the Japanese themselves believed present.

In the propaganda war, the battle of the communiqués continued apace. The U.S. Navy issued a fairly detailed description of the cruiser action but very little on the battleship engagement. In fact, only on November 19 did the Navy admit that American battleships had participated at all. The Japanese description, issued on November 18, modified Kondo's claims but followed his essential description:

> On Nov. 14, while escorting our transport fleet in the face of a
> fierce counterattack by enemy aircraft, the Imperial naval forces

encountered an enemy reinforcement fleet with two battleships and more than four large-size cruisers at a point northwest of the island and at night, after a heated encounter, destroyed the major part of the enemy auxiliary units and heavily damaged two large battleships, routing the enemy fleet in a southerly direction.

Through the sequence of battles from November 12 through 14, the Japanese admitted to the loss of a battleship, a cruiser, and three destroyers, and to sustaining damage on a second battleship and a cruiser. The U.S. Navy texts covering these two battles claimed to have sunk a battleship and damaged two more, sunk eight cruisers and damaged another, and sunk six destroyers while damaging seven more. Both sides could lie with statistics.

Kondo Nobutake explains his decision to terminate the battle in terms very different from his damage claims. The fleet had almost exhausted its torpedoes. He considered that he had achieved substantial results against two battleships, either sinking them or leaving them in a sinking condition. Yet, "[A] continuance of that night engagement in the face of still sound enemy battleships as well as land- and carrier-based air forces, would cause us to subject our fleet to powerful enemy air attacks from early morning . . . [and] consequently would result in sacrificing our important striking force which could hardly be supplemented afterward."

Writing of World War I, Winston Churchill once famously named the commander of Britain's Grand Fleet as the only man on either side who could lose the war in an afternoon. That person, Admiral Sir John Jellicoe, was inclined toward caution, and Churchill sought to explain his attitude. Kondo Nobutake could not make an equivalent claim to importance. Admiral Kondo could not lose the war in an afternoon, so the enormity of stakes did not justify his caution. Moreover, Jellicoe won his war, whereas Kondo and his nation went down to defeat. And while Kondo could not have lost in an afternoon, it might be that Kondo Nobutake *did* lose Japan's war in a month, the month starting at Santa Cruz and ending with the Naval Battle of Guadalcanal.

As seen earlier, at Santa Cruz, Admiral Kondo's halfhearted pursuit of a defeated U.S. carrier force had left the victory incomplete. At the Naval

Battle of Guadalcanal, in his capacity as overall tactical commander, Kondo had exercised weak leadership over Vice Admiral Abe Hiroaki during the first inning of this multiday match. Here was a case where Imperial Navy predilections for subdividing forces was truly counterproductive.

In the second sortie, now known as the "Battleship Action," Kondo held the direct responsibility. By not sailing with all his battlewagons, Admiral Kondo transformed a tactical situation where the Japanese would have held a decisive advantage into one in which the balance was much narrower. But there was more. Kondo's one-day postponement also had a determinant effect. The same sortie carried out the previous night would have left Halsey's battleship force too far away to intervene while his cruiser unit had been destroyed. Kondo could have demolished Henderson at leisure—*before* the Army convoy entered the Cactus Air Force's kill zone. Losses to both Tanaka's convoy and Mikawa's cruisers would have been avoided. Kondo's fuel shortage—his rationale for delay—cries out for much deeper investigation. Even as it was, the Japanese ended the battle with the only warships around Cactus—a success of sorts—to which Kondo responded by leaving the scene rather than pressing on to plaster Henderson.

In fairness to Admiral Kondo, it needs to be said that Japanese experience with previous cruiser bombardments (and this is what he had left after the crippling of the *Kirishima*) had been that these had only had limited impact. Without battleship firepower his fleet would indeed have been in peril. But what needed to be taken into account were the strategic considerations: Was it worth Kondo's *entire force* to ensure the safe landing of the Army troops on Guadalcanal? After the heavy losses to the Tanaka convoy during the daylight hours, probably not. Before them, assuredly so. This intermediate observation puts additional weight on the first sortie, the Abe mission. That too could have been beefed up—and Kondo could have sailed in closer support. He did not. And his delay of the second foray had the same consequence. Failure to cripple the Cactus Air Force brought Yamamoto's entire Z-Day strategic plan to naught.

The common denominators in all of Kondo's actions and omissions are two, both subsumed in his defense of leaving the Battleship Action: fear of airpower, and the sense that the Navy was a limited, irreplaceable quantity. Allied airpower could not be discounted. World War II brought the ascendancy of the warplane, and sailors ignored that at their peril. In the Battleship Action too, the distant presence of the *Enterprise* functioned as a wild card—Henderson Field was not the sole Allied asset. But that brings back the consequences of failed pursuit at Santa Cruz. Had Kinkaid's remaining carrier—the *Enterprise*—been trapped there, Halsey would have had *no* wild card now. On one (tactical) level Kondo's respect for aircraft was healthy, but strategically, in this situation, caution played against Japanese purposes. And Kondo Nobutake, as C-in-C Second Fleet, was a strategic commander.

Admiral Kondo's sense of the Imperial Navy as a limited quantity was also accurate on one level but detrimental at another. Starting from Pearl Harbor, Japanese strategy recognized that the Allies, in particular the United States, had far superior productive capacity. The essence of Japan's maneuver had been that its force be used to secure a predominance to play upon during the near term. The Solomons was the first big Allied offensive and Guadalcanal its opening act. To defeat that would set back the enemy's rising curve. If nothing else it would gain time for the weapons designers and shipyards to introduce the new plane designs and aircraft carriers that might give the Navy a fighting chance. The Japanese Empire hung in the balance. From a Japanese perspective, this was the time and here the place to hazard everything. Tokyo's chances would never again be as good. This was as true for the warships Kondo so zealously guarded as for the quality of Japanese pilots or their numbers relative to the Allies.

In short, the month from Santa Cruz to the Naval Battle of Guadalcanal should be seen as the instant when the pendulum began to swing in the Pacific war—and Admiral Kondo Nobutake was central to that development. Japan's inability to capitalize on success at Santa Cruz set the downward trend in motion.

These are judgments of history. At the time Imperial Navy officers, perhaps carried away by outlandish claims of the size of the enemy fleet and those for damage inflicted, seem to have thought the Naval Battle of Guadalcanal some kind of a victory. If so, they indulged in the same sort of misplaced pride as Americans who claimed too much for Santa Cruz. Perhaps the two acts of assertion cancel each other out. But for Japanese who considered the engagement a victorious one, it must have been shameful that immediately afterward the fleet needed to shift into emergency mode to funnel mere scraps of food onto Starvation Island. Had the result been as advertised, a triumphant Navy ought to have been able to succor Guadalcanal with impunity.

On the American side there were no doubts—immediately afterward William F. Halsey was promoted to four-star admiral, breaking a tradition that there be only a certain number at this rank in the U.S. Navy. Halsey sent his old stars to the widows of admirals Callaghan and Scott with testimonials that their husbands had won him his new ones.

Kondo Nobutake faced no consequences for his actions or the lack of them. Six months later Kondo still led the Second Fleet. His treatment contrasts vividly with that doled out to subordinates Abe Hiroaki of the battleship division and Nishida Masao of the *Hiei*. Abe was relieved in December, not surprising, since both his warships lay at the bottom of the sea. Yamamoto and Ugaki had previously lobbied the Navy Ministry for better treatment of officers whose vessels were sunk—Japan could not fight effectively if every captain knew he had to go down with his ship or commit *seppuku* once having lost it. But neither admiral lifted a finger to block the ministry when it convened disciplinary boards to investigate Abe and Nishida. Abe could retire. Captain Nishida was exiled to the small Chinese port of Amoy as a local force commander. By way of another comparison, Captain Iwabuchi of the *Kirishima* was immediately reemployed to lead naval troops on New Georgia and later given an important base force command at Manila, which he defended against the Allies when MacArthur returned to the Philippines. Iwabuchi received posthumous promotion to Vice Admiral, plus the Order of the Golden Kite, First Class.

At Truk on November 22, the Combined Fleet reviewed this sequence of battles. The exaggerated claims for losses were still credited. Commanders and staff, to include Admiral Ugaki, argued that the Imperial Navy had been at a disadvantage in all these actions and had done reasonably well. Admiral Kondo commented that officers could not rise above their conscious knowledge so the best training remained necessary to ensure that when the test came leaders would instinctively choose the right course. Ugaki was more practical. It had to be recognized that the reinforcement mission had failed, and Japanese forces now faced acute difficulties. Steady

Savo Island looms behind the American destroyer escorting the Guadalcanal invasion fleet as the task force reaches its destination, August 7, 1942. These were the waters of Ironbottom Sound.

Allied strike aircraft made the Solomons arena a zone of terror for the Japanese. Among the most redoubtable was the Douglas SBD Dauntless dive-bomber, mainstay of carrier air groups and Marine air wings throughout the campaign. Here a group of SBDs flies in close formation. Two planes sport auxiliary gas tanks but none carries a bomb.

Henderson Field, late August. There are no hangars and just a few open-sided sheds in which to perform maintenance work. The "Pagoda" control facility is visible just right of center. Roughly twenty American aircraft are on the field. This photo, taken from a plane that had just launched, shows eight others (in several flights of three) lining up to take off or taxiing behind them.

Marines were beset by their initial lack of supplies, and benefited enormously from captured materiél. Here Marines confer next to a Japanese-made 75mm antiaircraft gun.

American defenses took a steady toll on the Japanese Naval Air Force. Marines pose holding the wing of a destroyed Japanese aircraft. A PBY Catalina scoutplane is visible in the upper left-hand corner behind them, and two F-4F fighters are at the center just above the wing of the downed enemy plane.

The Japanese also made their marks. This is the wreckage of a Dauntless dive-bomber destroyed on Henderson Field. Parking it among the palms has not protected it. Note the gasoline drum. Allied ground crews had to refuel aircraft by hand until late in the campaign.

Bloody Ridge, September 14, 1942. A Marine surveys the detritus of battle from Colonel Edson's second position. Here the Marine Raiders and Paratroops halted the Japanese penetration of their initial defenses. The Japanese never got closer to Henderson Field than on that savage night. Ammunition crates scattered along the crest testify to the fight's intensity.

Desperate Japanese sailors ran the transport *Kyushu Maru* onto the beach at Tassafaronga Point on the night of October 14/15. Ammunition in her hold blew up, and Allied bombers finished the job. Her derelict hull marked the frustration of Japanese supply efforts at Guadalcanal.

The formidable Zero fighter became the single most important aircraft in the Japanese arsenal, flying from both carriers and land bases. Here, at the Battle of Santa Cruz, the Zero unit slotted to escort the Japanese first strike against the U.S. fleet prepares to launch from carrier *Shokaku*.

Captain Osborne Hardison maneuvers the *Enterprise* at the Battle of Santa Cruz, October 25, 1942, escaping a near miss in the carrier's wake. A destroyer, probably the *Smith,* is firing flak from her main battery. Smooth seas and scattered clouds show the ideal conditions under which this action occurred.

Enterprise, after sustaining early hits, is visibly emitting smoke from her hangar deck. This sequence of photographs was taken from battleship *South Dakota.*

The task force, maneuvering wildly, with the *Enterprise* on an opposite course, sustaining a near miss to port. Smoke is visible abaft her island superstructure. The ship is heeling, possibly listing, to starboard. Which it may be is not clear due to the "Big E's" course changes.

Brave damage-control efforts stopped the blazes aboard *Enterprise* and restored her ability to conduct flight operations. With the carrier now on a straight course to recover aircraft (an SBD is lost over the side at the moment of this photo), and her fires extinguished, it is revealed that the "Big E" indeed lists to starboard.

The USS *Hornet* in happy days, off Pearl Harbor in April 1942, after her return from the Doolittle Raid. Zooming past is a pair of then-newfangled PT boats. These swift patrol craft became a nemesis to the Japanese in the Solomons, who began to call them "devil boats."

A Japanese Kate torpedo bomber shoots past the heavy cruiser *Pensacola* and lines up for her attack run against the *Hornet*. The plane's deadly payload can be seen slung beneath her fuselage.

The heavy cruiser *Chikuma* under way at high speed at the Battle of Santa Cruz, her exhaust plume clearly visible from nearly overhead. This ship would endure the heaviest of all the American attacks that day.

The *Hornet* suffered considerable damage and blazing fires. Crewmen formed bucket brigades to fight the conflagrations. Sailors gained the upper hand when U.S. destroyers closed in to help with their high-capacity hoses. After that, the *Pensacola* attempted to tow the aircraft carrier away. In this picture *Pensacola* is off *Hornet*'s bow and a destroyer alongside. The lack of apparent damage misled enemy scouts, who reported a third U.S. carrier in the area, which had a key impact on Japanese decisions.

Afternoon attacks and additional damage kindled new fires aboard the *Hornet*, and she was judged beyond recovery. Smoke blows across the deck as destroyers stand by to evacuate crewmen. Sailors awaiting rescue dot the *Hornet*'s flight deck in this photo taken from the *Pensacola*.

In the aftermath of the surface battle off Tassafaronga, the heavy cruiser *Minneapolis* limped into Tulagi with her bow nearly sheared off. She remained until crewmen could jury-rig a flood barrier and torch off the wreckage crippling the ship. Here the *Minneapolis* appears under camouflage nets strung to fool the Japanese. Her bow is missing ahead of the forward gun turret.

For a time in the wake of Santa Cruz, the damaged *Enterprise* and then the *Saratoga* were in succession the only aircraft carriers available in the South Pacific. From Britain the United States obtained the loan of the HMS *Victorious* to fill the gap until new American flattops began joining the fleet. Here the *Victorious* lies at anchor at Nouméa in July 1943, watched from the veranda of the officers club, part of a recreational complex built at Ducos Cove by the crews of the *Saratoga* and the light cruiser *San Juan*.

Light cruiser *Helena* was an exemplar of the class of warships capable of delivering fire at an enormous rate. Some crewmen called her the "Tiger of the Slot." Off New Georgia on July 6, 1943, the *Helena* fell victim to Japanese torpedoes at the Battle of Kula Gulf.

At Kula Gulf the Japanese destroyer *Nagatsuki,* a hero of the earlier torpedo battle of Tassafaronga, ran aground while attempting to escape. Here she is stuck off Kolombangara, where the vessel was pounded by Allied aircraft.

The shifting pendulum: Just seven months after Tassafaronga, a battle that had eliminated the Allied cruiser force in the South Pacific, a similar level of damage at Kula Gulf left SOPAC striking power little impaired. On July 8, 1943, days after that engagement, a sailor aboard the destroyer *O'Bannon* snapped this picture of Task Force 18, another cruiser-destroyer unit, under way in the Slot.

War in the Pacific brought culture shock to indigenous populations. Here, in December 1943, Melanesians gape at the second American aircraft to alight on Mili atoll. While that was not in the Solomons, indigenous responses were quite similar.

The Grumman TBF Avenger, with its great survivability, longer range, and good payload, became one of the most effective Allied strike aircraft. Japanese sailors dreaded the planes, which seemed to be everywhere.

One of the last Japanese successes: The *John H. Couch,* one of two Liberty ships hit off Guadalcanal on October 11, 1943, was badly damaged and would finally sink.

The invasion of Bougainville on November 1, 1943, Operation Shoestring II, brought Admiral Halsey's South Pacific forces to the very parapets of Fortress Rabaul. Behind the broaching landing craft, note others headed for shore, and the anchored attack transports behind them. Techniques that had been novelties at Guadalcanal were now deeply ingrained.

Warships of Admiral Merrill's Task Force 39 at anchor off Tulagi. That place became a major waypoint for SOPAC operations and launching pad for forays up the Slot. Three light cruisers are in this picture, taken in July. Merrill's force also sailed for Bougainville from Tulagi. His firepower would be formidable at the Battle of Empress Augusta Bay on the night of November 1, 1943.

Rear Admiral Aaron S. Merrill on the deck of light cruiser *Montpelier,* receiving the Navy Cross for his actions at Empress Augusta Bay.

Determined to prevail in a direct strike on Fortress Rabaul, Rear Admiral Frederick C. Sherman's carriers *Saratoga (in the foreground)* and *Princeton* practice antiaircraft gunnery against a target sleeve towed by a Dauntless flown off the *Sara,* as she was affectionately known.

Heading for Rabaul, the *Saratoga* prepares her aircraft while planes from the *Princeton* protect the task force.

Pre-attack briefing in the ready room of carrier *Saratoga* on the morning of November 5, 1943. Commander Henry H. Caldwell of the *Sara's* air group was overall strike leader, directing the attack formation.

The first in a series of photos taken from Caldwell's TBF aircraft. The strike commander passes Crater Peninsula before turning in to guide the carrier planes over Rabaul town (*concealed under the cloud formation at center right*) and into Simpson Harbor. Just above the wing are the volcanic mounts known as Daughter and Mother. Past them, across the harbor mouth, is the crater of the volcano named Vulcan. Most Japanese vessels are at anchor with just a few in Blanche Bay. Only one major warship (*center left*) is showing a wake, heading east-southeast. (Refer to position A on the Fortress Rabaul map on page 341.)

The gathering storm: Caldwell's view just at the turn for the assault. Lakunai airfield is beyond the plane's left wing. Several Imperial Navy vessels are in motion. Cruisers have cast off from the oilers in the right-hand section of Simpson Harbor. Photographer's Mate Paul T. Barnett noted the time as eleven twenty a.m. The Avenger will turn southeast and fly down Crater Peninsula for Commander Caldwell to direct the action. (Refer to position B on the Fortress Rabaul map on page 341.)

Hornet's Nest: Mate Barnett snaps a picture showing numerous Japanese ships on the move. Flak bursts over Simpson Harbor. Two heavy cruisers (*center*) are about to debouche from its mouth; a third, with two speeding vessels ahead of her, is out and approaches Praed Point (*right foreground*). A number of ships are passing Vulcan Crater (*middle, left of center*) and one of them displays the black smoke of a bomb hit. Inside Simpson Harbor, a heavy cruiser is clearly on fire and two smaller ships show signs of damage. Caldwell's aircraft is almost directly above Praed Point. (Refer to position C on the Fortress Rabaul map on page 341.)

Commander Caldwell flies over St. George's Channel and circles to observe. Barnett's photo shows the Japanese vessels off Praed Point now hugging the coast along Crater Peninsula. Behind them a heavy cruiser in Blanche Bay is hit and on fire. Imperial Navy vessels scatter in all directions. (Refer to position D on the Fortress Rabaul map on page 341.)

A short time later, Caldwell is headed back into the mouth of Blanche Bay to open the view into the inner harbor, behind Crater Peninsula. One Japanese heavy cruiser is out into the open sea of St. George's Channel, another warship behind her just past Raluana Point. Most ships have cleared Simpson Harbor, but a heavy cruiser is ablaze near the exit to Blanche Bay. Zero fighters jumped Caldwell's TBF shortly after this picture was taken. Photographer Paul Barnett died, and the plane's gunner was wounded. Caldwell would land back aboard *Sara* on one wheel and with no control of flaps or aileron, a remarkable feat. (Refer to position E on the Fortress Rabaul map on page 341.)

Fighter pilots Lieutenant (junior grade) H. D. Fechtelkotter and Lieutenant "Bus" Albert of VF-12 report to *Saratoga*'s air intelligence officer following the Rabaul raid.

December 1943: Admiral Halsey visits the *Sara* once she returns to Nouméa. Here he toasts Admiral Sherman and salutes the Rabaul results.

March 1944: The siege ring around Fortress Rabaul is completed with Allied airstrips such as this one at Cape Torokina on Bougainville. Note the considerable air strength, with many Corsair fighters and other aircraft parked along the flight line.

supply could be ensured only by positioning air forces at new forward bases. The Japanese were already attempting to install them.

THE PENDULUM AND THE PIT

Perfectly predictable, the aftermath of Admiral Kondo's withdrawal from battle brought great pain to the Japanese. The Cactus Air Force and American artillery pulled out every stop to blast the transports their adversary had fought so hard to get to Guadalcanal. Stacks of stores landed from the beached ships were also shelled. Commander Emura reported through the day on November 15: At 9:00 a.m., two of the beached transports were burning; at 10:15 all of them were aflame; later several Allied destroyers were bombarding the area. A certain number of troops joined General Hyakutake, but not as a fresh infantry division in battle trim. Messages reported the salvage of 360 cases of ammunition for field guns and 1,500 bales of rice—just a few days' supply. On November 20 senior staff officer Kuroshima returned from a visit to the front. Captain Kuroshima warned that men at Rabaul were in despair. The pendulum hovered and Japanese were in the pit.

Americans on Guadalcanal, if not despairing, at least continued to feel themselves beset by the enemy. At the Cactus Crystal Ball, radioman Philip Jacobsen insists that through the end of the campaign the South Pacific bastion never experienced a moment of diminished threat. But in the map rooms of the high command, the tense atmosphere softened into one of opportunity, not desperation. There is an almost palpable sense of elation. Here is the CINCPAC war diary for the day after Kondo's battle: "It is now definite that the enemy offensive was completely stopped . . . it appears that now is the time to move in supplies and to relieve the tired Marine amphibious troops." Pearl Harbor knew that carrier *Saratoga* was crossing the equator on her way to SOPAC. With her was the battleship *North Carolina*. Both had been healed of their wounds. The older battlewagons *Colorado* and *New Mexico* lay at Fiji. Another new battleship, the *Indiana*, was transiting the Panama Canal. Two new escort carriers, two cruisers, and a passel of destroyers in the Atlantic had been alerted for Pacific duty. Aircraft reinforcements were arriving in increased numbers. The war had begun shifting in Allied favor.

The admirals had no difficulty attributing the margin of difference to the pillars of intelligence. At Pearl Harbor, Nimitz issued a commendation, perforce sent over the classified Copek circuit:

ONCE AGAIN RADIO INTELLIGENCE HAS ENABLED THE FIGHTING FORCE OF THE PACIFIC AND SOUTHWEST PACIFIC TO KNOW WHERE AND WHEN TO HIT THE ENEMY. MY ONLY REGRET IS THAT OUR APPRECIATION, WHICH IS UNLIMITED, CAN ONLY BE EXTENDED TO THOSE WHO READ THIS SYSTEM.

From COMINCH in Washington, Admiral Ernest J. King added, "Well Done."

The contrasting desperation among the Japanese is evident in the sudden switch of Imperial Navy submarines to supply work. Starvation, now rampant on Guadalcanal, demanded no less. The I-boats had been some of the Navy's best weapons—contrary to the impression of the Japanese submarine force as ineffectual, subs had sunk an aircraft carrier and two cruisers, and crippled another flattop and battleship, results on a par with those of the *Kido Butai*. In using subs for supply purposes, the Combined Fleet weakened its blockade of Torpedo Junction, advantaging the Allies. This diversion of combat forces shrank Japanese naval power without the Allies doing anything at all, virtual attrition akin to the reduced capability that followed the use of destroyers on the Tokyo Express. Combined Fleet issued the order to cut back the blockade and use the submarines for supplies on November 16. That date, immediately after the Naval Battle of Guadalcanal, testifies to Yamamoto's realization of the changed balance. Four days later the fleet learned of a new Allied convoy steaming through Torpedo Junction to Cactus. It was unable to respond. That furnished yet more evidence of the new conditions.

The Sixth Fleet, Japan's submarine force, was loath to accept supply duty. With his flag in light cruiser *Katori* at Truk, Vice Admiral Marquis Komatsu Teruhisa convened his senior officers to consider the task. Submariners uniformly opposed halting war patrols to become underwater trucks. Komatsu's staff, led by Rear Admiral Mito Hisachi and Captain Kanaoka Tomojiro, participated in the heated discussion. Komatsu finally held up his hand. "Our Army troops . . . are starving on Guadalcanal. They used the last of their rations several days ago. More than a hundred men are dying from hunger daily. Many of the rest are eating grass. Very few men are fit for fighting." Komatsu looked around the wardroom. "What are we to do," he asked, "let our countrymen starve to death in the jungle?" The answer was obvious: "We must help them, no matter what sacrifices must be made in doing so!"

Use of the subs proved awkward from the start. I-boats were not designed as cargomen and lacked storage capacity or such equipment as cranes—except those designed to carry seaplanes. Diverting *those*, of course, meant cutting into Japanese scouting potential. Manhandling the cargo was slow, cumbersome, and, when subs were unloading at Guadalcanal, with the Cactus Air Force close by, dangerous. But each boatload meant two days' sustenance for men on the island. The one distinct advantage of undersea transport was that vessels could approach shielded from attack until the last moment.

Supply specialists quickly hit upon a new technique: cleaning out oil barrels, loading them half-full with rice or matériel, then resealing them. The drums had buoyancy and would float. Sailors aboard *Yamato* experimented and confirmed feasibility. The drums could simply be tossed overboard for collection by men onshore or in motorboats. This limited the necessity to anchor and reduced vulnerability. It simplified unloading, though it also introduced supply collection difficulties—drums could drift away, and improperly sealed ones would sink. The men on Starvation Island also did not always have boats available for the recovery task, and sometimes lacked the strength to handle barrels on the beach. A further innovation greatly eased the unloading problem—strings of fifty drums could be tied together and lashed to the deck. Then submariners needed only emerge, cut the lashings, and the drum strings would float as the I-boat submerged. It was not long until the drum strings were in use on both subs and destroyers. Then Buna, on New Guinea, was added to the destinations. Tin cans, which quickly adopted the method also, typically carried four of the drum strings. Motorboats would recover them; then work parties of 200 men would roll them ashore.

The first submarine supply mission was carried out by Commander Nishino Kozo's *I-17.* She stopped to load at Rabaul and then headed for Guadalcanal. Orbiting aircraft and nearby PT boats stymied his initial attempt on November 24, but the next night Nishino succeeded in delivering about eleven tons at Kamimbo. Each night thereafter brought another sub. The procedure soon became loading at Buin and sailing to the western tip of Guadalcanal. The subs typically carried twenty to thirty-two tons, and sixteen trips succeeded in the first month. The chief of staff of the Seventeenth Army, Lieutenant General Miyazaki Shuichi, estimated that more than 20,000 supply drums were carried to Guadalcanal, but only 20 to 30 percent of them actually reached the troops. Postwar inquiries determined that approximately 300 tons of supplies were delivered to Guadalcanal in this fashion. Other studies find submarine transports conveyed 1,115 tons to the island—very close to Miyazaki's estimate.

Despite every precaution, submarine supply remained dangerous. The very first sub delivery had been cut short by the approach of American destroyer *McCalla*, which shot up the barges off Kamimbo and shelled the midget submarine base there. On the night of December 9, Lieutenant Jack Searles in the *PT-59* was on patrol off Kamimbo when he saw a surfaced I-boat, with barges shuttling from the shore. Commander Togami Ichiro's *I-3*, on her fourth supply run, was out of luck. Searles fired a pair of torpedoes. One crumpled the sub's stern. Togami's boat sank with all hands. Before the end of the campaign at least three more submarines would be lost on Guadalcanal supply sorties, off the beach or while returning from their missions. PT boats also routinely looked for floating drums, which they sank with machine guns and automatic cannon.

The I-boat gambit can only be seen as an expedient. Submarines could never move the quantities required for subsistence, much less to wage battle. That could be done only by surface ships, hence the Tokyo Express. It did not take Admiral Mikawa long to realize this, and he promptly ordered new destroyer missions. Mikawa had a free hand, since, during the last part of November, Combined Fleet was preoccupied with the fighting at Buna. The Eighth Fleet commander assigned Rear Admiral Tanaka to the effort, and planned a series of five Tokyo Express runs at three-day intervals to be confined to delivering supply drums. The critical inaugural sortie would establish the method.

Admiral Tanaka recalled destroyers on the Buna run and began preparations for his Tokyo Express. A practice exercise showed that the drum strings could be pushed overboard and recovered by barge operators. Tanaka summoned his officers to go over the mission. Briefings indicated that the Army had consumed its staples and would exhaust its supplies before the end of the month. Tanaka planned to take eight destroyers, six loaded with barrel strings, in all 1,089 drums. He himself would sail in Commander Kumabe Tsutae's ship *Naganami.* There would also be a guardship, the *Takanami.* Both would carry full armament and be prepared to fight. The other vessels were stripped of torpedo reloads to reduce weight and free space for the drum strings. The Tokyo Express left Shortland soon after midnight on November 29–30. To outfox snoopers, Tanaka spent the morning steaming east before setting course for Cactus and Kamimbo Bay. Sure enough the aerial scouts kept watch. About noon the Tokyo Express changed its heading and went to twenty-four knots, and, hidden under rain clouds at midafternoon, accelerated to thirty knots.

SOPAC prepared a hot reception. Bull Halsey had reconstituted his cruiser-destroyer force as Task Force 67 under Admiral Kinkaid. The latter, finding the old problem of scratch units of ships that were strangers, had begun to whip them into shape when Nimitz suddenly recalled Kinkaid for the North Pacific command. Rear Admiral Carleton H. Wright succeeded him at the head of Task Force 67. In between exercises at Espíritu Santo, he compiled a generic battle plan. At 7:40 p.m. on November 29, Admiral Halsey ordered Wright to raise steam to intercept a Japanese force of eight destroyers and, possibly, half a dozen transports. At 11:00 p.m. SOPAC sent the execute order, telling Wright to place his ships off Cape Tassafaronga twenty-four hours later.

Although research has yet to uncover the actual intercept, this information had to be from radio intelligence. The precision of the notice, enumerating Tanaka's exact force and its expected position a day in advance, leaves no room for doubt. Even the error in the warning—the mention of transports—suggests that the codebreakers, whose garble had the correct numbers for both the overall force and the loaded ships, but mistook cargomen for destroyer-transports. Halsey's staff, well aware of previous Japanese attempts to get convoys to Cactus, filled in the blanks. The American PT boats at Tulagi were also ordered to stand down in the expectation that heavy ships would slug it out in Ironbottom Sound—more evidence of advance knowledge. Ultra had struck again. Wright left Espíritu only an hour later than Tanaka departed Shortland. By 3:00 a.m. on November 30, Wright's Task Force 67 was at twenty-seven knots on its way through Torpedo Junction, where Japanese submarines had been thinned out.

Tanaka Raizo would not be taken by surprise. The simple fact that air reconnaissance had seen his Tokyo Express warned Tanaka that there could be opposition. At midafternoon he learned from JNAF scouts of numerous Allied destroyers off Lunga Point. The Eighth Fleet communications unit also warned Tanaka of transmissions indicating heavy ships in the vicinity. Tanaka had his destroyers clear for action and instructed them that if battle eventuated, the force would fight without thought of unloading.

That is exactly what happened. Tanaka's two transport units had broken formation and were on the verge of putting out their drum strings when, at 11:12 p.m., Commander Ogura Masami's *Takanami* came on the radio to report enemy ships, shortly afterward seven destroyers. Admiral Tanaka suspended unloading and ordered battle stations. Aircraft flares suddenly illuminated the Japanese and, at 11:20, Wright's warships began shooting. Commander Kumabe's *Naganami* turned to parallel the Americans. *Takanami* launched her torpedoes, and both destroyers, plus Lieutenant Commander Shibayama Kazuo's *Suzukaze*, replied shell for shell, setting two American destroyers ablaze. The U.S. fleet shone in the light of the burning ships. Tanaka's destroyers put their Long Lances into the water all down the line.

Admiral Wright plotted his assault carefully. The heavy cruiser *Minneapolis* actually acquired the first target at 11:06, and the force commander adjusted his dispositions. Ten minutes later Wright's destroyer leader asked to make the torpedo attack. Judging the range, then 14,600 yards, excessive for U.S. torpedoes, Wright asked him to wait. He delayed, in part, due to his own confusion—sailors assured him the Japanese were destroyers—there were no transports to be seen. The distance was down to 7,600 yards at 11:20 when the admiral freed everyone for a general assault.

The battle had all the confusion and floundering that characterized night combat, save that Japanese tactics worked while American ones did not. Tanaka's lookouts erroneously identified a battleship among Wright's fleet, which had only cruisers and destroyers. American cruiser *Pensacola* picked out a Japanese *Mogami*- or *Yubari*-class cruiser to shoot, yet no such ships were present. The *Pensacola* was really firing at light cruiser *Honolulu*.

Japanese Long Lances ran hot and true. Admiral Wright's flagship, the heavy cruiser *Northampton*, practically blew up, the consequence of a magazine explosion following a Long Lance hit. Three of Wright's other big ships, heavy cruisers *Minneapolis*, *New Orleans*, and *Pensacola*, were all torpedoed. American destroyers waited their tin fish launches but eventually made them. The *Naganami*, at least, had to evade torpedoes. Tanaka emerged feeling that only high speed—Commander Kumabe had raced at thirty-five knots—prevented *Naganami* from being hit. Not so the *Takanami*, carrying the chief of Destroyer Division 31, Captain Shimizu Toshiro. Splitting off from the rest, Shimizu deliberately ordered her into danger. American shells blasted *Takanami* to smithereens.

Typical track charts drawn for this battle portray the Tanaka force acting in concert as a single unit. Yet according to Japanese records compiled after the war, this wasn't the case. In addition to *Naganami*'s turn to port, *Kawakaze* and *Suzukaze* split to starboard, while the four vessels of Captain Sato Torajiro's Destroyer Division 15 continued ahead, eventually breaking into two groups and advancing toward the Americans. Captain Toyama Yasumi, Tanaka's chief of staff, exercised the tactical command through these evolutions. Given chart positions, times of launch, and when U.S. ships recorded hits, the Long Lances that inflicted the most grievous harm came from Tanaka's flagship, Lieutenant Commander Wakabayashi Kazuo's *Kawakaze*, and Commander Hajime Takeuchi's *Kuroshio*, though several of her torpedoes seem to have detonated in transit. All operated independently at the moment of launch. Sato's ships divided into two groups, and *Oyashio* with *Kuroshio* probably loosed the torpedoes that sank *Northampton*.

By about 2:00 a.m., Admiral Tanaka had re-formed his unit and begun withdrawing. Most torpedoes had been used up, and he was low on ammunition. The remaining Japanese destroyers arrived at Shortland at 10:30 a.m. the next morning. Under Rear Admiral Mahlon S. Tisdale in the *Honolulu*, the American fleet licked its wounds back in Ironbottom Sound, preparing damaged warships to get them to Nouméa, where preliminary repairs could be accomplished.

This Battle of Tassafaronga, undeniably a Japanese victory, had been won despite the Allied intelligence advantage, considerable U.S. material superiority, the technological marvel of radar, *and* SOPAC's preparation of the battlefield. But the Imperial Navy delivered no supplies that night. Tanaka Raizo never lived that down. Years later, visited by one of his former ship captains, Tanaka shed tears for the *Takanami*, which absorbed all the punishment during the first critical moments, making the rest possible. "It was an error on my part not to have delivered the supplies on schedule," Tanaka told Hara Tameichi in 1957. "I should have returned to do so. The delivery mission was abandoned simply because we did not have accurate information about the strength of the enemy."

As the Japanese on Guadalcanal continued to starve, Bull Halsey poured it on. The 5,500 troops landed during the period of the Naval Battle of Guadalcanal gave the Allies an edge. The Cactus Air Force grew to 188 aircraft—and Halsey hastened preparations for B-17 heavy bombers to fly from Cactus on a routine basis. The Army's 164th Regiment would be followed by the full Americal Division, led by Major General J. Lawton Collins. Some units of the 2nd Marine Division also went to Cactus. General Vandegrift was told to prepare his men to pull out beginning on November 26. The idea that the Americans on Guadalcanal could rotate their troops, while the Japanese could not even feed theirs, confirms the changed strategic balance. Commander Ohmae Toshikazu of Mikawa's staff went to the island after Santa Cruz to help organize a renewed offensive. There Ohmae encountered the ubiquitous Colonel Tsuji. The fit, well-fed figures of Ohmae and his assistant disgusted Tsuji, who saw walking skeletons all around him.

Meanwhile the pendulum began to acquire momentum. SOPAC commanders pushed hard. An advance across the Matanikau River began just as the battleship guns fell silent. Except for some Marine preliminaries, this weeklong attack would be carried out by U.S. Army troops. Among the Japanese soldiers driven back was the 16th Infantry, hailing from Admiral Yamamoto's home prefecture. At Truk, trying to lighten the mood surrounding the Combined Fleet staff's initial meetings with the new leaders of the Southeast Area Army and Eighteenth Army, Yamamoto tried to joke about his hometown regiment. Admiral Ugaki told him to shut up.

Strength returns in late November showed that little more than 40 percent of the Japanese Army and Navy troops on Guadalcanal were still in the ranks. There were more than 6,000 wounded and sick. By early December, General Miyazaki would note later, Japanese troops were in such need of ammunition they hardly shot back except in the direst circumstances. Captain Monzen Kanae, the Navy's senior officer on Guadalcanal, sent a note to Admiral Ugaki by the hand of Lieutenant Funashi, who was returning to the *Yamato*, reporting shortages that had gone beyond the limit of endurance.

With supplies more critical than ever, the Navy ran another Tokyo Express on December 3. This time Tanaka brought ten destroyers. Despite coastwatcher warnings, the only opposition came from the Cactus Air Force, which inflicted slight damage on Commander Hitomi Toyoji's *Makinami*. Admiral Tanaka took a dozen destroyers on the Express run of December 7, when Allied aircraft were joined by PT boats. Whereas the first sortie had gone off without a hitch, this time PTs induced part of Tanaka's force—Captain Sato's Destroyer Division 15, which had covered itself in glory at Tassafaronga—to give up its resupply mission. For the successful destroyers, ropes attaching some barrel strings broke and made them impossible to recover. Two tin cans were damaged. After this fiasco, Navy officers from the Solomons and the Combined Fleet informed Army staff at Rabaul that the Tokyo Express would have to stand down. Horrified, General Imamura Hitoshi, the new Eighth Area Army commander, appealed to Tokyo and begged the Navy to relent. The Army-Navy differences sharpened after December 9, with the loss of the *I-3*, when the fleet suspended submarine transport as well.

Admirals Kusaka and Mikawa agreed on one more Tanaka unit mission. Aviation ship *Chitose*, which had furnished air cover for both previous operations, needed to leave for Empire waters for conversion to an aircraft carrier. The new Express required stronger escort, so five of the eleven vessels on the December 11 run functioned as guard ships. Tanaka took no chances—good for him, since this time Ultra warned SOPAC and precisely outlined Tanaka's force.

As a result of the Tassafaronga disaster, however, Bull Halsey no longer had a usable cruiser force to put against the Express. But the aggressive SOPAC commander had no problem with that. Marine dive-bombers accosted Tanaka coming down The Slot, but they came away with no score. That night the PTs went out and boats *-37*, *-40*, and *-48* let fly their torpedoes, gaining a solid hit on flagship *Teruzuki*. The fish impacted her stern, wrecking the rudder and one propeller shaft, and ignited a fire that spread to an after magazine, which exploded. Admiral Tanaka, wounded, transferred to destroyer *Naganami*. Only a few of the barrel strings ever reached the troops. Tanaka, once recovered, was reassigned to Singapore. Command of the Reinforcement Unit was realigned. On December 20 the JNAF began diverting some bomber aircraft to parachute supply bundles on moonlit nights. The Navy's cancellation of Tokyo Express stuck.

The events of mid-November did not dissuade Imperial General Head-quarters. The concept for a big new offensive was refined into a formal plan that the Navy General Staff promulgated in its Directive No. 159 on November 18. This called for the preparation of new airfields in the lower Solomons that, when ready, would enable the Japanese to regain air superiority over Guadalcanal, after which Army troops could capture Henderson Field and Tulagi. Operations on New Guinea would follow. The offensive would be timed for January 1943. Admiral Yamamoto's early conversations with General Imamura had focused on this scheme. But barely a month later IGHQ reversed itself. During this period of five weeks, Tokyo conducted its first true strategic review of the war.

At Truk, the assumptions built into the plan did not sit right with Ugaki Matome, though the Fleet proceeded assiduously with such elements as building a new lower Solomons airfield. Admiral Ugaki feared that the Army's fixation on Guadalcanal might pull the Navy into a bottomless quagmire. He recognized New Guinea as more important, but reinforcing there seemed hopeless. Japanese estimates were that SOPAC supplied Cactus at a rate averaging two merchantmen a day, while the Japanese managed only their paltry submarine runs. Not wanting to miss an opportunity for strategic change, Ugaki put Captain Kuroshima's team to work assessing the conditions that would make recapture of Guadalcanal impossible, and the moment these might occur. Admiral Yamamoto, in a notable divergence with Ugaki, was not sure how to proceed. The C-in-C had pursued the campaign determinedly and had never yet abandoned a position.

On November 26, just a few days after the Army-Navy conversations about an offensive, Ugaki resolved to ask the NGS to send its senior operations planner to Truk to consider the opposite course—withdrawal. Not willing to commit these thoughts to a dispatch others might see, the fleet chief of staff sent a letter to Vice Admiral Fukudome Shigeru, recently appointed head of the NGS Operations Bureau, delicately probing his view. As a first step the fleet wished to reorient operations, sending the Army's 51st Division to New Guinea instead of Cactus. If Fukudome did not detail Baron Tomioka to Truk, Ugaki would order Kuroshima to Tokyo. Ugaki entrusted his letter to a visiting flag officer on his way home.

The initial response seemed not to take Ugaki's concerns seriously. Baron Tomioka asked the Combined Fleet to send someone to Tokyo, but to study the movement of the 51st Division to Guadalcanal instead. On December 5, Fukudome finally answered Ugaki directly, warning him against infecting the field forces with pessimism. Fukudome would dispatch an emissary to Truk, but not until the end of the month. Meanwhile, an Army-Navy conference at Truk brought a slight break in the stalemate, with Tomioka's assistant, Commander Yamamoto Yuji, newly reassigned from Kondo's staff, informing the group that IGHQ had approved sending some 51st Division troops to New Guinea.

The resupply fiascos of early December, plus the Army's appeal to Imperial Headquarters, brought the dilemma to a head. Prodded by Admiral Fukudome, Nagano of NGS insisted on war gaming the supply flow. Colonel Tsuji, irrepressible as ever, saw such studies as more delay while men starved. But the war games, carried out at Rabaul, showed that barely a quarter of the matériel should be expected to arrive. Yamamoto of the NGS and Watanabe of the Combined Fleet were in Rabaul when the December failures occurred, and they witnessed the war game. General Imamura had no confidence in the Solomons effort. While he refused, as did many of his staff, to speak directly of withdrawal, Imamura vowed to do everything necessary to save the men at the front. He also war gamed an evacuation and found it dangerous but doable.

Commander Watanabe observed. When he reached Truk, Watanabe

found Admiral Yamamoto reluctant to accept these conclusions. The C-in-C pressed his staff officer to explain why Guadalcanal's recapture had become impossible. Watanabe cited the war game. To Yamamoto this fell short of a personal assurance. The next day Watanabe Yasuji was back on a plane to Rabaul. Imamura's associates thought he looked like a ghost. Watanabe met Imamura's chief of staff, who forthrightly declared that the Army could not recapture Guadalcanal, but went on to say that the general could not assert that. Puzzled, Watanabe asked why. He was told that Imamura had been appointed in audience before the emperor for the declared purpose of retaking Guadalcanal. Several Army staffers confirmed this. When he heard it, Yamamoto remarked upon how difficult it could be to say a true thing. The admiral finally gave way on the issue of withdrawal.

The instant Commander Watanabe returned to Truk, Ugaki sent him on to Tokyo. The fleet's strategy study went ahead of him. Given the growing interservice animosities, Ugaki was anxious that the initiative come from the Army, which necessitated IGHQ involvement. "The time for changing the future policy might come sooner than expected," he speculated on the first anniversary of Pearl Harbor. The chief of staff widened the circle, briefing Captain Miwa, about to leave Truk to become senior staff officer for the Eleventh Air Fleet. By December 10, hardly three weeks after Kondo's phantom naval "victory," Ugaki's view had hardened: The most urgent operational problem was to find some way to rescue the men on Starvation Island.

Soul-searching in Tokyo accelerated. On December 12, Emperor Hirohito began an unusually extended visit to worship at the Ise Shrine. That same day the NGS signaled its doubts. Not only were Baron Tomioka and Admiral Fukudome now in accord with Combined Fleet views, but they reported the Army General Staff as having initiated its own study. Truk was privately informed that the two armed services had reached a preliminary agreement. The Army General Staff sent planners on a South Pacific fact-finding mission, led by incoming operations section chief Colonel Sanada Joichiro, Tsuji's replacement. At Rabaul, Kusaka Jinichi advocated fighting for New Guinea and not "hurrying" efforts to retake Guadalcanal. Mikawa's senior staff officer, Captain Kami Shigenori, said that which was necessary: "To withdraw from Guadalcanal island temporarily to stabilize the general situation . . . must be considered." Colonel Tsuji had been agitating for a pullout for weeks.

Passing through Truk on his way back to Tokyo, Colonel Sanada admitted that the situation was even bleaker than he had expected. But the Army still wanted to send 10,000 replacements to Guadalcanal in January and two full divisions for an offensive in February. Stunned, Admiral Ugaki brought up the need to decide on the basis of the overall situation, not the simple desire for a successful outcome at Guadalcanal. Colonel Sanada "took him to be talking through his hat," but a colleague, Lieutenant Colonel Imoto Kunao, at one time Ugaki's student at the war college, accepted his analysis. That night Ugaki had several staffers warn the Army men of the fleet's weakness. Captain Kuroshima told them, "If the present situation continues, the Navy will not be able to move at all." Before leaving, Colonel Sanada told Ugaki that, after all, he would recommend that the fight for New Guinea be pursued without respect to the Solomons. An IGHQ directive to this effect could be expected.

The Army fell into line with the "New Guinea first" proposition before any decision on the Solomons. Bitter fights over the allocation of shipping had been ongoing in Tokyo since November. The Army had gotten its way, but the Tojo government warned that the additional merchant ships added to the Army roster would necessarily limit raw material imports, reducing Japanese steel production by nearly 15 percent in 1943. Losing more ships in the Solomons was unacceptable. An interim directive IGHQ issued on December 23 aimed entirely at New Guinea—just in time, for MacArthur's attacks captured Buna shortly afterward.

Tokyo's studies proceeded. On December 25, General Hyakutake of the Seventeenth Army reported that supplies were gone. He could no longer even send out scouts. Hyakutake asked to be allowed to die an honorable death by flinging his whole army at the Americans. Imperial Headquarters considered the situation. Major reinforcements—with convoys—the Allies were sure to resist in strength. Shipping losses were already a headache, and a renewed Solomons effort meant even more vessels lost.

Colonel Sanada's return with the results of his inspection settled the last doubts. The importance of the decision is signified by Admiral Nagano and General Sugiyama's audience with Emperor Hirohito on December 27. The next day the emperor expressed frustration to his military aide. Grave as was the situation, Hirohito complained, the supreme commanders had said nothing regarding how they intended to force the Allies to submit. He wanted an imperial conference to consider the matter, and professed himself ready for one at any time. The meeting was held on New Year's Eve. The group included Prime Minister Tojo. The emperor almost never spoke on these occasions, but here he stepped out of character. Hirohito demanded to know what would be done to stem the losses. The emperor said explicitly that withdrawal from Guadalcanal must be accompanied by offensive action elsewhere. Hirohito received reports on that point, but with no alternative, he approved the new policy. On New Year's Day, the Army operations chief left for Rabaul to announce that Japan would evacuate Guadalcanal, defend the Central Solomons, and move forward in New Guinea.

On January 4, 1943, Imperial Headquarters made it official. Admiral Nagano issued Navy Directive No. 184, which foresaw an end to efforts to recapture Guadalcanal, mandated that the Army should defend the central and northern Solomons, and specified, "During the period from about the latter part of January to the early part of February, the Army and Navy will, by every possible means, evacuate the units on Guadalcanal."

At Truk, gloom increasingly descended over Combined Fleet leaders. Still aboard the *Yamato*—though the C-in-C already anticipated moving his flag to the newer superbattleship *Musashi*—an ominous sign came with the New Year ceremony for 1943. Broiled sea bream and salt were put at the C-in-C's table. The admiral's steward was somehow off his excellent service that evening. Omi Heijiro placed the *tai* fish head to the left, both a breach of etiquette and, in Japanese culture, a portent of evil. Yamamoto shrugged it off with a smile. When the year changed, the admiral told his steward, a change of manners could be permitted. But for the Japanese starving on Guadalcanal everything remained the same.

Back at Cactus, on December 9, Marine Alex Vandegrift handed the command over to Major General Alexander Patch of the U.S. Army. The reinforcement proceeded apace, and the Army soon created the XIV Corps under Patch. Collins's American Division resumed the offensive in mid-December, clearing some Japanese positions in the interior and beginning a drive toward the western end of the island. Faced with Allied dominance in the air, on December 27 the JNAF gave up its desultory effort to parachute supplies, but the fleet resumed submarine missions. Several Tokyo Express sorties also conveyed at least a modicum of comestibles and delivered a few fresh troops to help shield the retreat of the others. Mount Austen was threatened. General Patch issued orders for a last-phase offensive on January 5. His forces included the American and 25th Infantry Division, plus part of the 2nd Marine Division. The Marines pushed along the coast while the 25th Division slogged ahead inland. The offensive opened on January 10. The attacks made steady progress. So far the Americans were completely unaware that their adversaries were going to leave altogether.

THE CACTUS SPRINGBOARD

Despite the Tassafaronga disaster, a developing perception of advantage led to the revival of Allied debates over the future. General MacArthur, pressing hard at Buna and Gona, in parallel to the Guadalcanal campaign, agitated for activation of "Task Two" of the original U.S. Cartwheel plan, which would give him the supreme command. The SOWESPAC chief exerted pressure both at the local level, with Admiral Halsey, and with Washington headquarters. MacArthur wanted to redeploy SOPAC forces to expedite his New Guinea operations. Halsey's units could afford him a seaborne supply line around the tip of New Guinea, and the seizure of Rabaul would be executed to protect MacArthur's flank. Admiral Halsey remained leery of that idea. The Bull preferred to create a solid framework within which the reduction of Rabaul could be conducted with confidence. Halsey answered MacArthur in detail in a dispatch sent on November 28:

OUR COMMON OBJECTIVE IS RABAUL. UNTIL JAP AIR IN NEW BRITAIN AND NORTHERN SOLOMONS HAS BEEN REDUCED, RISK OF VALUABLE NAVAL UNITS IN MIDDLE AND WESTERN REACHES SOLOMON SEA CAN ONLY BE JUSTIFIED BY MAJOR ENEMY SEABORNE MOVEMENT AGAINST SOUTH COAST NEW GUINEA OR AUSTRALIA ITSELF. SEABORNE

SUPPLY OF BASES WE TAKE ON NORTHERN COAST OF NEW GUINEA NOT FEASIBLE UNTIL WE CONTROL SOLOMON SEA, IN OTHER WORDS RABAUL. PURSUANT FOREGOING AND WITH HISTORY PAST MONTHS IN VIEW, CONSIDER RABAUL ASSAULT CAMPAIGN MUST BE AMPHIBIOUS ALONG THE SOLOMONS WITH NEW GUINEA LAND POSITION BASICALLY A SUPPORTING ONE ONLY. I AM CURRENTLY REINFORCING CACTUS POSITION AND EXPEDITING MEANS OF OPERAT-ING HEAVY AIR FROM THERE. IT IS MY BELIEF THAT THE SOUND PROCEDURE AT THIS TIME IS TO MAINTAIN AS STRONG A LAND AND AIR PRESSURE AGAINST THE JAPANESE BUNA POSITION AS YOUR LINES OF COMMUNI-CATION PERMIT, AND TO CONTINUE TO EXTRACT A CON-STANT TOLL OF JAPANESE SHIPPING, AN ATTRITION WHICH IF CONTINUED AT THE PRESENT RATE HE CAN NOT LONG SUSTAIN. I BELIEVE THAT MY GREATEST CONTRIBUTION TO OUR COMMON EFFORT WOULD BE TO STRENGTHEN MY POSITION AND RESUME THE ADVANCE UP THE SOLO-MONS AS SOON AS POSSIBLE.

General MacArthur had also begun, as early as October, to press Washington to confirm his supremo status. MacArthur had emphasized his need for the command with Hap Arnold when the Army Air Force chief visited the South Pacific, and General Arnold's report advocated a top command for the entire Pacific be placed under MacArthur. The recommendation embroiled the Joint Chiefs of Staff in questions of Pacific command and their corollary, the next steps in fighting the Japanese. By late November progress on Guadalcanal had begun to make it urgent to resolve these matters.

The Joint Chiefs reliably split along service lines. General George C. Marshall, the Army Chief of Staff, supported MacArthur's bid for control. A Pacific Theater command would be fine by him if MacArthur could have it. Admiral Ernest J. King, the Chief of Naval Operations, was more circumspect. The COMINCH regarded direct assault on Rabaul as a frontal attack doomed to failure or likely to bog down in an extended stalemate. King solicited Nimitz's opinion, and the CINCPAC responded early in December along lines very similar to those Halsey had used directly to MacArthur. New Guinea suffered from poor overland communications (an understatement) and could not be a useful center of operations so long as its real transport lines—by sea—were flanked by Japanese bases in the Solomons. It would be tempting to bypass the intervening enemy positions to strike directly at Rabaul, but by now the enemy possessed an interlocking set of bases that were mutually supporting and could be used to outflank an advanced Allied force. CINCPAC felt that "Task One" of the original Joint Chiefs of Staff directive could not be considered fulfilled until the Japanese base network had been neutralized. Since that mission belonged to SOPAC, Admiral Halsey should retain control.

The CINCPAC also made an observation that soon figured in Admiral King's arguments—that no Allied superiority in naval forces could be foreseen until at least the spring of 1943. In his exchanges with the Army, King broadened that observation: In fact, the truth was not just that naval forces were limited, but that the overwhelming majority of the U.S. Pacific Fleet was engaged in the South Pacific. When General Marshall pressed for a theater supreme command, Admiral King countered that CINCPAC held responsibility for naval defense throughout the ocean area, so that putting the Pacific Fleet under a ground officer in Australia would impinge on Nimitz's ability to act anywhere else. The Army continued pressing for a Pacific supremo, at which point the Navy responded that it would agree if that officer were Admiral Nimitz. MacArthur could take over the SOPAC forces provided his orders came from Pearl Harbor. General Marshall was loath to agree to that formula—and Douglas MacArthur would undoubtedly have rejected it—so the end result was to preserve the existing command structure. Almost tacitly, though later confirmed by formal directive, SOPAC would conduct operations farther up the Solomons, first to complete securing Guadalcanal, then to prepare for the capture of Rabaul.

Neutralization of Rabaul remained an Allied goal, ratified at the Roosevelt-Churchill summit at Casablanca in January 1943. The next steps were important. In both Washington and at Pearl Harbor, some suggested a leap ahead to Buin to seize the Japanese base complex on Bougainville. But the truth was that at the moment, SOPAC/SOWESPAC forces remained weak while the enemy were strong. Japanese forces in the Solomons–New Guinea area in January 1943 were estimated at 132,000 troops in place, with

60,000 more on the way, along with 547 aircraft. The pendulum might be swinging toward the Allies, but it had not gone far.

Under the circumstances SOPAC needed an initial operation that would be unopposed or only lightly so. This led to the scheme for an amphibious landing in the Russell Islands, just a step up The Slot from Guadalcanal. Coastwatchers reported no Japanese there. It might be easily seized, and could become a new airfield bastion. As the end of January approached, both sides had plans in motion. These led to the next phase of the fight for the Solomons arena.

V.

INCHING FOR GROUND

Preparing to shoot the movie *Tora! Tora! Tora!*, producers for the Japanese segments of the film built full-size wooden replicas of Imperial Navy warships, including the battleship *Nagato*, on a beach in Kyushu. That was in the late 1960s, and it was a huge project—the *Nagato* was 660 feet long and ten stories high. Had the Japanese had that building capacity in the 1940s, the Solomons campaign might have ended differently. Their nightmare began with an airfield built too slowly and deepened with the flimsiness of a network that left bases so far distant that losses multiplied. Only in the period after Santa Cruz, in planning a renewed offensive, had Navy leaders put their efforts into constructing a new field close to Guadalcanal. The site chosen was on the island group called New Georgia, at a place called Munda.

Japanese surveyed the area and found a suitable location at a plantation on Munda Point. At Truk the fleet staff studied the project, and, about the time of the Naval Battle of Guadalcanal, Admiral Yamamoto decided to proceed. The first thousand troops, with supplies, were delivered a week after the battle. When Combined Fleet staff officers visited IGHQ late in November, they obtained agreement, included in the next operational directive. Initially conceived as an emergency airfield, the IGHQ order envisioned Munda as an operating base. A convoy reached there in the face of Cactus air and PT boat attacks on November 24, and another five days later. The 17th Construction Unit and Sasebo 6th SNLF were the first to arrive. Captain Iwabuchi Sankichi took command from an interim leader, Commander Shimada. The flat terrain and carefully spaced plantation trees allowed rapid progress—already Imperial Navy construction had gained efficiency compared to Guadalcanal. By mid-December enough had been accomplished for the JNAF to carry out test landings using Zeroes and Vals. These were successful, and the fleet planned to deploy aircraft to Munda on December 22.

Coastwatchers supplied early indications of something afoot. Missionary schoolboys working for Donald Kennedy on New Georgia watched the first Japanese disembark. On nearby Vella Lavella, where Henry Josselyn and Jack Keenan spied, scouts saw barges loaded with heavy equipment and bags of cement, which sheltered in coves by day and continued to New Georgia at night. The Japanese also installed an outpost at Viru and a barge station at Vangunu, the island in this group closest to Guadalcanal, but the traffic didn't seem right for those places. Halsey suspected the worst. The Bull ordered up scout planes, but they found little at first.

Meanwhile the Cactus Crystal Ball tracked enemy vessels stopping and not going on to Guadalcanal, and radio intelligence tracked several Japanese units to Munda. Within days of their arrival codebreakers had identified the construction unit and SNLF naval infantry. On December 3, after the coastwatchers' barge warning, Allied aerial reconnaissance photographed Munda. Japanese engineers had disguised the airfield carefully, wiring fronds in place of removed trees to preserve an apparent canopy of coconut palms, but Commander Quackenbush's photo interpreters penetrated the deception. By December 5 AIRSOLS had hard evidence of construction, including a runway and gun emplacements, demonstrating the synoptic impact when pillars of intelligence worked together.

Only 180 miles from the Cactus bases, Munda posed a threat to them. Slowing the enemy became Halsey's goal. He committed SOPAC to early, sustained neutralization. Army fighter-bombers attacked on December 6, followed several days later by a B-17 strike. Night harassment began with a Catalina over Munda on December 13. Then the JNAF deployed a Zero detachment of the 252nd Air Group. Christmas Eve brought a fighter-escorted dive-bomber attack that caught the Japanese mostly on the ground. Pilots claimed ten planes destroyed taking off and a dozen smashed on the airfield, with half the eight combat air patrol Zeroes flamed in dogfights. "It's deplorable indeed," chief of staff Ugaki lamented, "that everything is on the way to retreat due to the inferiority of our airpower."

Ultra struck again on December 14, with news of Japanese destroyer sorties planned for several succeeding nights. Decrypts included information on planned times of arrival and the course to be followed from Shortland. Using this data, SOPAC diverted the submarine *Plunger*, on her way from Australia to Pearl Harbor, and laid on strong coverage by the Cactus Air Force. Aircraft damaged destroyer *Kagero* on the night of the sixteenth, and the *Plunger* was credited with sinking a destroyer from that group and hitting, perhaps crippling, one from the next Tokyo Express, though Japanese records do not confirm it. In any event, Admiral Mikawa canceled the Tokyo Express scheduled for December 18. Around Christmas two more tin cans were damaged, one by collision with the freighter *Nankai Maru* after Cactus aircraft had hit her. During the final week of 1942, Ultra identified a rapid succession of fresh Japanese formations: the 15th Antiaircraft Unit, the Kure 6th SNLF, and—for the first time—Army units, including an infantry battalion, an artillery battery, and engineers.

Now Bull Halsey sent in the big boys, taking a page from the Imperial Navy playbook with a bombardment of Munda carried out by Rear Admiral Walden L. "Pug" Ainsworth soon after midnight on January 5, 1943. Halsey had grabbed Pug, then holding an administrative billet at Pearl Harbor, as the latter visited SOPAC, much as Halsey himself had suddenly been drafted as theater commander. Admiral Halsey put Ainsworth in charge of Task Force 67, the unit smashed so badly at Tassafaronga. By January, Pug Ainsworth had rebuilt the cruiser-destroyer group and would lead it with distinction. The Munda bombardment represented its coming-out party. In less than an hour, Ainsworth's warships hammered the Japanese with more than 3,000 six-inch shells and another 1,400 rounds of five-inch fire. Air scouts reported Munda heavily damaged the next morning, but on the evening of January 6 one of Ainsworth's light cruisers, the New Zealand ship *Achilles*, lost a six-inch turret to a direct hit from a JNAF Val dive-bomber, one of four that made a sudden attack and were likely from Munda. All the other airplanes scored near misses on U.S. cruiser *Honolulu*. Perhaps the Japanese now had their own Henderson Field. On the ground, Lieutenant Yunoki Shigeru, formerly of the *Hiei* and now a flak gunner at Munda, found his men restive under shelling, but the damage did not appear serious. Munda seemed destined for an important role in the next phase of the war.

LAST ROUND ON GUADALCANAL

Bull Halsey liked fighting Marines but had a soft spot also for solid soldiers. One of his favorites was Joseph—or "J."—Lawton Collins, whose rise in the Army at that moment was meteoric. In barely a year Collins had gone from instructor at the Army War College—as a lieutenant colonel—to major general leading the Americal Division, the first big Army unit in the South Pacific. Along the way he had been chief of staff of the Army's Hawaiian Department, while Halsey, recuperating from serious dermatitis, marked time at a Pearl Harbor desk as commander, aircraft, Pacific. The quiet Collins turned up whenever CINCPAC and the Army held talks, and Halsey was impressed with his unflappable competence. The Bull had gone to the South Pacific when Collins, upon promotion to temporary general's rank, was given the division command. Collins understood the Americal was intended for MacArthur, but Admiral Nimitz drew him aside to warn that he might be diverted. When Lawton Collins reached Nouméa, Bull Halsey invited him to dinner, where the Army general was surprised to also encounter Alex Vandegrift. The Marine, on his way to Australia to arrange rest camps for his men, described conditions on the 'Canal. General Collins was happy to go wherever SOPAC wanted him, asking only for time to combat-load his transports and cargo ships. Admiral Halsey replied the Americal was indeed going to Guadalcanal, leaving *the next day*.

After December 9, the Army took the lead. General Alexander Patch commanded, and in early January formed the XIV Corps. Lawton Collins's troops would be his original division-size unit. One Americal regiment, the 164th Infantry, plus most of the 182nd, were already on Cactus. The Americal was unique in that it had been scratch-built outside the U.S., its name a contraction of "America" and "New Caledonia." The troops with General Collins were primarily divisional artillery and support units. His 132nd Infantry Regiment had landed from the transports that took away the initial tranche of Marines. By mid-December, Patch had ordered the Army men to take Mount Austen. Also under Patch were the 25th Infantry Division, the Army's 147th Infantry, and two regiments of the 2nd Marine Division, plus assorted other units. By January, even with the departure of Vandegrift's troops along with the 7th Marine Regiment, there were more than 50,000 Allied troops on Cactus, the vast majority Americans. A Japanese intelligence appreciation at the end of that month estimated Patch's strength accurately: three divisions with more than 118 guns, 44 flak guns, and about 300 mortars.

Generals Patch and Collins made a good team. Patch had been on Cactus long enough to learn the lay of the land, while Collins brought energy and enthusiasm. Together they ground away at Hyakutake's Japanese. The difficulties of the terrain were enormous. Even with the enemy's meager supplies and the huge Japanese losses, by January, Patch was still throwing troops against Mount Austen. The hitherto fresh 132nd Infantry sustained enough casualties fighting for one of Austen's bastions, and had so many succumb to sickness that it became ineffective. General Collins had to substitute other troops. The final fall of Mount Austen on January 16 eliminated the last Japanese position east of the Matanikau. It had taken more than a month.

Patch did not wait long before renewing his offensive. He selected his least-weakened units, relying upon a composite Army-Marine division. Once this force linked up with the 25th Infantry Division around Kokumbona, Patch stopped fighting for the rugged interior and advanced along the coast. The fall of Kokumbona showed the campaign nearing its end. But, concerned lest the Japanese renew their attacks, Patch instructed Collins to concentrate on defending the Lunga Point airfield complex—by now no fewer than *two* satellite airfields supplemented Henderson. Lawton Collins was intensely disappointed at these orders, for he wanted to finish off the enemy. Others would do that. His cameo appearance in the Pacific nearly completed, Lawton Collins would soon leave for Europe. General Patch persisted to the final fight, but he too neared the end of his Pacific involvement. Both went on to great things in the war against Germany.

While the Americans ground ahead, the Japanese retired. Once Imperial Headquarters made its decision to evacuate, the course became clear. Some of Hyakutake's regiments, formations that had landed with two thousand or more soldiers, were down to fewer than a hundred. The loss of effectiveness among the units could be added to other weaknesses as reasons the Army could not endure. The Imperial Navy did what it could to succor Hyakutake's remnants. More submarines, more aerial resupply, and the Tokyo Express brought a few supplies. The fresh infantry battalion that delayed the Americans at the end was also there courtesy of the Navy. Given their situation, the Japanese fought very hard.

Plans for the evacuation, code-named the "KE Operation," were agreed between Combined Fleet and the Eighth Area Army on January 9. Commander Watanabe continued as the fleet's action officer. Army war games at Rabaul evaluated the concept of lifting out the troops in several Tokyo Expresses. General Imamura estimated half the destroyers might be lost, and worried that the Navy's extraction of a few men by submarine or barge would be used to excuse cancellation of the larger enterprise. Historian Richard Frank comments that such suspicions were not fair to the Navy, and he is right. The Imperial Navy remained solidly committed. Admiral Yamamoto blanched at the potential losses—he feared forfeiting up to a third of his destroyers—but he went ahead. Commander Watanabe took the prize for optimism, expecting that 80 percent of those on Guadalcanal could be saved.

In a carefully parsed sequence, initial resupply came by all delivery modes, the new troops were sent, and General Hyakutake began recoiling toward the westernmost tip of the island. The Navy installed a barge base in the Russell Islands, between Guadalcanal and New Georgia. Five I-boats successfully delivered supplies between January 5 and 9, and the Tokyo Express was active after the tenth. Its missions on the nights of January 10–11 and 14–15 were opposed by PT boats. Two PTs were lost, against a destroyer damaged. Meanwhile, Japanese Army aircraft made their initial appearance in the Solomons. The JNAF reinforced Admiral Kusaka's Eleventh Air Fleet. As part of this augmentation, the Navy for the first time deployed a medium bomber unit especially trained for mass night operations. In all there would be roughly 436 aircraft, including a hundred Army planes, sixty from the R Area Force, and an equal number from carrier *Zuikaku*, whose newly retrained air group advanced to Buin. At Shortland, Admiral Mikawa assembled a massive group of twenty-one destroyers for the transport missions. Heavy cruisers *Chokai* and *Kumano* plus the light cruiser *Sendai* stood by to contribute surface support. With the beginning of January, the Imperial Navy also went to a new version of its JN-25 fleet code.

Yamamoto's evacuation plan was predicated on a deception. Several times already the Japanese had attempted major operations to capture

Henderson Field. Indeed, they had intended another such offensive until just recently. The Allies expected that, so the Imperial Navy would give them something to believe in. Eleven hundred miles to the east, in the Marshalls, the Japanese sent an air flotilla to make it appear that forces were gathering, sent the cruiser *Tone* to mimic the activities of a task force, and had a submarine shell Canton Island. To the west the JNAF resumed bombing Darwin in Australia and upped radio traffic to suggest activity.

But the centerpiece was the *Kido Butai.* Yamamoto sent Admiral Kondo to sea, accompanied by Rear Admiral Kakuta's Carrier Division 2 with the *Junyo* and *Zuiho.* Kondo's two battleships, four heavy cruisers, and a screen completed the force. The Kondo fleet weighed anchor and began leaving Truk shortly before 7:00 a.m. on January 31. In the lagoon Yamamoto retained the *Yamato* and *Musashi,* plus fleet carrier *Zuikaku.* The *Musashi* was abuzz with excitement because the admiral was about to transfer Combined Fleet headquarters to her. Kondo, meanwhile, cruised northeast of the Solomons as the fleet had done so often. Each time before, this maneuver had accompanied a Guadalcanal offensive. The Japanese hoped the Allies would assume as much now. Ultra revealed Kondo's sortie within forty-eight hours.

Careful preparations were required, since the Allies were now much more powerful than had been the case in October–November. The *Saratoga* gave SOPAC a fully capable aircraft carrier, while the *Enterprise*—still with her damaged elevator—provided a second, less effective flight deck. A half dozen of the small "jeep"—or escort—carriers were now in the Pacific. Halsey incorporated a pair of them into one of his cruiser groups. With thirteen cruisers Halsey had enough to create *two* separate cruiser-destroyer forces plus furnish escorts. Three fast battleships and forty-five destroyers completed his fleet, which SOPAC divided into no less than a half dozen task forces. Compared to where the South Pacific command had been a few months earlier, Admiral Halsey possessed a veritable armada. Enough, in fact, for offensives of his own.

Long anxious to reach beyond Cactus, Halsey was well aware of the strategic debates on the "tasks" of Operation Cartwheel. Like Nimitz at Pearl Harbor, he did not feel strong enough to strike directly at Rabaul.

Command boundaries remained in flux. Even New Georgia lay outside the SOPAC region, falling within MacArthur's domain. Halsey made a start with the cruiser bombardments on Munda in early January, and at Vila toward the end of the month. The *Saratoga* task force covered that sortie. But Admiral King agitated for more action. Chester Nimitz visited in late January, accompanied by Navy Secretary Knox. The night of their arrival, staging through Rekata Bay, a couple of JNAF patrol bombers struck Espíritu Santo, startling the brass. Halsey and Nimitz agreed on a small foray to capture the Russell Islands, just thirty miles past Guadalcanal. While SOPAC completed preparations, the Japanese began their evacuation.

With Admiral Nimitz headed back to Pearl, the Imperial Navy conducted a series of strong fighter sweeps against AIRSOLS. On January 25, with eighteen Bettys as bait, seventy-six Zeroes came hunting. Some turned back in soupy weather, and the bombers wheeled away short too, but dozens of fighters went on to dogfight Cactus defenders. Two days later the bait was nine Army medium bombers and the hammer seventy-four Army fighters. Neither mission inflicted much damage, but the strikes, the first major raids since November, were the latest piece of the intelligence puzzle to fall into place. Aerial reconnaissance had found large Japanese shipping concentrations at Rabaul for weeks—as many as ninety-one ships on December 30. With the first big air raid, CINCPAC immediately warned of an imminent offensive. On January 29 the fleet intelligence summary noted that one "impended," speculating on whether carriers would be involved.

Bull Halsey deployed his strength to counter the offensive. He ordered the *Enterprise* task force into the Solomon Sea, and sent a cruiser unit to make a daylight incursion up The Slot. With fighter cover from SOPAC's jeep carriers, and the "Big E's" bombers to back them, this force could break up an enemy fleet. Led by Rear Admiral Robert C. Giffen, the cruiser unit aimed to pass Guadalcanal and enter The Slot. Among the crews was Seaman James J. Fahey, an antiaircraft gunner aboard the recently arrived light cruiser *Montpelier*. Like so many others, Fahey found life trying in the South Pacific. Too hot to sleep below deck, sailors lay down topside on the hard steel. Fahey put his cap atop his shoes for a pillow. Walking brought the danger of stumbling over crewmates slumbering in every conceivable place. After a long day of combat exercises on January 28, Fahey conked out as accustomed, only to be soaked when it rained in the middle of the night.

Seaman Fahey was soon glad of the battle practice. Giffen's ships were spotted by Japanese scouts off Rennell Island, south of Cactus. On January 29, Admiral Kusaka canceled a planned Henderson raid in favor of striking the cruisers. For this he relied on the new night attack force drawn from the 701st and 705th air groups. They reached the target amid gathering darkness and attacked into the night. For an instant Fahey thought another rehearsal was under way, but then he saw fountains of water erupting into the sky, planes all over the place, and an enemy peppering the ships with machine guns as they passed. Strings of tracers from flak and the lightning bolts of the five-inch dual-purpose guns lit the darkening sky. One five-inch mount was right next to Fahey's quadruple 40mm, and when the heavy flak spoke, it was tremendous. Cotton-stuffed ears didn't help. The concussion made him feel like the insides of his chest and throat were being ripped out. The previous day's combat exercises gave Fahey confidence in his comrades. Their 40mm mount made *Montpelier*'s first score of the war, a JNAF torpedo plane. But the Japanese were determined—and good. Fahey felt his ship struck by a tin fish, a dud. Heavy cruiser *Louisville* evaded another torpedo by combing its wake, but when a second wave of Japanese attacked twenty minutes later they hit her—fortunately also a dud. Something was wrong that day with Japanese torpedoes, if not airmen. A third dud hit light cruiser *Wichita*. Not so lucky was heavy cruiser *Chicago*. She lost engines and power and began listing after two torpedoes struck home. Damage control restored some power, and late that night the *Louisville* successfully rigged a towline. The *Chicago* was being pulled to safety the next day, surrounded by half a dozen destroyers, with *Enterprise* fighters overhead for cover, when the Japanese returned to blow the cruiser out of the water.

Radioman 2nd Class Philip Jacobsen had the watch at Station AL, the Cactus Crystal Ball, when they began to intercept Japanese aviation transmissions. The excitement in the stream of contact reports was almost palpable. A message soon reported the destruction by torpedo of a battleship. Because the JNAF were still using the aircraft code captured on the destroyer *Smith* at Santa Cruz, decryption was fast and accurate. Ensign C. A. Sims's mobile radio unit on the *Enterprise* copied the same transmissions. By noon, January 30, the Japanese had rectified their identification mistake. There was no doubt of the result: A further intercept specified the target as the *Chicago.* Bull Halsey was furious. In Washington Admiral King took it hard, for Giffen had been a favorite of his and had now messed up. At Pearl Harbor, Chester Nimitz was unusually acerbic—possibly because he was coming down with malaria after his recent South Pacific visit. The CINCPAC exhibited a fury more typical of Ernie King. Nimitz had been upset several times previously when U.S. warship losses—the destroyer *Porter* and the carriers *Wasp* and *Hornet*—had been revealed before families of crews were notified. Now Nimitz threatened to *kill* anyone who spoke of the *Chicago*'s sinking.

Immediately after these events, CINCPAC issued an all-hands warning of an enemy offensive. The fleet intelligence bulletin that day was the first to put a time frame on the expected attack: between January 29 and February 12. Ultra yielded a tabulation of available JNAF air strength: 142 at Rabaul (including forty-nine twin-engine bombers and seventeen dive-bombers) plus forty-nine to sixty-nine at Buin (including thirty-five to fifty-five dive-bombers). There were also the carrier air groups, plus significant Japanese Army air strength. On January 31 the intelligence mavens became quite explicit:

> A major action . . . is expected soon. This will probably consist of an attempt similar to the one on November 13–15 where transports attempted to land at Guadalcanal covered by fleet units. Whether or not carriers will be [i]nvolved is unknown as yet. It is known that a detached group of carrier aircraft is now operating in the Shortland area.

The intelligence bulletin now put timing at February 3 or 4. The next day analysts added that "the major operation predicted yesterday appears more and more probable."

On the Japanese side, the naval attack delayed the Henderson neutralization provided for in the KE plan. Admiral Kusaka requested postponement. Suspicious as ever, the Army wanted none of that. So the Tokyo Express would run on time, starting the next day. But the *Chicago* diversion proved a blessing in disguise. The ship's destruction told Halsey he could not yet hazard heavy ships in The Slot. That precluded surface interdiction.

Fooled by the warnings of an offensive, Halsey now determined to hold his cards and see what developed before committing his forces.

This put the onus on the Cactus Air Force, now under Marine Brigadier General Francis Mulcahy. He had eighty-one planes, among them roughly sixty-five bomber types. There were far more in the South Pacific, but not at the tip of the spear. About eighty patrol planes based in the New Hebrides had sufficient range to participate, and SOWESPAC had thirty B-17s that could contribute. Halsey's choice to hold back his carriers took 161 planes off the table, slightly more than 200 if the two jeep carriers are included. There were more than that number of additional U.S. aircraft in SOPAC, but merely to replace warplanes lost from Guadalcanal. Events put the Cactus Air Force at the center of battle. Only the planes and PT boats would oppose the Japanese withdrawal.

Imperial Navy planners were very precise with their arrangements. Pickup would take place exactly at midnight. The arriving Express would flash a blue signal light. Every destroyer carried five rubber boats preloaded with supply drums and powered by a dependable (American) Johnson outboard motor. Crewmen would push the drums overboard about 600 yards from shore and continue to the beach. The troops would wade out and hoist themselves into the boats, then use rope ladders to climb to the destroyers' decks. Every ship would carry two or three hundred men. The loading had to be completed quickly. With no time to spare, the rubber boats would be left for later missions and finally abandoned.

Rear Admiral Kimura Susumu of Destroyer Squadron 10 was to lead the first sortie. But he was injured when the U.S. submarine *Nautilus* torpedoed the *Akizuki* off Shortland some days earlier. Rear Admiral Hashimoto returned to mastermind the evacuation. Hashimoto, like Tanaka Raizo, had worked himself to exhaustion in the Solomons and had been moved to less demanding duty. But the KE Operation was *that* important. Koyanagi Tomiji, former skipper of battleship *Kongo*, had been promoted to rear admiral and given command of Destroyer Squadron 2. Having plied The Slot with the Express for six weeks, he also had been relieved, and arrived at Truk only to be sent back. Koyanagi led the transport unit. Hashimoto calculated that to make the schedule he would need to leave Shortland unusually early—about 10:00 a.m. So they were passing Vella Lavella in the afternoon when they were spotted. Coastwatcher Josselyn reported the Japanese, which brought two powerful attacks by the Cactus Air Force. Though the Express had a strong combat air patrol, the U.S. planes overwhelmed it, but the best they could accomplish against the flotilla was to damage the destroyer *Makinami*, Admiral Hashimoto's flagship. Koyanagi stepped up to take over, leaving a couple of ships to stand by Hashimoto. The latter transferred to *Shikinami* and rushed to catch up, but could not do so until much later. The Japanese were running late, and Koyanagi's reassignment of ships to replace those detached from the screen left the transport unit understrength by two destroyers.

The next hurdle was a PT attack. Tulagi sent out eleven PT boats that night. Seven of them made the Japanese and in various combinations launched torpedoes. Several PTs bored in from behind the enemy at Cape Esperance. Lieutenant Yamamoto Masahide of the *Akigumo* recalls his ship firing her five-inch main battery directly over the stern at the PT boats. Yamamoto thought they blasted three. There *were* three boats lost that night—PTs -*111*, -*37*, and -*123*—but only one here. Another boat was actually destroyed by Louie the Louse—the greatest known combat exploit of the nighttime JNAF floatplane operation. Among the Americans missing was John H. Clagett, a legendary PT skipper. The PT boats achieved no clear results. Japanese destroyer *Makikumo* was lost after chasing *PT-124*, but whether the cause was a -*124* torpedo or a mine—Americans had laid 300 mines in these waters that day—remains in dispute.

Kusaka's Eleventh Air Fleet also played its part, with pairs of Bettys shuttling over Henderson to keep Cactus Air Force heads down. They were unable to prevent some U.S. planes from taking to the air, or a morning attack on the retreating flotilla, but this time the Cactus aircraft achieved nothing. About noon the Tokyo Express reached Shortland. Nearly 5,000 Japanese soldiers had been saved. Admiral Koyanagi recorded that the survivors wore only shreds of uniforms, were sick with dengue and malaria, and so emaciated they could not stomach real food, only porridge. Aboard the *Akigumo*, Lieutenant Yamamoto found the men did not even ask to eat, only for cigarettes.

Meanwhile, General Patch's Americans stolidly continued their advance. On the morning of February 2, word reached Cactus Crystal Ball that a complete Japanese radio station, abandoned, had been captured undamaged. Crystal Ballers knew the enemy emitter at Tassafaronga had gone off the air a week before. Petty Officer Jim Perkins, radioman Phil Jacobsen, and a Marine intercept operator volunteered to recover the equipment. They set off in a two-and-a-half-ton truck, spent a full day bouncing along rutted trails, and finally reached their goal. What they found was strange: The Japanese radio and a generator were completely functional. The only document was a radio frequency list that U.S. intelligence knew all about. The enemy had clearly taken the trouble to secure their documents but had done nothing to destroy the equipment. Perhaps they had lacked the means? An Army officer raised the possibility that the enemy were withdrawing. Perkins and Jacobsen passed that along, but Commander McCallum decided against reporting it up the line, on grounds that Station AL would be exceeding its mandate as a direction-finding unit. Melbourne, Pearl Harbor, and Washington were left to draw their own conclusions.

Philip Jacobsen, who retired as a lieutenant commander after a full career in signals intelligence, came away from Guadalcanal convinced the Allies had penetrated the secret of the enemy withdrawal. He points to the numerous position and mission reports put out by FRUMEL and FRUPAC as evidence. Movement reports, however, absent knowledge of Japanese intentions, could fit many interpretations. More striking was a partial Ultra decrypt of a message to one of the destroyer units assembling for the Tokyo Express. The Washington office that circulated this information commented that the KE Operation might be intended for evacuation. That very word appeared in a late-January dispatch regarding submarine movements. Jacobsen also recalls quiet rumblings among codebreakers at FRUMEL, but Duane Whitlock, who was on the scene at Melbourne, remembered no great excitement there at the time, the opposite of what one would expect if codebreakers held the view that the Japanese were escaping their grasp.

Whatever doubts existed never made their way into the intelligence summaries. Indeed, on February 1 in Washington, COMINCH released a cable for transmission to Nimitz, Halsey, and MacArthur: "INDICATIONS ARE THAT JAP OFFENSIVE OPERATION NOW IN FULL SWING ON MAJOR SCALE PRIMARILY DIRECTED AGAINST SOUTHERN SOLOMONS." With the Tokyo Express in motion, Pearl Harbor intelligence, which had also predicted an offensive, and observed that it appeared more and more probable, reported no change in its estimate, an observation repeated throughout the withdrawal. On February 6 the doubters in Washington finally managed to get out a cable that asked, "ARE THERE ANY INDICATIONS THAT RECENT TOKYO EXPRESSES MAY HAVE BEEN FOR THE PURPOSE OF EVACUATING NIP FORCES FROM GUADALCANAL?" Halsey's SOPAC intel people answered the next day: "AS YET NOTHING DEFINITE."

The second Tokyo Express, also under Admiral Hashimoto, left Shortland the morning of February 4. Its combat air patrol was again pushed aside by a big Cactus Air Force formation, some thirty-three Dauntlesses and Avengers. They damaged the destroyer *Maikaze*. Two ships in the Koyanagi unit suffered minor impairment. Once more Hashimoto's flagship was crippled, this time by engine failure. But the armada voyaged to Cactus and loaded about 4,000 more men, including General Hyakutake and his staff. The third Express took place on February 7, with the strongest air escort yet—but was again overcome by the Cactus Air Force. Fifteen SBDs bombed Hashimoto. Lieutenant Commander Soma Shohei of the *Akigumo* startled his sailors with his bad mood. Soma had a premonition of doom. In fact, she came through fine. A different destroyer was knocked out, and another damaged insufficiently to stop her. Hashimoto closed the last Cactus evacuation beach, and Koyanagi led his second unit to pull out the men holding the barge station in the Russell Islands. The Japanese were gone. Estimates of the sum total of Japanese rescued from Starvation Island range from 10,652 to some 13,030. The Imperial Navy escaped with a single destroyer sunk and others damaged.

When Admiral Koyanagi returned to Truk, he reported to the Combined Fleet chief. Yamamoto confessed that he too had feared when he heard, early on, that Hashimoto had lost a destroyer to damage, but that he had consoled himself with the thought that Koyanagi Tomiji was on the scene. Yamamoto congratulated Koyanagi on a job well-done.

The date-time group on the SOPAC message replying to Washington's query regarding a Japanese evacuation indicates that dispatch was sent twenty-nine minutes after the final Tokyo Express reached Shortland safely. Bull Halsey had kept his big ships for news of Yamamoto's carriers and their expected offensive. Now it was too late. On February 5, a B-17 at the limit of her search actually caught sight of the Kondo fleet. Halsey strung his bow to shoot it, but Kondo stayed beyond his reach.

Several days later, according to Lieutenant Commander Ito Haruki of Imperial Navy radio intelligence, the Japanese extended their deception, using the frequency of a Catalina patrol plane, whose own communications had become scrambled, to send a carrier sighting report in its name. Ito, who survived the war without participating in any other major battle, observed that "the fake message which helped the total evacuation of Guadalcanal will be my only consolation." Senior officers reprimanded Ito for violating Imperial Navy security regulations with this gambit.

Americans who researched this claim found that a PBY had been in the area but could not verify that any Allied command had circulated the phony report. The CINCPAC intelligence summary for that day actually noted that the major enemy fleet appeared to be returning to Truk. The summary for February 9, twenty-four hours later, is worth quoting:

> The return of the Advance Force to Truk along with the comparatively rapid advance of U.S. Army forces as far as Visale from the southwest and the Doma Cove area from the east may indicate that the enemy is indeed evacuating from Guadalcanal and that the major operational stage [for] the present . . . is completed. If this be true it shows that the tide of war in the Pacific has changed and that the Nip is on the defensive at last.

At 4:25 p.m. that day, General Patch's GIs completed clearing Cactus. He messaged Halsey: "'TOKYO EXPRESS' NO LONGER HAS TERMINUS ON GUADALCANAL." Admiral Chester W. Nimitz's observations are also noteworthy:

> The end was as abrupt as the beginning of the struggle for Guadalcanal. Until the last moment it appeared that the Japanese were attempting a major reinforcement effort. Only skill in keeping their plans disguised and bold celerity in carrying them out enabled the Japanese to withdraw the remnants of the

Guadalcanal garrison. Not until all organized forces had been evacuated on February 8 [East Zone date—at Pearl Harbor] did we realize the purpose of their air and naval dispositions. Otherwise, with the strong forces available to us . . . and our powerful fleet in the South Pacific we might have converted the withdrawal into a disastrous rout.

POLISHING APPLES

Quite close to the end, an event took place that had a huge impact on the war. This was the loss of the submarine *I-1* off Kamimbo Bay on January 29. Fresh from the dockyards, where the *I-1* had gone to repair balky engines, this I-boat represented a more thoughtful approach to the "mole" (*mogura*) submarine supply duty. The boat's after deck gun had been removed and substituted with a waterproofed *Daihatsu* landing barge. After tests in Empire waters and at Truk, Lieutenant Commander Sakamoto Eichi's *I-1* went on a mole run to Guadalcanal with supplies and sixty soldiers.

Ultra intervened. A series of late-January messages had mentioned I-boat cruises to Cactus on several succeeding days. The *I-1* appeared in the traffic. Though only one decrypt confirmed a *mogura* mission, and two others actually spoke of cancellation, SOPAC warned Guadalcanal to be alert for subs over a three-day period. Several radio direction-finding stations in New Zealand tracked I-boat transmissions showing subs nearing Guadalcanal. Based on this, Cactus naval command alerted all units to a Japanese sub off Kamimbo. On the night of the twenty-ninth when Commander Sakamoto surfaced, lookouts reported torpedo boats in sight. The *I-1* dived. But the "torpedo boats" were actually the New Zealand corvettes *Moa* and *Kiwi*. The latter detected the sound of Sakamoto's I-boat. Lieutenant Commander Gordon Bridson's *Kiwi* dropped depth charges. The *I-1*, now with damaged steering, engines, batteries, and leaks, went into an uncontrolled dive far past her design depth. Desperate to save his ship, Sakamoto managed to regain control and blew his ballast tanks to bring the *I-1* to the surface, where he rushed toward shore on his one good engine, trying to beach the submarine.

Commander Bridson went to full speed, intending to ram. He rejected the complaints of officers who warned of the danger of collision damage, holding out the possibility of shore leave during repairs. *Kiwi*'s four-inch gun, illuminated by star shells from *Moa*, set afire the landing barge on *I-1*'s deck and killed Sakamoto and most of those on the conning tower. The executive officer, Lieutenant Koreda Sadayoshi, took command and tried to defend the boat, now unable to submerge. Bridson rammed the *I-1* three times. During one of these collisions the sub's navigator tried to board the New Zealand corvette and attack with his sword, but ship movements shook him loose and he fell into the sea, rescued to enter the POW cages. The sub ran aground on a reef 300 yards from the Guadalcanal shore.

Loss of the *I-1* set back the Imperial Navy's effort to develop specialized transport subs—but far worse was the loss of secrets of enormous value. Of the Japanese soldiers, nineteen survived. Of the sailors, forty-seven reached shore, taking with them papers that included the current version of the JN-25 code, alternately reported burned or buried. But later they realized that a case of documents had been left behind. With little time, a working party of Koreda and a couple of crewmen, along with sailors from the Japanese evacuation flotilla, were unable to demolish the sub. The survivors left with the destroyers. Koreda reached Rabaul, where NGS officers questioned him. Now the Japanese were anxious to gut the wreck with its secret trove. By February 8, Ultra had intercepted a message expressing dismay that codes had been compromised. On February 10, a strike by Buin-based Vals of the 582nd Air Group made a bomb hit on the wreck, though most planes failed to find it. The next day Lieutenant Koreda sailed from Shortland aboard Lieutenant Commander Inada Hiroshi's *I-2* in yet another desperate attempt. Ultra revealed that too, and the Allies interfered. The wreck eluded the *I-2* twice. On the first try Inada could not find her in the dark bay at night; on the second, during the night of February 15, PT boats depth-charged Inada's sub and an aircraft finally drove him away.

By then it was too late anyway. The New Zealand corvette *Moa* had nosed around the wreck the morning after the battle. By some accounts codebooks were taken then. On February 11, Army G-2 officers went to the site aboard *PT-65* and discovered much intelligence to exploit. Submarine rescue vessel *Ortolan* returned on the thirteenth, and divers salvaged documents including five codebooks, which were delivered to the Cactus Crystal Ball. Phil Jacobsen remembers the red-bound books, weighted with lead to be thrown overboard if necessary, and how the signals intelligence people worked to restore the waterlogged pages. Clean sheets of dry paper were placed between each leaf and the codebooks put on a hot radio receiver whose vacuum tubes did the job. On February 15, Cactus naval base reported acquiring seven codebooks, including two in the JN-25 code. CINCPAC immediately instructed the South Pacific command to forward the material by aircraft as quickly as possible.

Some historians have objected to an estimate in a history of Japanese naval communications that the *I-1* disaster resulted in the loss of 200,000 codebooks. This is a misinterpretation. The number refers to the copies of various code publications throughout the Imperial Navy that *had to be replaced* as a result of the compromise, not to the books actually lost in the submarine. Others have minimized the importance of the windfall, arguing that the current version of the code had actually been destroyed. That observation fails to take into account how codebreaking worked. JN-25 was a "book code" of groups of letters that stand in for words—and there were thousands of words in the Imperial Navy's fleet code. Until the *I-1* incident, Allied codebreakers never even knew what all the words were, did not know how the Japanese rendered certain technical terms, and remained free to dispute meanings. Even an old codebook settled those matters. Commander Thomas Dyer, codebreaker extraordinaire at Pearl Harbor, would later comment, "It was very useful to have a complete code, fleet vocabulary. It settled a number of arguments." Suddenly the codebreakers had a panoramic view of JN-25's structure.

In addition, the *I-1* yielded lists of the Imperial Navy's geographic designators, radio call signs, short-time and area codes, and a wealth of technical data on Japanese subs. A petty officer rescued from the crew furnished supplementary detail. Equally important, *the Japanese* considered the loss an intelligence crisis of the first order. The Imperial Navy immediately declared a cryptologic emergency, changed the additive tables used with JN-25, and began compiling a new codebook with different values. But they did not change the basic codebook. After the *I-1*, Allied codebreakers were two steps ahead on JN-25 throughout the war.

The Guadalcanal intelligence bonanza burst upon an Allied intelligence community morphing into new configurations. In the works for months, these changes created an even more dominant juggernaut. Some changes resulted from sincere efforts to improve the information that underlay operations, some from personality clashes; others could be traced to officers jockeying for position. Several strands of this story began and evolved through the first year of the war, but they came together early in 1943.

On the technology side there were two key developments. One resided in the increasing use of punch cards and mechanical sorting devices. The basic work of penetrating JN-25 and the other Japanese codes was accomplished by hand. Progress remained dependent on the ability to cross-reference possible discoveries, and there the card sorters proved critically important in accelerating the pace. The machines were not new, but the war brought great numbers of the sorters into service, and that injected fresh vigor and speed. "Radio Fingerprinting" (RFP) *was* a new development. It had long been recognized that experienced radiomen became so familiar with the circuits they monitored that, much like handwriting, over time they could recognize the "hand" of a given Japanese operator. The RFP technique capitalized on this phenomenon and regularized the process. An oscilloscope would be connected to the radio receiver, and whenever monitors overheard a new enemy operator, oscilloscope photos would be taken of his transmission, identifying his method and "hand." Over time intelligence accumulated an extensive file of these "fingerprints," which helped radio traffic analysts follow changes in the Japanese system. RFP helped identify the key enemy messages—which would be given to the most trusted operators for transmission—and it could reveal the character of a given ship or unit or even its identity when call signs were not available.

The most important organizational change concerned merging different pillars of intelligence to produce "all source" data. When the Central Intelligence Agency in the 1990s trumpeted so-called "fusion centers," it was really reviving this concept from World War II in the Pacific. Not long after Pearl Harbor, Washington began considering fusion centers, and soon after that the Marine Corps commandant suggested these be created in the field, starting with Pearl Harbor. A Washington delegation went to Hawaii to talk up the fusion concept, its Navy representative Commander Arthur H. McCallum, longtime chief of the Japan desk at the Office of Naval Intelligence. McCallum knew everybody in intel, but not Admiral Nimitz, and he was also afraid to broach the subject with Captain Edwin Layton,

CINCPAC's fleet intelligence officer, who might feel threatened by a joint center. McCallum was right about Layton, but that turned out not to matter. Shortly before Midway, Chester Nimitz put his name to a paper accepting the concept. A week after that battle, Admiral Ernest J. King approved the creation of an intelligence center. Layton, meanwhile, was wrong about the bureaucratic threat—his job with CINCPAC was secure so long as he wanted it.

Admiral Nimitz was notorious on the subject of staffs—none could be small enough for him. When Commander McCallum first broached the intelligence center with CINCPAC, Nimitz laughed as the emissary suggested a unit of 120 people. He couldn't fit that many on his flagship, Nimitz countered. But the realities of command across the Pacific soon forced the admiral to move CINCPAC headquarters ashore, and size became less problematic. In July 1942, seventy-six officers and men were ordered to Pearl Harbor to create the Intelligence Center Pacific Ocean Area (ICPOA), which grew like Topsy. The center absorbed Commander Jasper Holmes's combat intelligence unit, then an Army map unit, then newly trained language officers to interrogate prisoners, and later Pearl's photographic interpretation group. Station Hypo, reconstituted as FRUPAC, worked alongside ICPOA. At a December 1942 conference with Nimitz, despite his opposition Admiral King affirmed the decision to expand the center and have the radio spies report to it. In September 1943 the fusion took final shape, becoming the Joint Intelligence Center Pacific Ocean Area under an Army brigadier general. By war's end 1,700 people worked there, and Admiral Nimitz appreciated every single one of them.

The codebreaking group mushroomed too, even with the transfer to ICPOA of Commander Holmes's unit, by then a virtual FRUPAC ancillary. At the time of Midway there had been 168 persons—including radio operators—in the Station Hypo codebreaking unit, with just two cryptanalysts and three traffic analysis experts. By Eastern Solomons, FRUPAC had grown to 283 people, among them fifty-four experts in the code or traffic work or in the Japanese language, plus forty-six additional radio intercept operators in training. The Navy soon ordered FRUPAC personnel increased to 500, with seventeen more code experts and twenty-four extra language officers. Having outgrown its quarters, in early 1943 FRUPAC moved to a huge new wood frame building near CINCPAC headquarters on

Makalapa Hill. The Intelligence Center moved with it. Construction mirrored the burgeoning expansion: Before the end of the war FRUPAC had taken over the entire building, and an identical one had been built next door for the Joint Intelligence Center, which would also have an advanced echelon on a captured Central Pacific island. By then the U.S. Navy alone was operating 775 receivers across the Pacific entirely devoted to intercepting Japanese message traffic.

One man who did not make the move was Commander Joseph J. Rochefort, FRUPAC's eccentric chief. Until the fall of 1942, Rochefort had personally handled every Ultra decrypt at Pearl Harbor. Smoking his pipe, sitting at his desk in a bathrobe, Rochefort had penciled code solutions on pads used for that purpose. In a way, what happened was a harbinger of codebreaking come of age: The exponential growth of the effort, the increasing numbers of messages in the system—tokens of Ultra success— forced a mass-production approach. Joe Rochefort was an icon of a past age, when the gentleman codebreaker held sway. But he was also a victim of envy and ambition.

The codebreakers' head office in Washington—Station Negat in the cable addresses and Op-20-G by its Navy Department title—was headed by Captain John R. Redman and seconded by Commander Joseph N. Wenger. Redman, a communications expert, went to CINCPAC in the fall of 1942, leaving Wenger, promoted to captain, in charge. They denied Rochefort the award of the Distinguished Service Medal after Midway. Captain Wenger disliked the Hypo chief and hated the way Rochefort ignored Op-20-G directives. But Hypo had been right about Midway and Op-20-G wrong, and Rochefort saw no reason why FRUPAC should abandon work on key codes of which it had the deepest knowledge just because Wenger wanted the glory for Negat. Rochefort got Admiral Nimitz to approve a cable stating that FRUPAC worked only for CINCPAC, and only through him for Washington. Captain Layton also believed that Op-20-G harbored unduly alarmist fears of Japanese masterstrokes and counseled Nimitz to listen to Rochefort. Thus Nimitz protected Rochefort, untouchable after Midway.

Captains Redman and Wenger had the ear of Admiral King. Op-20-G officials saw the COMINCH almost every day. Over time Wenger convinced Ernie King the FRUPAC chief was a disruptive influence. At any rate, King got sick of the backbiting. If Rochefort had to be sacrificed to promote comity, those were the fortunes of war. With the reorganization going on perhaps Rochefort's departure would be more understandable. In October 1942, Admiral King summoned Commander Rochefort to Washington on temporary duty. He ended up as skipper of a floating dry dock. Jasper Holmes recorded that Rochefort "became the victim of a Navy Department internal political coup." Commander William B. Goggins succeeded him at the head of FRUPAC. His deputy would be Jasper Holmes. In later years Negat partisans claimed that 75 percent of the biggest breaks had happened there. FRUPAC veterans insist that 80 percent of the significant breakthroughs were made at Pearl Harbor.

Behind the scenes of the codebreakers' secret war, another conflict raged between the Office of Naval Communications and Office of Naval Intelligence (ONI) over control of the Ultra empire. John Redman's brother Joseph, already a rear admiral, was director of naval communications. Admiral Redman coveted Op-20-G and wanted Ultra for himself. Others maintained that Negat's function was intelligence and it should be within the ONI bailiwick. This dispute triggered continuing friction and reduced effectiveness to a degree, but since it continued past our period here, it will be noted only as a persistent problem.

As contentious as were issues between Washington and Pearl Harbor, those in General MacArthur's command were equally thorny. MacArthur wanted primacy for his SOWESPAC G-2 staff, yet he had to contend with the Australian government, with its own intelligence services, including such special services as the coastwatchers, a Dutch special services unit, and support to guerrilla forces in the Philippines. The organizations multiplied. SOWESPAC created an Allied Translator and Interpreter Section, which specialized in reporting on captured Japanese documents, and incidentally became a major employer of Japanese-American Nisei. Also established in 1942 was the Allied Intelligence Bureau, which handled special warfare activities like support to the Filipino partisans. Commander Feldt's coastwatcher organization Ferdinand became Section C of the Bureau. SOWESPAC also served as locus for another intelligence fusion center, the Seventh Fleet Intelligence Center (SEFIC), up and running by 1943 under Captain Arthur McCallum. Meanwhile, the Australian government's codebreaking unit, the Central Bureau, became yet another part of this constellation. And, of course, there was Fleet Radio Unit Melbourne (FRUMEL), officially existing since March 12, 1942.

Under Major General Charles A. Willoughby, G-2 was an Army shop, and that brought trouble with the naval codebreakers of FRUMEL. Lieutenant Commander Rudolph Fabian, its chief, crossed swords with Willoughby on numerous occasions. With Ultra, Fabian's practice was to relate the information in decrypts but not permit access to the documents except to the top commander, General MacArthur. On one occasion, when Willoughby demanded to see a dispatch, Fabian carried a copy to the G-2's office, took out his cigarette lighter, and burned it in front of the enraged general.

Security was a top worry for Fabian. At the time of Coral Sea, Fabian had briefed MacArthur—as he did daily—and found the general unconvinced when the FRUMEL expert informed him that the Japanese were really going to go for Port Moresby. That did not surprise Fabian much—His own notion of the enemy strategy had been that they would go for New Caledonia first, to isolate Australia. Commander Fabian launched into an explanation of the entire Ultra process, and the SOWESPAC boss ended up diverting a transport scheduled for New Caledonia to Port Moresby instead. General MacArthur seemed so excited, the Navy officer worried the SOWESPAC leader would reveal his source. Meanwhile, British codebreakers laboring as part of the Allied common effort complained that Fabian and FRUMEL were denying them appropriate access. On the Australian side, Commander Eric Nave was a big player in Royal Australian Navy codebreaking and came aboard at FRUMEL. Fabian repeatedly upbraided Nave for lax security discipline until the latter left for the Central Bureau. Commander Fabian felt relieved to see him go.

Rudy Fabian's headaches only began there. At FRUMEL some of the language officers, including his Australian Navy deputy, Commander Jack B. Newman, as well as U.S. lieutenant commanders Swede Carlson and Gilbert M. Richardson, actually outranked him. Commander Newman was content to let Fabian take the lead. The others had been with Fabian in the Philippines during the desperate siege of Corregidor, and they had escaped with him by submarine. At the old Station Cast, they had had an informal understanding: Fabian would be in charge, freeing them for practical work. Both Carlson and Richardson preferred translation and code work to administration, so they were happy with the arrangement. On the British side, despite the problems with coordination, a Japanese linguist who had escaped from Singapore, Lieutenant Commander Meriman, became one of FRUMEL's best translators. Relations with the Central Bureau were always delicate. Both did the same kind of work. Once Eric Nave started a small naval codebreaking cell within Central Bureau there was a danger of direct competition. Mostly the two Ultra units went their own ways.

Unlike Rochefort, Commander Fabian did not fall victim to internecine squabbling. He served out a full term. When Captain McCallum arrived to set up the SEFIC intelligence center, he drafted Fabian to help him with the key players. Then, for his sins Fabian was sent to Colombo as U.S. intelligence liaison to the British. Fabian continued to earn British ire there. In mid-1943, FRUMEL, Station Belconnen in the Copek network, had 203 personnel on staff, with a projected need for 300. Fabian was followed by Commander E. S. L. "Sid" Goodwin. By then most of FRUMEL's work—Sid Goodwin estimated 90 percent—concerned Japanese submarine messages. Of course, that was after the year of Guadalcanal and the big naval battles. In early 1943 some of the fiercest engagements were yet to be fought.

STOCKTAKING

Both sides tried to measure themselves against the enemy. At CINCPAC, Chester Nimitz put his staff to work on a variety of studies, and put his impressions in a letter to Ernie King on December 8, 1942, when COMINCH was debating the Joint Chiefs of Staff on war strategy. Neither side had any advantage in determination to fight, Nimitz observed. The Japanese were full equals in that department. In terms of surface naval units, Nimitz went on, the sides were roughly equal save that U.S. fire control radars seemed to be a lot better under low-light conditions. He also found American antiaircraft batteries considerably better than Japanese. Allied air forces were superior in quality. American ground forces had proved themselves more skillful, but Nimitz was not willing to bet on this and wanted to be in greater numbers whenever battle was joined. The CINCPAC admitted to perplexity on the question of torpedoes. American ones just seemed not to work, while Japanese torpedoes wreaked havoc time after time. Solving that technical problem required patience and hard work.

Admiral Nimitz's opinions provide a good point of departure for a review of the balance in the Solomons. Guadalcanal had been secured. Henderson, now a complex of several airfields and about to operate heavy B-17 aircraft, became an offensive base once SOPAC fed in enough airplanes to perfect its striking power. The island furnished the stepping-stone for the implementation of Cartwheel. Naval forces were strong enough that after the *Chicago* episode Halsey felt able to detach the *Enterprise* to return to the U.S. for real repairs to her deck elevators and aircraft hangars. Negotiations with the British for the loan of an aircraft carrier had been completed; the Royal Navy had selected the HMS *Victorious*, and by January 1943 she was being refitted at Norfolk Navy Yard. This included replacing her antiquated Swordfish torpedo bombers with modern Grumman TBF Avengers. Disguised in radio messages as the USS *Robin* (for Robin Hood, the wags had it), the *Victorious* transited the Panama Canal and reached Pearl Harbor by March. A month later she went to the South Pacific. Captain L. D. MacIntosh's *Victorious* became a crucial SOPAC asset in a critical category at an important time.

At the moment troops were the worst problem. Expectations were that the 1st Marine Division would not again be ready to fight until March 1943. That was tentative and depended on restoring the Marines' health and retraining the units. The 2nd Marine Division, now mostly at Guadalcanal, had been projected late in 1942 to be on hand by February, but after the exhausting finish of the battle, it too needed rest. No Army troops beyond those already present were ready or even assigned to the South Pacific, and the Americal and 25th Infantry Divisions were worse off than the 2nd Marines. The 43rd Infantry Division, pulled together from various island garrisons that were no longer required, presently became available, but it was green and needed experience. A 3rd Marine Division would materialize later in the year. In short, the paucity of ground forces required an operational pause.

Admiral Halsey recognized that, but he wanted to retain the momentum gained at Guadalcanal. He needed a close-in target with some intrinsic value. The Bull and Nimitz had already discussed the Russell Islands, and now Halsey settled on that. Like the Japanese with their barge base there, the Americans could put down a PT base. Such a base could project PT boats up The Slot to blockade New Georgia and the Japanese airfield at

Munda. Air bases on the Russells could extend AIRSOLS power to and past Munda. Halsey decided to go ahead. Coastwatchers scouted the Russells. So did a party of American and New Zealand officers. They found nothing but abandoned Japanese equipment and the roughly 350 islanders who before the war had cultivated the coconut plantations for Lever Brothers. Operation Cleanslate, the invasion of the Russells, took place on February 21. Major General John Hester of the 43rd Infantry Division, Halsey's only fresh formation, led the landing force, composed of a few of Hester's units, some Marines, plus engineer and construction troops. For all practical purposes, Cleanslate proved a routine landing. Ironically, in view of the Japanese withdrawal from Guadalcanal, one of the worst headaches in Cleanslate turned out to be failures of the outboard motors on rubber assault boats.

Once ashore the Americans turned to their main purpose: converting the Russells into a base area. Banika, one of the Russells, actually seemed free of malarial mosquitoes, so the engineers concentrated there. The 118th Engineer Battalion of Hester's division built roads and fortifications and installed water pumps. The 37th Seabees were the airfield specialists and began to lay runways and PT boat base facilities. The Japanese tried their best to slow progress with air attacks, starting March 6. In spite of every obstacle, by late April, Banika was available for emergency landings, and a month later the Russells opened for business. Remarkably, its first denizens would be Marine Air Group 21, among the stalwarts who had pioneered at Henderson Field.

Bull Halsey continued trying to suppress the Japanese on New Georgia. His main instruments were air strikes from Guadalcanal, now rebranded "Mainstay," and naval bombardments. On a March 6 excursion to shell Vila, Rear Admiral Aaron S. Merrill caught a pair of Japanese destroyers returning from an Express run. Seaman Fahey was aboard the *Montpelier*, which led the cruiser line and was first to open fire. In moments the lead destroyer, *Murasame*, transformed into a mass of flames and explosions. *Minegumo* put on speed and tried to flee but was smashed in her turn. "It looked like the 4th of July," Fahey noted. Two Japanese seamen were rescued and questioned by intelligence; some 175 survivors reached the Kolombangara shore and eventually the Vila base; the rest of the sailors went down with their ships. Merrill proceeded to execute his bombardment. *Montpelier* alone lashed out with 1,800 five- and six-inch shells in a mere quarter of an hour, producing a spectacle: "There were many big explosions from the shore as our guns hit their targets. . . . We did an awful job on the Japs, we left the place in shambles, we hit troop barracks, ammunition dumps, radio towers, airfield planes, and broken bodies were everywhere." Halsey then switched Rear Admiral Ainsworth's task group for Merrill's and kept up the pressure. Ainsworth adopted the novel approach of splitting his cruisers and destroyers into two units so he could alternate sending them up The Slot, attempting to keep the Tokyo Express away from New Georgia. Pug Ainsworth led the combined force back for another bombardment of Munda and Vila on April 2.

Meanwhile the top brass hammered out their strategic approach in memos, dispatches, a Pearl Harbor staff conference, and Joint Chiefs of Staff deliberations. Halsey wanted to assault Munda, or at least neutralize it, in April. MacArthur insisted the SOPAC advance on New Georgia be held back pending his next offensive jump in New Guinea, projected for May, which would include a landing in the Trobriand Islands to install an airfield at the virtual doorstep of Rabaul. The Joint Chiefs accepted MacArthur's strategy, but also Admiral Nimitz's proposal that operational command throughout the Solomons would continue to be exercised by SOPAC and Halsey. Cartwheel assumed its ultimate form at the end of March. Though MacArthur's offensive would be delayed for six weeks while amphibious forces assembled, the directions of action and lines of command had finally been set.

As did the Allies, the Japanese reassessed their position. The Guadalcanal campaign had been exhausting, but it at least ended on the positive note of a successful evacuation. Losses had been staggering, the pace relentless. General MacArthur's U.S. and Australian troops were thrusting ahead in New Guinea and had captured Buna. Halsey's invasion of the Russells might have followed a minimum-energy trajectory from the Allied perspective, but to the Japanese it seemed like the next step in a continuing onslaught. The IGHQ directive currently in effect required Combined Fleet and the Japanese Army to contest both the Solomons and New Guinea.

Much had changed at Rabaul. Just before Christmas the Imperial Navy finally created a theater command along lines similar to the Allies. This Southeast Area Fleet controlled both the Eighth Fleet's surface ships and the

Eleventh Air Fleet airplanes. Vice Admiral Kusaka Jinichi led it, and also his air fleet. Rear Admiral Nakahara Giichi, a Navy Ministry bureaucrat, assisted Kusaka as chief of staff in his area fleet capacity. There were new faces. Some old warhorses left. Kusaka's cousin, Kusaka Ryunosuke, supplanted when Admiral Nagumo turned over command of the *Kido Butai*, later appeared in Rabaul as air fleet staff boss. Captain Miwa Yoshitake, recently of Combined Fleet staff's inner sanctum, acted as air fleet senior staff officer. Genda Minoru, having contracted malaria, returned to Japan. Fighter expert Commander Nomura Ryosuke took over the air operations staff slot. Captain Kanai and Commander Kaneko arrived to coordinate the flow of replacement planes.

Though this would be the admiral's time, he had not anticipated it. The fifty-five-year-old Kusaka had served more than three decades and had expected to retire as superintendant of Etajima. His war had been China. On December 7, 1941—Kusaka Jinichi's birthday—his daughter had become engaged. After celebrating he went to bed—and awoke next morning to discover Japan had bombed Pearl Harbor. Kusaka had known war threatened—temporary duty as staff chief of the Eleventh Air Fleet in 1941 had led to his participation in the tabletop war games that rehearsed the invasion of Southeast Asia—but he had known nothing of Japan's Pearl Harbor plan. Thoughts of retirement evaporated. Kusaka was a good friend of Yamamoto, who had been on the training ship *Soya* during Jinichi's midshipman cruise, notable because their circuit of Australia had been in company with a Russian warship that Yamamoto helped sink in the Russo-Japanese War. Refloated, that vessel sailed with them now, enemies no more. Friendship with Yamamoto was a plus in Kusaka's selection for the Rabaul command. His assignment to replace Tsukahara Nizhizo had been sudden, and came when the latter fell sick in the fall of 1942.

Kusaka Jinichi was an unusual choice for an air command. His only exposure to aviation had been that short stint with Tsukahara before the Philippine campaign. A gunner by trade, Kusaka had been gunnery officer aboard the *Nagato*, skippered the *Fuso*, and directed the Naval Gunnery School once making his stars. He had also been naval attaché in London. But the compact, careful Kusaka—one historian likened him to the actor Alec Guinness—was a flexible thinker, and no one carped at his skimpy aviation knowledge. Plus he was well supported by cousin Ryunosuke, a true aviation expert. Kusaka made up for ignorance with evident concern. The aviators saw him often, and he would witness their departures or returns. Once, when JNAF ace Nishizawa Hiroyoshi was late returning from a mission, Kusaka had stood for hours at the runway, an admiral attending a warrant officer. Nishizawa was among those whom Kusaka honored with the award of a ceremonial sword.

In early 1943 there were a few good elements in Kusaka's picture. Another airfield had recently been added to the Rabaul complex. Facilities at Buin had been expanded. Meanwhile the arrival of Army air forces increased strength considerably. Another airfield was planted in the New Georgia group, on Kolombangara, and the Army planes soon deployed there. Admiral Kusaka had good relations with General Imamura, his Army counterpart. As for supplying the far-flung bases, the Japanese were now well practiced in barge, submarine, and Tokyo Express activities, and had even developed specialized equipment, for example the submarines that carried their own barges. The first two months of 1943 were very good for the Imperial Navy in terms of losses, with only two destroyers sunk and four damaged, a toll almost sustainable.

Night-attack tactics were also a plus for Kusaka. Training this force had been difficult, for many units had had to practice while keeping up standard operating routines. The 751st Air Group was a good example. A storied unit, with battle honors for sinking the British capital ships *Repulse* and *Prince of Wales*; and a mainstay of the Philippine, East Indies, and China campaigns (under its previous identity as the Kanoya Air Group), the 751st had reunited at Rabaul in September 1942. Thereafter it had participated in the Henderson Field bombing as well as the raids at the time of Santa Cruz. The night missions had actually sharpened aviators' skills, as the 751st demonstrated when it helped sink the American cruiser *Chicago* in January.

Completion of the air base at Munda created another new bastion, soon protected by eighteen heavy flak guns, twenty of 40mm caliber, and fifty quick-firing 25mm pieces by the count of Q-bush's photo interpreters. They were well protected, their worst problem ammunition supply. Through the first half of 1943 there were only a couple hundred casualties among the flak crews, which, considering the weight of Allied attacks, amounted to very little. Repeated Allied naval bombardments damaged Munda's runway, but it was never out of action for long. Halsey's neutralization campaign convinced Kusaka not to station Navy planes at Munda, yet it remained vital as a bolt-hole for damaged aircraft or those low on fuel. By mid-1943 there were 12,000 Japanese at Munda, with several months of food and one month of ammunition supplies.

Gloomier aspects were also apparent. The Japanese Naval Air Force had been shorn of hundreds of its best pilots and crews. While the total number of aircrew had grown since Pearl Harbor, the percentage of less experienced fliers increased rapidly, and the Navy had no system for regular rotation of flying personnel. Men flew until they were shot down, they were assigned to another air group, or their units redeployed. The 751st Air Group, to take one case, had been so sharply reduced that after eight months in action it would be withdrawn to Tinian for retraining and reinforcement. Some 150 airmen were lost in just the first four months of 1943. Captain Sato Naohiro brought the group back to Rabaul in August. By then only a dozen of Sato's crews were qualified for night attack. For the remainder of the campaign the 751st flew out of Vunakanau and Buka. Having returned at full strength—fifty-two aircraft—the unit would be given another fifty replacements, and in November it absorbed fifteen Bettys from the 702nd Group, which had to be disbanded. Yet when the 751st left for Tinian again it possessed just twenty planes—and eight of them were flyable but not capable of combat. In short, the air group had lost nearly a hundred warplanes. At that point officer pilots were nearly extinct in Sato's group—two of his squadrons (*hikobutai*) were led by junior lieutenants and one by an ensign. The Solomons arena burned through JNAF units.

Captain Sato's headaches regarding mechanics matched his problem with aircrews. The group had two maintenance units, each responsible for servicing the planes of a pair of 751st Group flying squadrons. With losses, one of the maintenance outfits had to be converted into a training unit. Melding Sato's formation with the 702nd Air Group actually proved advantageous, for it brought a new gang of mechanics to replace the men reassigned as instructors.

Individual pilots were funneled in to replace losses, but reassignment usually happened in conjunction with debilitating sickness or unit withdrawal. One example would be Warrant Officer Shimakawa Masaki of the 204th Group, so badly afflicted with malaria that he was put on a hospital ship that departed in March. Another was ace Nishizawa, sent home from the 253rd Air Group in late 1943 to become a pilot instructor. A third was Warrant Officer Ohara Ryoji of the 204th, the so-called "Killer of Rabaul." Air officer Nomura believed that an inability to keep up the level of experienced fliers and maintenance men, shortfalls in aircraft production, and the quality of Allied planes, were key reasons for high loss rates.

Averages tell the story. The percentage of pilots rated expert, with more than 600 hours in the air, had declined by a quarter. Worse, around the beginning of 1943, the JNAF reached the fifty-fifty point in terms of experts versus less experienced fliers with 300 to 600 air hours. By February those with fewer air hours exceeded expert airmen for the first time, and within a matter of months the Navy would begin sending pilots into battle with just 200 to 300 air hours. In February there were 104 combat losses but 161 aircraft destroyed by accident or mishap. By spring the ratio of operational to combat losses would rise to two to one, a rate that improved only occasionally and would often be exceeded. Despite the experienced airmen reassigned as instructors, larger numbers of trainees meant less personal attention, while diminishing supplies of aviation gas reduced training hours in the air.

Commander Ohmae, who had been at Rabaul since the onset of the Solomons campaign, estimated that barely 15 percent of the expert pilots who had flown against the Americans still manned their cockpits. The 582nd Air Group, though up to strength, had just four fighter pilots left from its original complement. By July the 204th Air Group had not a single officer pilot. In mid-July the 201st Air Group, a Zero fighter unit, arrived in Rabaul. Commander Nakano Chujiro, its boss, assessed his pilots as eight experienced, twenty competent, and twenty-four novices. Fresh-faced young fliers developed a fear of Allied interceptors, especially the F-6F Hellcats, but even of the trusty older Wildcats. An American intelligence study prepared in October 1943 captures this well:

> They made glaring tactical mistakes, unnecessarily exposed themselves to gunfire, got separated and lost mutual support, and at times seemed to be completely bewildered. Both bomber and fighter pilots ceased to display the aggressiveness that marked

their earlier combat. Bombers ceased to penetrate to their targets
in the face of heavy fire, as they had formerly done; they jettisoned bombs, attacked outlying destroyers, gave up attempts on
massed transports in the center of a formation. Fighters broke off
their attacks on Allied heavy and medium bombers before getting within effective range, and often showed a marked distaste
for close-in combat with Allied fighters.

On the other hand, a U.S. intelligence commentary a few months later
observed that between February and June 1943 there had been a partial
resurgence of high-quality performance among JNAF fliers. But in June
alone, the 204th Group lost five of its most experienced prewar pilots.

The crews resigned themselves to fighting at a disadvantage yet with
determination.

Early in the year there had been a daylight air raid on Rabaul, an ominous sign. But only a dozen B-17s participated. That was a big strike. General Kenney's air force was stationed on primitive bases—like the Japanese
themselves—with gaping spare parts shortages and the challenges of flying in the tropical climate. Bomb squadrons that typically possessed twelve
aircraft had trouble keeping more than seven in flying shape. These were
the units that went against Rabaul. "We'd go in individually," recalled Lloyd
Boren, a bombardier with the 19th Bomb Group. "We only flew in formation twice." On many nights a few planes circled above the base, occasionally dropping a bomb, utilizing intruder tactics identical to those of
"Washing Machine Charlie" over Cactus. Kenney's airmen made more than
twice as many sorties against the fortress in January 1943 than in the previous month, though their effort overall (127 flights) remained at a low level,
fewer in February (110 sorties)—and these would be high points until the
summer. A couple of larger night raids in February inaugurated the use of
incendiary bombs. One Japanese airman at Vunakanau thought the incendiaries were like lightning bolts.

Meanwhile the Japanese aircraft industry confronted major headaches
in getting its own innovations through engineering development into production. Meeting specifications required more powerful aircraft engines,
and the Japanese had trouble there. Engine problems delayed both the J2M
("Jack") and the Zero follow-on A7M ("Sam") fighters. The Sam failed to

perform with its first engine and had to await a new one, delaying the program two whole years. Tooling the manufacturing plants to produce new
planes posed other difficulties. Production of the "Judy" (D4Y), a new carrier scout plane, remained so sluggish that during the Guadalcanal battles
the Navy's carriers had only small detachments of these craft. The Jack was
accepted for production in October 1942, but by April 1943 only fourteen
had been delivered. Over the next year the plants manufactured just 141
more of these planes. With the N1K1-J ("George") the factories turned out
only seventy aircraft by the end of 1943. Japanese predilection for light-
weight designs caused additional problems. The Judy had been designed as
a carrier bomber but became a scout when it was revealed that carrying
bombs damaged aircraft structural components. The "Jill" (B6N2), the next
alternative, was revealed to have understrength arresting gear and failed its
carrier landing tests aboard the *Zuikaku* and *Ryuho* in early 1943. Redesign
retarded production. Deliveries by midyear numbered 133. Accidents
and teething problems with the "hot" Jack fighter that summer required
further design modifications and triggered more factory delays. During the
time of decision in the Solomons, the new aircraft hardly made an impact.
The Imperial Navy would be obliged to fight with the weapons at hand.

Such problems did not go unnoticed at the highest level. Emperor Hirohito, a scientific adept, took an interest in aircraft and the aviation industry. Lord Kido, the privy counselor, records that at the end of March the
emperor spent much of an unusually long audience with him ruminating
on the setbacks in the Solomons. Heavy losses in aircraft especially concerned him. From a Tokyo perspective the future seemed bleak.

Given the fragility of naval aircraft—Army planes were actually better
armored and protected—and the steadily increasing numbers of new-
generation Allied fighters, the trends were distressing. At the point when
the Allies occupied the Russells, Admiral Kusaka's air strength remained
respectable, at 200 serviceable planes, though the Guadalcanal withdrawal
cost about fifty effective aircraft. The JNAF had become inferior in both
numbers and quality.

Combined Fleet chief of staff Ugaki complained incessantly to his diary
of Japanese air forces found wanting. At Truk, where the fleet flagship moored, the picture was actually brighter than nearer the front. The
deployment of the night-attack force bombers seemed a plus, quickly

rewarded by destruction of the *Chicago.* But at Rabaul the high losses of experienced airmen and the poor aircraft upkeep, leading to low serviceability rates, were petrifying. It was symptomatic of this situation that some of
the unit commanders and best crews in the night-attack force had perished
in its first engagement. On the other hand, Allied bombing of Rabaul declined after February—to a low of just nine sorties in April. Another good
sign, in May, would be the first JNAF night fighters, twin-engine Irvings
converted from scouts. Commander Kozono Yasuna of the 251st Air Group
suggested replacing the observer's position in the cockpit with upward-
firing 20mm cannon. The Irvings represented the first aerial opposition to
the Allies' nocturnal bomber raids, which returned to a high level in June
with 141 sorties dropping 284 tons of ordnance. Ensign Kudo Shigetoshi
would score the first B-17 kill with an Irving on the night of May 21. A half
dozen more victories followed before August, when Admiral Kusaka gave
Kudo a sword.

The Japanese high command understood the necessity to regain control
of the air. No matter the weakness of the forces, this was a prerequisite to
success. Admiral Nagano exhorted the Combined Fleet both privately and
through Imperial Headquarters. The November IGHQ directive that underlay base construction at Munda and Kolombangara had dictated special
attention to strengthening air defenses. A month later, setting operational
policy for New Guinea, Imperial Headquarters again underlined the need
for aerial strength. The orders that mandated the KE Operation provided
for Navy and Army air forces to "display their all-out joint might." Other
activities should be conducted under this air umbrella. The Navy was to
concern itself especially with the Solomons, the Army with New Guinea.
Admiral Nagano hinted to the emperor that Munda would be abandoned
if the base became endangered. When they next met, on January 26, Hirohito opposed that course, and the naval command backed down. Munda
would be held and New Guinea contested. Recognizing the growing threat
of General MacArthur's offensive, the high command diverted to Papua,
where Japanese positions were threatened, the troops earmarked for the
next, now forgotten, Guadalcanal offensive.

At Rabaul the high command's intentions boiled down to collaboration
between Admiral Kusaka and General Imamura on a major reinforcement
of New Guinea, with the bulk of the 51st Infantry Division to be sent there

in a troop convoy at the end of February. Kusaka and Imamura believed MacArthur's forces would need to catch their breath after their exertions at Buna, so the opportunity seemed to be offered for this maneuver. Admiral Mikawa laid down detailed plans for the scheme, called Operation 81. Eight transports would be stuffed with men and supplies, escorted by an equal number of destroyers under Rear Admiral Kimura Masatomi. Because a convoy to Lae had gone without incident in January, Mikawa felt this could succeed also. He had no illusions that the convoy would emerge unscathed—at their speed of seven knots the transports would be within attack range for as long as two days—but Guadalcanal experience suggested that at worst half the 7,000 troops would reach their destination, doubling the Lae garrison even at that level of losses. The risk seemed worth taking, given the stakes involved.

Mikawa made careful arrangements with Eleventh Air Fleet. For a few days prior to the convoy there would be neutralization attacks on Allied air bases around Port Moresby, Buna and Rabi. With Army planes participating and the arrival of the 25th Air Flotilla, as many as 200 fighters would take turns patrolling above the ships. Desperate for sustenance, the Japanese were determined to succeed. The first bad omen came when poor weather and overconfidence combined to nullify the precursor raids. Reconnaissance flights either were canceled or returned few results. The Japanese would have scant knowledge of the opposition. No one realized the great danger that lay ahead.

SLAUGHTER IN THE BISMARCK SEA

As with the bloody tales of the Guadalcanal convoys, the story of the Lae transport fleet again demonstrated the vulnerability of slow ships to mass air attack. This Allied triumph, with a minor assist from the codebreakers, was the product of energetic SOWESPAC airmen both innovating new techniques and executing their missions. As early as February 19, General Willoughby's G-2 warned of probable enemy attempts to reinforce Lae. Two days before the Japanese convoy sailed, Ultra had enough of an inkling to issue a warning. While the picture remained fuzzy—the codebreakers were not sure of the convoy's size, its escort, or whether the Japanese intended prior or concurrent "mouse" missions—Allied intelligence was certain that transports were involved, that their destination was Lae, and they projected a date of arrival. This was enough to alert the Fifth Air Force to search with special care, and it gave General Kenney a chance to marshal his strike planes for the appointed days. Though a number of worn-out units were resting in Australia, Kenney put together 129 bombers and 207 fighters for the battle. The Australians contributed fifty of those planes. Kenney's bomber command even planned for contingencies, creating three different options depending on which way the Japanese turned as they approached New Guinea.

Rear Admiral Kimura, an experienced officer, had been in some tight spots already. He had had an important role in Kondo's naval battles off Cactus, and was another of those who had witnessed the *Hornet* ablaze at Santa Cruz. Kimura was old-school, sporting a splendid mustache, and had risen through the ranks as a mine and torpedo expert, just recently promoted to flag rank. His experience might have helped, except that General Kenney had an enormous strike force, plus the benefit of a newly innovated technique called "skip bombing." With this method an airplane would toss its bombs at an enemy vessel, like skipping a rock across a pond, resulting in a very flat trajectory and minimizing the ability of a ship to react. Bombs were armed with delayed-action fuses to permit the skip action to take effect. Kenney also modified his bombers with rigs of eight forward-firing machine guns to strafe as they made their attack runs. The Allies would suppress the flak gunners by having some fighters strafe alongside the bombers and by simultaneous attacks from low and medium altitude.

Familiarity with standard torpedo tactics would not help Admiral Kimura here, for turning into or directly away from an aircraft using skip bombing actually *increased* the target aspect. The old salt also would be poorly served by Japanese air cover. While the JNAF and the recently created Fourth Air Army had plenty of fighters to protect a westerly run to New Guinea, their bases were under SOWESPAC attack, and the nearest airfield on New Britain, at Gasmata, could not handle masses of aircraft. The headache of Japanese aircraft flying at extreme range repeated. The Army interceptors had less endurance than JNAF Zeroes. Some forty Navy and sixty Army fighters would patrol. Lieutenant Sato Masao brought the fighters of his *Zuiho* air group to Kavieng to be available for the operation. Despite preparations, Kusaka's Eleventh Air Fleet found itself hard-pressed to keep as many as forty fighters orbiting the convoy. They would be no match for Kenney's Fifth Air Force. Admiral Kimura steamed into a trap.

Kimura set the time of departure from Rabaul shortly before midnight of February 27. The admiral flew his flag in destroyer *Shirayuki*. Senior Army commanders also sailed in the tin cans, General Adachi Hatazo of the Eighteenth Army in the *Tokitsukaze*, and General Nakano Hidemitsu in the *Yukikaze*. The first day passed peacefully, a deceptive prelude to hell. Admiral Weather helped the Japanese, with a storm front above New Britain—gale-force winds, recurrent rain, plenty of mist. But late on March 1, one of Kenney's snoopers saw the Japanese convoy for the first time. SOWESPAC tried an immediate attack with some B-17s, but the weather closed in and they could not locate Kimura. The next morning Kenney had his scouts deliberately looking and found the convoy, leading to a bombing late that day by B-24 Liberators. Kusaka's land-based Zeroes had some success distracting the bombers, but one transport, struck aft by a heavy bomb, settled and sank. Kimura's destroyers hovered next to her and rescued many of the embarked soldiers and crew. That night Australian PBY Catalinas followed the convoy and made harassing attacks but obtained no results. Two of Kimura's destroyers dashed ahead to land their Army troops, including General Nakano, at Lae. The warships rejoined the convoy early in the morning of March 3.

Aboard the *Tokitsukaze*, Yoshihara Kane, a lieutenant general and Adachi's chief of staff, was up to greet the dawn. With the convoy rounding the Huon Peninsula, the general could see the coast of New Guinea for the first time. Suddenly he glimpsed a plane in the distance, coming up from the south, but it disappeared in mist. Yoshihara felt apprehensive, a premonition of evil, but this was an Imperial navy show. Any decision would be made by Kimura. The admiral could have put about, withdrawing, or made for Finschhafen, the nearest port. He radioed Rabaul for instructions. Shades of Eastern Solomons: neither Mikawa nor Kusaka made any immediate reply. Because an arrival time at Lae had been set, Kimura held his course. Bending on every ounce of steam, the convoy accelerated to nine knots.

General Yoshihara went below for breakfast. His impression was that that plane, rather than being some casual morning flight, had been looking for them specifically. As Yoshihara climbed back topside, the dawn mists were giving way to a sparkling day. All was calm, so he returned to his cabin, then went to consult his senior staff officer on what they should do upon debarking. Ten minutes later, at about 10:00 a.m., sirens sounded and *Tokitsukaze* went to battle stations. Machine gun bullets from strafing planes began to perforate the destroyer's unarmored hull. The ship groaned and vibrated as her skipper, Lieutenant Commander Motokura Masayoshi, maneuvered under the bombs. The *Tokitsukaze* shuddered with a blow. She lost way. Motokura thought they had been torpedoed. Yoshihara felt it miraculous that there had been no explosion, but there was no remaining aboard, so the nearby *Yukikaze* was asked to take the Army men off.

By then General Yoshihara could already see smoke rising from more than half the surrounding vessels. The air assault succeeded brilliantly. As it happened, Kenney's planes struck just as the JNAF fighter patrol was to hand over to the next unit. Fighters of the 253rd Air Group had had the first shift, reinforced by planes of the 204th later. Around 10:00 a.m. there were twenty-six land-based Zeroes orbiting at 20,000 feet as eighteen *Zuiho* aircraft approached. Some of the patrolling Zeroes had started for Gasmata. Hearing panic on the radio, the interceptors returned. American and Australian fighters engaged them as the strike waves pounced. Half the Zeroes were lost. B-17 Flying Fortresses attacked from medium altitude, while B-25s and A-20s came in very low to skip bombs. Much of the carnage took place in just twenty minutes, though follow-on attacks occurred throughout the day. The American official historian estimates that twenty-eight of thirty-seven 500-pound munitions from the skip bombers hit, an amazing success rate. Fifth Air Force losses were a mere three P-38 fighters and a single B-17.

On the Japanese side the toll was horrendous. There were six transports and two cargo ships in the convoy. Every one disappeared beneath the waves. In addition to *Tokitsukaze*, Kimura lost his flagship and two more destroyers, half his total escort. In all, the losses amounted to eight merchantmen, four destroyers, and about fifteen aircraft. In his memoirs, George Kenney claimed the losses as six destroyers or light cruisers sunk, two more damaged, eleven to fourteen merchantmen sunk, and ninety-five aircraft definitely or probably destroyed or damaged. Naval historian Samuel Eliot Morison investigated this huge discrepancy after the war and discovered that captured documents had revealed the true strength of the Japanese convoy before the end of March 1943. The inflated numbers appeared in pilot claims—always exaggerated—and had been used in MacArthur's press releases, soon to be corrected. Yet even after the war General Kenney repeated the demonstrably false claims.

Back at the battle, Admiral Kimura was wounded when his flagship *Shirayuki* had her fantail blown off. Commander Kawahashi Akifumi brought his *Shikinami* alongside and rescued the crew. When General Yoshihara came aboard to consider what to do, Kimura lay on a couch in *Shikinami*'s wardroom, blood seeping through the bandages covering his arm. Yoshihara wanted the destroyers to take his men on to New Guinea. Kimura agreed that might be desirable, but his warships were now low on fuel, and he had no desire to risk them on the anvil under the Allied planes. They were still wrestling with this decision when orders came to return to Rabaul immediately. In Tokyo, informed of the disaster, Emperor Hirohito immediately asked Yoshihara's question: Why had the Navy not immediately shifted gears and landed the troops elsewhere than Lae? The high command had failed to learn the lessons of the Guadalcanal convoy battles.

Kimura's remaining destroyers saved as many as they could. A couple of submarines in the area, *I-17* and *I-26*, also helped, rescuing 275 men. That night New Guinea–based PT boats came to finish off the derelicts. In at least one case, the PTs drove an I-boat underwater and machine-gunned refugees who had thought themselves saved. Some 2,734 Japanese soldiers were taken aboard rescue vessels. A couple hundred destroyer crewmen were recovered later. More than 900 troops had already been deposited at Lae. Some 3,000 men of the 51st Division were missing. The lucky few survived. Yamada Masayoshi drifted for ten days and finally reached Goodenough Island, only to be captured by Australians. Two more soldiers, Lieutenant Iki and Sergeant Namiki, who rescued the battle flag of the 15th Regiment, endured a whole month and providentially reached shore near Gasmata. Most of the missing men perished. The Imperial Navy never sent another transport convoy to New Guinea.

The Bismarck Sea slaughter stunned the Imperial high command, Combined Fleet, and everyone else. Despite precautions, the convoy had been crushed. That showed the swing of the pendulum, but it also raised leadership questions. The Navy decided to revamp its command structure and recalled Mikawa Gunichi. Samejima Tomoshige, a baron and vice admiral, replaced him. Until the previous October, when the fifty-four-year-old Samejima went to Truk to head the Fourth Fleet in the Central Pacific, he had been Emperor Hirohito's senior naval aide-de-camp. The question of an Imperial Navy gambit to placate Emperor Hirohito is relevant here. The emperor's impatience had become increasingly apparent from his repeated, if indirect, criticisms. Much of our knowledge of Hirohito's anxieties resides in the diary of Samejima's associate Captain Jyo Eiichiro, another Navy aide, of whom the monarch was quite fond, and with whom Hirohito even relaxed, playing cards and other games. Jyo, an aviator, exemplified the thoroughly modern element of the Navy. When off duty he explored facets of science, which fascinated Hirohito as well. The two were close enough for Captain Jyo to furnish informal advice. Although this is speculative, it is possible the aide encouraged the emperor to get his own observer near the front by inducing the Navy to send Samejima to the Central Pacific, where he could keep an eye on the Combined Fleet command. Aware of Hirohito's concerns from his remarks, as well as Captain Jyo's reports, the Navy Ministry no doubt saw an advantage in assigning an officer close to the imperial household to a command position from which the emperor might obtain a deeper understanding of the challenges facing the fleet.

Admiral Samejima was renowned for leading Navy troops at Shanghai during a 1932 incident that had prefigured war with China. He had skippered cruisers and battleships, and led an aircraft carrier division. Samejima's combination of surface and aeronaval experience could be useful. But at Truk, Vice Admiral Samejima had outranked Combined Fleet chief of staff Ugaki, something of a delicate personal situation. The same arguments that lay behind posting the admiral to the fleet applied to sending him to Rabaul, at the very tip of the spear. And there were other advantages: The baron was an Etajima classmate of Kusaka Jinichi's, which might improve relations among the brass at Rabaul. The baron's assignment was also desirable because, having come from Truk, he was au courant with the furious strategic planning then under way. Within weeks of Baron Samejima's arrival, the hotheaded staff officer Kami Shigenori was packed off home. Given mounting losses, the Imperial Navy needed to fight deftly, not rush around out of control.

At Tokyo, the IGHQ huddled to craft a fresh strategy. In mid-February,

Emperor Hirohito had questioned why there were no signs of Japanese offensive action. He pressed Admiral Nagano to use the bases at Munda and
Kolombangara to bomb Guadalcanal. That concept was already pregnant
with the notion of an aerial onslaught in the South Pacific. On March 25,
the Navy General Staff promulgated Directive No. 209. This conceded that
the war had entered a new, third phase. Unsurprisingly, the order called
for thorough steps to protect convoys, and now made formal the arrangement whereby supplies to forward posts would be carried by submarines or
fast warships. More important, the directive provided that "enemy fleets in
advance bases will be raided and destroyed," that immediate efforts should
be made to establish air superiority, with the main strength of the JNAF
dispatched to the South Pacific for that purpose. In the Solomons, Allied
strength would be annihilated by seizing the initiative.

In a separate NGS order (No. 213) issued directly to Yamamoto the same
day, Imperial Headquarters provided for the fleet to cooperate closely with
the Japanese Army and concentrate their main effort in New Guinea. Army
air forces were to relocate there, while the Navy would defend the islands
and the Bismarck Archipelago with the ground forces allotted them. The
fleet should expand large-scale air operations and secure a network of airstrips and supply transit bases. Imperial Headquarters wanted the Navy and
Army to work as one unit—a fantasy—but it did assign explicit responsibility to the Army for the Rabaul area (New Britain) and Bougainville, and
to the Navy for the Central Solomons. Admiral Nagano's staff also alluded
obliquely to a specific air campaign to consist of counterair missions, attacks on Allied transportion, interception of enemy attacks, and defense of
communications lines. This instruction became the genesis for Admiral
Yamamoto's last, fateful operation.

Because of what happened to Yamamoto, the fact that Ugaki did not
survive the war, and the loss of the latter's diary for this period, the specific
planning for what became a huge enterprise is obscure. It is known that
Kusaka and JNAF commanders had agitated for the assignment of carrier
air groups to land bases. Until then carrier aircraft had flown from land
only as a temporary expedient or when their ships were sunk or put out of
action. As early as February, Commander Ohmae had personally raised the
issue. *Kido Butai* officers insisted on the integrity of the carrier force, and
Ohmae's fervid appeals were denied. It is likely that right after the Bismarck

Sea debacle, Ugaki put staffers to work on how to counter the Allied air advantage, with conversations at a staff level between Truk and Rabaul, and that Combined Fleet staffers carried the results to Imperial Headquarters. It is known that Watanabe of the fleet staff visited Tokyo at this time. In any case, the concept went into the NGS directives. The offensive, to be called the "I Operation," was on. Regardless of what IGHQ might say about priorities of New Guinea versus the Solomons, Yamamoto fully intended to hammer both.

Preparations consumed the next weeks. For the first time the Japanese built their strength in the Solomons to three full JNAF flotillas. The matter of the carrier air groups was reconsidered and their deployment approved in March. To the base air force the Japanese would add *Kido Butai*'s groups, though the flattops themselves remained at Truk. Admiral Kusaka, controlling the land-based force, would be the major player, but Vice Admiral Ozawa Jisaburo, now leading the carrier force, came to Rabaul to oversee his own units. To be sure all the leaders worked together, Admiral Yamamoto went to Rabaul too, taking along Ugaki and the Combined Fleet staff. The C-in-C certainly had his own doubts. Before departing, Yamamoto played shogi into the night with an officer he was leaving with the rear echelon. He confessed misgivings about moving the high command so near the front. Yamamoto would have preferred a return to Empire waters. But his presence would be good for morale. At home the citizenry were complaining about commanders who did not lead their men into battle. In any case it had become necessary to make this venture go just right.

Never before had fleet headquarters been located ashore. Any doubts that Yamamoto intended to lead in person, not simply visit the front, were dispelled when the admiral and Ugaki turned up replete with their stewards and the fancy dishware, tablecloths, and silverware used to serve meals aboard flagship *Musashi*. On the morning of April 3, the staff group took a launch to Truk's seaplane base and packed into a pair of Emily flying boats. The big four-engine patrol bombers took wing, circled the *Musashi*, and laid in their course for Rabaul. Yamamoto landed in Simpson Harbor at midafternoon. Admirals Kusaka, Ozawa, and Mikawa, the latter soon to leave, received him. Yamamoto's staff would work out of Southeast Area Fleet headquarters. He and Ugaki stayed at the colonial governor's villa on Residence Hill. The war's toll could be seen on the faces of the men and in their health. The C-in-C's friend Kusaka Jinichi had dysentery and could hardly keep his food down. Yamamoto picked a cucumber and tried to get Kusaka to eat it. Yamamoto himself was off-kilter, looking tired. Okumiya Masatake, the air staff officer, noticed his physical decline. Medical experts studying Yamamoto believe he may have gotten beriberi, with swollen ankles and shaking hands plus potential mental impairment. The admiral was getting vitamin C shots from his doctor and was said to be changing shoes four or five times daily. But the I Operation would be the big show. Yamamoto pushed at the hinge of fate.

VI.

WAR OF ATTRITION

Already the tentacles of Allied power had begun to wrap around Japan's Central Solomons outposts, replicating the headaches of Guadalcanal. Well might Admiral Yamamoto want to change the rhythm. Chief of staff Ugaki records that the Combined Fleet had concluded that if the big offensive did not work, "[T]here will be no hope of future success in this area." Admiral Ugaki wondered whether the point had been driven home sufficiently to the sailors and airmen who were about to fight. The entire I Operation was fraught with consequence.

At the end of March a Munda-bound Tokyo Express had recoiled in the face of fierce aerial attacks. Twenty-four hours later, April Fools' Day, the Express tried again, with six destroyers to Kolombangara. This action took place simultaneously with a big AIRSOLS raid on Munda. Japanese fighters intercepted the attackers and pursued them toward the Russells, over which nearly sixty JNAF fighters furiously battled a hundred Americans. Kusaka's fighter groups claimed to have destroyed about half of the enemy aircraft but incurred nine losses. American records note only six planes lost. Meanwhile the destroyers completed their voyage undisturbed. But the Americans had been tougher than ever and the JNAF achieved little.

The Allies quickly struck back. On April 3, hours after Yamamoto flew into Rabaul, the 43rd Bombardment Group bashed Kavieng, where Captain Yamamori Kamenosuke's heavy cruiser *Aoba* lay anchored outside the port. Especially upsetting about this attack was that the B-17 aircraft skip bombed—the Americans had found a way to make their heavy bombers effective at sea. Japanese officers also cringed because the *Aoba* had just returned from repairing damage taken at Cape Esperance. She had yet to get back into action. A 500-pound bomb made a direct hit, cooking off two of

the cruiser's torpedoes. Though Yamamori's crew extinguished the resulting fire within an hour, he had to beach *Aoba* to prevent steady flooding
from sinking her. It took two weeks to pump her out and apply a temporary patch. The Imperial Navy could not afford incidents like this.

The events at Kavieng put a dark cloud over the I Operation. Already
misgivings had sprung up in the ranks. The dogfight over the Russells had
been another mission for the Eleventh Air Fleet fighters, which had battled
over the islands twice in the previous month. Kusaka's fighter strength,
though powerful, was increasingly limited. The 204th Air Group had a
full complement of forty-five Zeroes, the 253rd some thirty-six, while the
fighter component of the 582nd Group possessed twenty-seven planes. Admiral Yamamoto's plan depended on massive reinforcements. The air
groups of Carrier Division 2—the *Hiyo* and *Junyo*—just up from Empire
waters, formed one major source of augmentation. The carrier planes flew
from Ballale when attacking and withdrew to Rabaul when not in action.
Air staff officer Okumiya Masatake accompanied Rear Admiral Kakuta.
Full of foreboding, Okumiya saw young men, many just out of flight school
with barely a month of carrier training before this aerial offensive. The
pilots—supposed to be Japan's best—were proof positive of the decline. He
feared for both crews and aircraft. "More than once this lack of experience cost us our valuable warplanes, as the unqualified pilots skidded,
crashed, and burned on takeoff," Okumiya wrote.

Ozawa of the Third Fleet, *Kido Butai*'s boss, arrived at Rabaul on April 2,
his Carrier Division 1 planes alighting there from the *Zuikaku* and *Zuiho*. The
latter's fighters were actually returning to the Solomons less than a month
after a previous stint there. The carrier air groups added more than 180
aircraft to the JNAF deployment. Of Kusaka's land-based air fleet, the 21st
Flotilla set up shop at Kavieng with half its seventy-two Betty bombers, the
rest at Vunakanau. The 26th Air Flotilla concentrated at the complex of
fields around Buin on Bougainville. With the 25th Flotilla, Kusaka's fleet
brought 190 warplanes to the table. The concentration was huge for the
Japanese, the biggest since the *Kido Butai* at Pearl Harbor—but a measure of
the changing war was that at Pearl Harbor the carriers by themselves had
fielded a force of practically this size.

Admiral Yamamoto was not to be deflected. But sometimes determination is not enough. With Yamamoto and his staff at Rabaul, a weather front

closed in over the northern Solomons. Yamamoto and Ugaki were pelted with rain their first night and into the morning, but more than that, delay became necessary to dry out runways and obtain better flying conditions. By midmorning the C-in-C had pushed back the onset of his offensive by twenty-four hours, to April 6. As the awful weather continued into the fifth, Ugaki considered changing the initial target from Guadalcanal to Port Moresby, but finally agreed to another twenty-four-hour postponement. Yamamoto and Ugaki inspected Lakunai Airfield, the *Zuikaku* planes there, and Captain Sugimoto Ushie's 204th Air Group Zeroes. Ozawa deployed the *Zuikaku* and *Zuiho* aircraft to Bougainville later that day. Yamamoto directed Kakuta to move his carrier aircraft to Buin also, and the latter followed suit the next morning. On April 6, Admiral Mikawa handed the Eighth Fleet command over to his successor, Baron Samejima.

Yamamoto's assembly of forces did not go unnoticed. An Allied reconnaissance flight over the Buin complex returned photos of 114 aircraft at Kahili, where there had been forty the day before. At Ballale were ninety-five JNAF planes where the field had been bare. Quackenbush's Photographic Interpretation Section, now installed on Guadalcanal, quickly generated a report. Meanwhile, on April 2, Pearl Harbor intelligence predicted possible imminent attacks in the central Solomons. By April 4 the CINCPAC fleet intelligence summary had refined this to anticipate "increased air activity expected soon." Two days after that the intelligence had hardened: "Large air action by land-based planes, possibly supplemented by carrier planes [is] expected within one week."

Yamamoto launched the thunderbolt of Japan's "sea eagles." The air assault began with a night raid on Guadalcanal. Some of the soldiers there were watching the heroics of the recent film *Wake Island* when the night stalkers struck. Movie antics were forgotten as GIs dashed for cover. The raid lasted nearly an hour. The JNAF inflicted barely any damage, but they disrupted sleep and relaxation very well. The intruders dropped flares at intervals, using the tactics of "Washing Machine Charlie" so familiar to the Marines of Cactus.

Kusaka's dawn scout over Guadalcanal on April 7 reported Pug Ainsworth's cruiser-destroyer group on its way to another bombardment of Munda. Fourteen merchantmen were also counted. Yamamoto hurled an armada of seventy-one bombers and 117 Zero fighters. The lead wave were fighters of the 253rd Air Group, closely followed by those of the 204th. Lieutenant Miyano Zenshiro personally led his 204th Group fighters. Behind them Ozawa's carrier Zeroes escorted Val dive-bombers. Next in were Vals of the 582nd Air Group, with its own fighters plus some from the *Zuiho*. Cloud cover frustrated this attack unit. Rear Admiral Kakuta's bombers struck in two last waves. Kakuta's aircraft flew from Rabaul and refueled at Buka or Buin before heading on, affording them maximum air time over Guadalcanal. Yamamoto went to Lakunai to encourage the "sea eagles."

Making up for Santa Cruz, *Zuiho* fighters participated in nearly every attack unit.

Coastwatchers duly reported the aerial stream. But the Allies seem to have had multiple warnings derived from Ultra. Lieutenant Ray Calhoun of the destroyer *Sterett* remembers a message foreseeing an air raid with at least a hundred planes for April 7. Aboard another tin can, the *Maury*, escorting a nearby convoy, Lieutenant (Junior Grade) Russell S. Crenshaw comments on the work of both the aerial spies and the codebreakers, and assumes Captain H. E. Thornhill, the convoy commander, was being appraised of their results. Ashore, notice of the air raid had percolated so far down the food chain that GI journalist Mack Morriss was aware of it. Through the morning, men hurried preparations. As the raid approached, at 12:20 p.m. Cactus control issued Condition Red.

Destroyers and other ships milled around in Ironbottom Sound. The *Aaron Ward*, escorting supply vessels to the Russells, left them off Savo Island to pick up the arriving *LST-449* and shepherd her out of Ironbottom Sound. The LST, a new-type large landing ship, carried a couple of hundred Army soldiers and naval officers for Guadalcanal assignments. One of them, Lieutenant (Junior Grade) John F. Kennedy, bound for the PT-boat base at Tulagi, was a long way from his native Boston. Destined to be a future president of the United States, Kennedy began his combat career with an eye-opening display of the violence of war. Several dive-bombers dropped out of the clouds to cripple the *Aaron Ward* right in front of him. Flak gunners were powerless to stop them. The tin can sank that night.

As usual Carney Field—the former Henderson—had had enough notice to loft an ample number of interceptors. Of course, the Japanese were in huge numbers also. "There's millions of 'em!" exclaimed Lieutenant James E. Swett, on his first mission leading a division of four Wildcats of Marine

Fighter Squadron 221. Lieutenant Swett waded into a flight of Val dive-bombers about to hit Tulagi and quickly shot down three. He followed another formation right into their attack, flaming four more even as U.S. flak damaged his F-4F. Swett's engine seized and he had to ditch off Tulagi, nose broken by the water impact and face lacerated from glass shards when bullets shattered the windshield. Swett, an instant ace, earned the Medal of Honor. He went on to sixteen and a half kills and nine more probables in the war, starting with this dogfight.

The Condition Red notice did not last long. An unprecedented Condition *Very* Red followed. The sky filled with AA shell bursts, flashes of swirling planes catching the sun, smoke, flames, or explosions as aircraft were damaged or disintegrated. Some seventy-six fighters met the Japanese, and fifty-six of them engaged. Army Captain Thomas G. Lanphier, with his flight of three twin-tailed P-38s, claimed seven planes smoked. Air intelligence credited twenty-seven Zeroes and twelve Vals destroyed. In his memoirs Bull Halsey would gush that as many as 107 JNAF birds were clipped. Halsey was usually more careful about his claims, and this one bore no correspondence either to Air Intelligence findings or the numbers contained in the Navy's own communiqué, public knowledge at the time. The Japanese recorded nine Zeroes and twelve Vals destroyed. The Americans lost seven warplanes.

Again damage was minimal, especially for such a huge effort. The Japanese concentrated on Tulagi, about twenty miles across the sound. Reporter Morriss saw AA shells detonating over the island, the tall water spouts of bombs exploding in the sea, a few columns of smoke, and the flash of something pulverized. Near him the only damage was a tree limb dislodged by muzzle blasts of the AA guns. In Tulagi harbor the New Zealand corvette *Moa*, refueling, did not get the warning and could not cast off quickly enough. She was holed and sank in minutes, perhaps a measure of retribution for *Moa*'s role in the capture of the Japanese codes from the *I-1*. The tanker *Kanawha* also went to the bottom. A number of other ships were attacked, threatened, and sometimes suffered lightly, but there were no huge disasters either to vessels off Guadalcanal or to Ainsworth's cruiser group. The early news disappointed Combined Fleet headquarters, but Admiral Kusaka had sent a scout to the battle area just to observe proceedings, and it confirmed the Tulagi result, though misidentifying the ships. Overall claims were much more optimistic (and inaccurate): a cruiser and a destroyer sunk, ten merchantmen (two large) put down, two more damaged. That seemed more satisfactory. When Admiral Nagano reported it to the emperor, Hirohito seemed pleased.

The next day in Rabaul passed with reviews of New Guinea events. The responsible Army general, plus Navy staff officer Ohmae, had both done surveys. The military situation appeared better than in the Solomons. On the other hand, the need to cross high mountains complicated air attacks. Bad weather crossed the Bismarcks toward Papua. At the final briefing on April 9, with admirals Kusaka and Ozawa both pleading for more preparation time and the weather still uncertain, Yamamoto approved a delay. As the planes were prepped, staff chief Ugaki visited the command posts of the 21st and 26th air flotillas. Plans were altered again to protect the vulnerable Betty bombers, postponing their participation so as to arrange stronger fighter escorts. The initial New Guinea strike took place on April 11 against Oro Bay.

It was a Sunday, like Pearl Harbor. Oro Bay, a dozen miles south of Buna, was one of MacArthur's supply centers for the area. Milne Bay, the other, not far away, was stuffed with shipping. Kusaka's Eleventh Air Fleet had been flying against Oro Bay for a month, and the raid of April 11 had been preceded by a half dozen others. This strike would be carried out by carrier aircraft alone, with *Zuiho* fighters in an initial sweep, a *Zuikaku* formation following, and Kakuta's warplanes bringing up the rear. Without Guadalcanal's extensive warning net, the defenders got just a few minutes' notice. Fighter interceptors scrambled from nearby Dobodura, but many engagements occurred only as the enemy retired. Ozawa's *Kido Butai* air groups contributed a swarm of seventy-two Zeroes and twenty-two Vals. The "sea eagles" sank a 2,000-ton freighter and damaged another merchantman plus an Australian minesweeper. They lost four dive-bombers and two fighters, though Allied claims amounted to seventeen JNAF aircraft. General Kenney could not understand why the enemy had not hit Milne Bay, and ordered most of his interceptors, more than a hundred fighters, to Dobodura, north of the Owen Stanleys, where they would be in ideal position.

Admiral Yamamoto rose early the next morning, at Lakunai by 4:30 a.m.

to send off the medium bombers for their ambitious Port Moresby strike. Next to Guadalcanal, Moresby, having endured more than a hundred air raids since the war started, was undoubtedly the favorite Japanese target. It was also the most heavily defended, with many airfields and many Fifth Air Force warplanes. Forty-three Betty bombers, directly escorted by seventy-six Zeroes of the land-based air groups and the carriers, made the hit. They were in two assault formations led by Commander Nakamura Tomo of the 705th Air Group and Lieutenant Commander Suzuki Masaichi of the 751st. Some fifty-five Zeroes of the *Zuikaku*, *Hiyo*, and *Junyo* conducted a roving fighter sweep. Warrant Officer Morinio Hideo claimed three planes flamed, a substantial contribution to the nineteen planes believed destroyed with six probables that day.

This time the Allies had warning. The CINCPAC intelligence summary predicted an air attack. Radar picked up the attackers northeast of New Guinea. General Kenney scrambled his Dobodura fighters to defend Milne Bay, the supposed target. But radar lost the Japanese, only to reacquire them near Port Moresby. There the Fifth Air Force had just eight P-38s and twelve P-39s. Allied airmen could not stop the bombers, which attacked from 18,000 feet, but they inflicted losses. Despite direct escort by thirty-two Zeroes from the *Zuiho* and the 253rd Air Group, Commander Nakamura's unit lost half a dozen Betty bombers. Suzuki's second wave, covered by forty-four Zeroes of the 204th and 582nd air groups, had several Bettys damaged. Kenney, meanwhile, ordered the mass of his fighters toward Lae, where he assumed the JNAF would land. When the strikers headed for Rabaul instead, fewer than two dozen interceptors had the fuel to catch them and flame a few more enemies. The Japanese believed they had damaged eleven airfields. While that was exaggerated, as usual, even American accounts concede injury to four, with nineteen aircraft hurt or wrecked on the ground and two shot down, against the loss of six Bettys and two Zeroes (Fifth Air Force claimed fifteen bombers and nine to ten fighters downed). This success did not prevent American B-17s from harassing Rabaul with a bombing of their own.

Then came the Milne Bay attack, on April 14 shortly after noon. The CINCPAC intelligence summary, partly right, partly off, tentatively predicted a strike, but not on the scale of Guadalcanal or Moresby. Dobodura was fog-bound at the critical moment, and most of Kenney's fighters were unable to launch. Out of more than a hundred planes, eight P-38s and thirty-six P-40s engaged. Not enough, though only a couple were lost. Two of the P-38s that fought were those of the 9th Fighter Squadron's Lieutenant Richard Bong and his wingman. Befogged early on, Bong managed to catch the later wave and thought he bagged at least one before a Zero damaged his plane and sent him home. Analyzing historical data, aviation historian Henry Sakaida concluded that Bong had actually destroyed *three* JNAF bombers. Lieutenant Bong soon ranked among the top American aces of the Pacific war.

In waves totaling 187 aircraft, a third of them bombers, the Japanese attacked. The lead strike unit comprised Bettys accompanied by fifty-six land-based fighters. The follow-on force consisted of Ozawa's carrier planes, Vals, plus no less than seventy-five Zeroes. The raiders claimed to have sunk six transports, damaging nine; and to have set afire land targets, destroying forty-four aircraft. A gasoline dump was indeed blown up, and a ship sunk. Two merchantmen suffered damage. These results were paltry. Under the circumstances, the statement that day from Emperor Hirohito, which lauded the I Operation, seemed overdone. Ten JNAF aircraft never came back. SOWESPAC informed Washington it had downed ten bombers and five fighters, with eight more bombers and a fighter as probables, plus four bombers and two fighters damaged, a total of thirty planes.

At this juncture, mindful of the need to preserve the air units, Admiral Yamamoto curtailed his offensive. Possibly the main impact was on morale. Petty Officer Igarashi Hisashi of the 705th Air Group told his diary that the carrier pilots had been "a good stimulus to our land-based attack units as they tend to be in low spirits." Yamamoto ordered Ozawa's carrier planes back to their ships on April 16. Chief of staff Ugaki, ill with dengue, recovered enough to preside over an operational review at Eighth Base Force headquarters. The Japanese believed they had destroyed ninety-five aircraft (plus thirty-nine probables), sinking a cruiser, two destroyers, and twenty-five transports. The true results were a tiny fraction of that. Ugaki praised the "sea eagles" but observed that airpower remained the key long-term problem. He exhorted everyone to greater effort. In the audience Commander Okumiya listened as officers fussed that just four missions had cost fifty planes. In particular the bomber losses could not be sustained. The aircraft needed more protection. Allied air was better—and stronger. Japanese striking power was waning. "The meeting concluded in a pessimistic air," Okumiya recalled.

Before returning to Truk, Yamamoto Isoroku wished to visit Bougainville. The C-in-C knew that Army troops from his hometown had been evacuated there after Guadalcanal. A trip to the bases could also buck up the airmen. Yamamoto broached the idea on his second day at Rabaul and later reaffirmed his intention. Admiral Ugaki desired to inspect outposts as far afield as Munda and Vila. That was simply not practical. He put Commander Watanabe Yasuji to work on the arrangements. Ugaki concerned himself with the public relations aspect—he wanted pictures of Yamamoto in the Imperial Navy's combat utility uniform—all existing photos of the fleet commander had him in service blues or whites, more formal garb. The afternoon of April 17, Ugaki also fretted over whether the travel party should go in neckties or with open-necked shirts (not regulation uniform). He decided the former.

That evening Yamamoto dined at the officers' club with Kusaka and Ozawa along with several other classmates of Etajima 1909. Yamamoto was not of that class, but he had been on their training cruise. Yamamoto brought a bottle of Johnnie Walker Black Label Scotch, his favorite drink since living in America. Perhaps it was fitting that the admiral should enjoy some before meeting his destiny. Ozawa begged Yamamoto not to fly, or at least to take along a cloud of his carrier fighters. The C-in-C brooked no change. Not just Yamamoto and Ozawa had an inkling of disaster— two more men warned the C-in-C that very day. General Imamura went to Yamamoto and recounted how, several months earlier, his plane had been accosted by a pack of American fighters and had escaped only by hiding in a cloud bank. Imamura intended this as a warning, and encouraged Yamamoto to go by boat. Rear Admiral Joshima Takatsugu of the R Area Force had also warned Yamamoto not to fly. Joshima had seen the cable traffic on the Bougainville visit. Disturbed at the large number of addressees, plus the detailed schedule and itinerary, Joshima became apprehensive when he learned that two bases had exchanged the identical trip information in a less secure aviation code (it remains unclear whether this was the one the Americans possessed). Admiral Joshima hopped a seaplane to Rabaul and laid his fears before Yamamoto. The C-in-C shrugged it off. Yamamoto invited Joshima to breakfast together upon his return. Yamamoto's bravura gesture proved empty.

"WE'VE HIT THE JACKPOT!"

Commander Watanabe took a little more than a week to complete Yamamoto Isoroku's itinerary. The admiral would fly from Lakunai, first stop Ballale in the Buin complex. Five days in advance, on April 13, Watanabe put details into a dispatch he sent to all concerned commands. The message included a schedule, specified what transportation Yamamoto would use at each stage, and noted the admiral's intention to inspect facilities and see the sick and wounded. Helpfully, Watanabe noted that if the weather was bad the trip would be postponed a day. Watanabe took such care that he calculated the extra time required to boat back from one location due to running against the tide. Watanabe specified that the travel party would be escorted by six fighters. Almost the only detail he left out was to note the fleet staff's practice of putting C-in-C and chief of staff in different aircraft so the top leadership could not be wiped out by a single plane crash. As far as radio intelligence was concerned, Commander Watanabe had some doubts about the security of Army codes, so he ordered that the message be sent only in the D Code—that is, JN-25. The dispatch went out from Southeast Area Fleet late that afternoon.

The Yamamoto trip notice promptly found its way to Allied codebreakers. FRUPAC and Negat picked it up immediately, and FRUMEL obtained a later retransmission as well as the text recirculated by U.S. intelligence on the Copek circuit. Both Pearl Harbor and Washington immediately plunged into recovering this message. Though the Imperial Navy had changed its additive table on April 1, complicating work with JN-25, many values had already been recovered, especially oft-repeated terms like names of commands and places.

Lieutenant Roger Pineau at FRUPAC later recorded that the large number of addressees for Watanabe's dispatch had instantly drawn attention. The cryptanalysts—at FRUPAC the aces were Tommy Dyer and Ham Wright—worked to strip the additives off the code groups. Traffic analysts—here the experts included Tom Huckins and Jack Williams—established the address information and geographic locator designations, assisted by Jasper Holmes. Then the code groups of the underlying message were revealed. By now the codebreakers were using new technology, the IBM mechanical card-sorting machines, to help break messages. Each code group in a message would be punched onto a card, and the sorter would run the cards against another set containing known JN-25 meanings. Experts penetrated the unknowns by considering their position in sentences, and comparing the appearance to their usage in other messages. Once a basic version of the original—or "plaintext"—had been recovered it was ready for the language experts, in this case Marine Major Alva B. "Red" Lasswell and Lieutenant Commander John G. Roenigk. The Navy officer saw the Marine leap to his feet.

"We've hit the jackpot!" Lasswell exclaimed.

Red Lasswell remembers, "I personally did the whole thing overnight." Having been a key participant on the Midway decrypts, Lasswell contributed to possibly the two greatest radio intelligence achievements of the Pacific war. "I didn't feel, somehow or other, the joy in this [the Yamamoto decrypt] that I did in the other, because I sort of felt more of a snooper," Lasswell remembered. He was glad he did not have to make the call. Lieutenant Donald M. Showers plotted the itinerary and checked times and distances on maps to verify plausibility.

The same thing happened in Washington. At Negat, Lieutenant Commander Prescott Currier had the predawn watch when the intercept arrived. He took it to the "Blitz Additive Room." In the morning, code maven Commander Redfield "Rosie" Mason practically skipped through the office, yelling at everyone to double-check *everything*. He assigned linguists Phillip Cate, Dorothy Edgars, and Fred Woodrough to make the translation. Rosie Mason, whose private passion was Greek and Roman mythology, was hard to please, but decided the result was "good"—high praise. A touch of spring hung in the air and the weather was mild, recalled linguist Edward Van Der Rhoer, on watch when the final version appeared. It stunned Van Der Rhoer, who read it with growing excitement, realizing that the intelligence was "actionable"—it offered the opportunity to kill Yamamoto Isoroku. Such a death would rise to the Olympian heights of Rosie Mason's favored mythological tales.

Both units put their versions of the decrypt on Copek on April 14. Pearl Harbor was out of the starting gate a bit faster—about an hour and a half.

FRUMEL contributed a decrypt of another message between Japanese sub-ordinate commands—possibly one of the dispatches Admiral Joshima had worried about. OP-20-G reported the result to Admiral King and Navy Secretary Knox. At CINCPAC Red Lasswell and Jake Holmes took the message file to Eddie Layton.

The fleet intelligence officer immediately realized the importance of this message and carried it to Nimitz. Captain Layton met with Admiral Nimitz shortly after 8:00 a.m. Nimitz asked whether Layton thought it worthwhile to take a shot at the enemy commander, and the latter responded that Yamamoto's death would shock Japan. Nimitz worried that the enemy might be able to bring in a better commander, but when they discussed the possibilities—Nimitz was surprisingly well acquainted with the enemy's senior officer corps—they agreed the Imperial Navy had no one better than Yamamoto. Another consideration was the danger that such action would confirm to the Japanese their codes had been breached. Admiral Nimitz decided to proceed, then wrote a cable to SOPAC commander Halsey order-ing him to try the ambush. This chronology is confirmed in the CINCPAC war diary for April 14, which records that Yamamoto would inspect Buin four days hence, arriving from Rabaul by plane—and on April 16 the diary notes, "[A]n attempt will be made to intercept an enemy high commander when he makes a projected visit to the Buin area the 18th."

Because several authors, including Nimitz biographer E. B. Potter, have written that this move was cleared with President Roosevelt and Secretary Knox due to Yamamoto's stature, the question of approval is worth com-ment. This writing is very shortly after the May 2011 U.S. commando raid into Pakistan to kill the terrorist leader Osama bin Laden, personally or-dered by President Barack Obama. The Yamamoto ambush is an obvious parallel. Roger Pineau spent decades attempting to determine whether FDR made an affirmative decision on Yamamoto. Pineau came up empty. This writer walked the same path with a similar result. There is no evidence in Roosevelt's papers, the records of COMINCH, CINCPAC, or the National Security Agency; and, in fact, the president was traveling during this period and out of touch. Nimitz's cables were routinely copied to King and Knox for information, and in the records there are no answering messages on April 14 or 15 that comment on the Yamamoto kill order either pro *or* con. Certain books have printed quotations of an alleged message from

Secretary Knox, but this appears to have been fabricated. The SOPAC mission planner recalls *seeing* a cable from Knox, but the document has never materialized and the timing given suggests it may have been an exhortation to the field forces, not an execute message. There seems little reason to doubt that Nimitz, at his own level, made the decision to get Yamamoto, and higher authority did not impede him. The world was simpler then.

Be that as it may, it was up to Admiral William F. Halsey's South Pacific forces to do the deed. A few argued for hitting Yamamoto's boat en route to one or another inspection site, but he might survive a boat sinking more easily than an air crash. Halsey convened his aviation specialists, including his new air boss, Rear Admiral Marc A. Mitscher, who had arrived just days before. It happened that April 18, the day of the trip, was the anniversary of the Doolittle Raid, and Mitscher wanted to do something special. The ambush, soon called the "Y-Mission," seemed just the thing. Marine Major John P. Condon, the AIRSOLS fighter staff officer, planned the operation starting on April 17. Condon decided that Army twin-engine P-38 fighters, if given extra fuel tanks, could fly to Bougainville with enough gas to afford them time for the interception. The 339th Fighter Squadron, the "Sun Setters," got the assignment.

Under Major John Mitchell, then the leading ace on Guadalcanal, the force consisted of a covering unit of fourteen P-38s, and an attack unit of four planes led by Captain Thomas G. Lanphier Jr. Mitchell distrusted the compasses in the Lightning aircraft, important because Condon had planned an indirect approach, taking a route west of New Georgia until heading northeast, then north to make Bougainville. Condon found Mitchell a nautical compass, eliminating the problem. Mitchell chose the intercept point; then Condon calculated the necessary parameters. Dissatisfied with Condon's planned course, Mitchell recalculated it. Departure from Fighter Two was timed precisely to bring Lanphier to the intercept point just as Admiral Yamamoto's planes reached there. Mitchell's group would fly very low—as low as ten to thirty feet altitude—to avoid detection by Japanese radars.

Palm Sunday, April 18, dawned clear and humid. Mitchell's planes took off at 7:25 a.m. One of Lanphier's attack group blew a tire on takeoff and another found its extra fuel tanks were not feeding properly. Those aircraft returned to base. Thus sixteen P-38s winged toward Bougainville.

At Rabaul/Vunakanau, Captain Konishi Yukie of the 705th Air Group selected two of his best pilots to fly the Bettys that would carry Admiral Yamamoto's traveling party. For security reasons the crews were not told until after bedtime. They were shaken awake and given detailed instructions. Petty Officer Hayashi Hiroshi thought this just a routine mission until Konishi warned him to wear full uniform. He had been used to utility gear. Hayashi was told they would fly to Buin—not Ballale, as the Americans had decoded—and that bothered him, since he had never landed there. The six Zero pilots of the 204th Air Group at Lakunai, also carefully selected, had a similar experience. Captain Sugimoto Ushie, however, informed his fliers the previous afternoon. The escort might not be strong but they were good men. Petty Officer Hidaka Yoshimi was an ace with twenty victories. The Bettys would shuttle over to Lakunai, closer to Yamamoto's billet; then the entire sky train would leave from there.

Admiral Yamamoto's group assembled for an 8:00 a.m. departure. At the last moment senior air staff officer Commander Toibana Yurio convinced Watanabe to give up his place. Though Toibana's assistant was already going, the air officer was anxious to speak to frontline aviators. Commander Watanabe had a myriad of matters to take care of before the fleet staff returned to Truk. So Toibana flew on Yamamoto's airplane. In an eerie twist of fate—perhaps exacting retribution—it had been Toibana, in China in 1937, who had been a key figure in the *Panay* incident, convincing superiors to delay word to their attack planes that an American gunboat cruised in their strike area.

Vice Admiral Ugaki recorded that the songbirds were pleasant that morning. He and Yamamoto left Governor's Hill ten minutes before plane time. Toibana, his deputy, and others came from the direction of the control tower. Ugaki was puzzled to discover two officers in dress whites when he had decreed field uniforms, but they turned out to be the fleet surgeon and paymaster. One would fly in each airplane. The men boarded. Yamamoto's Betty took off first, then Ugaki's. Petty Officer Hayashi piloted the aircraft carrying Admiral Ugaki. The fighters formed up over Lakunai. A V of three stationed itself above and to the side of each transport. Hayashi kept such tight formation with the lead plane, Ugaki remembers, that he feared their wingtips might touch and cause an accident. The flight plan, designed to enable Yamamoto to see something of the war theater, took them to the southern tip of New Ireland, then along the eastern coast of Bougainville. The Bettys descended to lower altitude for optimal viewing. The route took them over the bases at Buka and Kieta, turning inland to head toward Buin. The planes rose to about 6,500 feet.

Admiral Ugaki had just been handed a note telling him to expect landing in fifteen minutes when lightning struck. Major Mitchell's P-38s came from below. Warrant Officer Yanagiya Kenji, flying one of the escort, about 2,000 feet above the Bettys, looked down and saw them under attack. The Japanese fighters were surprised, because Allied fighters most often dived from above. Before they could intervene, the Bettys were already embattled. Major Mitchell's covering Lightnings interposed. Captain Lanphier and Lieutenant Rex Barber made the crucial gun runs. While the American pilots have disputed credit for the success, what matters is that both Bettys were smoked and both crashed, Yamamoto's in the jungle and Ugaki's just off the Bougainville shore. One P-38 was lost in the clash, but the strike team returned without further incident.

No one, including Commander Toibana, survived the crash of the airplane carrying Yamamoto Isoroku. The admiral's body would be found by Commander Watanabe, who grabbed the first plane he could get and mounted a frantic search for survivors. Pilot Hayashi, chief of staff Ugaki, and paymaster Kitamura Gen escaped from the Betty crashed in the surf. Badly injured, already sick, Admiral Ugaki spent months in the hospital.

At the daily staff meeting the next morning in Nouméa, Richmond Kelly Turner whooped it up when the shoot-down was announced. Admiral Halsey, privately exulting, chose to tease Turner. "Hold on, Kelly! What's so good about it?" the Bull groused. "I'd hoped to lead that scoundrel up Pennsylvania Avenue in chains."

Commander Watanabe Yasuji understandably obsessed over everything that preceded Yamamoto's death. He discovered that his original message, supposed to have been confined to Navy radios, had in fact passed over Army circuits also. This bit of confusion created an obstacle to the Imperial Navy's realizing its codes had been cracked. Watanabe nursed his suspicions. In 1949 Roger Pineau interviewed him on behalf of Samuel Eliot Morison. Watanabe's one question for Pineau concerned the Yamamoto trip message and which radio net had betrayed it. Pineau, sworn to secrecy about Ultra until the codebreaking was declassified in 1978, begged off answering. Watanabe Yasuji had had a hearty reputation in the Imperial Navy as a ladies' man. In the 1950s he—and Kusaka Jinichi also—morphed into devotees of Zen Buddhism.

The Yamamoto shoot-down had huge consequences for Japan. Nimitz and Layton had been right that the Japanese lacked admirals of his stature. Tokyo managed to keep Yamamoto's death secret for a month. His body was cremated, Commander Watanabe accompanied the ashes to Truk, and the remains were carried home aboard fleet flagship *Musashi*. A state funeral was held. Yamamoto's ashes were divided in two parts, one buried on the grounds of the Imperial Palace, the other in his hometown. But while the nation grieved, the war in the Solomons heated up to fever pitch.

THE YEAR OF THE GOAT

In the animistic, twelve-year cycle common in many Buddhist countries, 1943 was the Year of the Goat. Though the Asian image of that is different, more positive than the Western one, Japan would need to overcome adversity. In particular, since Imperial Japan's fiscal year started with April, the death of Admiral Yamamoto was an especially bad setback at the outset of a new year of war. Aboard the Carrier Division 2 flagship *Hiyo*, Commander Okumiya was standing near recently promoted Vice Admiral Kakuta at Truk when the *Musashi* lowered her flag in honor of Yamamoto. Only a few days earlier Kakuta and Yamamoto had stood together in Rabaul. Now the C-in-C was dead. Okumiya's heart skipped a beat when he saw the color drain from Kakuta's face. The air officer struggled with his emotions too.

The feeling of shock was universal. Hara Tameichi arrived at Truk aboard the destroyer *Shigure* a week after Yamamoto's death. Upon recuperating from his exertions off Guadalcanal, Hara had been elevated to command a full division of destroyers, though his promotion to captain had yet to come through (he gained that rank on May 1). Captain Hara went to the *Musashi* to report to Admiral Ugaki. Hara worried that the Imperial Navy's repetition of formulas led to unnecessary losses, and he wanted to make this argument through Ugaki, whom he knew, to Yamamoto. Climbing the superbattleship's Jacob's ladder from his launch, Captain Hara found only a single warrant officer to greet him, a breach of protocol in receiving a unit commander. The whole ship seemed odd and somber, and when the captain declared that he wished to visit Admiral Ugaki, the man stared at him as if he were mad. The warrant hesitated, but finally led Captain Hara into the *Musashi*. "No officers were evident along our route, and the men I saw looked bewildered and depressed," Hara later wrote. The man conducted him to Yamamoto's cabin, which opened to wafting incense and dim light. Suddenly Hara recognized an urn of ashes on a draped table. The sailor explained, "These are the remains of our Commander-in-Chief and six of his staff officers. Admiral Ugaki and the others were critically injured." Captain Hara teared up, and he offered a silent prayer for the dead.

Sagging morale was evident, disturbing, and could be dangerous to performance. Four of the six fighter pilots who flew escort on Yamamoto's fated trip would be dead within months. No doubt morale worries figured among Emperor Hirohito's reasons for visiting the *Musashi* on June 24, during her sojourn in the Empire after she delivered Yamamoto's remains.

Meanwhile, the more Captain Hara learned, the more alarmed he became. Reporting to his fleet commander, Vice Admiral Kondo Nobutake, Hara discovered his division existed only in name. All his vessels except one were on loan to other units. Kondo's haggard appearance and hoarse, slow voice also shocked Hara, who knew the admiral's reputation as a dapper gentleman. And once Captain Hara read the files, he went from anxiety to deep gloom. Allied airpower constricted Japanese naval operations like a python snake, while Halsey's South Pacific naval forces steadily grew, their strength presently towering over the Imperial Navy's. The record of the Bismarck Sea battle was especially shocking. Leaving Kondo's flagship *Atago*, Hara stopped at the officers' club, where he encountered Koyanagi Tomiji, now chief of staff to Admiral Kurita. Koyanagi explained the Allied skip-bombing method. Hara quickly realized that unless the Navy could develop a counter, the jig might well be up. At Rabaul even the water was being rationed. No one had bread. Meat and vegetables went first to high-command messes, while the clever supply clerks of the base forces managed to divert much of what was left. The destroyermen got the dregs. Koyanagi had led Tanaka Raizo's destroyer squadron, in which Hara had sailed. He trusted Koyanagi. Hara felt like a student on his first day in college.

Japanese officers might be depressed, but on the other side of the mirror Allied leaders were not quite riding high. Admiral Halsey saw the enemy redoubts at Munda and Vila becoming major thorns in SOPAC's side. The need to retrain troops and the disagreements with MacArthur hindered Halsey's grinding ahead. The delay attendant in preparing new Russells bases also retarded an offensive. Even as codebreakers put finishing touches on their Yamamoto shoot-down decrypts, Halsey flew to Australia to coordinate with MacArthur. It was the first time they had met, and in person they cooperated very well.

In the meantime Admiral Halsey wore the enemy down. The Imperial Navy had begun sending the Tokyo Express to its new outposts as early as February. It had also run a few merchant ships into those places. Interdicting the traffic led the Bull to order offensive mining. While not a desperate measure, the mining represented a double-edged sword—with Halsey fully expecting to operate SOPAC forces here, minefields sown to catch the Japanese might very well cripple Allied vessels. Once the PT boat base in the Russells became active, and patrol craft were plying these waters regularly, the mines could become even more dangerous to Americans. The aspect of calculated risk was manifest.

Halsey also pursued the neutralization of Munda and Vila. By the time of Yamamoto's I Operation, which obliged SOPAC to cancel a cruiser bombardment that Rear Admiral Ainsworth was to have carried out, the Japanese bases had been hit a good half dozen times. Beyond the cruiser forces, Admiral Halsey assigned destroyer units to these missions as well. Much like the Japanese at Guadalcanal, SOPAC commanders discovered that cruiser and destroyer bombardments appeared more effective than they actually were. Regardless of the weight of shells fired, the enemy air bases were typically in working order the next day. Naval bombardments supplemented constant air action. Three times Allied warships shelled Munda, the last on the night of May 12–13. The Vila base and nearby Stanmore Plantation were the targets on four occasions. Sometimes the bombardments were simultaneous, as on May 12–13, when Ainsworth's cruisers hit Vila while Captain Colin Campbell's destroyers shelled Munda. Since the JNAF had stopped actually basing aircraft, the number of planes vulnerable to these bombardments was small. Every cruise involved a danger of being caught by enemy warships or air strikes, so Halsey used the sorties to punctuate an aerial campaign.

Aerial interdiction did not suppress Munda or Vila, but it did exact a price. And the campaign would be extended beyond New Georgia to hit the enemy farther up The Slot. Buin, Ballale, and Kieta went on the target lists. With B-17s and B-24s now flying from Guadalcanal—the Thirteenth Air Force was formed to lead Army air units in the Solomons—Halsey's airmen ranged far afield. The air attacks were never milk runs. Japanese flak took a toll of strike aircraft, enough so that night missions became the primary tactic, at least against Bougainville. AIRSOLS and the Thirteenth Air Force also ran a vigorous night-intruder operation. JNAF night-fighter capability was quite limited. In any case the air campaign would be massive and constant.

The Navy's communiqués tell the story. The department's press office issued releases almost daily, sometimes more than one, reporting events as news reached Washington. Typically the information office ran a day or two behind operations, and, of course, the releases were shorn of such relevant information as the size of attacks, specifics of combat action, and so on. But the contours are readily apparent. In the seven-week (forty-nine-day) period through Yamamoto's death, Munda was hit at least twenty-two times and Vila twenty-one. From the releases it is clear that some of these were multiple attacks, some were mass efforts, and some were simultaneous strikes at both places; a few were fighter sweeps, and some seemed to be intruder operations. Bombers struck the Buin complex twenty-one times. Kahili was by far the most popular target, but most "attacks" appear to have been harassment. Bombings or fighter sweeps engaged Rekata Bay on six occasions. Other places were also hit, but these targets absorbed by far the greatest effort. The massive I Operation strike at Guadalcanal did not prevent AIRSOLS from hitting Vila early that same morning, or Rekata Bay in the afternoon. Rabaul was not struck even once.

The handling of the Yamamoto shoot-down is quite interesting: Where news usually ran days behind, Navy Department Communiqué 348 of April 18 stated: "A number of Lightning (Lockheed P-38) fighters engaged two Japanese bombers, escorted by six Zero fighters, over Kahili in the Shortland Island area," and went on to claim destruction of both bombers.

Everything else in the release concerned April 16. The mention of two bombers, information that *had not been* in the radio intercepts, reveals that authorities must have arranged in advance for the press office to run this current item, quite likely for the purpose of suggesting that the ambush had been nothing more than a routine air battle.

An Allied reorganization in March designated SOPAC naval forces as the Third Fleet and those under SOWESPAC the Seventh Fleet. Though the latter did not yet truly merit that appellation, Halsey's Third Fleet had become a potent force. His major weakness remained lack of aircraft carriers. The *Saratoga* still represented the only fully capable flattop. The *Enterprise* continued to be hampered by her damage from Santa Cruz. Following a last round of training maneuvers, the "Big E" left the South Pacific at the beginning of May. At that moment the Royal Navy's *Victorious* was en route to the Third Fleet. The *Victorious* and the *Saratoga* made up Halsey's fast carrier force. He had several jeep carriers too, but they did not sail in the battle line. The *Victorious* served in the South Pacific throughout. Crewmen who had expected a long-term deployment were astonished when she was recalled. America's industrial behemoth had begun to spew forth the new warships that would overwhelm Japan. Indeed, the same week the Americans hustled to prepare Yamamoto's ambush, higher authority informed CINCPAC that *eight* new aircraft carriers would join the Pacific Fleet before the end of the year. By June 19, Nimitz had decided to release the *Victorious* to Royal Navy control on August 1. The light carrier *Princeton* replaced her.

Meanwhile SOPAC initiated its mine-laying campaign on March 20, initially focusing on Bougainville waters, especially Shortland harbor. Avenger aircraft from Guadalcanal laid most of the mines. They were credited with damaging a destroyer and a merchantman, and sinking another. Aerial mines laid in Blackett Strait—off Vila—and in the Munda area did not seem to faze the Tokyo Express, however. Accordingly, on May 6, Rear Admiral Ainsworth's cruiser-destroyer group sauntered through Blackett Strait to clear it. Then, under Commander William K. Romoser, the modern destroyer *Radford* led three older tin cans converted into minelayers into the strait to deposit a standard three-row field. In no time this outing produced a signal success. The next day Captain Tachibana Masao led four Japanese destroyers from Buka to Buin, loading supplies for Vila, where they arrived after midnight on May 8. While getting under way, the *Kuroshio* touched off a mine, rendering her unnavigable. About half an hour later the *Oyashio* also hit a mine. Less heavily damaged, she took off many crewmen of the other vessel. The *Kuroshio* drifted onto a couple more mines, broke up, and sank. In the morning the *Oyashio*'s engines failed. Australian coastwatcher A. R. Evans promptly reported the enemy presence. They were set upon by SOPAC aircraft. Supported by destroyers *Kagero* and *Michishio*, *Oyashio* drove off the first strike, but the Americans returned in the afternoon to sink both *Oyashio* and *Kagero*. Tachibana's single remaining ship, damaged by strafing, rescued survivors of all the others. Thrilled by such results, Halsey's mine group repeated the exercise a week later in Kula Gulf, covered by Ainsworth's cruiser bombardment of Vila. Alerted this time, the Japanese swept the mines. Repetition of operational formulas did not work on either side.

The hapless heavy cruiser *Aoba* staggered into the lagoon at Truk on April 25. The cruiser tied up next to repair ship *Akashi*, which labored to make her seaworthy enough to sail home for a proper fix in a shipyard. The *Aoba*'s brief return and almost instant crippling were a metaphor for Japan's desperate condition. The ship would be hors de combat for seven long months. At midafternoon that day an Emily flying boat landed from Yokosuka. The patrol bomber carried Admiral Koga Mineichi, chief of the Yokosuka Naval District, ostensibly down for an inspection. Upon his arrival Admiral Koga assumed command of the Combined Fleet.

The *Aoba* held special meaning for Koga. The admiral had skippered that cruiser in 1930, a moment that from the Navy's perspective might be considered the twilight of peace, before Imperial Japan had gone far into the machinations in China that led ineffably to the Pacific war. Koga had been a member of the so-called "treaty faction," those who favored naval disarmament as part of a program to avoid conflict. The faction had been outplayed by others who aggressively sought advantage, and disputes begun in north China had embroiled Japan in a progressively deepening crisis, now extended across the Pacific. With the Imperial Navy increasingly tested, and its acknowledged finest leader—Yamamoto, Koga's good friend—now dead, Koga was summoned to pick up the pieces.

The advent of Koga Mineichi surprised no Japanese. As early as January

1941, Yamamoto had written a memorandum advising on officers who could succeed him. Koga's name was at the top of that list. That paper was secret, but opinion in the fleet put Koga in line for the top command. Only ten men stood ahead of Koga on the Navy List, including admirals who were retired, elevated to the supernumerary Supreme War Council, dead, or serving in indispensable positions, such as NGS chief Nagano or Navy Minister Shimada. Toyoda Soemu was just ahead of Koga, and the latter's promotion to full admiral in May 1942, eight months after Toyoda, made Koga junior in rank. But Koga had Imperial household connections that Toyoda lacked, while Yamamoto's secret advice had specifically counseled Koga over Toyoda. Both had graduated Etajima in 1905, a year behind Yamamoto, who had known them well.

When Admiral Nimitz mulled over the Yamamoto ambush, he and Captain Layton had discussed Koga's potential. They agreed he would be a step down from his illustrious predecessor. But beyond a small circle of former American naval attachés, intelligence professionals, or officers with service in China, Koga Mineichi remained a cipher to the Allied camp. "In a race of unknown men," *Time* magazine prattled, "he is an especial anonym."

Koga wholly lacked Yamamoto's flamboyance, probably the main reason for his not being better-known. The admiral was a stolid, competent officer who acted with caution and care, advancing steadily through the ranks. In the officer corps Koga was considered able, prudent, and amiable. He and Yamamoto had been shipmates as well as midshipman contemporaries, and political allies in the treaty faction. Koga was knowledgeable on both naval matters and international affairs, spoke French and some English, and was viewed as friendly to the United States. In 1937, when the fighting in China became generalized, Admiral Koga as vice chief of the Navy General Staff had participated with Yonai Mitsumasa in a last-ditch effort to settle the crisis. As a subordinate fleet commander in 1940, when Japan made demands on Vichy France that increased America's hostility, Koga Mineichi had objected to the myopic policy. Before Pearl Harbor, informed of even more aggressive policies sure to bring war, Koga—who knew Yamamoto opposed them—complained of measures being taken without consulting the Combined Fleet leader.

Born in Saga prefecture of samurai stock, the fifty-nine-year-old Koga

Mineichi had graduated Etajima near the top of his class. His braininess showed in many ways. Hardly a year after passing the course at the Naval War College, Koga returned as an instructor. He had spent nearly five years assigned in France, including a tour as naval attaché. Koga had been a Combined Fleet staff officer. There were several berths on the Navy General Staff, including a stint in charge of the intelligence bureau and an unusual three-year tour. He had also been active on technical boards and worked for the staff of the emperor's special inspector.

But Koga Mineichi was a battleship man amid an upheaval in the nature of warfare. In addition to the *Aoba*, Koga had skippered the battleship *Ise* and led a cruiser division. He had preceded Kondo Nobutake in command of the Second Fleet. Koga remained a solid surface warrior imbued with the traditional doctrine of decisive battle. With the NGS in the late 1930s, the admiral had argued that surface ships need not fear airplanes. The *Aoba*'s misfortune contradicted that view. As Second Fleet commander in 1941 he had opposed the transfer of his attached carrier unit to become part of the new all-flattop *Kido Butai.* In part, Koga's opposition had been overcome by reassignment to lead the China Area Fleet, in which capacity he had blockaded Hong Kong when war began. Much now depended on Koga Mineichi's flexibility and intellect.

The emergency nature of his appointment at least afforded Admiral Koga the opportunity to have his pick of subordinates, and the new C-in-C prevailed on the Navy General Staff to send him its vice chief, Fukudome Shigeru, as his staff boss. Vice Admiral Fukudome, who had been with Koga on the NGS in the 1930s, had much more experience with aviation, and that was a help. But a certain fatalism had set in. On several occasions when the press of business let up, Koga reflected to Fukudome that Yamamoto had been lucky to have passed while the war situation still seemed favorable.

Admiral Koga told Fukudome that the fleet would not stop its effort to force a decisive battle. On the plan for third-phase operations, necessary once IGHQ declared the war had entered this new period, Koga altered Combined Fleet's contingency plans. He took account of changed conditions by designing a new kind of decisive battle. Completed in the summer, Koga's plan divided the broad expanse of the Pacific into sectors and made local commanders responsible for preparing numerous air bases and fortifying each one. The various air flotillas could shuttle—as they had been doing into Rabaul—among threatened sectors. Once an opportunity arose, the main strength of Combined Fleet would join with land-based air to smash the enemy. Under Koga the Navy began creating a new First Air Fleet as an elite JNAF formation—but it would not be ready for many months. Koga also engineered Kondo Nobutake's relief. Vice Admiral Kurita Takeo, promoted to replace him at Second Fleet, had a reputation as an aggressive surface commander. Kondo went to the China Area Fleet.

In short, Koga Mineichi intended an aggressive strategy. Admiral Koga said as much in the order of the day he issued on May 23, when Japan revealed the death of Yamamoto and the appointment of his successor:

> No matter how many times the enemy shall advance against us, we shall always welcome combat with him and in exterminating him and assuring for ourselves the ultimate victory, we shall by united effort and perseverance forge for ourselves a greater and greater military power. At the same time that we manifest a relentless spirit of attack, we shall be prepared to meet the changing conditions of warfare with new strategies and new weapons, always keeping one step ahead of the enemy.
>
> The war is now at its peak. We defend what is ours and the task of meeting and striking the enemy must be the prerogative of the Imperial Navy. We shall defend ourselves to the last breath and shall totally destroy the enemy.

Pious words, perhaps. At the moment Admiral Koga issued this exhortation, the Aleutians seemed threatened and much of the fleet had concentrated in Empire waters. Koga would keep his biggest ships there for several months, taking the opportunity to dry-dock them for upkeep. He returned to Truk in August. By then the war in the Solomons had brewed up. A week before the *Aoba* was sufficiently repaired to voyage home, the test began.

REDRAWING THE BATTLE MAPS

After two postponements, SOWESPAC completed preparations for its next leap ahead. In the Coral Sea this included assault landings at Kiriwina and Woodlark islands, below New Britain. Once those places had airfields, Allied fighters would be in easy range of Rabaul itself, not to mention all the other Japanese bases. The enemy were not blind to the peril. It was apparent the Allies were poised to leap. In May the 25th Air Flotilla returned to Rabaul, followed in June by the 24th, reinforcing what the Eleventh Air Fleet already had. Aerial reconnaissance over Guadalcanal on May 21 showed forty four-engine bombers, thirty-two twin-engine ones, and no fewer than 275 single-engine aircraft. When Halsey and MacArthur sent fifty-plane raids against Lae and Shortland and a hundred-plane raid on Munda, Admiral Kusaka decided to strike back. He used his added strength for new lightning bolts. On June 7, Kusaka sent a swarm of eighty-one Zeroes on a fighter sweep to the Russell Islands bases. Among the casualties was Warrant Officer Yanagiya Kenji of the 204th Air Group, who had failed in escorting Yamamoto's fatal flight. Seriously wounded, Yanagiya had his arm amputated. Redeploying 25th and 26th flotilla planes to Buin, on June 12 Kusaka repeated the sweep using seventy-seven fighters, and four days later he struck at Ironbottom Sound with twenty-four bombers and seventy fighters. Veterans remember this as the "Big Raid." Two ships were damaged badly enough to beach, another hurt more lightly, and half a dozen U.S. planes crashed, against thirty Japanese. As with the I Operation, results disappointed. A submarine concentration against Halsey's carriers, sighted in Torpedo Junction, failed to accomplish anything.

In contrast to vigorous air activity, now Admiral Kusaka became reluctant to use his surface ships. With the bulk of the Combined Fleet in Empire waters and oriented toward the Aleutians, Kusaka had little support. A staff meeting on June 10 revealed the dismal state of Vice Admiral Samejima's Eighth Fleet. Heavy cruiser *Chokai*, previously the flagship, had been recalled by the Combined Fleet. Samejima's main strength comprised the 3rd Destroyer Squadron. Light cruiser *Yubari* of that unit had damaged the shafts for two of her three propellers, restricting top speed to twenty-four knots. Equally perplexing, *Yubari* was undergoing crew transfer. Two-thirds of her officers plus 35 percent of enlisted men were new. Destroyer *Yugiri*, torpedoed during an antisubmarine sweep, was undergoing local repair. She would be ready before the end of June. The commander of Destroyer Division 22 reported his ships had not been dry-docked for seven to nine months, depending on the vessel, and steamed at reduced efficiency. They had off-loaded reserve torpedoes to reduce displacement and maintain speed potential. Those ships and two others all needed dry-docking. Destroyer *Nagatsuki* had a leak in a propeller shaft casing and was shipping two dozen tons of water a day, double that under way. Desperate for bottoms, Kusaka nonetheless rated her battleworthy. Half the destroyers had just changed skippers or were about to. Rear Admiral Akiyama Teruo of the 3rd Squadron, himself a new face, had come from a shoreside billet. The one bright light was that light cruiser *Sendai* had joined and settled in. Admiral Samejima's Eighth Fleet faced grave challenges.

All this would have made Bull Halsey happy. Photos of Rabaul and Shortland showed Japanese heavy cruisers and more destroyer types than there were. This was coincidental. The Imperial Navy had been using Vice Admiral Nishimura's Cruiser Division 7 to shuttle replacement seamen into Rabaul. As for the *Chokai*, for weeks she had been at anchor off Truk's Dublon Island. Meanwhile the Eighth Fleet had patrol boats and some old destroyers converted to other uses, often mistaken for tin cans. Halsey's aerial snoopers were reporting a stronger fleet than Kusaka, in fact, possessed.

In tandem with MacArthur's advance, Halsey had laid on Operation "Toenails," his next move, against New Georgia. He began with assault landings. Rendova, an island just five and a half miles across the water from Munda, offered a prime location for a PT boat base from which the devil boats could mount a close blockade. It would be invaded at several points. On New Georgia there were landings at Segi Point, Viru Harbor, and Wickham Plantation. The first, actually undertaken by the Marines' 4th Raider Battalion on June 21, was the opening chord in the ensemble. In preparation SOPAC made a forty-plane raid on Vila on June 19, and fifty-plane attacks on Munda on June 25, and both on the twenty-sixth. Then on the twenty-ninth, Merrill's cruisers bombarded Munda while Halsey's minelayer unit took on Vila. The real landings took place the next day.

News of the invasion electrified Rabaul. The Japanese fleet, alerted at dawn on June 30, soon learned of Americans storming Rendova. One who got the alert was Lieutenant Commander Hanami Kohei of the destroyer *Amagiri*. Until recently skipper of a tin can at Singapore, Hanami had taken over the *Amagiri* less than two weeks earlier. He found the ship in sore need of rest and reconditioning and planned to replace some sailors and effect such repairs as could be done in place. Hull, weapons, and engines had all been affected by war service. Commander Hanami was coping with the frustration of futile requests for spare parts when Rendova changed everything. "The information created a tumult at Rabaul Base," Hanami recalled. The fleet moved out "in full strength with determination to blast the enemy on the sea but efforts to locate him finally ended fruitlessly." That night Rear Admiral Akiyama brought the light cruiser *Yubari* with nine destroyers, including *Amagiri*, to pound the Rendova beachhead. Without observers to correct their aim, the Japanese blasted the jungle, inflicting no damage.

None of the invasion sites directly threatened Munda. The strategy was rather to seize a foothold, develop Rendova, then mount the offensive on Munda and Vila from there. The covering force, under Halsey's direct command, would be Task Force 36. It included both Ainsworth's and Merrill's cruiser groups and a carrier unit built around *Saratoga* and HMS *Victorious*. As a historical artifact, it is interesting that the Royal Navy here participated in a U.S. amphibious landing in the South Pacific.

At Rabaul, Admiral Kusaka knew of the general threat but not specific Allied intentions. On New Georgia the Japanese now had 10,500 troops, built around two regiments of the Army's Southeast Detachment, under General Sasaki Akira, and Rear Admiral Ota Minoru's 8th Combined SNLF, divided between Munda and Vila, with a few scattered outposts elsewhere, including Rendova. Preparatory bombardments did nothing to destroy the defenses. As the invasion fleet dropped anchor, only a few miles away shore batteries at Munda opened fire. Their very first salvo hit the destroyer *Gwin*. But two others replied, and American troops going ashore quickly set up artillery at Rendova and added their counterfire. The Japanese guns fell silent.

American amphibious ships just beginning to learn their trade at the time of the Guadalcanal landing were now well practiced. The command ship *McCawley* not only put ashore 1,100 soldiers but landed supplies at a rate of 157 tons per hour. This proved fortunate, for the first important Japanese reaction was an afternoon strike by two dozen torpedo bombers, one of which put a fish into the *McCawley*. That night an overenthusiastic PT boat launched her spread at the "Wacky Mac" and finished her off. The only other naval casualty was the destroyer *Zane*, run aground on a reef in the dark.

General Sasaki updated Rabaul in a stream of radio messages. Startled when no landings were attempted against Munda itself, Sasaki soon understood. Seabees went ashore at Rendova in the early assault waves. They had strict orders to fabricate an airfield within two weeks, along with a new PT boat base and other facilities. The Seabees worked through rain and dark. They almost never stopped. Admiral Kusaka added his bit. The day after the landing he sent in a bomber attack that arrived undetected at noon, with GIs in their chow lines. Bombs smashed the hospital, damaged boats, and inflicted more than 130 casualties. New Zealand Squadron No. 14 participated in the defense. Pilot Officer Geoff Fisken, flying the P-40 called the "Wairarapa Wildcat," splashed two Zeroes and a Betty. Bombings continued, with Japanese Army aircraft participating during the early days.

On July 5 came the first surface naval engagement. Tip Ainsworth brought his cruiser group back to punish Vila. Starting after midnight, Ainsworth dumped more than 3,000 rounds of six-inch fire on the enemy base. While that happened, other Allied ships moved 43rd Infantry Division troops and the 1st Marine Raider Battalion across from Rendova to make the first landing near Munda. A Tokyo Express did the same for the Japanese. The Express had been unloading when the Japanese heard Ainsworth's thunder and they hurriedly put to sea. As the Americans completed fire missions, the *Ralph Talbot* reported radar contact. Moments later a torpedo plowed into the destroyer *Strong*. The Japanese were so far away that no one could believe their destroyers had launched these deadly fish.

That injury became insult the following night. Halsey flashed word that intelligence called a Tokyo Express run from Buin. Rear Admiral Ainsworth, who had been retiring down The Slot, reversed and came back hunting bear. Ainsworth far outgunned the enemy, with light cruisers *Honolulu*, *Helena*, and *St. Louis*, plus four destroyers. Admiral Akiyama led a full-bore Express, with a guard unit of three ships escorting seven destroyers crammed to the gunwales with troops and supplies. At 1:40 a.m. of July 6, American radars acquired Japanese targets inside Kula Gulf. Akiyama had just detached his second transport unit to Vila, having already sent the first. He was headed north-northwest, hugging the Kolombangara shore. Lookouts spotted the Americans minutes later, but surprise had already been lost—though lacking radar, Akiyama's flagship, destroyer *Niizuki*, had a radio receiver designed to detect radar emissions. More than half an hour earlier she recorded the Allied signals. Akiyama knew the enemy was out there, just not where. Ainsworth began clearing for action and maneuvering to trap the Japanese. He ordered guns at 1:54 a.m., but it was several minutes until the cannonade began. The initial salvo smashed the *Niizuki*, but her mates instantly launched torpedoes. Despite 2,500 six-inch shells, only the *Niizuki* sank, taking Akiyama to his grave. Three other destroyers were lightly damaged. But on the American side Captain Charles P. Cecil's *Helena* was destroyed by torpedoes. A single hit between her forward six-inch turrets simply blew off the bow, sluicing water into every deck—and above deck too as she forged ahead at twenty-five knots. Seaman First Class Ted Blahnik, whose action station was in an AA gun director tub far aft on the 600-foot-long ship, could not figure out why water coursed over the deck and poured into his tub. But in moments the "Happy *Helena*" shuddered as a second Long Lance hit, and a third shattered her keel. For extra ignominy a final hit was a dud torpedo. The *Helena* sank in little more than twenty minutes, except for her prow, which jutted from the water like an arrowhead pointed at the Southern Cross. Almost 450 sailors were lost.

Amid the confusion the battle had a second act. Destroyers that stopped for rescues or were late out of Vila faced a pair of Ainsworth's tin cans that had stuck around to rescue *Helena* survivors. The *Nagatsuki* ran aground. In daylight she would be pounded into a wreck by SOPAC airmen. Some *Helena* sailors, convinced they faced an enemy force of four new cruisers with eight destroyers, insisted they had blown every one out of the water. Admiral Ainsworth himself reported eight Japanese craft, claiming all of them sunk save one or two left as cripples. The CINCPAC war diary recorded that result. The truth was that no Japanese were visible because the Imperial Navy had disappeared into the night.

Even worse from the American point of view would be what became known as the Battle of Kolombangara, in the same waters a week later. Ainsworth was back with Task Group 36.1, the *Atlanta* replaced by New Zealand light cruiser *Leander*, with six extra destroyers for a total of ten. Every ship had radar and an integrated combat information center. They now sported a combination of search and microwave radars that enabled actual spotting of the fall of shells, optimally at 10,000 yards or less. Radar-controlled gunnery had become a reality. Ainsworth was there because of

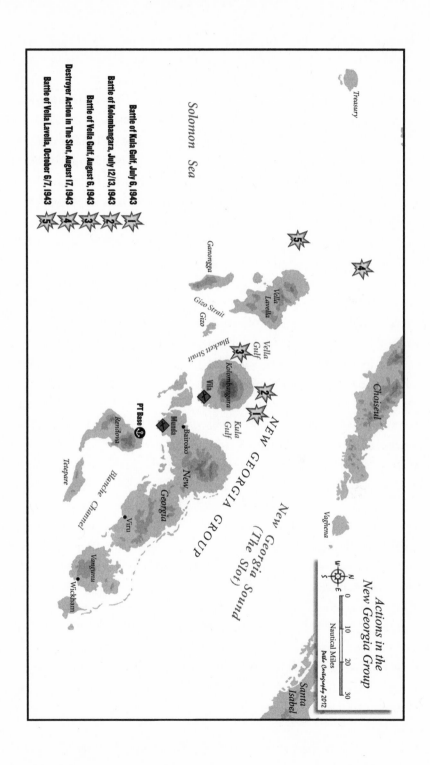

Actions in the
New Georgia Group

Battle of Kula Gulf, July 6, 1943 ⭐1
Battle of Kolombangara, July 12/13, 1943 ⭐2
Battle of Vella Gulf, August 6, 1943 ⭐3
Destroyer Action in The Slot, August 17, 1943 ⭐4
Battle of Vella Lavella, October 6/7, 1943 ⭐5

Ultra, confirmed by coastwatchers. So well-informed were the Allies that he could delay departure until late on July 12 and still be in position at the appointed hour. Ainsworth had a crushing superiority.

The Japanese made some changes. Eighth Fleet headquarters moved forward to Buin. But the Imperial Navy no longer had the resources to accomplish wholesale unit rotation. A fresh fighter unit advanced to Rabaul—but the fighter component of the 582nd Air Group had to be disbanded. The air groups of carriers *Ryuho* and *Junyo* were also thrown into the meat grinder. Admiral Koga ordered a fresh destroyer squadron to Rabaul to replace the battered ships with the Eighth Fleet. But much like Captain Hara Tameichi's destroyer division, its vessels farmed out to others, Rear Admiral Izaki Shunji's 2nd Destroyer Squadron had a few original ships with a hodge-podge of others glommed onto it. The flotilla on July 12 included several destroyers that had fought with the 3rd Squadron, plus others drafted in from the outside. In the U.S. official history Samuel Eliot Morison complains of the late-inning addition of unfamiliar destroyers into Ainsworth's force creating "once more the setup of Tassafaronga." This condition had become the norm on the Japanese side.

Izaki's force left Rabaul before dawn, loaded 1,200 troops at Buin, and stood down The Slot. He sailed in the light cruiser *Jintsu* with a covering unit of five destroyers. The transport unit with four more carried the load, departing Shortland in the afternoon. Captain Sato Torajiro's cruiser launched a floatplane at 8:15 p.m. to scout Kula Gulf. After nightfall a bright moon lit the sea, enabling an Allied snooper to spot Izaki soon after midnight. The Catalina carried an observer from Task Group 36.1's flagship, so premeditation is clear. Ainsworth was already within thirty miles of Izaki. The admiral had to have been expecting action. Izaki detached his destroyer-transports to slide by the Americans and they did so. Whether he based this on a general understanding of the combat environment—Izaki was an Etajima classmate of codebreaker Ushio Fujimasa, then heading the Owada Group—or on detecting Ainsworth's radars is unknown. One destroyer, *Yukikaze*, carried her own radar and acquired the enemy thirty minutes before visual contact. The bright moon now worked to Japanese advantage. Izaki's vessels saw the Americans before they had closed to optimal range.

Admiral Ainsworth instructed his ships to launch torpedoes before shooting, but Izaki beat them to the punch—and Japanese torpedoes were faster and more powerful. Captain Sato's *Jintsu* spit seven torpedoes, and the destroyers more. Sato ordered his ship to illuminate the enemy—as fatal here as it had been for the *Hiei* off Guadalcanal. *Jintsu*'s main battery had been in action only a couple of minutes when she was hit. The Allied cruisers pummeled her—2,630 six-inch shells in about twenty minutes. American light cruisers in particular had awesome firepower. At least ten hits slammed the *Jintsu*, and she was also struck by a torpedo. Seaman Toyoda Isamu, one of the ship's oldest salts—he had been with *Jintsu* since the spring of 1939—was at his action station just forward of the aft smokestack when there was a tremendous explosion on the port side. Admiral Izaki, Captain Sato, and the ship's executive officer were all killed. There were no fires. *Jintsu* listed slightly to port but then rolled to starboard. After just ten minutes, at 1:48 a.m. the cruiser broke in two and sank. A handful of men were rescued by the submarine *I-180*, and the Americans picked up a few more. Seaman Toyoda was captured on New Georgia four days after the battle. The vast majority of 484 sailors perished.

But by this time Rear Admiral Ainsworth's battle plan had already gone wrong. Captain Shimai Zenjiro of the *Yukikaze* took charge of the remaining Japanese warships. He turned away under a squall and ordered torpedoes reloaded, a vital chore completed at 1:36 a.m. Twenty minutes later Shimai's destroyers regained sight of the Allies. They flung thirty-one torpedoes at 2:05. At about that moment Ainsworth, confused over the identity of the targets on his radar, ordered star shell illumination. Shortly thereafter, within a hellish six minutes Long Lances detonated against cruisers *Leander* and *St. Louis*, Ainsworth's flagship *Honolulu*, and the destroyer *Gwin*. Both American cruisers' bows were opened to the sea. The *Leander* had a starboard list. As a final act, the PBY that had been observing all this made her own bombing run against the retiring Japanese. She missed. The damaged warships returned to Guadalcanal under their own power, but *Honolulu* and *St. Louis* would be out of action for four months and the *Leander* laid up the better part of a year. The destroyer *Gwin* sank. At Pearl Harbor, Admiral Nimitz decided that Pug Ainsworth had handled a succession of difficult situations with aggressiveness and skill. At Rabaul, learning the details, Hara Tameichi concluded this had been a greater victory even than Tassafaronga. But not all Imperial Navy officers were so pleased. Another

destroyer captain, Hanami Kohei of the *Amagiri*, emphasized the technological balance: "While night fighting had long been regarded as a unique
prowess of the Japanese Navy, the results now had become entirely the reverse. This was because US forces were using radar and we were powerless from preventing them from approaching us suddenly with . . . guns
blazing."

The young John F. Kennedy's story epitomizes this moment, its trials and
anguish, and the relentless rhythm of the conflict. Kennedy had arrived at
Tulagi under the hammer of Japanese air attack, a fresh-faced PT boat officer hungry for a command. The boat he would skipper, *PT-109*, claimed to
have downed one of the Japanese raiders that day. The tender *Niagara*, serving the PT boat base, claimed seven. Patrol boat methods and missions were
changing to reflect burgeoning Allied strength and the new texture of the
war. PT patrols that had been a matter of one or a few boats from Squadron
3 on Tulagi first became mass sorties to block the Express at Guadalcanal,
then switched to a variety of activities. Flotilla One, a collection of squadrons, replaced the single unit. Tulagi harbor became a receiving center. The
need for room drove the PT flotilla to set up a satellite base on Florida Island. Lieutenant Kennedy spent his early weeks at Sesapi on Florida with
Squadron 2, integrating his basic training with the practical experience PT
boat hands had acquired and now passed along. Florida too had become a
backwater. The advance up The Slot moved the nexus of PT operations first
to the Russells, then Rendova.

PT-109, the boat Jack Kennedy made famous, distinguished herself in the
Russells invasion before he arrived. She recovered some of the scouts sent
to reconnoiter the islands. During the landing phase the PTs, including the
109, turned out en masse to help screen the transports. Two-boat sections
of PTs then patrolled Russells waters. But Squadron 6 became the denizens
of the Russells base, while Squadron 2 pulled back to Sesapi for the boats to
be overhauled, their hulls scraped. The *109*'s radar proved troublesome, but
in itself this detail shows the difference between sides in this war: The Allies
now had radars even in individual patrol boats, whereas this crucial technical development was only beginning to trickle down to reach Japanese destroyers. Lieutenant Commander Rollin Westholm, flotilla operations

officer and a former skipper of *PT-109*, assigned Jack Kennedy as her new captain. He took command on April 25. Her crew included only a couple of men from the boat's original complement, and some sailors boarded with Kennedy himself.

For a period of weeks Lieutenant Kennedy made familiarization patrols and did shake-down runs with *PT-109*. He was off Lunga Point on April 18 when fighter pilot Tom Lanphier, returning from the Yamamoto shoot-down, made a celebratory rollover down the runway of the airfield to mark his success. Kennedy's patrol boat investigated strange lights on Savo Island, charted water obstacles, and looked for stray supply drums off the coast. Kennedy experienced the dangers of cruising in fog—near zero visibility, throttling up the PT boat's three engines was an invitation to disaster—and the fear of seeing a light at sea that might turn into a Japanese warship. At Sesapi Kennedy lived in a native hut and employed a Melanesian houseboy, who confessed that he'd helped eat a missionary. The Melanesians were friendly and the houseboy helpful, but one day he disappeared. Scuttlebutt had it that he had been apprehended by authorities who sought to punish indigenous cannibalism.

This is a good place to spend a moment on the impact of the war on this primitive society. Throughout the Solomons lived tribes of headhunters, fishermen, or others who practiced slash-and-burn agriculture. Shell money remained standard currency. Many Melanesian ways had not changed in decades, if not centuries. Excepting those who crewed island steamers, most experiences of the outside world were limited to contacts with missionaries, colonial officials, and plantation owners or overseers. New Zealand and Australian colonial authorities, in succession to the British, and in particular missionaries like the Seventh Day Adventists, whose South Seas Evangelical Mission made them possibly the most enthusiastic proselytizers in the islands, introduced a modicum of modernization. The main island of the New Georgia group suggests the degree of missionary penetration: It had settlements called Jericho and Nazareth. Developers came to the Solomons to install plantations, primarily for coconuts and gum trees. This led to a reduction in nomadization, some wage-based employment, the growth of villages into towns around the ports, and the establishment of new settlements, particularly around missions. The colonizers introduced notions of "law" and legal norms that clashed with traditional adjudication and lineal descent, not to mention the concept of "property" as against tribal lands. Traditional ways were diluted, though not eliminated. Close connections among the islands remained. An example springs from Jack Kennedy's experience when his PT boat was later smashed and the young officer worked desperately to save his crew. Years afterward Kennedy thanked the islanders who helped rescue them. By then the ten men lived on seven different islands. Two resided at Munda, another at Rendova. One had taken the name "Moses." One, Eroni Kumana, later donated a bracelet made of seashells to the Kennedy Library, asking that it be laid on the former president's grave. That was done in 2009. In the Solomons the cream-colored shells were money still. Modernity had arrived in the islands, yet tradition remained strong.

The clash of cultures did not come to the Solomons because of World War II, though war accelerated many trends and brought tremendous agitation. Sophisticated ships and planes, cannon, mechanisms people had hardly seen, and alien men with guns who tried to enlist the natives or demanded they take sides were major features of the indigenous experience. The sheer scale shocked the Melanesians. On Guadalcanal the indigenous population amounted to perhaps 15,000 people. The warring sides flooded the island with soldiers numbering many times that—and more men died there than the entire native community. Some indigenous people took the war as an opportunity to better their lot, others to break free of the colonial mold; still others sought to flee.

With a colonial tradition already spanning decades, the Melanesians mostly sided with the Allies, who represented the whites they had long known. Vicious Japanese reprisals for real or imagined slights made that choice easier. Coastwatchers, in particular, depended on these traditional loyalties. Roughly 400 Melanesians served alongside the coastwatchers on the various islands. Such cooperation explains how Australian coastwatchers could be active on New Georgia while the Japanese held bases on the same islands. In addition there was a Solomon Islands Protectorate Defense Force that carried 680 natives on its rolls. Some of these people, like Sergeant Vouza, fought with the Americans on Guadalcanal. The war sparked demands for native labor. Indigenous men from Guadalcanal, Tulagi, Florida, and Malaita became the mainstay of supply handling for the huge Allied bases on Cactus. Eventually this phenomenon would be recognized by the establishment of an official Solomon Islands Labor Corps in which 3,200 Melanesians served.

But the war also challenged the fabric of indigenous society. Malaita Island—never invaded, never occupied, never a battleground—gives the example. The closest Malaita came to the war was the quiet presence there of a couple of Australian coastwatchers. Natives returning from work on Guadalcanal brought tales contrasting their treatment with that meted out by plantation overseers. Even African-Americans in the U.S. forces—themselves visibly oppressed—behaved more graciously than the compradors. An emancipation movement formed on Malaita and spread through the Solomons. After 1945, protectorate security authorities regarded these self-government advocates as revolutionaries, which led to a hysterical response.

The Allied commanders at least took some pains to avoid the worst of culture shock. Native villages were typically off-limits to Allied troops. Often there were only chance contacts, or ceremonial occasions when officers were invited to native rituals. Most outsiders, both American and Japanese, were left with their fantasies of half-naked natives frolicking at village festivals. Some encounters were less convivial. When PT boats moved to the new Russells base, a couple of sailors who had rustled up a skiff with an outboard went off exploring a little river. Startled by black snakes, they ran away from the boat and saw some native women, only to confront tribesmen with spears, who followed them, pounding their spears on the ground in the manner of Zulu tribesmen in the British-African colonial wars. The sailors hightailed it for their skiff, ignoring vines and snakes alike.

Most PT sailors' encounters with the tribesmen more resembled Jack Kennedy's attempt to teach his houseboy soccer than that of the crewmen in the Russells, but there was no escaping the fact that Allied bases, wherever they were, shared the islands with the indigenous. Soon enough Kennedy arrived in the Russells himself with *PT-109.* Jack, who had participated in such antics as keeping his men in instant ice cream, and turning a blind eye to their concocting moonshine, was ready too. Lieutenant Kennedy lost a coin toss for a PT boat assignment to New Guinea and went to the Russells instead. Toward the end of May his boat, rated combat-ready, his crew "Tulagi-groggy," moved up and into the war. There were three PT formations at the base. Commander Allen P. Calvert led the group, as he had the original force at Tulagi. *PT-109* belonged to the Russell Islands Motor Torpedo Boat Squadron.

PT patrols now frequently escorted small ship movements, or went as outriders for the tin cans and other vessels screening larger convoys. Kennedy guarded the 4th Marine Raider Battalion when it was inserted at Segi Point, and *PT-109* helped screen one of the Rendova landings. The Seabees installed the Rendova PT base at Lumberi, an islet at the southeastern end. It was named Todd City after Leon E. Todd of PT Squadron 9, the first devil boat skipper killed there. Lieutenant Commander Thomas G. Warfield led the force to which *PT-109* soon belonged. The boats here aimed at Munda and Vila. Their exploits exasperated the enemy, who could be dangerous, but Allied air was nearly as bad. On July 20, *PT-164*, *-166*, and *-168* were returning to Rendova when they were set upon by Army B-25s. They shot down one of their own planes. Another night Kennedy's PT would be attacked by a Catalina snooper.

The whole New Georgia venture turned out to be much more complicated than anyone, Admiral Halsey included, had anticipated. The passel of little landings that led to Rendova became a kind of amphibious infiltration. When the first three U.S. battalions assaulted New Georgia, they landed only five miles from Munda. The troops were supposed to prepare the way for a much bigger force of the 43rd Division that would wrest that place from the enemy. Terrain proved so difficult that more than six weeks of mud and misery would sap the energy and consume the strength of the GIs sent to New Georgia to cover those five short miles—more properly four, since the lead units moved a mile or so on the day of the invasion.

General Sasaki observed the American encroachment with mounting alarm, appealing to Rabaul for reinforcements and supplies. The series of naval battles off Vila demonstrated that running the Tokyo Express in these waters, if anything, would be more difficult than at Guadalcanal. But the Japanese gamely went at the task. On July 18, Admiral Kusaka issued his Operations Order No. 10, which provided for measures to secure Munda and Kolombangara and "sweep" the enemy from New Georgia. "The air units and surface units will cooperate with the submarine force, exerting every effort to cut enemy transportation lines, especially to prevent his unloading in the Kula Gulf region." Dusk or dawn "group fighter attacks" were favored, and submarines were to make surprise strikes.

Instead it seemed the Japanese themselves were being swept from the board. The submarine force tried hard. At one point Rabaul set two of the smaller RO boats to approach Munda from opposite directions and snare SOPAC vessels either there or off Rendova. No result. Commander Orita Zenji made seven patrols in The Slot during June and July. He found little except PTs until July 12, when the American destroyer *Taylor* caught his *RO-101* on the surface and opened fire. Orita submerged, escaped, and made Rabaul, but counted 127 dents in his boat from the destroyer's automatic weapons. Two other subs were not as lucky. The fleet also deployed heavy surface ships to Rabaul for the first time in many months. Vice Admiral Nishimura Shoji's cruiser force steamed off Kolombangara as cover unit for a Tokyo Express, ready to intervene against any SOPAC sortie into Kula Gulf. But on the night of July 19–20 it was Nishimura who was set upon—by half a dozen U.S. Marine Avengers, probably from Marine Torpedo Squadron 143 or 144. One TBF managed a near miss on cruiser *Kumano* that sprang hull plates and sent her to the repairmen for two months. Nishimura moved his flag to the *Suzuya*, but took Cruiser Division 7 back to Truk without attempting further operations.

Admiral Kusaka next tried a heavy Tokyo Express to Buin, sending the seaplane carrier *Nisshin* crammed with twenty-two tanks and eight guns, plus almost 1,200 soldiers aboard her and three destroyers. AIRSOLS planes piled on them on July 22, based on an Ultra intercept the previous evening that revealed the *Nisshin*'s time of arrival and planned anchorage. The aerial ambush was a fifty-plane raid, covered, since the action would take place in the heart of the Japanese base zone, by no fewer than 120 fighters. Several bomb hits crippled the *Nisshin*, which sank with the bulk of the troops and supplies and all the heavy equipment.

On July 20, Captain Hara was summoned to Rabaul and brought destroyer *Shigure* to join the Eighth Fleet transport unit. She carried a load of desperately needed aircraft spare parts and spent several days in transit. When *Shigure* dropped anchor in Simpson Harbor and the captain could get to headquarters, he learned that two of the destroyers responsible for the naval victory off Kolombangara were already sunk. Hara was stunned. Within a few days he had been scheduled for a Tokyo Express to Vila. Before that expedition, on August 1, another of the Kolombangara victors fell to the enemy. The Vila Express would have a nasty encounter with John F. Kennedy's *PT-109*.

Hara Tameichi dreaded formulas. What unfolded on August 1 was not an exact repetition, though the Express did follow the course of a previous mission, which had made a sort of backdoor passage through Blackett Strait. Captain Sugiura Kaju of Destroyer Division 4 led the Express and its transport unit. Admiral Kusaka kicked off the action by sending a dozen bombers to plaster Todd City and keep down the devil boats. That SOPAC knew of the expedition, in turn, is indicated by the fact that it ordered a full-press effort. At sunset fifteen PT boats put to sea under Lieutenant Henry J. Brantingham in *PT-159*. He also served as section leader for one group, posting himself farthest up the channel and other PT sections on down it. On the opposite side of Kolombangara, Admiral Halsey posted a destroyer group under Captain Arleigh A. Burke.

Captain Yamashiro Katsumori led the one-ship destroyer guard force for the Express. He had had some success on previous voyages, including reaching Vila with a transport unit the night of the Kula Gulf battle, and had taken over Destroyer Division 11 afterward. Yamashiro sailed in the *Amagiri*, with Sugiura's *Hagikaze*, *Arashi*, and *Shigure* bringing up the rear. That only a single vessel could be spared for the crucial guard role indicates the thinness of Japanese resources. Captain Sugiura's unit carried 900 reinforcements and 120 tons of supplies. The night was pitch dark as they entered Blackett Strait. Sugiura had his vessels hove to at the rendezvous, and barges came from shore to meet them. Yamashiro put the *Amagiri* to the west of the mission force, steaming in a loose square pattern. In the *Shigure*, Hara was astonished that all the men and supplies could be unloaded in just twenty minutes. They were under way within five more, and not long afterward were making thirty knots through waters so treacherous that in peacetime no one would dare a fraction of that speed. Yamashiro recalled that the entire business of approach, transshipment, and withdrawal was completed within ninety minutes. Once he saw Sugiura's bow waves, Yamashiro altered to starboard and increased speed to resume position at the head of the Japanese column.

Comparing historical accounts of this action leaves some mysteries. Hara clearly recollects that the engagement took place during the return voyage. Captain Yamashiro and Lieutenant Nakajima Goro, navigation officer of the *Amagiri*, both confirm Hara's observation. American accounts are replete with detail on all the PT boat sections firing at the enemy. In fact, the PT squadron after-action report erroneously cites five Imperial Navy destroyers and claims five or six torpedo hits. These claimed contacts would have been possible only if the action had taken place with Sugiura's vessels still inbound for Vila. Hara recounts only the single encounter with *PT-109*. Brantingham's PTs had been on station since twilight. The discrepancies cannot be resolved on the basis of available evidence. Either the PTs missed the inbound Express or the Japanese remained completely oblivious to torpedo attacks that resulted in five to six hits.

But no one contests the contact with Brantingham's "B" Section. The unit leader detected the Express on radar and soon had visual contact. *PT-159* shot four torpedoes at 1,400 yards; her consort the *157* boat launched two. Their presence revealed—grease in a torpedo tube caught fire during launch—Brantingham's vessels fled under fire. Remaining were Lieutenant (Junior Grade) John R. Lowrey's *PT-162* and Jack Kennedy's *PT-109*, joined by Lieutenant P. A. Potter's *PT-169*, which had become separated from its group. They saw flashes and heard radio chatter, but had no real knowledge of the situation. Kennedy called general quarters once he glimpsed a searchlight and the water spouts of exploding shells. Suddenly in the darkness the prow of a big ship loomed. For a second Kennedy thought it might be another PT.

Japanese lookouts also saw the other vessel only at the last moment. Lieutenant Commander Hanami of the *Amagiri* recorded this as a cloudy night with intermittent squalls and poor visibility. It was about 2:00 a.m. Petty Officer Kametani, the first to spot *PT-109*, reported Kennedy's boat when she was just 1,100 yards away. For a moment Captain Yamashiro, on the bridge as guard unit leader, thought the object might be a Japanese barge, but he swiftly decided she must be one of the devil boats. Navigator Nakajima later described the options for Australian journalists: "We had three alternatives—to turn to port and collide with the other destroyers, to keep ahead and go onto the reefs, or to turn to starboard and meet the M.T.B. [motor torpedo boat]." Skipper Hanami recounts that conventional wisdom in the Imperial Navy at the time was to meet a PT boat with a "crash strategy," and that he ordered a course change to run it down. Captain Yamashiro insists that *he* ordered a turn to port to *avoid* collision. Coxwain Doi Kazuto turned the wheel. Either way the *Amagiri* was just beginning to respond to her helm when she sliced into Kennedy's *PT-109* at thirty-four knots. Lieutenant Nakajima, in the charthouse as the collision occurred, felt a bump; Hanami heard a thunderous roar and felt the searing heat as flames erupted from the stricken PT. A sailor in one engine room heard a thud and feared they had been hit by a torpedo; in another a petty officer heard a scraping noise and thought the destroyer had stuck on a reef.

The *Amagiri*'s left-hand propeller had a blade sheared off as it ran through the American torpedo boat while turning. Scorched paint along the bow plus leaks were the main damage to the Japanese vessel—not serious but cutting her speed down to twenty-four knots for the return trip. At Rabaul, Captain Yamashiro took Commander Hanami with him to flagship *Sendai* to report to Rear Admiral Baron Ijuin Matsuji, who had replaced the deceased Izaki at the head of Eighth Fleet's destroyer squadron. The baron met them on the quarterdeck with a broad smile. He only wondered why Yamashiro had not broken radio silence to reveal this exploit. Japan, starved for good war news, made much of this ugly business, with newspapers headlining, "Unprecedented—Enemy Torpedo Boat Trampled Asunder," and "Enemy Torpedo Boat Cut Smack in Two." The Domei News Agency interviewed crewmen and presented the event as if it had been the achievement of a master swordsman.

Imperial Navy participants have their own dispute in the *PT-109* affair. It raged in Japanese media in the late 1950s, including articles in newspapers like *Yomiuri*, *Sankei Shimbun*, and *Nihon Keizai Shimbun*, and in television coverage on the NHK network. Officers Yamashiro and Hanami bickered over the events of that night, with Commander Hanami sticking to his claim that he had gone after *PT-109*. Captain Yamashiro insisted he had sought to prevent the collision. Both wrote letters to John F. Kennedy as if he could settle their argument. The question of whether the collision was deliberate turns on whether *Amagiri* altered to port or starboard and who ordered this change. Rightly enough, Yamashiro insists the ship's master could not have given the order against the wishes of his division commander, but the captain weakened his argument by telling Kennedy in a 1958 letter that the course change had been to starboard (a claim he subsequently reversed), and by writing in a 1960 article for the publication of an association of former naval officers that he could not remember whether helm orders had also been issued by Commander Hanami or by Lieutenant Yonemaru, the assistant navigator, who had had direct charge of the coxswain. The standard account with which American readers are familiar, Robert J. Donovan's book *PT-109*, relegates this dispute to brief mention in a footnote and declares that the case for an accidental collision is thin. In August 1962, Captain Yamashiro wrote Donovan and his publisher, McGraw-Hill, contesting Donovan's quotations from the accounts of certain Japanese sailors and demanding that changes be made to that book.

Back in 1943, when PT boat leader Lieutenant Brantingham saw the flaming carcass of Kennedy's boat and heard the shell fire of that engagement, he rejoiced that at least someone had gotten a hit. But the shoe was on the other foot. Fate tied together many threads that night. John F. Kennedy's war service later helped his political career. Arleigh Burke, whose destroyer unit had been too far away, smashed another Tokyo Express in November at the Battle of Cape St. George, one in which Captain Yamashiro led the transport unit. Yamashiro was subsequently banished to shoreside billets. And Commander Hanami's hometown, Fukushima, would be devastated by a nuclear plant meltdown. Japan, whose war ended in the awesome destruction wrought by nuclear weapons, had swiftly adopted nuclear power, and in 2011 the Fukushima plant complex succumbed to the climactic disaster of a tsunami.

So the *Amagiri* cut the *PT-109* in two. Two crewmen perished. Thus began a weeklong ordeal for Jack Kennedy and his eleven survivors. At great personal risk Kennedy rallied his sailors, saved several from the flaming wreck, and shepherded the disoriented men toward an island, swimming with one of them himself. After days of exposure Kennedy helped move them to another islet. He looked for ways to contact Allied commanders. A portion of the PT boat's wreck was found afloat in daylight, and in due course Station KEN, the Guadalcanal coastwatcher network control, circulated a notice to look out for American survivors. Reginald Evans, the Australian coastwatcher on Kolombangara, got the message. He confirmed the nature of the observed wreckage. Two of his native scouts, Eroni and Biuku, eventually encountered a pair of the *PT-109* crewmen, and Jack Kennedy was

able to get a note to Evans and then meet him. Natives took the news to a
U.S. outpost. Kennedy and his crew were picked up by *PT-157* on August 8.
While that day marked the end of an ordeal for Jack Kennedy and his men,
it also framed the moment Japan tumbled over the edge into an abyss.

TOWARD THE EVENT HORIZON

New Georgia continued to beg for help. Admiral Kusaka had to respond.
On August 4 he ordered another Express. In Tokyo the next day General
Sugiyama informed the emperor that Allied moves threatened every post
in the Outer South Seas. Sugiyama had to endure a very unusual imperial
outburst. "Isn't there someplace where we can strike the United States?"
Hirohito demanded. "When and where on earth are you ever going to put
up a good fight? And when are you going to fight a decisive battle?" The next
engagement would confirm all the emperor's worst fears.

At Rabaul naval officers gathered under an awning on the destroyer
Hagikaze for a briefing on their operation. Captain Sugiura Kaju, who had led
the previous Tokyo Express successfully, commanded this mission and
went over the plans. A torpedo expert, Sugiura had already been a senior
destroyer leader before the war, and he had a sterling reputation. But he
intended to replicate the approach of the previous sortie, so, even to an old
friend, Hara Tameichi objected. Sugiura countered that the details of the
Express had already been settled with Kusaka's headquarters and with the
Army. It was too late. Captain Hara sailed in the *Shigure*, last in Sugiura's
four-ship column.

Hara's misgivings were well-founded. While it is perfectly true that, with
the New Georgia campaign in full swing and the Japanese operational
tempo well understood, SOPAC could expect a Tokyo Express, Halsey's
preparations were based on Ultra intercept of an Eighth Fleet dispatch, enabling him to set the ambush. As on the night of the *PT-109* incident, when
SOPAC had put cruisers off Vella Gulf (on the other side of Kolombangara
from previous Express missions), with PTs down near Blackett Strait, this
time Halsey posted PT boats in the same place, with destroyers right inside
the gulf. He instructed Vice Admiral Theodore S. Wilkinson, his operational leader, to put the forces in motion. The preparatory order went to
Captain Frederick Moosbrugger the preceding day. The Japanese destroy-

ers, still at Rabaul, left at 5:00 a.m. on August 6. Moosbrugger had had nearly a day's notice. In any case, the American captain raised steam by noon and led a half dozen destroyers from the anchorage. They were in position by 10:00 p.m. Moosbrugger delivered on his instructions.

The standard practice with Ultra was to post an air scout in the vicinity of a predicted surface naval movement. While an air spotter tipped the enemy that the Allies were aware of their presence, more important was that it gave the Japanese an explanation other than codebreaking for why their actions were anticipated. Sure enough, as Sugiura's destroyers passed Buka Island at 6:30 p.m., they saw a snooper and then overheard its contact report. Sugiura pressed on without altering course or speed. By 9:00 p.m. the Express neared its goal. Captain Sugiura arrived in Vella Gulf at his appointed hour.

Moosbrugger had put his ships close off the Kolombangara shore, difficult to see against the dense jungle foliage. The last-quarter moon, obscured by clouds, was due to set near 10:30. The Southern Cross constellation was already dropping beneath the horizon. There were occasional squalls. This darkness completed the frustration of Japanese lookouts. At 11:18 destroyer *Dunlap* made radar contact. Captain Moosbrugger decided it was a ghost signal, but fifteen minutes later the same ship acquired a real contact, almost due north, twelve miles distant. *Craven* this time confirmed the contact. Moosbrugger immediately ordered his ships to set for torpedo attack. By 11:37 the tin cans knew there were four Imperial Navy warships. The launch took place at 11:43, with the Japanese at 6,500 yards, before a single gun had spoken. Commander Gelzer L. Sims of the *Maury* sent her fish against Sugiura's *Hagikaze.* These were classic night-destroyer tactics, the kind the Japanese had so often employed against American flotillas whose own tin cans were usually restricted by conforming to a battle line of heavy ships.

Captain Sugiura saw everything as nominal. His Tokyo Express had settled on a southeast course at thirty knots. At 11:30 p.m. he altered to south-southeast. On the *Kawakaze*, the second ship, Petty Officer Tokugawa Yoshio, an ammunition hoist operator, was grabbing some shut-eye, in common with his comrades. Aboard the other vessels only Hara Tameichi had any inkling of danger. His *Shigure*, an older tin can in need of a refit, had lagged behind. Seeing nothing but forbidding darkness, rather than speeding up Hara ordered the *Shigure* to battle stations and doubled his lookouts. At 11:42 a spotter on the *Hagikaze* reported dark shapes along the Kolombangara coast. American torpedoes were already in the water.

After that, bedlam. A *Shigure* lookout saw torpedo wakes. Captain Hara had hardly gone on the long-wave radio to warn of torpedoes when lookouts on *Arashi* and *Kawakaze* reported enemy ships. *Hagikaze* and *Arashi* heeled to port and *Kawakaze* to starboard, but none could avoid the deadly tin fish. The first two were hit amidships. On the *Kawakaze* the crew barely made it to battle stations before torpedoes struck. Petty Officer Tokugawa believed the first one hit the bow. Sailors claimed a PT boat had delivered it. She quickly began sinking. The Japanese later established that seven torpedoes struck home, including one no one noticed, right through *Shigure*'s rudder, apparently so encrusted with barnacles that the holed rudder was only slightly less efficient at turning the ship. It was Hara who put up the fight for the Japanese, and *Shigure* survived because she had lagged behind. Had she matched the speed of Sugiura's other ships, the *Shigure* would have been in the torpedo water. Hara turned away under a cloud of smoke and made for Rabaul, joining cruiser *Sendai*, returning from a supply run to Buin.

A number of Japanese survived tribulations as great as those of Jack Kennedy. Chief Petty Officer Kawabata Shigeo of *Kawakaze* swam fifteen hours before reaching land. Friendly natives gave him coconuts and young shoots to eat. Petty Officer Tokugawa drifted two days until the current took him to Vella Lavella, where he found more than two hundred survivors of the other ships. Seaman Kawahara Jihei drifted about twenty hours and cut himself badly on coral as he beached at Vella Lavella. The U.S. patrol that captured him was guided by a Melanesian tribesman.

The Battle of Vella Gulf, as this action is known, marked the onset of Japan's dark period. Suddenly a draw seemed the best that Japanese forces could accomplish. Amid the succession of inconclusive actions and actual defeats, Kusaka's position collapsed. Come to witness that sorry end would be Baron Tomioka Sadatoshi, the erstwhile NGS planner. After a time commissioning a new cruiser for the Imperial Navy, Tomioka arrived in Rabaul as a staff aide to Admiral Kusaka. Only a year earlier Tomioka had been debating the merits of South Pacific offensives versus an invasion of Australia. Now he had to assist his admiral in the desperate defense of a Japanese bastion, its power ebbing.

This transformation boggles the mind. Until very recently Halsey's SOPAC forces had not exceeded the Japanese. Indeed, for roughly the first half of Tomioka's year it was Japan that had been superior. Intelligence made the difference. Not that Japan lacked for resources in this field. The Japanese had aerial reconnaissance; they set up their own network of coastwatchers; the radio traffic analysts of the Owada Group and the communications units—like the 1st and 8th at Rabaul—were very good. But there were marked differences in the two sides' capabilities. The Japanese simply never devoted the weight of effort to intelligence that the Allies—the United States, Great Britain, Australia—all did. There were many thousands of officers and men involved with Allied activities. On the Japanese side the number was a fraction of that. While hard data are lacking, a reasonable estimate would put their personnel at a tenth to a quarter the size of the Allied intelligence force.

The professional spook in the Imperial Navy lacked standing. So did the Allied pros, but on their side wartime events, starting with Midway, ended any confusion over the value of their work. During Tomioka's year, intelligence proved so central to enabling meager Allied forces to trump the enemy that by mid-1943 it had become integral to the entire enterprise. The Japanese tolerated intelligence but regarded the product more as demonstrating the dimension of obstacles a commander must overcome to achieve victory. At root this was different from the Allied concept, in which intel identified targets; then operating forces blasted them.

Japanese intelligence nevertheless employed identical principles. Documents captured in the South Pacific show that the Japanese graded information for accuracy ("undoubtedly reliable," "probably reliable," "authenticity is undetermined"), collected topographical and other information from natives and friendly residents, had an actual propaganda strategy, exploited captured documents, recognized the value of prisoners as information sources, closely followed Allied radio news broadcasts, and, of course, valued radio intelligence and aerial reconnaissance. Japanese instructions placed special emphasis on this data: shifts in strength and movements of adversary air units, status and equipment of airfields, movements and status of warships and supply forces, the state of signaling and broadcasting, and adversary unit identifications. Japanese Army documents also emphasized data on enemy airborne raiding forces (MacArthur would conduct a parachute assault against Nadzab in New Guinea). Any Allied intelligence officer would recognize these collection targets immediately.

Much as IGHQ reached "central agreements" on operations, and local commanders negotiated parallel arrangements for their regions, the Imperial Navy and Army made formal agreements that assigned primary collection responsibility in given sectors to one service or the other. In the Solomons the Navy took the lead on intelligence.

The Japanese were careful statisticians. Captured documents showed they closely tracked attacks on their air bases in an effort to divine overall patterns. Ground observers recorded the numbers and types of aircraft in an attack or over an area, as well as the hour, altitude, and general technique of attacks. Halsey was thus gaming the Japanese system when he flung a 150-plane attack at Kolombangara but made his next amphibious landing on Vella Lavella. Kusaka expected SOPAC to invade the former.

Given the intelligence juggernaut that fueled Allied success, it is perplexing that their system fell short when it came to Japanese pullbacks. The Guadalcanal evacuation owed much to Allied tardiness in divining the enemy's true intentions. This happened again in the summer of 1943. The view from Rabaul was that supplying such exposed outposts as Munda and Vila had become too costly. Admiral Kusaka had also begun to suspect that Halsey would invade Bougainville—hence the sudden effort to build up Buin and surrounding bases, including Shortland, which Southeast Area Fleet believed a specific SOPAC target. Kusaka determined to regroup his garrisons, relinquishing Munda, which the Americans captured on August 4. He also ordered that troop movements be made primarily by barge.

What began as tactical maneuver soon became strategic necessity. Tokyo viewed the Solomons with increasingly jaundiced eyes. The Americans had just ejected Japan from the Aleutians—in the end without any intervention by Koga's Combined Fleet. In various encounters during early August the emperor raked both Army and Navy chiefs over the coals, and complained to Prime Minister Tojo as well. The Allies had to be stopped somewhere. Imperial Headquarters initiated yet another strategic review. Planners decided that positions throughout the Pacific needed strengthening and the Solomons were draining capabilities. As an interim measure while Army-Navy discussions progressed, on August 13, Admiral Nagano issued NGS Directive No. 267, providing that the Solomons battle be waged by forces in place, which should withdraw to rear positions from late September. Meanwhile at the front, the tenor of operations quickly changed. Naval officers at Rabaul found themselves dispatched to convoy barges or to distract SOPAC while barges sneaked past the the Allies. General Sasaki and Admiral Ota made it to Kolombangara with many of their troops. The Americans reckoned they had eliminated about 2,400 Japanese in the seven-week Munda campaign. That represented a fraction of the Japanese force. It soon became clear that the Allies were not going to assault Kolombangara. On August 15 Halsey's forces landed on Vella Lavella instead. The Japanese Army rejected any counterlanding. The Americans invaded more points on the island. Kusaka responded with air strikes. A transport was sunk off Guadalcanal and an LST at Vella Lavella, while a few other ships were damaged, but there was no halting SOPAC, which funneled 6,300 troops into Vella Lavella. Allied participation in combat reached a new level when New Zealand troops engaged there. The Japanese barges worked overtime to shuttle men to posts the Allies had yet to reach.

Bypassed, the 12,000-strong garrison at Kolombangara still needed recovery. To facilitate this, Kusaka decided to set up a barge station at Horaniu at the northeast end of Vella Lavella. Since the Allies on that island had stopped to form a perimeter and build an airfield, this remained possible. A small force loaded on barges at Rabaul. They were covered by a destroyer sortie. Rear Admiral Ijuin Matsuji of Destroyer Squadron 3 led the operation. Tall and gangly for a Japanese, with an optimistic disposition and wide-open eyes, the baron was a navigator of excellent reputation. Formerly master of the battleship *Kongo*, Ijuin had advocated reliance on barges. Intent on showing this would work, the baron gave his captains a free hand in making preparations. Only four destroyers could be used, but Admiral Ijuin picked the best tin cans at Rabaul, including Hara Tameichi's *Shigure*, and the *Hamakaze*, equipped with radar. Ijuin's force sailed before dawn on August 17.

American search planes discovered the baron's ships in The Slot. Admiral Wilkinson detached a destroyer division from the Vella Lavella invasion flotilla's screen and sent it after Ijuin in a high-speed chase. AIRSOLS also contributed a night attack by two flights of TBF Avengers. The torpedo planes failed to score, but they delayed Ijuin while Captain Thomas J. Ryan's destroyers came up on him. A surface engagement took place around midnight. The Americans were silhouetted by a bright moon behind them. The fight was inconclusive. One Japanese destroyer, slightly damaged by near misses, suffered a few casualties; another sustained even lighter damage. Two of Captain Ryan's tin cans had their prows battered by Japanese torpedoes. The barges sought refuge in a cove and continued to Horaniu the next night. Frustrations at home had reached such a point that when the emperor learned of the battle he erupted at Admiral Nagano, accusing the Navy's destroyers of running away and leaving the Army troops to their fate. In its essentials, however, the mission had worked.

For weeks the barge chain continued regrouping Japanese forces. Tokyo Express runs supplemented them on certain key evacuations. More Army troops were dispatched by convoy to the Outer South Seas. The Japanese reinforced Rabaul with nearly a full infantry division. This place became a fortress in more than name. General Sugiyama conferred with Hirohito on the plans. Their September 11 conversation shows the depths to which the Empire had fallen. In a talk replete with references to the historic Emperor Meiji, Hirohito expressed himself openly. He would not "tolerate" another episode where the generals came back to report their soldiers had "fought bravely, then died of starvation." Supplying Rabaul lay at the heart of the matter. Why defend the place at all? Sugiyama observed, "Rabaul is vital to the Navy and they have asked us to hold it somehow." General and emperor explored the implications of the initiative while Hirohito also harped on New Guinea, another of his sore points. But everything came back to the fortress. "If we lose Rabaul," Sugiyama admitted, "we will lose all mobility."

So the redeployment proceeded. The 3,400 Japanese at Rekata Bay returned aboard destroyers. Barges safely removed Japanese coastwatcher posts on Santa Isabel and Gizo. Troop strength at Vila and Choiseul was thinned out. At least one more Tokyo Express ran to the big island. Tip Merrill's cruisers made nightly forays up The Slot from September 12 in an effort to interrupt the barge traffic. One October night, Merrill thought he had nabbed a convoy and lit the sky with star shells to help his tin cans shoot—but results proved illusory. One officer concluded that the destroyers' five-inch guns could not track fast enough to follow barge maneuvers at close range, while the fuses on 40mm cannon shells were so sensitive they detonated prematurely. More than fifty PT boats patrolled constantly and slugged it out with the barges, but often got as good as they gave. On one occasion they claimed sinking twenty bargeloads of the enemy. The eye-opener came when the PT force started modifying boats, removing torpedoes and rearming them as gunboats.

For Allied sailors and airmen it seemed Japanese determination made them unstoppable. Day after day they went back to the same targets, blowing them to hell, but the enemy always came back—in numbers and with guns. Frustration eroded morale to a degree. One day at Espíritu the men were given a boost by the visiting first lady of the United States, Eleanor Roosevelt. Rear Admiral Aaron S. "Tip" Merrill's cruiser force happened to be there, revictualing. Sailors on liberty attended the rally, and others saw Roosevelt as she toured the base. James Fahey of the *Montpelier* noted that Mrs. Roosevelt was the first woman he had seen in nearly ten months. Lieutenant Commander Richard Milhous Nixon—another future president of the United States—saw Mrs. Roosevelt's jeep convoy as it moved between stops that September day. Nixon was a staff officer with the rear area forces. He too recalled the morale boost, and decades later remembered the first lady's visit as one of the most memorable moments of his war service.

The completion of the Vella Lavella airfield on September 24 strengthened Halsey's vise but did not stop the Japanese withdrawal. A couple nights later an I-boat narrowly missed light cruiser *Columbia* when she illuminated herself by opening up at a beach fire the Japanese had set. The major pullout from Kolombangara began on September 27. Wrapped up early the next month, only sixty-six men of the garrison were lost in the withdrawal. Admiral Halsey would claim that over a three-month period SOPAC forces sank 598 barges and seriously damaged another 670. These figures are hard to square with evident Japanese success.

Kusaka achieved his goals despite SOPAC intelligence, Halsey's knowledge that the movements were under way, and the strenuous Allied efforts to blockade Kolombangara by sea and air. The SOPAC leader claimed three or four thousand Japanese gunned down or drowned in the barges alone, but only about 1,000 of the 15,000 troops on Kolombangara and the surrounding posts ended up in Halsey's trap. The rest escaped. Captain

Yamashiro Katsumori of *PT-109* fame led the final Express mission to the island on the night of October 2–3. Had Japanese offensives been conducted as meticulously as their evacuations, the Allied Powers in the South Pacific might truly have been driven onto the ropes. Kusaka's bombers raided Guadalcanal, the Russells, Munda, Vella Lavella, and once even as far as Espíritu Santo, but accomplished no more than harassment.

In Tokyo a broad strategic review adopted a fresh approach. Japan would defend a restricted inner perimeter and adopt hugely expanded war production goals. But the Navy and Army differed on details yet again—and neither held fast to the plan's logic. Admiral Nagano plumped for the inner perimeter but, in accordance with Combined Fleet commander Koga's battle zone concept, held that opportunities for decisive action must be sought outside the perimeter. General Sugiyama favored holding on to what Japan already had, to gain time to build up the new defenses. Both supported more than doubling the existing rate of aircraft manufacture despite the fact that raw materials imports were already significantly below 1942 levels—and promised to diminish further as more merchant ships were requisitioned for war service. Even assuming the expanded production, Admiral Nagano refused to assure success. These issues were aired at an imperial conference with Hirohito on September 30. The IGHQ directive that followed sanctioned the new strategy without comment on its lack of realism. Rabaul lay hundreds of miles beyond the approved perimeter.

The last round would be fought over removal of the very barge station that Kusaka had placed at Horaniu, where there were now 600 men. On October 6, the Southeast Area Fleet sent Baron Ijuin with a strong destroyer group to escort a pair of transport units, one of tin cans, the other barges. An aerial scout spotted the Japanese en route, and Captain Frank R. Walker took six destroyers to meet them. This time Ijuin had "air" of his own. A floatplane saw the U.S. warships, and when Walker ducked into a squall to elude the enemy, his forces became separated. But any advantage the baron gained was canceled when the aerial scout reported U.S. strength at four cruisers and three destroyers. Ijuin maneuvered with caution in the belief that a greatly superior fleet aimed at him. Ijuin's own force had been divided when he detached Captain Hara with two destroyers as a close escort for the convoy. The subsequent action was another nasty scrap that began in confusion and ended with indecision.

In the initial phase, Admiral Ijuin was diverted just before rejoining Captain Hara, leaving him four destroyers against Walker's three. Ijuin sped to the southeast, closing, and in a position to cross the Americans' T. Moving too fast and executing a complex maneuver, the Japanese ended on Captain Walker's port side in torpedo water once the Americans launched on them. Ijuin turned, putting his own force in the trap he had hoped to spring on the enemy. Destroyer *Yugumo*, last in line, drew the American fire, quickly pounded by five hits. She failed to conform to Ijuin's maneuvers, advancing on the Americans instead, shooting and launching torpedoes. Walker's ships reduced Commander Osako Azuma's vessel to a sinking wreck. Walker had the advantage then, three tin cans against Captain Hara's ships *Shigure* and *Samidare*, while Ijuin was temporarily out of the picture. Then Imperial Navy torpedoes began to impact, and one took off the bow of destroyer *Chevalier*. The following ship, *O'Bannon*, collided with her, damaging her own bow. Returning to the action, Ijuin and Hara now had five destroyers against Walker's *Selfridge* and the damaged *O'Bannon*. Then a torpedo hit Walker's own ship, clipping off her bow, but the baron was headed away. Before Ijuin could turn back and resume the fight, Captain Harold O. Larson reached the scene with three fresh destroyers. Had the battle continued, the Americans would have been outnumbered, but with the advantage of radar-controlled artillery.

Because of the erroneous scout report, Ijuin thought there were cruisers out there he could not account for. He decided to break off. The *Chevalier* sank later that night, leaving the score one destroyer sunk on each side, plus two American vessels damaged. But by now Halsey's command could absorb those losses without breaking stride, while the single ship *Yugumo* represented more than 15 percent of Eighth Fleet strength. A couple dozen *Yugumo* sailors managed to reach a Japanese island base. Another seventy-eight became American prisoners after rescue by PT boats, fresh subjects for intelligence interrogation. Admirals Kusaka and Samejima could not afford many victories like this Battle of Vella Lavella.

Kusaka marked the success by presenting a ceremonial sword to Captain Hara, plus daggers to each of his destroyer skippers. There were no citations for Baron Ijuin or anyone in his unit. The presentations occurred at a banquet in Hara's honor at the Rabaul officers' club. Several geisha added a touch of glamour. Kusaka and Samejima hosted the event with all the top brass, including the other barons, Tomioka and Ijuin, the latter chagrined. Kusaka made a little speech and offered a toast to Hara and his colleagues. But the occasion turned into a disaster. Hara drank too much, and tried to exchange his sword for drinks for his crews. Ijuin promised to buy the sake for the men and led Hara away. The true embarrassment came from a fleet staff officer who had lost many friends on the *Yugumo*. He piped up, referring to the admiral's comments, "You have just noted the brief life expectancy of a destroyer. Must we put up with such a situation? Are we going to celebrate next October 26 as the anniversary of the last battle in history in which our carriers took part?"

The officer acknowledged the efforts of the Eleventh Air Fleet but complained of the prosaic Tokyo Express sorties, with all the danger borne by the destroyers—no wonder their life expectancy averaged less than two months—and came back to the big ships: "Why do destroyers have to shoulder the entire burden without the support of our carriers, battleships, and cruisers?" He lashed out, in effect, at Tomioka: "And what is Imperial Headquarters doing in Tokyo? Announcements blare every day that we are bleeding the enemy white in the Solomons. It is we who are being bled white."

Before he left, Captain Hara witnessed the end of this scene, with Admiral Kusaka in silent misery. Baron Samejima managed a flat reply: "I understand that Commander in Chief Koga is preparing for a decisive naval action in which all our big ships will be deployed."

The decision would come soon, and William F. Halsey and Chester W. Nimitz were setting the stage at that very moment. The South Pacific commander would invade Bougainville, on Rabaul's very doorstep. His strength was now such that he could hurl a multidivision force, the I Marine Amphibious Corps, into the fray. Its landing would be planned by Major General Alexander A. Vandegrift, in a brief reappearance as a field commander. Nimitz was going to attack in the Central Pacific, at a place called Tarawa. The Central Pacific action would have an indirect effect on events in the South Pacific. The combination of their efforts created Japan's last great crisis in the Solomons.

SOPAC's maneuver began in a low key, with diversionary attacks. A New

Zealand brigade landed in the Treasury Islands in the first autonomous action by troops from that nation. Meanwhile Americans—men of the 2nd
Marine Parachute Battalion—would hit Choiseul, the Solomon island next
down from Bougainville. This last operation illustrates the flexibility that
Allied forces could now apply. In finalizing the Bougainville invasion plan,
some attention to Choiseul seemed necessary. Admiral Wilkinson and
General Vandegrift had an interest in a PT boat base there, and some idea
an airfield could be built. But Bougainville remained the center ring. The
brass ordered up scouts. A five-man patrol spent a week on Choiseul, including time with local coastwatchers Charles J. Waddell and C. W. Seton.
The battle maps had changed so much that by now they were the only ones
still behind Japanese lines. The scouts transferred from a PT to a native
canoe to get ashore, and used canoes on their longer treks. In late September, two more patrols inserted from Navy seaplanes. The scouts found
about a thousand Japanese, mostly at the northern end. The coastwatchers
believed forces several times that size had abandoned the southern tip of
Choiseul to regroup, apparently awaiting barge transport. Based on this
information, on October 12 the brass ordered Marine paratroops to make a
diversionary landing. With luck the Japanese would be fooled, distracted
from the Bougainville target as well as the New Zealanders whose operation, though secondary, was intended to actually seize the Treasuries. If
nothing happened, SOPAC might reinforce the initial incursion and actually develop a Choiseul base.

The 2nd Parachute Battalion, under Lieutenant Colonel Victor H. Krulak, got the Choiseul assignment. Code-named "Blissful," the operation
was anything but. Krulak was to make as much noise as possible. It was the
battalion's first assault landing—and the men were green troops too. But
Krulak was first-rate, and he had the benefit of a personal meeting with
coastwatcher Seton, who came to Vella Lavella with two native guides to
brief the Marine commander. There were only a couple of weeks to prepare.
Some 650 paramarines landed at Voza bay the night of October 27. The
Marines drove the enemy out of a barge base, but Krulak and others were
wounded. His deputy took a strong patrol toward the north end of the island. They got lost. The boss radioed for PT boats to rescue them. The Marines' plea went to Navy Lieutenant Arthur H. Berndtson, whose torpedo
boat detachment had moved forward to Lambu Lambu Cove on Vella

Lavella. Berndtson had just two PT boats immediately available, and one of them, *PT-59*, was refueling at the time. Her skipper was John F. Kennedy.

After his ordeal, Kennedy had demanded another command. Superiors gave him the *PT-59*, among those rearmed as a gunboat. Lieutenant Kennedy, four of his original crew still aboard, had shaken down the boat and took it into action. It was Kennedy's *PT-59* with another that saved the Marine patrol. *PT-59* plus *PT-236* sailed from Lambu Lambu Cove. With his fuel tank just one-third filled, Kennedy had the gas to get to Choiseul but not enough for the return trip. From the beginning the plan was for the other craft to take her in tow when the time came. The PTs charged into the bay on the afternoon of November 2, guns ablaze. They covered two landing craft that managed to extract the desperate paramarines. One craft smashed up on reefs, and *PT-59* took aboard her passengers, whom they returned to Krulak's camp. A Marine too badly wounded to move stayed in Kennedy's bunk for the transit across The Slot. He died at sea, just before *PT-59* ran out of gas. Kennedy was towed back to Lambu Lambu, where Lieutenant Berndtson now had orders to take all five of his boats to shield the evacuation of Krulak's Marines. The entire force loaded into landing craft. Krulak's diversion had run its course. A couple weeks later, following several more missions, Lieutenant Kennedy was examined by a doctor and ruled physically and mentally exhausted. He was invalided home. Kennedy would miss the curtain rising on the last act of the Solomons campaign. There could be no doubt who had the advantage, but even now the Imperial Navy refused to concede defeat.

VII.

FORTRESS RABAUL

In important ways the diminutive General Kenney, a bantam rooster with an aggressive, perhaps bombastic streak, complemented Douglas A. MacArthur. Kenney gave MacArthur his real education in the use of airpower, and the two forged strong links in the fires of New Guinea. MacArthur had always wanted Rabaul. More than a year had passed since Kenney promised to burn it to the ground. That never happened. Preoccupied with SOWESPAC's New Guinea struggle, for two months during the high summer of 1943, the Fifth Air Force sent not a single bomber against the Japanese bastion. But as summer turned to fall and SOPAC girded to invade Bougainville, Rabaul's outer redoubt, the moment for action fast approached. Both generals realized that for Halsey to operate so close to the fortress he was going to need the strong arm of Kenney's bombers.

MacArthur wanted Bougainville too, because Allied aims in the South Pacific had changed again. Since June, Admiral Nimitz had been pressing for an offensive across the Central Pacific to match MacArthur's thrust from the south. The Joint Chiefs accepted CINCPAC's bid. Conducting a Central Pacific offensive, among other things, required drawing away Marines plus amphibious shipping from the South Pacific, as well as most newly arriving warships. The 2nd Marine Division, specifically slated for an invasion of Rabaul, went away. Reduced emphasis on the South Pacific meant changing the Cartwheel concept from capturing Rabaul to simply masking it by means of a ring of air bases. Strikes from them would suppress the enemy and make it impossible for the Japanese to supply the place. In August a meeting of the Combined Chiefs of Staff approved that strategy.

Bougainville, with its complex of bases around Buin plus facilities on the eastern and northern coasts, protected Rabaul and had to be smashed. At meetings between SOWESPAC and SOPAC staff, and in direct contacts with MacArthur, the general made it clear the capture of Bougainville was Halsey's highest priority. The Japanese withdrawn from the Central Solomons had mostly been deposited on Bougainville. Though Halsey had not been able to stanch the pullout, SOPAC intelligence understood the new dispositions. Admiral Kusaka would react promptly and in force to any move against that island. His response would come from Rabaul. Hence the need for a serious effort to contain the Japanese fortress.

The fifty-four-year-old George Kenney knew when his boss was serious, and it was clear that MacArthur was serious about Bougainville. SOWESPAC had spent a year pushing up the northern New Guinea coast, but before MacArthur could go much farther, Rabaul had to be dealt with. Kenney might be bombastic, but he was also resourceful and imaginative. An MIT grad who had honed his skills at the air engineering school and led the Army Air Corps technology development command, Kenney had put his Fifth Air Force in a position to undertake a serious aerial assault. The general not only had backed skip bombing, but he introduced new weapons, like incendiaries and the latest innovation, the parachute-fragmentation ("parafrag") munition, designed to enable bombers to hit from very low altitude without being blasted by their own ordnance. Kenney eagerly pressed for P-38 aircraft in his Fifth Air Force, and he prevailed on his airmen to accept the newer, even more powerful P-47 Thunderbolt, which SOWESPAC fliers initially resisted as inadequate. In April 1943 the Fifth Air Force had had 516 aircraft. Kenney planned for 1,330 before the end of the year, with a reserve of 25 percent on top of that. He sought a crew-to-aircraft ratio of two to one. General Kenney also obtained bases for the assault on Rabaul, championing the amphibious landings at Woodlark and Kiriwina islands, where other SOWESPAC staff viewed these as diversions from the war in New Guinea. Construction started within days of the June landings. Army engineers built the airfields at Kiriwina; Seabees, those on Woodlark. The first airplane alighted at the latter barely two weeks after the beginning of site clearance. Australian air force wings were based on the islands, and they served as recovery points for damaged aircraft or those low on gas.

Airmen had no illusions about Rabaul. The place was formidable. It was defended by 376 flak guns, both Navy and Army, including 118 of large caliber. The Japanese had nearly two dozen radars with ranges up to ninety miles. And there were fighters to repel the attacks. One B-25 pilot for the Fifth Air Force recalled, "Rabaul was the hardest target without a doubt." Years later at a squadron reunion a friend remembered how the crews looked scared to death before their first sortie against the fortress. General Kenney himself, writing of one of these Rabaul strikes, recorded it as "the toughest, hardest-fought engagement of the war." Though they flew for AIRSOLS, not Kenney's outfit, Halsey's aviators agreed. They began to hit Rabaul starting in November, when MacArthur, eager to return his focus to New Guinea, made the fortress an AIRSOLS concern. Edward Brisck recalled, "You would just grit your teeth and hold your position in the for-mation and concentrate on your job." Or LeRoy Smith: "In the early days when we hit Rabaul, it was a real killer." Or Charles Kittell: "You'd look around and you couldn't see the other airplanes because the sky was so full of flak." But the airmen went back again and again. They understood their purpose.

The men of the "Black Sheep Squadron," Marine Fighter Squadron 214, are representative. Led by the effervescent Major Gregory "Pappy" Boying-ton, VMF-214 was a first-team unit that could fight anybody. They reached the Russells in August and went on their initial mission against Bougain-ville on September 16. The squadron flew from Munda and Vella Lavella. Pappy Boyington, himself shot down over Rabaul just after the New Year, spent the last part of the war in prison camps. Boyington's intel-ligence officer, Frank E. Walton, later wrote, "Rabaul was the keystone to the entire Southwest Pacific. If we were able to neutralize it . . . the enemy would have to pull in their horns all the way back to the Philippines and the Marianas."

Allied airmen began their siege of Rabaul on October 12, when Kenney sent everything he had that could fly and go that far. The general had told one of Halsey's staffers that by the twentieth Rabaul would be "dead." That did not happen, but the fortress would be sorely tried. Kenney's strike force included 87 B-17 or B-24 heavy bombers, 114 B-25 mediums, 125 P-38 fight-ers, some 349 warplanes in all. Only fifty-six Japanese interceptors opposed them. Kenney thought there had been massive destruction to Japanese shipping, several of Rabaul's airfields, and other targets. The field at Vuna-kanau, at least, was indeed hit hard. There the Japanese 751st Air Group suffered its worst ground losses of the campaign. Caught in the open servicing planes, more than twenty of its scarce maintenance men were killed and more than fifty wounded. Adding to Captain Sato Naohiro's difficulties, a single squadron of his group lost a half dozen Bettys—and more 751st aircraft were undoubtedly among the thirty bombers smashed at Vunakanau that day.

Over the next week Port Moresby was socked in, precluding further attack, though the Japanese struck Oro Bay and mixed it up in dogfights over Wewak. Low cloud cover turned back most of the fighter escort on October 18, but fifty-four B-25s made it to Rabaul. From October 23 to 25, the Fifth Air Force raided the fortress every day. For the Japanese during the second of these raids, the ace Nishizawa Hiroyoshi led one of the intercepting formations. On the twenty-fifth the three P-38 squadrons of "Satan's Angels," the 475th Fighter Group, swept over Rabaul with the bombers and wreaked havoc. The JNAF opposition proved somewhat weaker than in the first big raid. Distances and aircraft range were such that escort fighters typically had to refuel at Kiriwina on their return leg before flying on to Dobodura. Another bombing took place on October 29. The weather zeroed out a Halloween attack. Though weather repeatedly interfered with planned raids, during October some 416 sorties by Kenney's bombers dumped 683 tons of munitions on Rabaul. Kenney's aerial offensive combined with Halsey's invasion to confront Kusaka with his greatest challenge.

PRELUDE TO DISASTER

Baron Tomioka had known Admiral Kusaka Jinichi since before the war. Tomioka thought him a cool customer, great in a crisis, never flinching. Kusaka needed all his powers now. In the Solomons the Imperial Navy faced oblivion. The difficulty of conducting surface operations had mounted steadily. But the dangers to ships almost paled next to those confronting the Japanese Naval Air Force. In the summer, already beset by mounting losses, the Navy had committed its Carrier Division 2, flying from Buin. The carrier men shared the Bougainville bases with the fliers of Rear Admiral Kozaka's 26th Air Flotilla. Half a dozen air strikes were carried out against the Allies on Vella Lavella and four against Rendova. As the planes flew off and did not return, the Navy finally merged the remnants of both flotillas and put Division 2 commander Rear Admiral Sakamaki Munetaka in charge of the combined unit, re-creating the carrier air groups in Singapore. With the merger, Commander Okumiya Masatake, Sakamaki's air staff officer, who had been planning the night missions, now found all distinction between day and night gone. The men ran on fumes. Malnutrition added to exhaustion, with particular effect on pilots, whose peripheral vision, nerves, and alertness were affected. Okumiya mourned one officer, a well-known ace, flying since the China Incident, who simply crashed into an Allied plane. Okumiya suspected the pilot had never even seen the aircraft with which he collided.

The warplanes themselves were worn out and beset with problems. Maintenance crews could hardly keep up with the damage. Spare parts were scarce and being run into Rabaul aboard destroyers. On paper the Eleventh Air Fleet was supremely powerful, with 144 Betty medium bombers, 96 Val dive-bombers, 24 Kate torpedo planes, an equal number of patrol aircraft, and 312 fighters, an aggregate of 608 aircraft. Yet Admiral Kusaka's serviceable strength amounted to barely 200 airplanes. Two-thirds of his flying machines were useful only as a boneyard to scavenge for parts to keep others in the air.

Commander Okumiya presently departed to help reorganize the Carrier Division 2 air groups. In the Solomons the fight went on. Heavy fighting over the Buin complex took place almost daily. By late July AIRSOLS was striking with eighty bombers at a time accompanied by more than a hundred fighters. In mid-September JNAF interceptors had to repel five air raids in a single day. The cumulative effects told. "Prior to the beginning of 1943," noted Chief Petty Officer Iwamoto Tetsuzo, Rabaul's top ace, "we still had hope and fought fiercely. But now we fought to uphold our honor. . . . We believed that we were expendable, that we were all going to die. There was no hope of survival—no one cared anymore." In a postwar study for the Occupation, former Imperial Navy officers, considering morale at this stage, chose to compare mid-1943 with that fall in order to set a baseline permitting them to conclude that until this point morale had remained stable.

Equally problematic, losses among the dive-bomber and torpedo plane units, combined with low production, condemned the JNAF to a critical shortage of striking power. That spring, attack formations like those in Yamamoto's big offensive were already being sent off with two to four fighters per bomber. By the fall, ratios of fighters to attack planes as low as two to one were unheard-of. Five or more fighters per bomber had become typical. Partly attributable to JNAF desperation to penetrate the curtains of Allied air patrols, partly to simple numbers of available aircraft, the trend took hold. Since the Zero had yet to evolve any significant fighter-bomber capacity, this deficit in Japanese attack capability was even greater than raw aircraft numbers suggest.

Not least among Kusaka Jinichi's worries was keeping his excitable cousin Ryunosuke in check. It was the other Kusaka who was the aviation expert, and he watched with increasing concern as the Eleventh Air Fleet proved completely unable to blunt Halsey's advance. The Rabaul command also faced continuing demands for action in New Guinea. Kusaka Ryunosuke coped by focusing Sakamaki's 26th Air Flotilla on the Solomons while the Rabaul-based 25th concentrated on New Guinea. The Japanese Navy was serious about New Guinea, continuing raids there even as Rabaul came under siege. Rear Admiral Ueno Keizo's 25th Air Flotilla attacked Buna, Lae, Oro Bay, Finschhafen, Woodlark, and Goodenough islands, and other targets. Finschhafen, just occupied by Australian troops, became a focal point, struck more than a half dozen times. The last significant offensive missions in the Solomons were against Munda and Vella Lavella at the end of September and beginning of October.

But the Allies compelled Japanese attention to the Solomons. Bull Halsey's air commanders, Rear Admiral Marc A. Mitscher of AIRSOLS and Brigadier General Nathan F. Twining of the Thirteenth Air Force, gave the enemy no respite. The proportion of Japanese supplies sunk in the Solomons, which had hovered at one-tenth the previous year, was up to a quarter. AIRSOLS carried out 158 attacks during October for a total of 3,259 sorties. Twining's Army air force was right behind. In that month the Army airmen flew 684 bomber sorties and 1,659 with fighters. The recently formed Thirteenth, though working through teething troubles, was emerging as a powerful force. Through the end of October Twining's airmen were credited with sinking nearly 20,000 tons of shipping, with a few more vessels rated as "probable," and to have damaged another 60,000 tons. Admiral Nimitz would recall Mitscher to lead Pacific Fleet carriers, with Twining left in the top command. AIRSOLS and the Thirteenth Air Force made the combination of Army, Navy, and Marine aviation that finally turned Rabaul into a smoking ruin.

Before that happened, the South Pacific airmen advanced the Allied aerial curtain to Rabaul's very gates. On October 4 the "Sun Setters" of the 339th Fighter Squadron swept in on Kahili with their P-38s ahead of a B-24 attack. Commander Shibata Takeo's 204th Air Group pulled out of Buin on October 8. AIRSOLS continued its harassment and threw a punch there on the tenth, in tandem with a Thirteenth Air Force attack on Kahili. By October 15 the enemy was reeling under another major attack on Buin, then similar raids almost daily. Japanese plane counters were tabulating 150 to 250 aircraft per mission. Each time, runways at the JNAF bases became unusable for hours at a time. Both Kusakas agreed conditions had become intolerable. Kusaka Jinichi ordered Rear Admiral Sakamaki to withdraw his 26th Air Flotilla to Rabaul. The last fighter unit, Commander Nakano Chujiro's 201st Air Group, retreated to the fortress after October 22. The forward detachment of Captain Sato Naohiro's medium bomber group held on at Buka until November 1, then abandoned it just before the base was creamed by a U.S. cruiser bombardment. Japanese power had shrunk to the hard kernel of Rabaul.

However, the Buin complex remained formidable, with the fields of Buin itself, Kahili, Ballale, and a new one at Kara. The Imperial Navy had real resources. In addition to almost a dozen big pieces of coastal artillery and twenty-one smaller cannon, a powerful array of flak guns defended the complex. These included ten 4.7-inch antiaircraft guns, seven 3.2-inch guns, twenty-seven 70mm weapons, seventy 25mm AA machine guns, and another forty of the 13mm variety. There were also sixteen searchlights. Protected by strong defenses, the Japanese could still slip planes through to strike the Allies farther south. Therefore SOPAC did not let up. By October 18, Japanese air commanders had to rate Ballale as beyond repair. Two days later they concluded that Buin itself could serve no further purpose. A week later Admiral Samejima moved Eighth Fleet headquarters from Shortland back to Rabaul.

In the meantime something happened in the Central Pacific that affected the siege of Rabaul. Combined Fleet C-in-C Koga, sensitive to an American advance, stood ready to implement his decisive battle scheme. For his part, Admiral Nimitz had created a Central Pacific Force in early August, and put his newly invigorated carrier unit to work raiding Japanese-held islands. Marcus was hit late in August and Tarawa in September. Ad-

miral Koga sortied from Truk in response to the latter attack. In early
October the Americans—now with *six* flattops—struck Wake. Radio traffic
analysis convinced Admiral Koga that Nimitz was about to raid the Marshalls. Koga led the Combined Fleet out of Truk on October 16. Measures of
how seriously Koga took the threat lie in his orders for an I-boat to reconnoiter Pearl Harbor, in his air reinforcements to the Marshalls—for which
planes were actually recalled from Rabaul—and in a surge of radio traffic
on Imperial Navy command circuits, combined with a change in the JN-25
code, making it temporarily unreadable. But there was nothing for Koga to
find. Disappointed, he returned to Truk on October 26. This is important,
because the frustrated Koga, having twice chased phantom menaces, suddenly faced an actual threat in the Solomons.

Without a doubt the acceleration of operations, from the Japanese
perspective, had become quite disturbing. Barely three weeks before, on
October 6, the Imperial Navy had fought a sharp destroyer engagement in
The Slot to protect its withdrawal from Vella Lavella. Then in short order
Fortress Rabaul had been attacked massively, the Japanese air force had
been driven out of Bougainville, and JNAF attacks in New Guinea had continued ineffective. When flagship *Musashi* dropped anchor off Dublon in
Truk lagoon, Rabaul had just endured three straight days of Allied air raids.
Shortly after dawn on October 27, a JNAF scout just south of New Britain
saw the fleet carrying New Zealand troops to invade Stirling and Mono islands in the Treasuries.

Koga Mineichi had a contingency plan for something called the RO
Operation. This involved rapid reinforcement of the Southeast Area Fleet
to regain the initiative in the Solomons and New Guinea. Admiral Koga
decided to put that into effect. He alerted Vice Admiral Ozawa of the *Kido
Butai* to prepare to send his carrier planes to Rabaul. Allied codebreakers
recorded a high volume of priority traffic on the Truk-Rabaul circuit. The
next day's Ultra summary noted "what appeared to be a short directive possibly modifying, canceling, or putting into effect a prearranged plan or
phase of operations, possibly as a result of recent Allied activity in the
northern Solomons." The message originated with the C-in-C of the Combined Fleet. It was addressed to commands charged with "frontier defenses."
The fat had gone into the fire.

INVASION

The Bougainville invasion was the Big Show. Everyone was there. Bull Halsey moved his SOPAC headquarters up to "Camp Crocodile" on Guadalcanal for the occasion. There he met with Rear Admiral Wilkinson, the amphibious force commander, and Lieutenant General Alexander A. Vandegrift, leading the I Marine Amphibious Corps. Even Vandegrift came back for Bougainville, though his participation resulted from tragic circumstances. The general leading the corps had fallen to his death from an open window at Nouméa. Vandegrift, headed to Washington to take charge of the entire Marine Corps, made a detour to help Halsey. But the selection of a new permanent commander had already been made—Major General Roy S. Geiger, once the Cactus air boss. The Bougainville landing was a gathering of the clan. On October 30 Vandegrift and Wilkinson embarked on transport *George Clymer* for the last leg of their voyage to the invasion area. The *George Clymer* too had been at Guadalcanal, where she had landed supplies and brought back Japanese prisoners.

Tip Merrill had his cruisers at the invasion; Arleigh Burke, his destroyers. Sailor Jim Fahey, fresh from liberty in Australia, manned his 40mm flak tub on the main deck of the *Montpelier*. As a result of Halsey's recent visit to Pearl Harbor and appeal to Admiral Nimitz, the Pacific Fleet had left the light aircraft carrier *Princeton* in SOPAC, and she, along with the *Saratoga*, were providing the carrier support, under Rear Admiral Ted Sherman, another South Pacific stalwart. Ray Calhoun aboard his destroyer *Sterett* soon arrived in a carrier group screen. Nimitz was now so flush with flattops he promised Halsey the loan of another group, even though he was set to kick off his Central Pacific offensive. John F. Kennedy had his *PT-59* working in the simultaneous Marine diversion on Choiseul. Ace pilots Pappy Boyington, with his "Black Sheep" squadron, and Jimmy Swett of VMF-221 were flying over the beach providing air cover. It seems the only ones not at the party were the Japs.

Admiral Halsey made an inspired choice of invasion site, Cape Torokina, at one end of Empress Augusta Bay. Bull Halsey was to secure airfields on Bougainville to aid in the suppression of Rabaul. Though Bougainville was replete with Japanese bases, those were the very places where the enemy concentrated. At the southern end, around Buin there were more than 12,000 Imperial Navy sailors and 15,000 Japanese Army soldiers with their coast artillery, strong flak, and the stockpiled supplies that had supported all the Solomons. The main strength was the 6th Infantry Division with 17th Army headquarters under General Hyakutake Haruyoshi—the Japanese veterans of Guadalcanal, hardened by their ordeal. At Kieta on the east coast were another 6,000 troops plus some naval personnel. At Buka in the north were 6,000 more men, most of them from the Army. Across the island as a whole there were some 40,000 Japanese Army troops and 20,000 Imperial Navy men—again outnumbering a native population of about 40,000—but in the Empress Augusta Bay sector there were only two to three thousand of the enemy, and in the actual invasion area just 270 Japanese with a single gun.

So the landing would be easy. Even though scout parties had recently discovered swampy land behind the beaches, due to the prowess of the Seabees, who had refined their airfield construction techniques into an engineering marvel, the airfield part would be relatively easy too. While this gets ahead of our story, the 71st Seabees completed the first of two Torokina airfields in just forty days with the war raging all around them. Ground crews arrived the day before the Seabees finished, and Marine Fighter Squadron 216 became the first occupants of what became key bases for the siege of Rabaul.

Getting from here to there was still the problem, but Halsey began with a smart choice of objective and funneled the entire 3rd Marine Division and 2nd Raider Regiment through a narrow beachhead on L-Day, November 1. In the amazingly short time of eight hours the invasion fleet landed 14,000 men and 6,200 tons of supplies. The worst aspect was dangerous reefs and currents that swamped a number of landing craft. The Marines fought their way inland. Japanese troops inflicted some casualties but fell back before this host. The Americans soon had a mile-deep beachhead they continued to expand. The real fight on Bougainville would not take place until weeks later, once Hyakutake had had time to march big units down from Buka and up from Buin. During that interval, in a series of transport echelons, General Geiger, who replaced Vandegrift shortly after L-Day, brought in additional troops and equipment. A great novelty would be the return of the coastwatchers, infiltrated from submarine *Guardfish*, the first time these spies inserted behind enemy lines as part of an invasion.

Japanese commanders knew the threat posed by Allied forces on Bougainville. They reacted instantaneously. Nothing was possible from Buka—Tip Merrill with his cruiser group administered a drubbing to that base area the night before the landing. During the predawn hours Merrill raced south to do the same at Shortland. Sherman's carrier planes busted up Buka too, and AIRSOLS helped suppress the Buin complex with a nightmarish succession of air strikes—more than a dozen, totaling 344 planes.

That left Rabaul. On the basis of an air scout's report the previous day, Admiral Kusaka had already sent a surface action group to intercept the invasion fleet. Rear Admiral Omori Sentaro with his Cruiser Division 5 had just escorted a convoy to the fortress, so his heavy ships formed the fleet's backbone. Omori believed the Allies bound for the Shortlands. A succession of confusing reports pulled him in different directions and finally he returned to Rabaul, arriving on L-Day morn. Admiral Samejima thought it better to hustle Omori back to Truk, but Kusaka overruled him. Omori's chance to meet the Americans in a battle royal at just the point when they were nearing Cape Torokina was lost. But Southeast Area Fleet now learned the invasion had begun. Kusaka ordered troops assembled for a counterlanding, and Samejima instructed the Omori fleet to escort them. The cruiser commander received his orders in the early afternoon.

Rabaul's airfields were busy that day. Admiral Ozawa's Carrier Division 1 planes were streaming in. Ozawa departed Truk and flew off his air groups 200 miles north of the fortress. Vice Admiral Ozawa brought *Kido Butai* headquarters to Rabaul, establishing his command post on land on November 1. Receiving this substantial reinforcement of 173 warplanes, Kusaka might yet smash the Bougainville landing. Air strikes could soften up the enemy; Omori would hit them with a compact but powerful force. Allied intelligence made up the fly in this ointment. On October 30, traffic analysis indicated aerial reinforcements en route to the Southeast Area. Then came Halloween. Ultra revealed Kusaka informing Koga that his disposable force numbered only seventy-one fighters and ten dive-bombers. A series of messages discussed urgent reinforcements. The Allies detected movement of a number of fighter and bomber squadrons alongside "possible" deployment of *Kido Butai* carrier planes. Kusaka's increased air strength would be no surprise. Another decrypt disclosed the arrival of Admiral Omori's cruiser unit. On November 1, Ultra reported the Japanese expecting a surprise U.S. landing, perhaps even on the coast of New Britain. Bougainville happened instead.

The Japanese response could just possibly have worked. A one-two punch might drive Halsey's fleet away. Bougainville could then be sealed tight by Kusaka's pumped-up air force. Roy Geiger's Marines would become beleaguered the same way the Americans had been on Cactus in that now dimly remembered past. General Hyakutake could assemble his ground troops and obtain revenge. The Japanese were in an excellent position to do this. But since August 1942, their power had deteriorated markedly. The consequences became apparent in the air strikes against Empress Augusta Bay. The first came early in the morning. The JNAF mustered only seven dive-bombers with forty-four Zero fighters. Then came a pure fighter sweep by eighteen Zeroes. Early in the afternoon there was a mission flown by seven Vals accompanied by forty-two fighters. Though JNAF fliers claimed sinking cruisers and transports and setting many landing craft afire, the Allies seem to have suffered no damage whatsoever. Against that nugatory result, the Japanese lost seventeen fighters and six bombers, with ten more planes damaged, two of them seriously.

That night Kusaka sent seven torpedo-armed Bettys accompanied by scouts and flare planes against Sherman's carriers off Buka. Admiral Sherman recounts that his crews had reached the point of complaining they never saw any action, grousing that land-based air got the juicy assignments. The Buka strikes supplied a corrective, while the pyrotechnics of a Japanese torpedo attack at night woke them right up. Several attack aircraft were splashed.

The daring of Halsey's landing at Empress Augusta Bay is demonstrated with blinding clarity by the fact that the invasion site was but a few hours' voyage from Fortress Rabaul, all of it under the Japanese air umbrella. This would be no Tokyo Express. A Japanese Navy force could leave Rabaul at speed, engage in a surface battle, and return in the space of a single night and dawn, before the bulk of Allied airpower could respond. The other major action of L-Day illustrates the point. That was Admiral Omori's sortie to Empress Augusta Bay.

In a fitting bookend to Guadalcanal—and Mikawa's triumph at Savo—
Omori intended to go after the invasion transports that his predecessor had
missed. Indeed, at the mission briefing in the gun room of heavy cruiser
Myoko, Omori referred to the earlier battle and indicated they might surpass
Mikawa's achievement. One participant was Captain Hara Tameichi, who
would bring along all three vessels of his division. Hara found it far-fetched
that Omori Sentaro, who had not been in battle since Santa Cruz, could
perform under the new conditions. A torpedoman par excellence, Omori
had passed out with a distinguished record and returned to the torpedo
school as an instructor no less than three times, in all spending more than
a decade familiarizing Imperial Navy officers with the intricacies of these
weapons. Omori had commanded destroyers, destroyer squadrons, and big
ships too, including battleship *Ise* and now the heavy cruiser unit. It was
Omori who had led the *Kido Butai*'s screen at Pearl Harbor, and he had played
a role in the Japanese seizure of the Aleutians. But perhaps Hara was right.
What Japan needed that South Pacific evening was a Blackbeard, a pirate
destroyerman along the lines of the British Napoleonic hero Sir Edward
Pellew. Omori Sentaro, well-informed and conscientious, better fit the
mold of Alfred Thayer Mahan.

Admiral Omori gamely accepted the mission. In addition to the heavy
cruisers *Myoko* and *Haguro* he would have two destroyer squadrons, each
with a light cruiser and three tin cans. Hara's unit sailed under Baron Ijuin
of Squadron 3, who was in the *Sendai*. Ijuin made a point of telling his captain that he would depend especially on Hara, for the baron did not trust
his aged flagship, which Ijuin had left behind on many previous missions.
Squadron 10, under Rear Admiral Osugi Morikazu in the *Agano*, added
another unfamiliar unit, though his light cruiser was among the most
modern in the fleet. Admiral Omori himself noted the lack of experience
working together as a disadvantage when the senior officers met, but
pointed out that this had also been true for Mikawa off Guadalcanal.

It was not only Imperial Navy officers who had Guadalcanal on their
minds. Bull Halsey code-named the Bougainville invasion Operation
"Shoestring II."

The Omori fleet sailed from Rabaul about 4:00 p.m. on L-Day. Before he
could exit St. George's Channel, Admiral Omori learned of a delay in loading troops aboard the five destroyers that were to transport them. He was

forced to mark time in submarine-infested waters, already distressing him. It was past dark when the units finally joined together. As they exited the channel there was a contact Omori understood to be a real submarine. The southerly course he adopted to skirt it further delayed the mission. The admiral's ambition to catch the Allied amphibious ships had already been frustrated—Halsey made sure those precious craft cleared before nightfall.

Awaiting the Japanese instead was Rear Admiral Merrill with his light cruisers *Montpelier*, *Cleveland*, *Columbia*, and *Denver*, along with eight destroyers in Empress Augusta Bay. The tin cans were under Captain Arleigh A. Burke, commanding Destroyer Squadron 23, the "Little Beavers." Burke himself led the van of the American formation. Tip Merrill's worst problem was that Burke's destroyers had gone to refuel, but they rejoined before midnight. Halsey had carefully saturated the channel from Rabaul and the northern part of The Slot with night snoopers. The sea was calm. It was dark and drizzly, with the moon setting early and overcast obscuring the stars except where they shone through holes in the cloud. Captain Hara estimated visibility at about 5,500 yards but thought the night murky. A fateful encounter impended.

Omori's cruisers were barely out of the channel when they began to overhear radio contact reports. In view of the delays in loading the troop force and avoiding the submarine, and the slower (twenty-six-knot) speed of the transport destroyers, Admiral Omori recommended that the counterlanding be canceled. Kusaka agreed—but ordered Omori ahead to attack the Allied invasion fleet anyway. The dispatch came through at 11:30 p.m., with Omori less than two hours from the invasion area. The fleet commander leaped ahead at thirty-two knots.

The Americans had radar-equipped aircraft (of the 5th Bomb Group) watching from above the clouds. Tip Merrill made a point of commending the accuracy of the aerial scouts in his after-action report. Early on one plane dived to bomb the *Sendai*; later a bomber tried its luck against *Haguro*. She was hit amidships, opening up some side plates. Omori altered course to follow one mistaken sighting report, then pressed forward at a reduced speed of eighteen knots. Scouts claimed several battleships plus many cruisers and destroyers were in Empress Augusta Bay. At 1:40 a.m., a *Haguro* floatplane reported ships only twenty miles away.

The Omori fleet went to thirty knots after another erroneous report that U.S. transports were unloading off the invasion beaches. The admiral discovered that the *Haguro*'s damage now restricted him to that speed. With the conflicting reports Admiral Omori ordered a course reversal to await clarification. Rain pelted the warships. After about ten minutes Omori again headed for Empress Augusta Bay. The double course change threw the formation into confusion. Shortly after they came about the second time, Captain Hara spotted a red flare in the distance and ordered a warning message.

At about the same moment, 2:27 a.m., American radars spotted the Omori fleet, beginning with Baron Ijuin's column. Tip Merrill intended to withhold fire with his cruisers while the tin cans executed a torpedo attack. Burke, whose estimate of when the Japanese would be seen was almost precisely correct, took his "Little Beavers" ahead immediately, and without further order launched half salvos of torpedoes. Commander Bernard L. Austin, with the trailing tin can unit, Destroyer Division 46, waited his own attack until Merrill came around to a southerly course. Omori's task force had more difficulty detecting the Allies. Some of his ships were equipped with modified air search radars, but the admiral had little confidence in them. But Merrill watched the enemy carefully. The Japanese prompted his course change after *Shigure* detected warships at 2:45, and Omori began to react. All three Japanese columns turned to starboard, which Merrill interpreted as their assuming a line of battle. Admiral Omori never commented on his intentions. Hara saw the maneuver simply as turning away from torpedo water. Merrill's cruisers opened fire four minutes later.

The Japanese fleet never regained its poise. Cruiser *Sendai* narrowly avoided colliding with the *Shigure* and became the prime target for Merrill's cruisers. Following behind the *Shigure*, Lieutenant Commander Sugihara Yoshiro's *Samidare* sideswiped the last destroyer in the column, *Shiratsuyu*. The latter's hull crumpled under the shock. Her guns were disabled. Both ships, their speed now restricted to only fourteen to sixteen knots, simply left the battle area. Seaman Fahey on the *Montpelier* had a ringside seat, as only the five- and six-inch turrets were involved. He watched an inferno. "You sense a funny feeling as both task forces race toward each other," Fahey told his diary. "It is very dark and heat lightning can be seen during the battle along with a drizzle. Our ship did not waste any time."

Captain Shoji Kiichiro's *Sendai* was surrounded by shell splashes and hit at least five times. Her rudder jammed. She coasted to a halt while the battle moved southward. Baron Ijuin signaled Captain Hara in the *Shigure* to come alongside and take off the crew, but the destroyer leader could not see any way to close with the blazing *Sendai*, and he hesitated to put his own destroyer in the American crosshairs. Hara conformed with Omori's movement instead. Commander Austin came upon *Sendai* a half hour later and finished her off with torpedoes. Baron Ijuin and thirty-seven sailors were rescued by an I-boat. The rest went to Davy Jones's locker.

Admiral Omori made the best of a bad lot. Captain Natsumura Katsuhiro's *Myoko*, the flagship, saw Task Force 39 at 2:49 a.m. Natsumura ordered torpedo action to starboard, then to port as the ship circled and steadied on a southwesterly heading. At 3:07 the destroyer *Hatsukaze* collided with the heavy cruiser, scraping her beam to port, tearing off two torpedo tubes. The destroyer was cut in half. Captain Natsumura ordered star shells to illuminate the scene, but apparently they were duds. He opened fire with armor-piercing shells at 3:17. *Myoko* launched four torpedoes and the *Haguro* six more. Captain Matsubara Hiroshi's *Agano* fired eight torpedoes from 2:51. American shells fell thick around her starting seven minutes later, and Matsubara's evasive action confused the formation, which could not re-form until a half hour later. Squadron commander Osugi ordered torpedo action, but the *Haguro* now lay between *Agano*, her consorts, and the Americans, so Rear Admiral Osugi canceled it. Cruiser *Haguro* fired on Merrill's ships. Jim Fahey saw shells falling all around. The *Montpelier* was struck by two torpedoes, duds at the end of their runs, which bounced off instead of opening her hull. The *Denver* caught a shell that fell right down a stack but apparently was a dud too. She was hit four more times. Destroyer *Foote*, crippled by a torpedo, lay dead in the water. The tin can *Spence* absorbed a shell hit without serious damage, and she too was sideswiped, by another American destroyer.

To maintain a steady course for gun laying, Admiral Merrill coolly ordered a series of simultaneous turns by his cruisers, despite his fifty-year-old navigation charts and a near collision with a U.S. destroyer. Fahey recorded, "They say the maneuvers Admiral Merrill pulled off in this sea battle would put German Admiral Scheer of World War I fame to shame. Scheer pulled his tactics in daylight off Jutland but Merrill had darkness to cope with and twice the speed." In a display of their enormous capacity for volume gunfire, the American cruisers fired more than 4,500 six-inch shells, the *Montpelier* alone accounting for a third of that total. Considering that Merrill had just carried out surface bombardments of Buka and Short-land, and that his crews had gotten only two hours' sleep, this gunnery is remarkable. The cruisers also fired 700 five-inch shells, while destroyers expended 2,600 rounds.

At 3:37 a.m. Admiral Omori ordered his fleet to withdraw. He told U.S. interrogators after the war that he based his decision on several factors. He remained uncertain of the composition of Merrill's force, and feared it might have as many as seven cruisers and a dozen destroyers. Omori him-self had already lost the equivalent of one of his two destroyer squadrons—*Sendai* and *Hatsukaze* sunk and two tin cans disabled by collision. Formation speed was down due to the *Haguro*'s bomb damage, *Myoko* had sustained structural damage in her collision, the supply of star shells had been exhausted—and Omori wanted to be beyond the range of Allied airpower, or at least under a Japanese air umbrella, before dawn. Merrill pursued until about 5:00 a.m. Omori's battered ships entered Simpson Harbor that afternoon. The crippled destroyers *Shiratsuyu* and *Samidare* arrived the next day.

Captain Uozumi Jisaku's *Haguro* absorbed half a dozen shells—Omori notes that four of them were duds—and the *Myoko* had been hit twice. Mor-ison mentions hits on the *Agano* only as a possibility, and indeed that cruis-er's action record notes none. The *Hatsukaze*, crippled by her collision with *Myoko*, sank with all hands. In terms of breaking up the invasion, Admiral Omori accomplished nothing. The Imperial Navy's vaunted superiority at night combat had eroded. In fact, Admiral Omori would cite a lack of train-ing in night operations as the main reason for the hapless collisions among his vessels that night. The Japanese warships smashed into each other like kids playing at crash cars in a theme park. The Americans had per-fected the marriage of technology and manual efficiency that made their radar-controlled gunnery so formidable.

Inevitably the Allied riposte went against Rabaul itself. George Kenney's air force returned determined to make good for the weather that had bedev-iled its strikes. On November 2, Kenney's airmen executed a large-scale low-altitude attack. Using B-25 bombers adapted for strafing, skip bombing, and

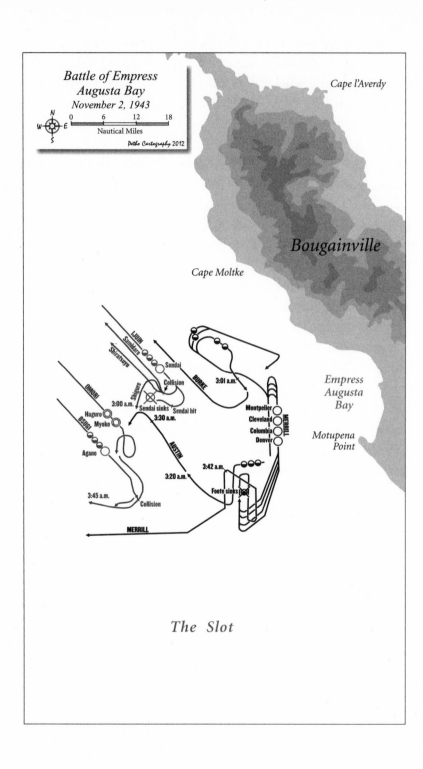

Battle of Empress
Augusta Bay
November 2, 1943

N
W—E
S

0   6   12   18
Nautical Miles

Petho Cartography 2012

Cape l'Averdy

Bougainville

Cape Moltke

Empress
Augusta
Bay

Motupena
Point

LAUIN
Samidare
Shiratsuyu

BURKE
3:01 a.m.

Sendai
Collision
Shigure
3:00 a.m.
OMORI
Sendai sinks   Sendai hit
Haguro   3:30 a.m.
Myoko
OSUGI
Agano

AUSTIN
3:20 a.m.

Montpelier
Cleveland
Columbia
Denver

MERRILL

3:42 a.m.

Foote sinks

3:45 a.m.
Collision

MERRILL

The Slot

all the tricks in the bag, the raid aimed at Simpson Harbor, not just the airfields. This was the action Kenney recalled as his toughest. More than a hundred JNAF fighters rose to fight, half of them crack carrier pilots. The assault formations had seventy-five B-25s and eighty P-38s—Japanese plane counters tabulated more than a hundred of each.

Imperial Navy fliers had begun calling Rabaul the "graveyard of the fighter pilots," and this battle shows why. Captain Jerry Johnston led the P-38s. His deputy was Dick Bong. Then the Army's leading ace, Bong had splashed two Japanese during the October 29 attack. This time he came up empty-handed. "Fate determines at birth where and when you will die," ruminated Petty Officer Tanimizu Takeo. "Since there was nothing I could do about it I didn't worry too much." P-38s of the 431st Fighter Squadron had a field day. Lieutenant Marion Kirby saw Zeroes hammering a B-25 and swung in on them, flaming two. The third got behind him, but wingman Fred Champlin came from nowhere and flamed it. Elsewhere a determined Japanese trying to ram P-38s was taken on by Leo Mayo of the 432nd. Mayo's P-38 was actually crippled when the JNAF fighter exploded in front of him, shearing off his wing. Ensign Okabe Kenji off the *Shokaku*, an ace since the Coral Sea, added to his score. But the heavy flak made the air as dangerous for JNAF interceptors as for the Americans. Most of the action took place between 4,000 and 7,000 feet altitude, where even light AA could be lethal. Americans claimed forty-one Zeroes destroyed plus thirteen probables (with thirty-seven more destroyed or probables by the bombers). By Japanese count their loss amounted to twenty aircraft.

It was early afternoon, so the sun blinded pilots when the enemy dived on them from above. Petty Officer Tanimizu notes, "P-38s at low altitude were easy prey. . . . Their weakest spot was their tail. A 20mm hit and their tails would snap off." The Japanese kept up the fight past the end of the attack, pursuing retreating aircraft for sixty miles beyond Rabaul. But no one had a lock on accurate reporting. The Japanese claimed to have downed thirty-six B-25s and eighty-five P-38s. General Kenney admits to nine bombers and ten fighters lost.

The bombing was another matter. Omori's flotilla, just returned from the debacle at Empress Augusta Bay, was a juicy target. Captain Hara got his destroyers under way quite quickly. His *Shigure* sat right under the attackers' flight path. "The enemy planes practically flew into our gunfire," Hara wrote. "I saw at least five planes knocked down by *Shigure*." The bigger ships were equally alert. Captain Uozumi of *Haguro* had her on emergency standby and immediately raised anchor. He used all his guns—eighteen rounds of eight-inch fire, 158 shells from the high-angle weapons, more than 3,000 rapid-fire rounds—and claimed eight bombers. The *Myoko* recorded a dozen B-25s for twenty-seven heavy shells, seventy-seven rounds of high-angle fire, and 3,200 25mm and 13mm rounds. Captain Nakamura's ship endured a near miss that cracked the cradle of a low-pressure turbine.

Major Raymond H. Wilkes, who led one of the B-25 squadrons and was awarded a posthumous Medal of Honor, went in with the last attack wave. By now the Japanese were blanketing the harbor with flak. According to his citation, Wilkes blew up a destroyer with his 1,000-pound bomb, hit a transport, and then strafed a heavy cruiser to attract her fire and enable his mates to escape. Kenney claimed to have wrecked half of Rabaul, blown up depots with 300,000 tons of supplies, taken out thirty planes on the ground, and destroyed or damaged 114,000 tons of shipping. All of this in twelve minutes. George Kenney wrote, "Never in the long history of warfare had so much destruction been wrought upon the forces of a belligerent nation so swiftly and at such little cost to the attacker." Given the evolution of the strategic balance, this hyperbole was not necessary. It was also transparent. Before Kenney wrote, developments such as the atomic bombs or the fire raids on Japan had occurred. Postwar record checks put actual losses at a minesweeper plus two small freighters aggregating 4,600 tons. Samuel Eliot Morison comments, "Never, indeed, have such exorbitant claims been made with so little basis in fact—except by some of the Army Air Forces in Europe, and by the same Japanese air force which General Kenney believed he had wiped out."

Disputes over results aside, there could be no doubt Rabaul was besieged. If the October strikes had not made that clear, the attack of November 2 put the writing on the wall. With grim determination Combined Fleet now poured its most mobile surface asset into this cauldron. Admiral Koga believed himself following up on Omori's achievements—to save face the latter had reported sinking and damaging cruisers and destroyers. Koga wanted to send Vice Admiral Kurita's fleet to administer the coup de grâce. Area commander Kusaka, aghast at the vulnerability revealed in the latest attack, tried to dissuade the C-in-C. Koga let the maneuver proceed. The heavy cruisers of Kurita Takeo's Second Fleet sailed. About to put his head into the lion's mouth, Kurita believed in victory. The Kurita fleet weighed anchor at 9:00 a.m. on November 3, departing by Truk's south channel.

BROKEN ARROW

Admiral Kurita's voyage at first went without incident. Unknown to him, however, before the day was out so was his secret. In his memoir William F. Halsey makes a point of noting that the first he learned of the Kurita fleet, "the most desperate emergency that confronted me in my entire term," was when it was sighted by a scout plane. Written soon after the war, this was for public consumption, intended to preserve the Ultra secret. In reality, as early as October 28, Halsey exchanged messages with Nimitz predicting a Japanese fleet move from Truk in response to the Bougainville invasion. Nimitz promised a carrier group to reinforce the South Pacific, but it was still on the way. Ultra furnished concrete opportunity to craft an actual plan—on November 3, with the Second Fleet barely out of Truk, the code-breakers placed Kurita at sea headed south. Better than that, they reported his time of departure and the precise composition of Kurita's force—eight heavy cruisers plus Destroyer Squadron 2. Ultra had again broken into JN-25.

The CINCPAC war diary records Halsey's request for fast battleships as a result of "information that a force of cruisers and destroyers left Truk headed south." Halsey's dispatch noted that Merrill's task force, while still effective, needed rearming. Nimitz sent some additional cruisers and destroyers to the South Pacific but warned he would have to call them very quickly to the Central Pacific. He added, "IN CIRCUMSTANCES BELIEVE REINFORCEMENTS BEING FURNISHED COUPLED WITH HEAVY AIR SUPERIORITY HELD BY COMSOPAC AND CinCSOWESPAC WILL MEET YOUR REQUIREMENTS."

In return Halsey objected that actions would undoubtedly be fought at night, when air superiority could not be applied, that the Japanese could reinforce from Truk more quickly that he from Efate, and that fighting on many fronts "usually" prevented "consistent attacks on Rabaul." The date/time group on this cable, sent on November 3 from the South Pacific, makes clear that SOPAC was lining up an air assault against Rabaul before Kurita's cruisers ever arrived there. Until then the conventional wisdom saw carrier units at a disadvantage striking powerful land bases, but Rabaul had been battered already, and the opportunity to wipe out Kurita was too good to pass up. Halsey ordered Ted Sherman to prepare the carrier attack. The premeditated nature is clear in what the Halsey memoir *does* say—that he had sufficient time to coordinate with Kenney for a near-simultaneous Rabaul strike by the Fifth Air Force. Halsey's dispatch to Nimitz finished: "AS IN THE PAST WE WILL HURT JAPS AND ATTACK THEM WITH EVERYTHING WE HAVE BUT HATE TO GIVE THEM AN EVEN BREAK." Thus the admirals planned a trap for the Imperial Navy.

Kurita Takeo steamed blithely into this iron storm. That an aerial snooper had not simply made a preliminary sighting that November 4 might have become clear when an air attack followed almost immediately. North of New Ireland the two tankers detailed to fuel the Kurita fleet were set upon. Both were damaged, one badly enough to be towed into Kavieng. The other returned to Truk accompanied by heavy cruiser *Chokai* and a pair of destroyers. *Chokai* was lucky. Otherwise she would have been on the hook with the rest of Kurita's vessels. Half past noon the cruiser *Mogami* actually fired her main battery at a scout 23,000 yards distant. No one attacked except a snooper near New Ireland late that night. Allied aircraft avoided the Second Fleet for a reason. A warship maneuvering at sea always had better odds against aircraft than one tied up in port. Halsey *wanted* the Kurita fleet inside Rabaul.

With his fleet carrier *Saratoga* and light carrier *Princeton* taking on fuel from oiler *Kankakee* not far from Rennell, Admiral Sherman received Halsey's dispatch late in the afternoon of November 4. Sherman was to make an all-out attack on shipping in Rabaul and to the north of it. The SOPAC commander, in keeping with his private Ultra, explicitly made cruisers, then destroyers the priority targets. Halsey did not reveal his source, but the reference to cruisers and the instruction to focus on Rabaul plus the waters north of it—the sea between that fortress and Truk—are a dead giveaway. To maximize striking power, he directed AIRSOLS to furnish Sherman's defensive cover, freeing all of Task Force 38's planes for the attack. Ted Sherman sped through the night, coming up from the south. The weather cooperated. Overcast protected the carriers from JNAF snoopers, and calm seas enabled destroyers to keep station. At Sherman's maximum practicable speed of twenty-seven knots he reached a dawn position 230 miles southeast of Rabaul in time to put a morning strike over Simpson Harbor.

Carriers began launching at 9:00 a.m. Air Group 12, of the *Saratoga*, sent out twenty-two SBD Dauntless dive-bombers, sixteen TBF Avenger torpedo planes, and thirty-three F-6F Hellcat fighters under air group boss Commander Henry H. Caldwell. The *Princeton's* Air Group 23 put up seven TBFs and nineteen F-6Fs under Commander Henry Miller, its chief. The rain and cloud at the launch point gave way to clear skies as the aircraft thrummed toward New Britain. Approaching Rabaul, visibility was estimated at fifty miles. It was a brilliant day for a killing. The strike wave swung into St. George's Channel on its final approach shortly after 11:00 a.m. Commander Caldwell led the overall force and directed it from his Avenger torpedo bomber.

Admiral Kurita also voyaged through the night. His Second Fleet skirted the eastern coast of New Ireland, crossed north of Bougainville, and entered St. George's Channel to make Simpson Harbor. Predictably, around dawn there was another aircraft contact. The fleet began entering Blanche Bay, Rabaul's roadstead, around 8:00 a.m. Kurita had with him the heavy cruisers *Atago*, *Takao*, *Maya*, *Suzuya*, *Mogami*, and *Chikuma*, the light cruiser *Noshiro*, and destroyers. Within fifteen minutes of entering Simpson Harbor, the first ships, cruisers *Chikuma* and *Noshiro*, thirsty for oil, were tying up alongside tanker *Kokuyu Maru*. At 11:16 a.m., flagship *Atago* and the *Maya* took their places. Captain Takahashi Yuji's *Suzuya* was gulping fuel from fleet oiler *Naruto*. Some destroyers fueled from cruisers. *Takao* apparently pulled away shortly before the moment of crisis. Kurita wanted to be ready to sail that evening.

There is some confusion about Japanese warning. Morison's official history indicates that the Rabaul area command issued a brief warning at 11:10. *Suzuya's* action record, however, records first sighting of aircraft at 11:15, notes verification of identity and *then* the alert by 8th Base Force at 11:18. Cruiser *Chikuma's* record agrees the sighting was at 11:15; *Mogami* makes the time 11:16; *Maya* 11:20; the *Noshiro* puts the clock at 11:21. Light cruiser *Yubari*, just back from an escort mission to Kavieng, saw enemy planes at 11:23. Other ships' action records are missing or lack detail. In any case the key point is that the Americans achieved surprise. Rabaul on November 5, 1943, would be Pearl Harbor in reverse.

Lack of warning impacted Japanese air defense. The number of fighters on patrol is variously cited as fifty-nine or seventy. JNAF pilots are reported to have held back, expecting escorts to break away to engage them, whereupon they could pounce on the bombers. Instead, American fighters stuck to the strike aircraft right into Simpson Harbor. Japanese air patrols were effectively useless. The escort fighters made their own contribution. One Hellcat peeled off to strafe the small boat carrying Commander Ohmae Toshikazu out to flagship *Atago*. The staff officer's routine delivery of a message from Kusaka to Kurita almost cost him his life.

Morison notes that one cruiser used her main battery in a desperate effort to obliterate the attackers. Kurita's vessels had the time to do this because Commander Caldwell circled the shoreline past Crater Peninsula to come in over Rabaul town. This gave his dive-bombers an approach vector enabling them to attack fore-to-aft, the most effective target aspect for dive-bombing. Available Japanese records show that *all* the warships fired their big guns, the heavy cruisers expending more than 356 eight-inch shells, the light cruisers at least ninety-five six-inch munitions. The cruisers also put up a hail of fire from five-inch high-angle guns, more than 1,421 rounds. And they expended nearly 24,000 light cannon and machine gun bullets in close-in defense. No doubt destroyers put up storms of fire also, since they collectively claimed downing ten aircraft. All this was in addition to the flak from Rabaul's extensive antiaircraft array. Given the curtain of fire, it is amazing that total American losses amounted to just five bombers and an equal number of fighters.

On the flagship, Captain Nakaoka Nobuyoshi ordered AA action to port and cast off from the tanker. His *Atago* was just under way when Commander Caldwell split the attack into several units headed for different parts of the harbor. One element aimed at Nakaoka's cruiser. At 11:28 three SBDs dropped on the *Atago*. All scored near misses to port, forward of the beam. Splinters opened steam lines and set fire to torpedo oxygen flasks. The ship listed. A splinter shot across the bridge, carrying away half of Captain Nakaoka's face. Sailors bore him from the bridge on a stretcher. The flag captain managed a weak, "Banzai!" as he passed Admiral Kurita. There were more dive-bombers—with another near miss—and seven Avengers

launched torpedoes without effect. By 12:11 p.m. counterflooding had returned the *Atago* to an even keel. By then Captain Nakaoka was dead.
Twenty-one seamen were killed and sixty-four wounded. Kurita was
stunned, as was Nakaoka's classmate Rear Admiral Komura Keizo, Ozawa's
chief of staff; and Baron Tomioka, another Etajima comrade. His friend had
died senselessly in the harbor of the impregnable fortress for which Tomioka was now responsible.

Cruiser *Takao* exited to Blanche Bay. Captain Hayashi Shigetaka watched
the attack planes turn in over Rabaul town. Every gun on his ship was firing by 11:25. As the *Takao* gained speed, destroyer *Wakatsuki* cut in front of her.
Hayashi ordered hard right rudder. The bombers came as the 12,000-ton
cruiser responded. She shuddered with an impact starboard of the number
one gun turret that holed its side, pierced the deck, and damaged the bar-
bette of the next turret back. Twenty-three sailors were killed and another
twenty-two wounded. A torpedo attack followed but obtained no result.
By 11:50 Hayashi's ship was out of Simpson Harbor and the enemy had
disappeared.

Next to the *Atago*, the worst affected would be Captain Kato Yoshiro's
cruiser *Maya*, caught just casting off from her oiler. Kato had held command for less than a month—not so familiar with his vessel as he could
have been. His ship was a sitting duck. Lieutenant Commander James New-
ell, leader of VB-23 of the *Independence*, put a bomb right down one of *Maya*'s
smokestacks. The weapon detonated in her engine rooms. The *Maya* suffered the most severe casualties, with seventy dead and sixty wounded. Fires
blazed into the night.

On the heavy cruiser *Chikuma*, Captain Shigenaga Kazue ordered AA action just two minutes after the initial sighting. By 11:24 his main battery and
secondary were both engaged. Any hope of escape evaporated in the two
minutes starting at 11:30 when, in close succession, the *Chikuma* was hit next
to her forward turrets and abaft the beam on her catapult deck. The latter
explosion started a fire that spread to the engine spaces. Shortly thereafter
came a near miss off the stern. The *Chikuma* was among the first to reach
speed and attain Blanche Bay, at 12:10, where Captain Shigenaga's violent
weaving put off the Americans' aim. Her damage turned out to be only
superficial.

Captain Aitoku Ichiro of the *Mogami* was also quick on the trigger, and for a little while it seemed his ship might escape. But SBDs re-formed over-head at 11:32, and a minute later Dauntlesses dropped on Aitoku's vessel. He ordered full left rudder, and the *Mogami* was turning when a bomb hit be-tween the forwardmost turrets. Black smoke billowed into the sky. A glide bomber and a torpedo attack were fended off by destruction of the aircraft, which crashed in the harbor nearby. The *Mogami* reached the wider waters of Blanche Bay fifteen minutes later, but at 11:45 a.m. Aitoku had to stop engines and flood the forward magazines. Crewmen extinguished the fires before 1:00 p.m. An hour later *Mogami* was pumping out. In all, thirty-one sailors were wounded.

The other Japanese warships proved luckier. Breaking away from the oiler that had been fueling his *Suzuya*, Captain Takahashi Yuji ordered full speed and joined the stampede for the harbor exit. His ship put up flak and endured only strafing attacks that wounded eight men. Also strafed was light cruiser *Agano*, which had stayed at Rabaul after Admiral Omori's debacle at Empress Augusta Bay. One sailor was killed and seven wounded, her damage bullet holes in the hull. Captain Tahara Yoshiaki's *Noshiro* sustained a near miss, which wounded a single sailor and damaged one high-angle flak gun. The *Yubari* also came through with nothing worse than a couple of men wounded. Destroyer *Fujinami* was hit by a torpedo that failed to explode, but dented her hull, killing a sailor and injuring nine others. Another tin can, the *Wakatsuki*, sustained damage from a near miss.

Admiral Kurita's ships were milling about, some in Blanche Bay, the others headed there, when another wave of American planes arrived. The *Takao* reports sighting these at 12:02 p.m., the other vessels variously between 12:17 and 12:19. This was General Kenney's complementary land-based attack, with twenty-seven B-24 bombers plus sixty-seven P-38 escorts. To Kurita's relief they made for Rabaul town, not the fleet. The action incensed Admiral Halsey, who notes Kenney had promised an attack in strength that would "lay Rabaul flat." His formation not only lacked the strength to do that, it arrived only as Navy carrier planes were leaving. In fact, Sherman's fliers could see only eight Army planes as they made off. The poor timing and weak strength, Halsey felt, were not the promised maximum effort. General Kenney's defense is that, after the exertions of recent weeks against Rabaul, his forces had damage that outstripped repair capacity. Kenney maintains he told MacArthur, "[M]y maximum effort

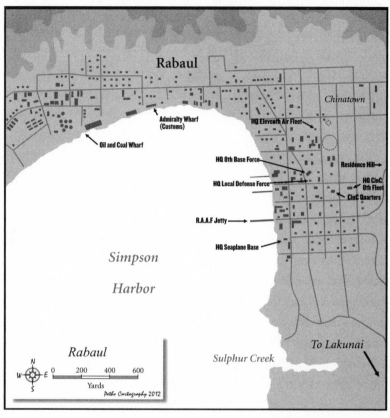

Rabaul

Chinatown

Admiralty Wharf
(Customs)

Oil and Coal Wharf

HQ Eleventh Air Fleet

HQ 8th Base Force

HQ Local Defense Force

Residence Hill →

HQ CinC
8th Fleet

CinC Quarters

R.A.A.F Jetty →

HQ Seaplane Base

Simpson

Harbor

Rabaul

N
W ⊕ E
S

0   200   400   600

Yards

Petho Cartography 2012

Sulphur Creek

To Lakunai

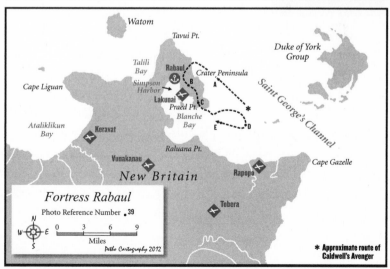

Watom

Tavui Pt.

*Duke of York
Group*

*Talili
Bay*

Rabaul

Crater Peninsula

B

A

Cape Liguan

*Simpson
Harbor*

Lakunai

Praed Pt.

C

*

Saint George's Channel

*Ataliklikun
Bay*

Keravat

*Blanche
Bay*

E

D

New Britain

Vunakanau

Raluana Pt.

Rapopo

Cape Gazelle

Tobera

Fortress Rabaul

Photo Reference Number .39

N
W ⊕ E
S

0   3   6   9

Miles

Petho Cartography 2012

✴ Approximate route of
Caldwell's Avenger

would be pretty low until I got some replacements and repaired all the shot-up airplanes." The SOWESPAC commander, Kenney writes, told him to proceed on that basis, and the actual attack force would be a bit larger than Kenney had estimated he could field. But the general was aware from communications with Washington that no replacements were in the offing and he should not have left Halsey expecting major cooperation.

Kenney notes his attack had excellent results. Japanese materials available at this writing, however, associate no particular damage with the bombs of November 5 other than the destruction of the Kurita fleet. Even the codebreakers had little to show except that Rabaul radio went off the air from 11:29 a.m. until 2:18 p.m.—less than two hours after the end of Kenney's attack. Two Japanese fighters fell to P-38s, both to the ace Dick Bong. Navy fighters claimed over two dozen more in dogfights as the carrier planes made for Sherman's task force. Over the two attacks, the Japanese claimed to have destroyed forty-nine American planes. The attack stirred Rabaul like a hornets' nest. By dint of strenuous efforts the Japanese made a sighting and sent as many planes as they could. Radio Tokyo would assert that a fleet carrier and a light carrier were both sunk in what the Japanese would term "the First Air Battle for Bougainville," but in fact the JNAF attack completely miscarried, going against a PT boat and a couple of landing ships. The most they accomplished was to damage one. It was an ignoble performance. At the Imperial Palace, where Nagano Osami reported the same claims for American carriers sunk, the news was believed and greeted with joy.

As for Admiral Kurita's glorious purpose of mopping up the Americans off Bougainville, that evaporated in the heat of Halsey's daring raid. Captain Shigenaga left for Truk almost immediately with his *Chikuma* and the destroyer *Wakatsuki*. Admiral Kurita sailed for the same place with most of the fleet that night. Heavy cruiser *Suzuya* stayed with the *Mogami*, making temporary repairs to her plant. Those vessels departed the next day. Captain Kato also stayed to effect temporary repairs to his *Maya*. Combined Fleet recalled a reinforcement unit it had sent from Truk direct to Bougainville. The heavy cruiser *Chokai*, hastening from Truk to rejoin the Second Fleet, reversed her course. The Imperial Navy never again sent heavy ships to Rabaul. The light cruisers *Agano*, *Noshiro*, and *Yubari*, now the backbone of the Southeast Area Fleet, did not have long left to them in the Solomons either.

The players were already taking their places for the last act of this story. The Empire had crossed the event horizon, entering a state of negative entropy: Under this condition enormous efforts generated picayune results. How pernicious the situation had become would be demonstrated almost immediately.

"A FUNERAL DIRGE FOR TOJO'S RABAUL"

Bull Halsey exulted at the results of the carrier raid. Though the next time they met, the admiral would complain to MacArthur of George Kenney's performance, in the moment he expressed himself quite clearly to Ted Sherman, signaling, "IT IS REAL MUSIC TO ME AND OPENS THE STOPS FOR A FUNERAL DIRGE FOR TOJO'S RABAUL." Admiral Nimitz, pleased too, immediately assigned Rear Admiral Alfred E. Montgomery's Task Group 50.3 to the South Pacific and directed that officer, who had fleet carriers *Essex* and *Bunker Hill*, along with light carrier *Independence*, to make his best speed. Nimitz wanted exploitation, taking action "WITH VIEW EARLIEST POSSIBLE STRIKES REPEAT STRIKES ON DAMAGED AND OTHER SHIPS IN AND AROUND RABAUL."

But a campaign of repeated carrier raids on the Japanese fortress proved unnecessary. Ultra revealed the Japanese heavy units withdrawing and Koga hunkering down at Truk. On November 9, CINCPAC modified his order to provide that Montgomery, after a single strike, should proceed to the Central Pacific for Nimitz's offensive.

The last act of the Rabaul drama took place in the air, with the evolving Bougainville campaign in the lead. The Japanese would actually fight *six* "air battles of Bougainville" in the course of their RO Operation. The air battles afforded Kusaka's and Ozawa's pilots no greater success than the ineffectual attack on the American carriers following the November 5 raid. But JNAF losses were painful, eighty-three aircraft. Emperor Hirohito's satisfaction with the claimed (but false) U.S. carrier losses in the Rabaul raid continued when Admiral Nagano updated the palace on November 9. Hirohito joined Captain Jyo for toasts in the aide's duty office. But those combat results were illusory too. Throughout November, on 869 sorties flown (many of which were, however, fighter patrols over Rabaul), the fruit was a single transport sunk and a few ships damaged. Halsey's infusion of South

Pacific forces onto Bougainville proved more supple and enduring than Japanese efforts to blockade the island.

For the Marines, Seabees, and others on Bougainville—including the Japanese—there would be plenty of mud, mayhem, and misery. But enemy efforts to drive the Allies into the sea were no more successful than they had been on Guadalcanal. Imperial Navy support activities would be subject to the existing operational environment—now highly dangerous to the Japanese. The light cruisers left at Rabaul furnish a good example. The fleet ran a counterlanding mission to Torokina coupled with a supply run to Buka. Both succeeded. On the next Buka run the *Natori* was torpedoed and left the Solomons for the last time. Again like Cactus, the Japanese on Bougainville became isolated.

While action off Bougainville continued, George Kenney sent several more small air strikes against Rabaul, and Bull Halsey geared up for another big attack. That aerial assault took place on November 11. Kenney's follow-up strike was canceled due to weather, which had also dramatically reduced his activities during the previous forty-eight hours. On the appointed day, Sherman flung his carrier planes at Rabaul from the east, and Montgomery from the south. Overcast hampered Sherman's planes, which got in just a small attack on a few ships they spotted through a break in the clouds.

Montgomery's 199 aircraft stormed into Rabaul through rain. Kusaka's defenses put up sixty-eight Zeroes to contest the airspace. In an echo of Santa Cruz, Jim Vose, who had planted the damaging bomb on the *Shokaku*'s flight deck that terrible day, was now a lieutenant commander leading the *Bunker Hill* dive-bombers. But Vose got no major decision this time. Not only was the weather uncooperative, but the pickings were nothing like they had been. Most important of them was the *Agano*. She sighted the attackers at 8:57 a.m. Captain Matsubara ordered his flak gunners into action ten minutes later. At 9:12 Avengers began their level runs for torpedo attack. One tin fish hit the bow but failed to explode. Another struck the after section and detonated in crew quarters, leaving part of the structure dangling in the sea. Dive-bombers achieved no results. With the detritus acting as a stationary rudder, Matsubara lost steering control. The *Agano* had many casualties. Heavy cruiser *Maya*, still repairing, emerged unscathed. The *Yubari* also rode at anchor. Captain Sakai Takumi's light cruiser saw the approaching planes at 8:54. Sakai ordered his main battery into action and got off twenty-six 5.5-inch shells. But by 9:13, U.S. planes were close enough to strafe the *Yubari* and several tin cans with her. The cruiser's luck held and only a couple of seamen were wounded. The destroyer *Suzunami* was caught while she was loading torpedoes. She sank near the entrance to Simpson Harbor. The *Naganami* reached Blanche Bay but suffered a torpedo hit and had to be towed back.

Admiral Montgomery's instructions were to make a second strike. He had begun rearming when Kusaka struck back. At least the JNAF waves were detected on radar more than a hundred miles away. Montgomery launched some of his follow-up strike planes beginning at 1:25 p.m., but shortly after that defensive action began to predominate. The Japanese force included sixty-seven Zeroes, twenty-seven Vals, and fourteen Kates, with a unit of Bettys trailing behind. By 1:54 action was joined. Montgomery canceled his second strike and concentrated on the air battle. For the first half hour Japanese dive-bombers held sway; then came the torpedo planes. Some Bettys that missed the carrier task force found Tip Merrill's cruisers instead and put a torpedo into light cruiser *Denver.* But that would be it. The Japanese strike groups lost a few Bettys, all of their Kate torpedo planes, and all but ten of the Val dive-bombers. The loss of several dozen attack planes in exchange for a single torpedo hit against a nonessential U.S. warship measured Japan's decline in the year since Santa Cruz.

The air battles of November 11 marked the effective end of Rabaul as a Japanese offensive base. Combined Fleet recalled Ozawa's *Kido Butai* aircraft the next day. The proud legions of the "sea eagles" were heavily thinned. Hirohito issued an imperial rescript congratulating the carrier- and land-based airmen on their achievements. Only after the war would the Japanese discover how meager these had been. But the numbers tell their own story: 173 planes had gone to Rabaul; fifty-three returned to Truk. The losses included half the fighter planes, 85 percent of the dive-bombers, 90 percent of the torpedo planes. Every single scout plane had been destroyed. Between damaged planes that had managed to land and airmen rescued, the personnel losses were not quite as bad: 50 percent of scout crews, 40 percent of the torpedo-plane crews, 30 percent of the fighter pilots. But among the dive-bomber crews, three of every four had perished. Fighter sorties were expensive, but effective to some degree. Attack sorties were prohibitively costly regardless of their effectiveness, which was considerably less than the Imperial Navy believed.

Admiral Kusaka, unable to protect major warships any longer, ordered them to Truk. Captain Kato sailed with the *Maya* on November 12. The *Agano* also cleared harbor, with some help, then was torpedoed en route by the American submarine *Scamp*. She had to be rescued by the *Natori* and her destroyers, which towed Captain Matsubara's ship the rest of the way. The *Yubari* was bombed at sea. Captain Arleigh Burke with his acclaimed destroyer squadron put the finishing touch on Japanese surface activity in the Battle of Cape St. George on November 25, when he annihilated three ships of a five-destroyer Tokyo Express bound for Buka. Thanks to Ultra, Admiral Halsey gave "31 Knot Burke" twenty-four hours' advance warning of the Imperial Navy sally. Allied forces had achieved complete surface superiority.

From Rabaul, Admiral Kusaka continued to throw his Eleventh Air Fleet against Bougainville and New Guinea, at enormous cost. JNAF losses in the Solomons for November 1943 are estimated at about 290 warplanes. Without the carrier aircraft, Kusaka's attacks were even less potent. His effort almost immediately suffered cutbacks. Once Nimitz opened his Central Pacific drive—on November 20, barely a week after the second Rabaul carrier attack—the pressures on JNAF strength multiplied. Ironically, some of the last aerial reinforcements to Rabaul were planes drawn from JNAF forces in the Marshalls and Gilberts—precisely where Nimitz struck—and the less experienced fliers added little to Kusaka's capability, while, in return, very soon the Combined Fleet withdrew the 26th Air Flotilla, removing some of Kusaka's best air groups and reducing his serviceable strength to about 160 aircraft. Other reinforcements were composites, as in late December, when the three ships of Carrier Division 1 each sent seven fighters to augment the 253rd Air Group. That was the period of the largest JNAF defensive efforts, when formations of seventy-two, ninety-four, and even ninety-eight fighters attempted to blunt the raids. The Japanese enjoyed a degree of success through the end of the year.

While Kusaka did what he could, General MacArthur began to confect a siege ring, surrounding the beleaguered fortress with Allied garrisons supporting air bases that kept up a constant rain of bombs. In December, MacArthur landed SOWESPAC troops at Arawe and Cape Gloucester, at the western tip of New Britain, for the first time putting Allied troops on the same island as Rabaul. In January 1944, the target was the Green Islands, to the east, which Halsey captured using New Zealand troops. At the air station planted there, Lieutenant Commander Richard Nixon served as a supply officer for the SOPAC Air Transport Command, his most substantive wartime assignment and one for which he received a citation. Nixon is said to have been popular with the natives. The supremo seized Emirau and Manus islands, west and north of Rabaul, in March 1944, completing the encirclement.

The war had reached a juncture where the Imperial Navy, even in its bases, could no longer be safe. For a Christmas present in 1943, Rabaul received another of Ted Sherman's carrier attacks. Shortly after the New Year, fighter ace "Pappy" Boyington, hit over the fortress, had to ditch in St. George's Channel and would be rescued by an I-boat. The pilot was held prisoner at Rabaul for some weeks and then sent on to Japan by way of Truk. In the meantime, flying from the brand-new U.S. airfield at Stirling in the Treasury Islands early in February, Marine photo planes took pictures of Truk. Admiral Koga viewed this as an omen of worse to come, and sailed away with his Combined Fleet. Sure enough, on February 17, Truk was subjected to a massive attack by the American fast-carrier task force. Prisoner Boyington's air shuttle from Rabaul landed amid this chaos. Boyington became an American witness to the demise of Truk as a center of Japanese power.

The Allied siege strategy was infinitely preferable to direct attack on Rabaul. By the time MacArthur completed his ring, the Japanese had had two years to fortify the place, and its defenses were formidable. The Japanese Army had 76,300 troops in two infantry divisions, two brigades, an artillery brigade, and a tank regiment. Supporting weapons included 237 big guns or howitzers, plus eighty-eight 75mm cannon. Special Naval Landing Forces contributed another dozen cannon, and the Navy had thirty-eight coast defense guns, almost half of them six-inch weapons. Kusaka's naval personnel amounted to 21,570 men, including four garrison units and an SNLF. The forces possessed nearly 5,000 vehicles. There were 30,000 tons of ammunition and 45,000 tons of food. Stocks included roughly 2,900 tons of aviation gas and 3,600 tons of motor fuel. An invasion of Fortress Rabaul promised more heartache than anything ever done in the South Pacific.

The reduction of Rabaul by means of aerial attack posed far fewer difficulties. This became the main function of AIRSOLS and the Thirteenth Air Force. The air campaign began immediately after the carrier raids. During November, the Thirteenth Air Force flew forty-one sorties against Rabaul, but a month later the overall scale of Allied effort increased to 394 flights, and in January 1944 to 2,865. This was overwhelmingly an effort of the South Pacific forces—George Kenney sent exactly nine airplanes to Rabaul from the time of his Fifth Air Force raids through November 1944. Within SOPAC, Marine Corps airmen carried much of the burden. The height of the suppression campaign occurred between January and July 1944. It peaked in February, when 4,552 sorties dumped 3,324 tons of munitions on the Japanese. To put that figure a different way, at this level of effort the Allies were hitting Rabaul with a 150-plane raid every day, rain or shine. Marine air flew more sorties against the fortress in every month except May, and its effort amounted to nearly 44 percent of the *entire* Allied tally. After April the Rabaul missions were considered "milk runs." Targeteers divided the town into more than a dozen sectors, and strikes tried to level them. Efforts to burn out the town were abandoned once photo interpreters determined that just 122 buildings were still standing—less than 10 percent of the town. Through July, Allied air forces delivered an average of more than 1,800 tons of bombs on Rabaul every month. From July 1944 through the end of the war, the Allies kept heads down with some hundreds of sorties each month. By the end of the war the Allies had plastered Rabaul with 30,000 tons of munitions.

The weight of that attack could not fail to have effects. In January 1944, Koga sent in the planes of Carrier Division 2 once more, recalling some of the land-based air units. Shortly after the American carrier raid on Truk, the Japanese pulled out these planes, plus the last of their 26th Air Flotilla. As many mechanics as possible left with them, and some more departed by submarine or the few aircraft and blockade runners that sneaked in. Several hundred mechanics of the 751st Air Group crowded onto a pair of ships at Rabaul on February 20. Its commander, Captain Sato, boarded an escorting subchaser. AIRSOLS planes sank both the transports north of New Ireland the next day. Sato's subchaser escaped. Tug *Nagara* rescued a number of survivors. She, in turn, was caught and sunk by Arleigh Burke's destroyers not far away a day later. Burke's "Little Beavers" picked up about half the Japanese survivors, including more than forty men of the 751st Group. Others drowned themselves or resisted capture. Rabaul was truly isolated. Operation Cartwheel had succeeded.

After February the JNAF managed to field only a guerrilla air force, a handful of planes assembled from the boneyard, patched together with parts from the wrecks that littered Rabaul's airfields. The Imperial Navy gave up trying to maintain Lakunai Airfield in July 1944. Several other fields of the fortress complex fell into disrepair much earlier. Strenuous efforts kept Vunakanau operational through the end of the war. It was last used on May 27, 1945, when the JNAF slipped two bombers into Rabaul to stage a raid on Allied shipping in the Admiralties. Japanese soldiers and sailors went into farming, raising food to supplement their rations. The emperor's expressed fears of brave men starving had proven prescient. Admiral Kusaka and General Imamura exerted themselves to buck up morale. The Army had the best farms, and they graciously shared food with the Navy. As Fortress Rabaul declined to an isolated backwater, left behind by a ferocious war, the Japanese Army and Imperial Navy finally achieved cooperation.

VIII.

SOUTH PACIFIC DREAMS

So it was that the Solomons became the grave of Japan's dream. Here the pendulum of the Pacific war began to swing against Tokyo. The Battle of Midway robbed the Japanese of momentum and stripped their aura of invincibility. But after Midway the pendulum hung in balance. Japan retained numerical superiority and some distinct qualitative advantages. The dream was still attainable. In the Solomons the war was fought to a decision. In the months beginning with July 1942 it remained open to the Japanese, more specifically to the Imperial Navy, to blunt Allied progress. Instead Tokyo frittered away its forces in vain efforts to reverse, and then simply to halt accelerating adverse trends. The Japanese achieved momentary advantage at least twice, but each time squandered the opportunity. The Allies worked at a steady pace and eventually equaled, then surpassed their foe. The drama of the rise and fall of Fortress Rabaul encapsulates that progression.

Japanese commanders believed they could fight in the Solomons on the cheap. A few men, planes, and ships would suffice to control the Outer South Seas. Once the Allies contested their dominance, the Solomons absorbed greater and greater Japanese attention until it became the main arena of confrontation. But Japan's devotion to the battle continued to suffer—from a contradiction between the logic of its basic strategy and the expression of that in combat action, and also from a disconnect between the operations and the Imperial Navy's traditional battle doctrine. Not so the Allies. The United States, Australia, and New Zealand had no doubt the campaign was a matter of life or death, and no hesitation at a full measure of commitment.

A multitude of factors help explain the outcome in the Outer South Seas. Japanese expansion into the Solomons, first conceived as a protection for the Empire as Tokyo ran the board in the Pacific, became something much more. When Tokyo strategic planners began to think in terms of isolating or invading Australia, they were reframing the South Pacific as a major combat theater. Yet they deployed no additional forces. The mismatch between strategy and force was a major error. Tokyo should have known the Allies would perceive Japan in the South Pacific as a threat. To leave the Solomons so sparsely held invited attack. Here Japan inserted a contradiction into its war strategy.

It is important to bear in mind the dimensions of this conflict. A Japanese victory did not mean the defeat of the Allies, in particular the Americans. With its huge territory and enormous economy, the United States was impervious to capture by Japan. The same was true of the British Empire. In coalition warfare alongside Germany and Italy, Tokyo might hope to fight the Allies to a standstill and force a negotiated termination of hostilities. Yamamoto's maxim about marching into Washington and dictating peace terms in the White House referred to this reality: Victory was bounded by the possible. Japanese leaders understood that. The transcripts of the Imperial Conferences before Pearl Harbor, the succession of meetings at which Japan decided on war, clearly show Tokyo believed its limited capabilities were just then at a maximum relative to those of the Allies. Leaders differed on how much leeway Japan possessed. Yamamoto Isoruku put the period of "going wild" at six months to a year; Nagano Osami felt the nation could fight for three years before ending hostilities became a necessity.

Distilled to its essence, this meant that to maintain the relative position of December 1941, the Japanese had to eliminate enough of the enemy to shave the margin by which Allied strength must increase. That represented an enormous task. The Japanese had a fair sense of Allied productive capacity and an exact knowledge of their own. Between December 1941 and June 1943, American shipyards delivered four new battleships, two heavy and thirteen light cruisers, six fleet and five light carriers, seventeen escort carriers, and 150 destroyers. Imperial Navy construction programs brought additions to the fleet as well. Through the end of 1943 these included one battleship, two fleet and two light carriers, five light/escort carrier conversions, four light cruisers, and twenty-four destroyers. Japanese aircraft carrier deliveries—specifically the conversions—would actually have been fewer except for Midway, which convinced Japan to expedite carrier construction. As a rule of thumb, the Imperial Navy needed to eliminate three or four warships for each one it lost.

That basic logic translates into a strategic necessity for an objective important enough to force the Allies to fight on Japanese terms. The Solomons became an arena of decision precisely because Yamamoto and his cohorts considered that their threat to Australia would pull the Allies into battle. Unlike Midway, however, where the Imperial Navy brought the weight of its forces to bear, the admirals resisted putting down chips commensurate with their stake. That failure created the most fundamental contradiction in Japanese strategy: between its basic logic and the admirals' application of it. The Allied South Pacific and Southwest Pacific commands also waged war on a shoestring at first, but Allied commanders could look ahead to a future of plenty once they passed the present of penury. SOPAC needed to do its best with what it had.

One reason the Imperial Navy resisted making a proper correlation between the dimensions of strategy and the forces required to carry it out lay in traditional doctrine. For decades the Navy had planned, trained, and designed ships for a "decisive battle"—a very particular engagement, in which Japan, in a defensive mode, would progressively weaken an advancing American fleet and then face and destroy it in a single cataclysmic combat. This precise engagement concept was what Emperor Hirohito had referred to in speaking with military leaders at an August 1943 meeting. Carrying out such an action required husbanding naval power until the very eve of battle. The disconnect came between this approach to decisive battle versus the aim of preserving relative Japanese strength: Force was necessary to impose losses. The essence of traditional doctrine lay in withholding force, and that effectively conceded the initiative to the adversary. But an enemy with the initiative could choose not to engage until his military attained overwhelming superiority.

Preserving relative strength, to the contrary, required an offensive posture, reversing the traditional direction of Japanese doctrine. Only on the offensive could the Imperial Navy compel the Allies to fight often enough and in sufficient strength to be whittled away. Historians and observers after the war who traced Japan's defeat to "victory disease"—in its essence an unrelenting offensive posture—have neglected to think through the dimensions of the Japanese strategic problem. Although Imperial Navy officers *were* overconfident, the truth is that Japan's basic policy required that stance. More useful is to question the assumptions in Japan's decision for war—that the basic policy could be carried out in the real world, and that the Imperial Navy could adapt to the different requirements of this strategy.

Admiral Yamamoto was the man best suited to shake the fleet out of its hoary doctrine and endow it with an offensive posture, and he did accomplish that to a considerable degree. The Pearl Harbor attack first broke the old decisive-battle mold. The Midway plan was another attempt to compel the adversary to action. When the Navy General Staff and Combined Fleet wrestled with their FS Operation and the Australia isolation schemes—the South Pacific dream—they were furthering this enterprise. But Yamamoto himself, not just his peers, had been steeped in traditional doctrine, and, inclined to husband the fleet, he shortchanged the Solomons. Japan set the stage for the arena of decision without putting enough props in place. The unraveling of Japanese strategy began there.

All of this is not to say that the Allies themselves were powerful, supple, or united in their own approach. Marines on Guadalcanal were quite right to consider themselves on a shoestring. In the Outer South Seas the Japanese were weak by choice, the Allies of necessity. What made the Solomons an arena of decision was precisely that narrow margin.

Which brings us to intelligence. The pillars of intelligence made enormous contributions in the Solomons. Take away codebreaking and there would still have been an Allied advantage. In combination with Ultra, the insight into Japanese operations and preparations enabled thin Allied forces to meet the Imperial Navy on equal or superior terms time after time. Intelligence was not omniscient—mistakes have been noted with respect to Japanese fleet movements and losses—and coverage was lost from time to time as the Japanese changed codes or procedures, but on those occasions the other pillars helped fill the gap. Aerial reconnaissance and the coastwatchers would have been formidable even without Ultra. Together they came as close to eliminating the fog of war as can be imagined. The decrypts that enabled American aircraft to ambush Admiral Yamamoto, by themselves, probably ensured that Ultra would be graded positively.

But there is a good argument that the nickel-and-dime contributions of intelligence actually overshadow the Yamamoto shoot-down. In the Solomons arena it became impossible for a Japanese ship or plane to execute a mission unopposed, *despite* the Allies' at first inferior forces. This led to disruptions of tempo, frustration of Tokyo's aims, and a succession of air and naval battles. Since Allied units were individually of high quality, the Imperial Navy got no free ride, and the accumulating losses rendered impossible its larger goal of whittling at Allied strength. In addition to the simple destruction of units, the Japanese were obliged to accept virtual attrition—the diversion of warships and aircraft to missions other than combat. Every destroyer used as a transport, every submarine hauling supplies, every bomber shuttling food packets was a unit taken out of the line of battle. Intelligence made both direct and indirect contributions to Allied success. In recent years it has become fashionable to speak of intelligence as a "force multiplier." The Solomons campaign shows very concretely how that worked.

Intelligence proved better at some things than at others. Undoubtedly the biggest Allied intelligence failure of the campaign lay in misinterpreting the import of the Japanese operations that evacuated Guadalcanal. Fortunately that miscarriage occurred at a point when the strategic initiative had shifted to the Allies. The Japanese success had little influence on the progress of the campaign. The failure is overshadowed by greater successes.

What if the Japanese had broken the American codes? Multipliers work on both sides of an equation. The Japanese did have some success with low-grade Allied codes, and they developed the same pillars of intelligence. Their radio traffic analysis was very good. But neither the Imperial Navy nor the Japanese Army developed intelligence networks as extensive as those of the Allies. And for the Japanese, intelligence does not seem to have carried the same weight or credibility as it did for Nimitz, Halsey, or MacArthur. Had the Japanese had a code penetration equivalent to JN-25, it is not clear that this advantage would have equivalent impact. In particular the Japanese lacked a radio interception network as immense as the Allied one. Without the requisite large volume of enemy messages to work with, the Japanese would have had difficulty maintaining their entry into the codes. The most reasonable conclusion is that the Japanese might potentially have scored some spectaculars, like the Midway or Yamamoto breaks, but would not have attained the degree of penetration required to inflict virtual attrition. Allied intelligence would have retained the edge.

The point of intelligence is still to inform the men and women at the tip of the spear. Battle is the payoff. In the Solomons arena each side had advantages, some quite important. Technological developments infused Allied forces with capabilities vital to success. Radar and other electronics were nearly as important as intelligence. Introduced for early warning, radar was adapted to guide fighter interception, make night-fighting practical on the sea and in the air, facilitate navigation, and finally to guide the gunners at their bloody work. Encryption devices, improved and miniaturized radios, amphibious ships, proximity fuses, high-endurance gun barrels, PT boats, and the warship's combat information center were important technological innovations. The atomic bomb was a game changer but is outside our scope here. Given the prowess of the American scientific establishment, it is embarrassing that throughout this period the United States proved unable to produce torpedoes that worked. With an excellent torpedo plane in the TBF Avenger, as late as the Rabaul raids of November 1943, only two torpedoes of more than fifty expended actually functioned properly.

Aeronautical design proved a key technological area. Early on the Japanese had an important advantage with their Zero fighter. American aircraft designers met the Japanese first with nearly equal or slightly superior warplanes—like the F-4F Wildcat and the P-38 Lightning. But then they deluged the adversary with superior designs: the F-6F Hellcat, the F-4U Corsair, and the P-47 Thunderbolt, to name only the most prominent. With its huge industrial capacity and talented engineering community, the United States had a major advantage. Four of these five aircraft were introduced during the Solomons campaign. In that interval Japan barely got its new fighters past the prototype stage. The innovations that reached the field were largely modifications to existing designs—but the Allies did plenty of that kind of tinkering as well.

Much less known were innovations that played a direct role in making rapid amphibious advance possible. Already at Guadalcanal, SOPAC had landing craft designed to put men onshore. These were followed by a variety of larger and specialized landing craft and ships to carry tanks, trucks, bulldozers, and heavy equipment direct from embarkation ports and deposit them on invasion beaches. The LST, or "Landing Ship Tank," was based on a British design and introduced toward the end of 1942. Some of the later Solomons invasions—such as Rendova, Vella Lavella, the Treasury Islands, and Bougainville—were carried out importantly or even exclusively by LSTs. Knowing a good thing when they saw it, the Japanese produced their own version starting in 1943. Specialized amphibious assault ships, like the LSD ("Landing Ship Dock"), were in use before the end of the campaign. The Solomons educated the U.S. Navy in amphibious operations, developing a professionalism applied in every subsequent invasion from the Central Pacific to Normandy to the Philippines. American industry furnished large numbers of these craft to the field forces in a short time.

Because the Solomons campaign proved to be all about airfields, next to specialized amphibious vessels the most important element was professionalized construction and combat engineering units. The efforts of the Seabees were vital to keeping Henderson Field in action during the very first battle. Without them the Japanese naval and air bombardments would have been successful. Seabees and Army engineers multiplied the bases available to the Cactus Air Force and made possible its dominance over The Slot. The construction teams perfected their techniques to such a degree that airfields were built on Rendova in just over two weeks, and at Kiriwina and Bougainville in little over a month. Those and similar airfields became bases for the siege of Fortress Rabaul.

Conversely, Japanese difficulties at air base construction substantially increased the vulnerability of Imperial Navy surface forces and the cost of Japanese air operations, starting with Guadalcanal. Had the Japanese had a fully articulated base network at the outset of the campaign, the inadequacies of their aircraft designs would have mattered less. Had the Japanese air umbrella extended from Lunga Point and Munda, rather than Rabaul, the invasion would have cost the Allies dearly and come nearer to fulfilling Tokyo's strategy. Even with the Cactus Air Force implanted at Henderson, Japanese aircraft at Munda would have posed a much greater threat—and the expert pilots would have survived in greater numbers. The JNAF airfield at Guadalcanal neared completion in roughly six weeks. When eventually built, Munda took about the same. The fields of the Bougainville complex were built in six to eight weeks. Tokyo's engineers improved their efficiency but never matched the Seabees.

The larger question is one of aerial superiority, basic to Tokyo's goal. Aircraft attrition drove the equation. During the Solomons campaign the Imperial Navy lost 1,467 fighters and 1,199 torpedo or dive-bombers or land-based bombers. Fighters always get the attention, but JNAF strike capability resided in its attack forces. Losses among the attack groups reached the point where massive numbers of fighters were being sent off with tiny numbers of bombers. Japanese strike capabilities became inadequate to inflict significant damage. There was no escaping this vicious circle.

Given the increasing Allied stranglehold in the air and the technical proficiency of its naval forces, it is a tribute to the skill and bravery of Imperial Navy sailors, as well as the quality of its own ships, that the Japanese were able to accomplish as much as they did. Until very late in the campaign its specialized equipment, techniques, and intensive training enabled the Imperial Navy to hold its own fighting at night against an Allied fleet in growing numbers and with technological sophistication. So long as the Japanese retained that margin they remained dangerous, in spite of Allied airpower, whenever the surface fleets came to grips. That practical superiority evaporated in the Central Solomons, when Allied tactics matched the Japanese, technology provided an edge, and the Imperial Navy's heavy ships, so jealously hoarded, fought at a serious disadvantage. Once the Japanese became inferior on the surface as well as in the air, there remained no obstacle to the swing of the pendulum. The event horizon proved a true phenomenon. In contrast to the period up through the isolation of Fortress Rabaul—when Imperial Navy sailors exacted an Allied toll almost ship for ship—between the end of 1943 and Japan's surrender in 1945, Allied losses became minimal, Japanese ones enormous.

Some commentary regarding individuals and situations is also appropriate. The most important concerns Admiral Yamamoto. What if he had not fallen victim to aerial ambush? Had Yamamoto survived, it seems likely the Japanese would have concluded their codes were being read. He had paid close attention to radio deception activities in several fleet engagements, and, having received the warnings he did before that Bougainville visit, Yamamoto would have been compelled to pay attention. On the other hand, Yamamoto's continued command might not have been very detrimental from the Allied point of view. The Japanese admiral was capable of mistakes—Midway being the obvious example. He was also prepared to rely upon tired officers like Kondo Nobutake, and that too was to Allied advantage. By April 1943 the pendulum had swung irretrievably to the Allies. There seems little Yamamoto could have done to reverse that. Perhaps he could have forced an early abandonment of the Solomons, before the last great dissipation of Japanese strength, but the attitude of the high command would seem to argue against Tokyo's giving up the game at that time.

On the American side, Chester W. Nimitz, a superb leader of men, made a huge difference to Allied efforts. Nimitz listened to subordinates, gave leeway to his intelligence people, integrated their reporting into his battle plans, and provided the example that others followed to victory. His finely honed notion of calculated risk made the difference in several important battles. With good sense, flexibility, and patience, Nimitz held the line in the fall of 1942, when Allied commanders in the South Pacific might have inclined to panic. The CINCPAC's willingness to commit extra carriers to SOPAC for repeat strikes on Rabaul a year later, even with the timing so close to his Central Pacific offensive, is characteristic of his aggressive pursuit of success. Nimitz and Yamamoto were well-suited adversaries.

One of Nimitz's strengths—his loyalty to subordinates—while in general a desirable trait, could be detrimental if the people he protected were not pulling their weight. This was the case with Admiral Robert Ghormley, the first SOPAC. Ghormley's detached method, his diffidence, and his indecisiveness failed to energize the South Pacific command at a key time. Nimitz left him in place too long. But the CINCPAC's selection of William F. Halsey as Ghormley's successor was excellent. Aggressive to a fault, an inspirational leader, Halsey was the very tonic SOPAC needed. Had Ghormley remained in command, the aftermath of the Battle of Santa Cruz might have turned out quite differently. Another officer Nimitz protected was Vice Admiral Frank Jack Fletcher. The CINCPAC appreciated Fletcher's experience as a carrier commander while apparently discounting his excessive caution. Fortunately a cadre of new carrier commanders, including

Marc A. Mitscher of SOPAC fame, but also such others as Raymond A. Spruance and Bill Halsey himself, were coming to the fore and making it unnecessary to employ Fletcher.

Admiral Nimitz served within a command structure that was supportive. Though not without its faults, the Allied high command successfully integrated strategy with operational control, furnished good logistical support, and provided for excellent intelligence. It adjudicated disputes between theater commands such as those between Nimitz and MacArthur. President Roosevelt managed with a very light hand, intervening only very occasionally. Emperor Hirohito actually seems to have concerned himself more directly with military activities, but was hampered by the constraints of court etiquette as well as the rigidity of the high command, which reflected the semifeudal clan origins, fierce independence, and jealous prerogatives of the Japanese armed services. Interservice cooperation and joint planning remained distant dreams, while the services' sense of ownership—as in the allocation and control of merchant shipping—actually created obstacles to efficient military operations and even the expansion of the war economy. All that was magnified by the limited resources available to Imperial Japan. Jealous military and naval satrapies underestimated the dimensions of the Allied threat to the Solomons, exaggerated their capability to deal with the adversary, concealed their weaknesses from one another, and minimized the requirements of an extended campaign in the Outer South Seas.

The Japanese high command had two major moments of opportunity during the Solomons campaign. The first took place at and following the Battle of Savo Island. If Frank Fletcher had stayed at Guadalcanal and engaged with the aggressiveness of a Halsey or a Mitscher, Savo would not have been an enemy victory. If Fletcher had even pursued the retreating Mikawa with any energy, Savo could at least have been a Mexican standoff. The Allies' salvation lay in the Japanese not being prepared for the Watchtower landings and dismissing the Americans on Guadalcanal as raiders.

The Japanese did not follow through on the logic of their own policy. This is especially puzzling in the aftermath of Midway, since the critical losses there put the Imperial Navy on notice that its margin of superiority had much diminished. If Midway had been a failed decisive battle, afterward the need was a do-over to get it right. Yamamoto's formula of "running wild" required that. Anything else meant handing over a discreet portion of advantage every day. To a certain degree this fault can be traced to the peculiarity of Imperial General Headquarters—a joint command of independent fiefdoms, not really a common leadership at all. But the truth is also that the Imperial Navy was slow to appreciate that the Solomons could be its arena of decision, and loath to flood the theater with its forces. The Japanese could perfectly well have begun constructing an airfield at Munda in August 1942, rather than December, and that would have made a huge difference in, say, October.

Though bound by their Decisive Battle doctrine, oddly enough the Japanese did not follow that logic either. Once Imperial forces engaged at Guadalcanal, the Navy enmeshed itself in a succession of actions to control the sea and air off that place. The constant drain of losses among the light units, beset by the Cactus Air Force and SOPAC's scratch battle groups, induced Yamamoto and his fleet commanders to feed in their heavy ships in order to achieve results. This flew in the face of the husbanding presupposed by doctrine. Yet even the heavy units did not solve the Guadalcanal supply problem—in some measure due to effective Allied intelligence—and mounting frustration led to accepting ever greater risks. Mutual attrition the Imperial Navy could not afford. And this was even truer of air forces than of the surface fleet. Yet every day made it clearer that aerial superiority had become prerequisite to any other action.

Japan's second great opportunity came with the Battle of Santa Cruz and in the weeks thereafter. This time the Japanese had generated their forces and prepared for the fight. But they failed to prepare for exploitation at that critical moment. The fault was Yamamoto's. He appreciated the situation and hastened to throw forces at Cactus but still did not fully commit, sending home his best aircraft carrier and planning new offensives far in the future. The days lost afforded Halsey the chance to regroup, and the Japanese Army's inability to generate offensive traction on Guadalcanal completed the failure.

While Allied intelligence—Ultra especially—contributed every day to the success of SOPAC operations, arguably it rendered its greatest service in the five weeks or so from Santa Cruz to Tassafaronga. During that interval Halsey's legions stood on a knife's edge. Cactus might yet have been isolated—as Rabaul would be later. Halsey's inferior surface forces could have been swept from the sea, and his single, weakened aircraft carrier overwhelmed from the sky. Intel enabled Halsey to block the enemy. That the Halsey fleet did not always succeed—Tassafaronga being a notable calamity—is no reflection on the pillars' performance.

Yamamoto's error in planning for the future rather than acting in the moment stood revealed before the end of the year, when the Japanese on Guadalcanal had become so starved they were incapable of offensive action in any event, and by which time Allied naval forces had begun to grow powerful. Careful Japanese offensive plans had to be scrapped in favor of ones to save the men on Starvation Island. By then major Japanese air operations yielded small effects. The attrition of Japanese air, in turn, made ground and naval sallies increasingly ineffective. Halsey's South Pacific command first inched up The Slot, then advanced at an accelerating pace.

Allied intelligence still furnished key information—its failure to detect the Japanese evacuation from Guadalcanal at least balanced, if not eclipsed, by the Ultra breakthrough on the Yamamoto ambush—but as SOPAC's raw power grew, the value of secret information diminished. Intelligence continued to multiply force but by a lesser factor—although it had a last great contribution still to make: the secret knowledge that led to the slaughter of the Imperial Navy's heavy ships at Rabaul.

The logic of the Japanese approach would be completely vitiated after Guadalcanal, when the focus turned from whittling down the adversary to force protection. The decisive battle doctrine had prevailed. Suddenly the Japanese rarely committed big ships—never their battleships—and sent carrier air groups to fly from land bases, never their flattops. The Imperial Navy's light forces, already addled by virtual attrition, were left unsupported against an increasingly capable and technologically sophisticated SOPAC fleet. So deplorable did the situation become that a Rabaul staff officer publicly remonstrated with his superiors for the high command's attitude. Forty Imperial Navy destroyers were lost in the Solomons campaign, more than a third of its prewar strength. New construction did not make good those losses. The Americans (in all theaters) also had forty destroyers sunk to the end of 1943—but added two hundred. The Japanese fleet so carefully husbanded for decisive battle lacked escort protection when it did emerge.

When Admiral Koga finally sent in the heavy ships, they suffered a Pearl

Harbor in reverse. Soon after that Fortress Rabaul itself became powerless against the Allied aerial armada. From Pearl Harbor to Rabaul the war had gone full circle in just under two years. The rapidity with which the Solomons transformed from arena to backwater is a measure of Allied triumph and Japanese failure. There would be no Japanese dictation of terms at the White House. Instead there would be a Japanese surrender in Tokyo Bay.

ENDNOTES

PROLOGUE

"We realize our own fault": (p. 2) Ugaki Diary, June 10, 1942, p. 162. **"I am the only one who must apologize"**: (p. 3): Fuchida and Okumiya, *Midway*, quoted p. 188. **"This present setback"**: (p. 3): Ugaki Diary, op. cit. **"America's Enemy no. 2"**: (p. 7): *Harper's Magazine*, April 1942. **"What we need . . . is numbers"**: (p. 8) Ugaki Diary, June 21, 1942, p. 166. **"Small success"**: (p. 9) Ugaki Diary, June 30, 1942, p. 167. **"The Japanese Navy still had"**: (p. 10) Fuchida and Okumiya, *Midway*, p. 186.

1. ALL ALONG THE WATCHTOWER

"If ever a sledgehammer": (p. 22): Fuchida and Okumiya, *Midway*, p. 46. **"To invade strategic points"**: (p. 24): Navy General Staff Directive No. 47, January 29, 1942, Headquarters, Far East Command, Military History Section, *Imperial General Headquarters Navy Directives*, p. 20; U.S. Navy Microfilm J-27 (hereafter cited as IGHQ Directives). **"Our biggest loss"**: (p. 25): Robert J. Cressman, "Carrier Strike Through Mountain Passage," *World War II* Magazine, December 1986, quoted p. 41. **"The farthest advanced base"**: (p. 30): 8th Base Force Secret Order No. 1, April 28, 1942. Captured document translated and disseminated by the Combat Intelligence Center, Pacific Fleet, October 5, 1942 (SRH-278, War Diary, Combat Intelligence Center, Pacific Fleet, 1942, pp. 56–57. NARA: RG-457). **"The tea in this cup"**: (p. 31): John Toland, *The Rising Sun*, quoted p. 346. **Baird is truly scathing:** (pp. 37–39): These reminiscences can be found in "The Pacific War Through the Eyes of Forrest R. 'Tex' Baird," *Cryptolog*, v. 10, no. 2, Winter 1989, pp. 4–18. Historian John R. Lundstrom, who has mounted the broadest defense of Admiral Fletcher (*Black Shoe Carrier Admiral: Frank Jack Fletcher at Coral Sea, Midway, and Guadalcanal.* Annapolis: Naval Institute Press, 2006), completely fails to take Baird's recollections into account. **"This enemy employed a huge force"**: (p. 41): Ugaki Diary, August 7, 1942, p. 177. **"Exercise strategic command"**: (p. 52): George C. Dyer, *The Amphibians Came to Conquer: The Story of Admiral Richmond Kelly Turner.* Washington: Government Printing Office, 1971, v. I, quoted p. 303. **"Forces of the**

United States Pacific Fleet": (p. 54): CINCPAC Communiqué No. 6, August 8, 1942. USN Communiqués Nos. 1–300, p. 73.

2. UNDER THE SOUTHERN CROSS

"[It] is evident that [Allied] operational commanders were aware": (p. 56): Commo Intel in Pac War SRH. **"A real bull's eye"**: (p. 60): Kenney, *A General Reports*, p. 59. **"Someone told me that an air raid"**: (p. 61): Herbert L. Merillat, *Guadalcanal Remembered*, p. 57. **"INDICATIONS POINT STRONGLY"**: (p. 71): COMSOPAC-CTF61, 220910 Aug 1942. Nimitz Command Summary: Running Estimate and Summary (hereafter cited as CINCPAC Greybook), December 7, 1941–August 31, 1942 (declassified May 3, 1972), Reel 1, p. 808. Date-time groups ("220910") in U.S. message traffic are given in Greenwich Mean Time (GMT). The Solomons were twelve hours ahead of GMT. **"We were completely unable to see"**: (p. 76): Barrett Tillman, "The Carrier War Remembered," *Naval History* Magazine, October 2010, quoted p. 33. **"INTERCEPTS INDICATE"**: (p. 77): CINCPAC-COMINCH 242305 Aug 1942. CINCPAC Greybook, Reel 1, p. 809. **"A frightful blast"**: (pp. 77–78): Tanaka Raizo, "The Struggle for Guadalcanal," in David C. Evans, ed., *The Japanese Navy*, p. 168. **"Like a broken record"**: (p. 87): Harold L. Buell, *Dauntless Helldivers*, p. 138. **"At this rate we can whip ourselves"**: (p. 88): Samuel B. Griffith, II, *The Battle for Guadalcanal*, quoted p. 136. **"The ridge you insist on putting your new CP behind"**: (p. 95): Vandegrift, *Once a Marine*, quoted p. 151. **"Thinner than Gandhi himself" et seq**: (pp. 100–1): Agawa Hiroyuki, *The Reluctant Admiral*, quoted p. 328. Agawa (and Tsuji in the original) dates this on September 24, but it is clear from Ugaki's diary that this meeting took place four days later.

3. A CRIMSON TIDE

"I liked Ghormley": (p. 103): George Kenney, *General Kenney Reports*, p. 116. **"Will hold what they have"**: (p. 104): *Time*, October 26, 1942, quoted p. 30. **"This is the decisive battle"**: (p. 106): Morison, *Struggle for Guadalcanal*, quoted p. 143. **"The operation to surround and recapture Guadalcanal"**: (p. 106): Kenneth Friedman, *Morning of the Rising Sun*, quoted p. 243. **"For the past six or seven weeks" et seq**: (p. 110): CINCPAC, "Estimate of Enemy Capabilities, October 1, 1942 (declassified August 12, 1976). CINCPAC Greybook, Reel 1, p. 1072. **"The impression is gained that the enemy"**: (p. 111): CINCPAC Fleet Intelligence Summary, October 10, 1942 (declassified July 11, 1985). NARA: Records of the National Security Agency (RG-457): SRMN-009, CINCPAC Fleet Intelligence Summaries, 22 June 1942–8 May 1943. [Hereafter the National Security Agency records will be cited only by their "SR" numbers.] **"What are we going to do"**: (p. 112): James B. Hornfischer, *Neptune's Inferno*, quoted p. 171. **"Where is the mighty power of the Imperial Navy"**: (p. 115): Morison, *Struggle for Guadalcanal*, quoted p. 143. **"There's a million of 'em" et seq**: (p. 116): C. Raymond Calhoun, *Tin Can Sailor*, quoted p. 63. **"All at once the murmuring night exploded"**: (p. 119): Nikolai Stevenson, "Four Months on the Front Line," *American Heritage*, October–November 1985, p. 53. **"The shelter shook"**: (p. 119): Herbert Merillat, *Guadalcanal Remembered*, p. 175. **"It now appears that we are unable to control the sea" et seq**: (p. 123): CINCPAC Greybook, October 15, 1942; Reel 2, p. 1093. **"From all indications"**: (p. 126):

CINCPAC Greybook, October 22, 1942; Reel 2, p. 1100. **"Impatiently" et seq:** (p. 129): Hara Tameichi, *Japanese Destroyer Captain*, p. 124. **"STRIKING FORCE WILL PROCEED":** (p. 131): Hara, quoted pp. 126–27. **"THIS COMMAND HAS THE WHOLE RESPONSIBILITY:"** (p. 132): Ugaki Diary, October 24, 1942, p. 245. **"I admit I've objected to your suggestions":** (p. 136): John Toland, *The Rising Sun*, quoted p. 460. **"What you said before was true":** (p. 137): Ibid., quoted p. 461. **"The crescendo of the fighting ashore":** (p. 138): William F. Halsey with J. D. Bryan, *Admiral Halsey's Story*, p. 121. **"ATTACK—REPEAT—ATTACK":** (p. 138): Quoted, ibid. **"OPERATE FROM AND IN POSITIONS":** (p. 147): John Lundstrom, *The First Team and the Guadalcanal Campaign*, quoted p. 409. **"Our men have become quite proficient":** (p. 149): Okumiya and Horikoshi, *Zero*, quoted p. 193. **"Damn fool!":** (p. 151): Ugaki Diary, October 26, 1942, p. 250. **"Again? Am I to fly again today?":** (p. 152): Okumiya and Horikoshi, *Zero*, quoted p. 195. **"Apprehend and annihilate any powerful forces":** (p. 154): Basil Collier, *The War in the Far East, 1941–1945*, quoted p. 299. **"I got the impression":** (p. 155): Kondo Nobutake, "Some Opinions Concerning the War," in Goldstein and Dillon, eds., *The Pacific War Papers*, p. 314. **"Halfhearted advance" et seq:** (p. 155): Hara Tameichi, *Japanese Destroyer Captain*, p. 133. **"Largest part" et seq:** (p. 156): Imperial Navy, Destroyer Squadron 10 Records (Washington Document Center no. 160985), Naval Historical Center, Records of the Japanese Navy and Related Translations, box 37, folder: "WDC 160875." **"The Combined Fleet is at present striking heavy blows":** (p. 157): Imperial Rescript of October 29, 1942. Samuel E. Morison, *The Struggle for Guadalcanal*, quoted p. 224.

4. EMPIRE IN THE BALANCE

"Japanese Fleet Quits Solomons": (p. 160): *New York Times*, October 31, 1942. **"Naval quarters" et seq:** (p. 160): *New York Times*, October 29, 1942. **"GROUND SITUATION AT CACTUS CAN BE TURNED IN OUR FAVOR":** (p. 161): CINCPAC-COMSOPAC Dispatch 282225, October 1942. CINCPAC Greybook, Pt. 2, p. 965. **"On a grand scale":** (p. 166): CINCPAC Greybook, November 8, 1942, Pt. 2, p. 1158. **"All-out attempt upon Guadalcanal soon":** (p. 166): CINCPAC Fleet Intelligence Summary, November 9, 1942. SRMN-009, "CINCPAC Fleet Intelligence Summaries, 22 June 1942–8 May 1943" (declassified July 7, 1985), p. 178. **"ULTRA. INDICATIONS THAT MAJOR OPERATION":** (p. 167): CINCPAC-SOPAC et al., 092107, November 1942; CINCPAC Greybook Pt. 2, pp. 902–3. **"What is the range and bearing?" et seq:** (p. 175): Hara Tameichi, *Japanese Destroyer Captain*, quoted p. 140. **"Pandemonium":** (p. 176): Ibid., p. 141. **"Cease firing, own ships!" et seq:** (p. 177): James Hornfischer, *Neptune's Inferno*, quoted pp. 288, 291. **"We've got the bastards":** (p. 183): Halsey and Bryan, *Admiral Halsey's Story*, quoted p. 130. **"THIS FORCE TO OPERATE":** (p. 184): Ivan Musicant, *Battleship at War*, quoted p. 114. **"The sudden appearance of enemy battleships":** (p. 192): Kondo Nobutake, "Some Opinions Concerning the War," in Goldstein and Dillon, eds., *The Pacific War Papers*, p. 314. **"GUADALCANAL ATTACK FORCE":** (p. 193): Ugaki Diary, November 14, 1942, quoted p. 271. **"On Nov. 14, while escorting our transport fleet":** (p. 194–95): Imperial Headquarters announcement, November 18, 1942; *New York Times*, November 19, 1942, p. 2. **"[A] continuance of that night engagement":** (p. 195): Kondo Nobutake in Goldstein and Dillon, eds., *The Pacific War Papers*, p. 316. **"It is now definite":** (p. 199): CINCPAC War Diary, November

15, 1942 (Nov. 16 in the South Pacific). CINCPAC Greybook, Pt. 2, p. 1168. **"ONCE AGAIN RADIO INTELLIGENCE HAS ENABLED"**: (p. 200): CINCPAC-COMSOPAC et al., 170139 Nov 42. NARA: RG-457, NSA Records, SRH-306 "Exploits and Commendations, World War II" (declassified July 18, 1984), p. 7. **"Our Army troops . . . are starving"**: (p. 201): Orita Zenji with Joseph D. Harrington, *I-Boat Captain*, quoted p. 138. **"It was an error on my part"**: (p. 206): Hara Tameichi, *Japanese Destroyer Captain*, quoted p. 165. **"The time for changing the future policy"**: (p. 210): Ugaki Diary, December 8, 1942; op. cit., p. 301. **"To withdraw from Guadalcanal,"** et seq: (p. 211): Colonel Sanada Joichiro Interrogation (WDC 62081). NARA: Franklin D. Roosevelt Library, John Toland Papers, box 3, folder: "Guadalcanal." **"During the period from about the latter part of January"**: (p. 212): IGHQ Navy Directive No. 184, January 4, 1943. IGHQ Directives, p. 80. **"OUR COMMON OBJECTIVE IS RABAUL"**: (pp. 213–14): COMSOPAC-COMSOWESPAC, 280145 Nov 42. CINCPAC Greybook, Pt. 2, p. 1001.

5. INCHING FOR GROUND

"It's deplorable indeed": (p. 218): Ugaki Diary, December 28, 1942, p. 314. **"A major action . . . is expected soon"**: (p. 226): CINCPAC Fleet Intelligence Summary, January 31, 1943. NARA: RG-457, SRMN-009 (the fleet summaries quoted below are also from this source). **"The major operation predicted yesterday"**: (p. 226): CINCPAC Fleet Intelligence Summary, February 1, 1943. **"INDICATIONS ARE THAT JAP OFFENSIVE"**: (p. 229): COMINCH Dispatch 012330 February 1943. NARA: RG-457, SRMN-044. **"ARE THERE ANY INDICATIONS"**: (p. 230): COMINCH Dispatch 062149, February 6, 1943, Ibid. **"AS YET NOTHING"**: (p. 230): COMSOPAC Dispatch 080931, February 7, 1943. Ibid. **"The fake message which helped"**: (p. 231): Ito Haruki 1958 Interview. Naval Historical Center, Morison Papers, box 26. **"The return of the Advance Force to Truk"**: (p. 231): CINCPAC Fleet Intelligence Summary, February 9, 1943. **"'TOKYO EXPRESS' NO LONGER HAS TERMINUS ON GUADALCANAL"**: (p. 231): Message, Patch–Halsey, February 9, 1943. Morison, *The Struggle for Guadalcanal*, quoted p. 371. **"The end was as abrupt as the beginning"**: (pp. 231–32): Robert Sherrod, *History of Marine Corps Aviation in World War II*, quoted p. 127. **"It was very useful to have"**: (p. 234): Prados, *Combined Fleet Decoded*, quoted p. 401. **"Became the victim"**: (p. 238): W. J. Holmes, *Double-Edged Secrets*, p. 116. **"It looked like the 4th of July"** et seq: (pp. 242–43): James Fahey, *Pacific War Diary*, pp. 36–37. **"They made glaring tactical mistakes"**: (pp. 247–48): Office of Naval Intelligence (Op-16-FE), "Characteristics and Quality of Japanese Naval Pilots," October 25, 1943. NARA: RG-38, Naval Operations: ONI Reports, box 2, folder: "1943 ONI F-14 Serials." **"We'd go in individually"** et seq: (p. 248): Eric Bergerud, *Fire in the Sky*, quoted p. 541. **"Display their all-out joint might"**: (p. 250): NGS Directive No. 184, January 4, 1943. IGHQ Directives, p. 82. **"Enemy Fleets in advance bases"**: (p. 257): NGS Directive No. 206, March 25, 1943. IGHQ Directives, p. 104.

6. WAR OF ATTRITION

"There will be no hope": (p. 260): Ugaki Diary, April 3, 1943, p. 320. **"More than once this lack of experience"** (p. 261): Okumiya Masatake and Horikoshi Jiro,

Zero, p. 175. **"Increased air activity"** (p. 262): CINCPAC Fleet Intelligence Summary, April 4, 1943. NARA: RG-457, SRMN-009, p. 343. **"Large air action by land-based planes":** (p. 262): CINCPAC Fleet Intelligence Summary, April 6, 1943. Ibid., p. 345. **"There's millions of 'em":** (p. 263): *Washington Post*, January 23, 2009, quoted p. B9. **"A good stimulus":** (p. 267): Bruce Gamble, *Fortress Rabaul*, quoted p. 327. **"The meeting concluded":** (p. 268): Okumiya and Horikoshi, *Zero*, p. 176. **"We've hit the jackpot":** (p. 270): Roger Pineau, "The Death of Admiral Yamamoto," *Naval Intelligence Professionals Quarterly*, October 1994, quoted p. 4. **"I personally did the whole thing"** et seq: (p. 270): John Prados, *Combined Fleet Decoded*, quoted p. 459. **"An attempt will be made to intercept":** (p. 271): CINCPAC War Diary, April 16, 1943. CINCPAC Greybook, Pt. 2, p. 1510. **"Hold on, Kelly":** (p. 274): Halsey and Bryan, *Admiral Halsey's Story*, quoted p. 157. **"No officers were evident along our route"** et seq: (p. 276): Hara Tameichi with Fred Saito and Roger Pineau, *Japanese Destroyer Captain*, p. 176. **"A number of Lightning fighters":** (p. 278): Navy Department Communiqué No. 348, April 18, 1943. Department of the Navy, *Navy Department Communiqués 301 to 600, March 6, 1943 to May 24, 1945.* United States Navy: Office of Public Information, 1945, p. 17. **"In a race of unknown men":** (p. 281): *Time* magazine, November 8, 1943, p. 30. **"No matter how many times the enemy shall advance":** (p. 283): Address No. 4 to the Combined Fleets, May 23, 1943 (JICPOA Item no. 4986). United States Congress, Joint Committee to Investigate the Pearl Harbor Attack, *Report: Congressional Investigation Pearl Harbor Attack.* Washington: Government Printing Office, 1946, Pt. 6, p. 612. **"The information created a tumult":** (p. 286): Hanami Kohei, "The Man I Might Have Killed Was Kennedy," *Yomiuri Daily*, November 2, 1960. **"Once more the setup of Tassafaronga":** (p. 290): Morison, *Breaking the Bismarcks Barrier*, p. 181. **"While night fighting had long been regarded":** (p. 292): Hanami Kohei, op cit. **"The air units and surface units will cooperate"** et seq: (pp. 296–97): Southeast Area Force Operation Order No. 10, July 18, 1943. Naval Historical Center: Records of the Japanese Navy and Related Documents, SOPAC Translations, box 3, item no. 730. **"We had three alternatives":** (p. 299): quoted in "Japanese Captain Was in Ship That Sank P.T. 109," *Evening Post* (Sydney), August 1, 1963. **"Unprecedented"** et seq: (p. 300): Yamashiro Satsumori, "Collision with American *PT-109* Boat," *Suiko*, September 1960 (publication of the *Suikokai* Society, English translation provided to John F. Kennedy). **Japanese dispute over *PT-109*:** (p. 300–1): This discussion is based upon letters to President Kennedy from the Japanese participants, press clippings, and other material contained in the files "PT-109 Correspondence—Japanese," and "PT-109 Correspondence—Robert Donovan" in box 132 of John F. Kennedy's Papers (Personal Papers, Personal Secretary's Files) at the Kennedy Library. **"Isn't there someplace where we can strike":** (p. 302): Herbert P. Bix, *Hirohito and the Making of Modern Japan.* New York: HarperCollins, 2000, quoted p. 466. **"Undoubtedly reliable"** et seq: (p. 305): ONI, "Japanese Intelligence Activities in South and Southwest Pacific Areas," February 9, 1944 (declassified May 3, 1972). NARA: RG-38, ONI Series, box 8, folder: "Intelligence Organs." **"Fought bravely, then died of starvation"** et seq: (p. 308): Bix, *Hirohito and the Making of Modern Japan*, quoted pp. 466–67. **"You have just noted the brief life expectancy of a destroyer"** et seq: (p. 312): Hara Tameichi, *Japanese Destroyer Captain*, quoted p. 226.

7. FORTRESS RABAUL

"**Rabaul was the hardest target**": (p. 317): Eric Bergerud, *Fire in the Sky*, quoted p. 641. "**The toughest, hardest-fought engagement**": (p. 317): George Kenney, *General Kenney Reports*, p. 319. "**You would just grit your teeth**" et seq: (p. 317): Bergerud, op cit., pp. 650, 648, 649. "**Rabaul was the keystone**": (p. 317): Frank E. Walton, *Once They Were Eagles*, p. 89. "**Prior to the beginning of 1943**": (p. 319): Henry Sakaida, *Aces of the Rising Sun, 1937–1945*, quoted p. 107. "**What appeared to be a short directive**": (p. 322): COMINCH Ultra Summary, October 29, 1943. NARA: RG-457: COMINCH Summaries of Radio Intelligence, SRNS no. 0564. "**You sense a funny feeling**": (p. 329): James Fahey, *Pacific War Diary*, p. 71. "**They say the maneuvers**": (p. 330): Ibid., p. 72. "**Graveyard of the fighter pilots**": (p. 333): Sakaida, *Aces of the Rising Sun*, p. 115. "**Fate determines at birth**" et seq: (p. 333): Ibid., p. 107. "**P-38s at low altitude**": (p. 333): Ibid. "**The enemy planes practically flew into our gunfire**": (p. 333): Hara, *Japanese Destroyer Captain*, p. 241. "**Never in the long history of warfare**": (p. 334): Kenney, *General Kenney Reports*, p. 321. "**Never, indeed, have such exorbitant claims been made**": (p. 334): Samuel Eliot Morison, *Breaking the Bismarcks Barrier*, p. 288. "**The most desperate emergency**": (p. 335): William F. Halsey, *Admiral Halsey's Story*, pp. 180-81. "**Information that a force of cruisers**": (p. 335): CINCPAC War Diary, November 2, 1943. CINCPAC Greybook, pt. 2, p. 1679. "**IN CIRCUMSTANCES BELIEVE REINFORCEMENTS BEING FURNISHED**": (p. 335): CINCPAC-COMSOPAC 030915 September 43. CINCPAC Greybook, p. 1823. "**Usually . . . consistent attacks**" and "**AS IN THE PAST WE WILL HURT JAPS**": (p. 336): COMSOPAC-CINCPAC 040446 September 43. Ibid. "**Lay Rabaul flat**": (p. 340): Halsey, *Admiral Halsey's Story*, p. 183. "**My maximum effort would be pretty low**": (pp. 341–42): Kenney, *General Kenney Reports*, p. 322. "**IT IS REAL MUSIC TO ME**": (p. 343): Morison, *Breaking the Bismarcks Barrier*, quoted pp. 329–30. "**WITH VIEW EARLIEST POSSIBLE STRIKES**": (p. 343): CINCPAC-COMSOPAC 052111 September 1943. CINCPAC Greybook, Pt. 2, p. 1824.

BIBLIOGRAPHY

OFFICIAL SOURCES

Joint Chiefs of Staff

Grace Peterson Hayes, *The History of the Joint Chiefs of Staff in World War II: The War Against Japan*. Annapolis: Naval Institute, 1982.

National Security Agency

Sharon A. Maneki, *The Quiet Heroes of the Southwest Pacific Theater: An Oral History of the Women of CBB and FRUMEL*. United States Cryptologic History, Series IV, World War II, volume 7, CCH-S54-96-01. NSA, 1996.

United States Air Force

Maurer Maurer, ed., *Combat Squadrons of the Air Force, World War II*. Department of the Air Force, 1969.

United States Army

Army in World War II Series: The War in the Pacific
John Miller, Jr., *CARTWHEEL: The Reduction of Rabaul*. Center of Military History, 1959.
Army in World War II Series: The Technical Services
Karl C. Dod, *The Corps of Engineers: The War Against Japan*. Center of Military History, 1987.

United States Navy

Communiqués, 1–300. Office of Public Information, United States Navy, 1945.
Communiqués, 301–600. Office of Public Information, United States Navy, 1945.

United States Naval Operations in World War II

(All volumes are by Samuel Eliot Morison and were published by Little, Brown on the dates indicated.)

v. 4: *Coral Sea, Midway, and Submarine Actions, May 1942–August 1942* (1949).

v. 5: *The Struggle for Guadalcanal, August 1942–February 1943* (1949).

v. 6: *Breaking the Bismarcks Barrier, 22 July 1942–1 May 1944* (1954).

v. 14: *Victory in the Pacific, 1945* (1990).

United States Strategic Bombing Survey

Campaigns of the Pacific War

Interrogations of Japanese Officers

OTHER SOURCES

John A. Adams, *If Mahan Ran the Great Pacific War: An Analysis of World War II Naval Strategy.* Bloomington: Indiana University Press, 2008.

Agawa Hiroyuki, *The Reluctant Admiral: Yamamoto and the Imperial Navy* (trans. John Bester). Tokyo: Kodansha, 1982.

Allison Ind, *Allied Intelligence Bureau: Our Secret Weapon in the War against Japan.* New York: Modern Literary Editions, 1958.

Henry H. ("Hap") Arnold, *Global Mission.* New York: Harper & Row, 1949.

Daniel E. Barbey, *MacArthur's Amphibious Navy: Seventh Fleet Amphibious Force Operations, 1943–1945.* Annapolis: Naval Institute, 1969.

James H. Belote and William M. Belote, *Titans of the Seas: The Development and Operations of Japanese and American Carrier Task Forces during World War II.* New York: Harper & Row, 1975.

David Bergamini, *Japan's Imperial Conspiracy.* New York: Pocket Books, 1972.

Eric M. Bergerud, *Fire in the Sky: The Air War in the South Pacific.* Boulder (CO): Westview, 2000.

———, *Touched by Fire: The Land War in the South Pacific.* New York: Viking, 1996.

Herbert P. Bix, *Hirohito and the Making of Modern Japan.* New York: HarperCollins, 2000.

Clay Blair Jr., *Silent Victory: The U.S. Submarine War against Japan.* New York: Lippincott, 1975.

Carl Boyd and Yoshida Akihiko, *The Japanese Submarine Force and World War II.* Annapolis: Naval Institute, 1995.

Gregory "Pappy" Boyington, *Baa Baa Black Sheep.* New York: Bantam, 1977.

Max Brand, *Fighter Squadron at Guadalcanal.* New York: Pocket Books, 1997.

William Breuer, *Devil Boats: The PT War against Japan.* New York: Jove, 1988.

Harold L. Buell, *Dauntless Helldivers: A Dive-Bomber Pilot's Epic Story of the Carrier Battles.* New York: Dell, 1991.

C. Raymond Calhoun, *Tin Can Sailor: Life aboard the USS Sterett, 1939–1945.* Annapolis: Naval Institute, 2000.

Craig Collie and Marutani Hajime, *The Path of Infinite Sorrow: The Japanese on the Kokoda Track*. Australia: Allen & Unwin, 2009.

Basil Collier, *The War in the Far East, 1941–1945: A Military History*. New York: William Morrow, 1969.

Russell S. Crenshaw, *The Battle of Tassafaronga*. Annapolis: Naval Institute, 2010.

———, *South Pacific Destroyer: The Battle for the Solomons from Savo Island to Vella Gulf*. Annapolis: Naval Institute, 2009.

Burke Davis, *Get Yamamoto!* New York: Random House, 1969.

———, *Marine! The Life of Chesty Puller*. New York: Bantam, 1964.

Peter J. Edwards, *The Rise and Fall of the Japanese Imperial Naval Air Service*. Barnsley, UK: Pen & Sword, 2010.

David C. Evans and Mark R. Peattie, *Kaigun: Strategy, Tactics and Technology in the Imperial Japanese Navy, 1887–1941*. Annapolis: Naval Institute, 1997.

David C. Evans, ed., *The Japanese Navy in World War II: In the Words of Former Japanese Naval Officers* (2nd ed.). Annapolis: Naval Institute, 1986.

James J. Fahey, *Pacific War Diary, 1942–1945*. New York: Avon, 1963.

Edward I. Farley, *PT Patrol: Wartime Adventures in the Pacific and the Story of PTs in World War II*. New York: Popular Library, 1962.

Eric A. Feldt, *The Coast Watchers*. New York: Ballantine, 1966.

A. B. Feuer, *Coast Watching in World War II: Operations against the Japanese on the Solomon Islands, 1941–43*. Mechanicsburg, PA: Stackpole, 2006.

René J. Francillon, *Japanese Aircraft of the Pacific War*. New York: Funk & Wagnalls, 1974.

Richard B. Frank, *Guadalcanal: The Definitive Account of a Landmark Battle*. New York: Penguin, 1992.

Kenneth L. Friedman, *Morning of the Rising Sun: The Heroic Story of the Battles for Guadalcanal*. Privately Printed, 2007.

Fuchida Mitsuo and Okumiya Masatake, *Midway: The Battle That Doomed Japan*. New York: Ballantine, 1958.

Bruce Gamble, *Fortress Rabaul: The Battle for the Southwest Pacific, January 1942–April 1943*. St. Paul, MN: Zenith, 2010.

Carroll V. Glines, *Attack on Yamamoto*. Altgen, PA: Schiffer, 1993.

Donald M. Goldstein and Katharine V. Dillon, eds., *Fading Victory: The Diary of Admiral Matome Ugaki, 1941–1945* (trans. Chihaya Masatake). Annapolis: Naval Institute, 2008.

Samuel B. Griffith II, *The Battle for Guadalcanal*. New York: Ballantine, 1966.

R. Cargill Hall, *Lightning over Bougainville: The Yamamoto Mission Reconsidered*. Washington, DC: Smithsonian Press, 1991.

William F. Halsey with J. D. Bryan III, *Admiral Halsey's Story*. New York: McGraw-Hill, 1947.

Eric Hammel, *Carrier Strike: The Battle of the Santa Cruz Islands, October 1942*. St. Paul, MN: Zenith, 2004.

———, *Guadalcanal: Starvation Island*. New York: ibooks, 2004.

Hara Tameichi with Fred Saito and Roger Pineau, *Japanese Destroyer Captain*. New York: Ballantine, 1961.

Hata Ikuhito and Izawa Yasuho, *Japanese Naval Aces and Fighter Units of World War II.* Annapolis: Naval Institute, 1989.

Hattori Takushiro, *The Complete History of the Greater East Asia War* (U.S. Army translation), published in Japan by Hara Shobo, 1966.

William N. Hess, *Pacific Sweep.* New York: Zebra, 1978.

F. H. Hinsley and Alan Stripp, *Codebreakers: The Inside Story of Bletchley Park.* New York: Oxford University Press, 1994.

W. J. Holmes, *Double-Edged Secrets: U.S. Naval Intelligence Operations in the Pacific during World War II.* Annapolis: Naval Institute, 1979.

James D. Hornfischer, *Neptune's Inferno: The U.S. Navy at Guadalcanal.* New York: Bantam, 2011.

Edwin P. Hoyt, *Blue Skies and Blood: The Battle of the Coral Sea.* New York: Pinnacle, 1976.

————, *The Glory of the Solomons.* New York: Stein & Day, 1984.

————, *Guadalcanal.* New York: Jove, 1982.

————, *Japan's War: The Great Pacific Conflict 1853–1952.* New York: McGraw-Hill, 1986.

————, *The Marine Raiders.* New York: Pocket Books, 1989.

————, *Raider Battalion.* Los Angeles: Pinnacle, 1980.

————, *Submarines at War: The History of the American Silent Service.* New York: Stein & Day, 1984.

————, *Yamamoto: The Man Who Planned Pearl Harbor.* New York: Warner, 1990.

Frazier Hunt, *The Untold Story of Douglas MacArthur.* New York: Signet, 1964.

Ito Masanori with Roger Pineau, *The End of the Imperial Japanese Navy* (trans. Andrew Y. Kuroda and Roger Pineau). New York: Jove, 1984.

————, *The Japanese Navy in World War II.* Annapolis: Naval Institute, 1969.

George C. Kenney, *General Kenney Reports: A Personal History of the Pacific War.* New York: Duell, Sloan and Pearce, 1949.

Ken Kotani, *Japanese Intelligence in World War II* (trans. Kotani Chiharu). Botley, UK: Osprey, 2009.

Eric Lacroix and Linton Wells II, *Japanese Cruisers of the Pacific War.* Annapolis: Naval Institute, 1997.

Edwin T. Layton with Roger Pineau and John Costello, *"And I Was There": Pearl Harbor and Midway—Breaking the Secrets.* New York: Morrow, 1985.

Robert Leckie, *Challenge for the Pacific, Guadalcanal: Turning Point of the War.* New York: Bantam, 2010.

————, *Strong Men Armed: The United States Marines against Japan.* New York: Bantam, 1963.

Charles A. Lockwood, *Sink 'Em All: Submarine Warfare in the Pacific.* New York: Bantam, 1984.

————, and Hans C. Adamson, *Hellcats of the Sea.* New York: Bantam, 1988.

Walter Lord, *Lonely Vigil: Coastwatchers of the Solomons.* New York: Viking, 1977.

Bruce Loxton with Chris Coulthard-Clark, *The Shame of Savo: Anatomy of a Naval Disaster.* Annapolis: Naval Institute, 1994.

John B. Lundstrom, *Black Shoe Carrier Admiral: Frank Jack Fletcher at Coral Sea, Midway, and Guadalcanal.* Annapolis: Naval Institute, 2006.

————, *The First South Pacific Campaign: Pacific Fleet Strategy, December 1941–June 1942.* Annapolis: Naval Institute, 1976.

————, *The First Team and the Guadalcanal Campaign: Naval Fighter Combat from August to November 1942.* Annapolis: Naval Institute, 1994.

Douglas A. MacArthur, *Reminiscences.* Greenwich, CT: Fawcett, 1965.

Lex MacCaulay, *Into the Dragon's Jaws: The Fifth Air Force over Rabaul.* Mesa, AZ: Champlin Fighter Museum, 1986.

Paul Manning, *Hirohito: The War Years.* New York: Bantam, 1989.

Lida Mayo, *Bloody Buna.* Chicago: Playboy Press, 1979.

William L. McGee with Sandra McGee, *Amphibious Operations in the South Pacific during World War II* (3 v.). Tiburon, CA: BMC Publishing, 2002–2009.

Herbert C. Merillat, *Guadalcanal Remembered.* New York: Avon, 1990.

————, *The Island: A History of the First Marine Division on Guadalcanal.* New York: Houghton Mifflin, 1944.

Thomas G. Miller Jr., *The Cactus Air Force.* New York: Bantam, 1981.

John Monks Jr., *A Ribbon and a Star: The Third Marines at Bougainville.* New York: Pyramid, 1966.

Samuel Eliot Morison, *The Two-Ocean War: A Short History of the United States Navy in World War II.* New York: Ballantine, 1972.

Mack Morriss (ed. Ronnie Day), *South Pacific Diary, 1942–1943.* Lexington: University Press of Kentucky, 1996.

Wayman C. Mullins, ed., *1942: "Issue in Doubt": Symposium on the War in the Pacific by the Admiral Nimitz Foundation.* Austin, TX: Eakin Press, 1994.

Kenneth Munson, *Aircraft of World War II.* New York: Doubleday, 1968.

Ivan Musicant, *Battleship at War: The Epic Story of the USS* Washington. New York: Harcourt Brace Jovanovich, 1986.

Richard F. Newcomb, *Savo: The Incredible Naval Debacle off Guadalcanal.* New York: Bantam, 1963.

Nihon Kaigun Web site.

Okumiya Masatake and Horikoshi Jiro with Martin Caidin, *Zero: The Story of Japan's Air War in the Pacific, 1941–45.* New York: Ballantine, 1957.

Michael K. Olson, *Tales from a Tin Can: The USS* Dale *from Pearl Harbor to Tokyo Bay.* Minneapolis, MN: Zenith, 2010.

Orita Zenji with Joseph D. Harrington, *I-Boat Captain.* Canoga Park, CA: Major, 1976.

Albert Palazzo, *The Australian Army: A History of Its Organization, 1901–2001.* Melbourne: Oxford University Press, 2001.

Michael Patterson, *The Secret War: The Inside Story of Code Makers and Code Breakers in World War II.* Cincinnati, OH: David & Charles, 2007.

Jack Pearl, *Admiral "Bull" Halsey.* Derby, CT: Monarch, 1962.

Mark R. Peattie, *Sunburst: The Rise of Japanese Naval Air Power, 1909–1941.* Annapolis: Naval Institute, 2001.

E. B. Potter, *Admiral Arleigh Burke: A Biography.* New York: Random House, 1990.

————, *Bull Halsey.* Annapolis: Naval Institute, 1985.

————, *Nimitz.* Annapolis: Naval Institute, 1976.

John Prados, *Combined Fleet Decoded: The Secret History of American Intelligence and the Japanese Navy in World War II*. New York: Random House, 1995.

Matthew K. Rodman, *A War of Their Own: Bombers over the Southwest Pacific*. Maxwell Air Force Base, AL: Air University, 2005.

Theodore Roscoe, *United States Destroyer Operations in World War II*. Annapolis: Naval Institute, 1953.

Sakai Saburo with Martin Caidin and Fred Saito, *Samurai!* New York: Bantam, 1978.

Henry Sakaida, *Aces of the Rising Sun, 1937–1945*. Botley, UK: Osprey, 2002.

———, *The Siege of Rabaul*. St. Paul, MN: Phalanx, 1996.

Alan Schom, *The Eagle and the Sun: The Japanese-American War, 1941–1943: Pearl Harbor through Guadalcanal*. New York: Norton, 2004.

Frederick C. Sherman, *Combat Command: American Aircraft Carriers in the Pacific War*. New York: Bantam, 1982.

Robert H. Sherrod, *History of Marine Corps Aviation in World War II*. Washington: Association of the United States Army, 1952.

Paul H. Silverstone, *U.S. Warships of World War II*. New York: Doubleday, 1968.

Michael Smith, *The Emperor's Codes: Breaking Japan's Secret Ciphers*. New York: Arcade, 2000.

Peter C. Smith, *Fist from the Sky: Japan's Dive-Bomber Ace of WWII*. Mechanicsburg, PA: Stackpole, 2005.

Stan Smith, *The Battle of Savo*. New York: McFadden-Bartell, 1962.

———, *The Destroyermen*. New York: Belmont, 1966.

———, *The Navy at Guadalcanal*. New York: Lancer, 1963.

Ronald H. Spector, *The Eagle Against the Sun: The American War with Japan*. New York: Vintage, 1985.

———, ed., *Listening to the Enemy: Key Documents on the Role of Communications Intelligence in the War with Japan*. Wilmington, DE: Scholarly Resources, 1988.

Edward P. Stafford, *The Big "E": The Story of the USS* Enterprise. New York: Ballantine, 1974.

Alan Stripp, *Codebreaker in the Far East*. London: Frank Cass, 1989.

Tagaya Osamu, *Imperial Japanese Naval Aviator, 1937–1945*. Botley, UK: Osprey, 2003.

John Toland, *The Rising Sun: The Decline and Fall of the Japanese Empire*. New York: Bantam, 1971.

Richard Tregaskis, *Guadalcanal Diary*. New York: Popular Library, 1959.

Alexander A. Vandegrift (as told to Robert B. Asprey), *Once a Marine: The Memoirs of General A. A. Vandegrift, United States Marine Corps*. New York: Ballantine, 1966.

Edward Van Der Rhoer, *Deadly Magic: A Personal Account of Communications Intelligence in World War II in the Pacific*. New York: McGraw-Hill, 1978.

A. J. Watts, *Japanese Warships of World War II*. New York: Doubleday, 1967.

Glen Williford, *Racing the Sunrise: Reinforcing America's Pacific Outposts, 1941–1942*. Annapolis: Naval Institute, 2010.

Charles A. Willoughby, *MacArthur, 1941–1951*. New York: McGraw-Hill, 1954.

John Winton, *ULTRA in the Pacific: How Breaking Japanese Codes and Ciphers Affected Naval Operations Against Japan, 1941–45*. Annapolis: Naval Institute, 1993.

AIRCRAFT OF THE SOLOMONS

JAPANESE			
Name/Designation	Speed (mph)	Range (statute miles)	Bomb Load or Armament
FIGHTERS			
Mitsubishi A5M4 (Claude)	273	746	2x 7.7mm MG
Mitsubishi A6M2 (Zero, Zeke)	332	1,160	2x 20mm cannon, 2x 7.7mm MG
Mitsubishi J2M (Jack)	371	1,180	2x 20mm cannon, 2x 7.7mm MG
Kawanishi N1K1-J (George)	363	1,500	2x 20mm cannon, 2x 7.7mm MG
Mitsubishi A7M (Sam)	357	NA	2x 20mm cannon, 2x 13.2mm MG
Nakajima J1N1 (Irving)	315	1,677	4x 20mm cannon
Nakajima Ki-27 (Nate)	286	389	2x 7.7mm MG
Nakajima Ki-43 (Oscar)	320	1,095	2x 12.7mm MG
FLOATPLANES			
Nakajima A6M2-N (Rufe)	270	1,107	2x 20mm cannon, 2x 7.7mm MG
Aichi E13A1 (Jake)	234	1,128	1x 7.7mm MG
Nakajima E8A1 (Dave)	184	560	3x 7.7mm MG
Mitsubishi F1M (Pete)	230	460	3x 7.7mm MG, 2x 66-lb bombs
Yokosuka E14Y (Glen)	153	548	3x 7.7mm, 2x 66-lb bombs (submarine-based aircraft)

MG: Machine gun
Bomber listings give ordnance loads only.

| Kawanishi H6K (Mavis) | 150 | 2,600 | 2 torpedoes or 2,200-lb bombs (patrol bomber) |
| Kawanishi H8K (Emily) | 290 | 4,400 | 2x 20mm cannon, 5x 7.7mm MG (patrol bomber) 2 torpedoes or 2,200-lb bombs |

LAND-BASED BOMBERS

Mitsubishi G3M2 (Nell)	216	2,722	1 torpedo or 1,760-lb bombs
Mitsubishi G4M2 (Betty)	272	3,765	1 torpedo or 2,200-lb bombs
Mitsubishi Ki-21 (Sally)	297	1,350	2,200-lb bombs
Nakajima Ki-49 (Helen)	306		

CARRIER- OR LAND-BASED DIVE- AND TORPEDO BOMBERS

Aichi D3A2 (Val)	266	730	816-lb bombs
Nakajima B5N2 (Kate)	235	608	1 torpedo or 1,760-lb bombs
Nakajima B6N2 (Jill)	289	909	1 torpedo or 6x 220-lb bombs
Yokosuka D4Y (Judy)	350	950	1,650-lb bombs

ALLIED

Name/Designation	Speed (mph)	Range (statute miles)	Bomb Load or Armament

FIGHTERS

Name/Designation	Speed (mph)	Range (statute miles)	Bomb Load or Armament
Bell P-39 (Airacobra)	385	675	1x 37mm cannon, 4x .50-cal. MG, 500-lb bombs
Curtiss P-40 (Warhawk)	350	760	6x .50-cal MG, 1,500-lb bombs
Grumman F-4F (Wildcat)	328	1,150	4x .50-cal. MG
Grumman F-6F (Hellcat)	376	1,090	6x .50-cal. MG
Lockheed P-38 (Lightning)	414	2,260	1x 20mm cannon, 4x .50-cal. MG
Chance-Vought F-4U (Corsair)	446	1,562	6x .50-cal MG, 2,000-lb bombs
Republic P-47 (Thunderbolt)	429	590	6 or 8x .50-cal. MG
North American P-51 (Mustang)	437	2,080	4 or 6x .50-cal. MG

MG: Machine gun
Bomber listings give ordnance loads only.

SEAPLANE			
Consolidated PBY (Catalina)	179	3,100	5x .50-cal. MG, 1 torpedo or 2x 500-lb bombs

LAND-BASED BOMBERS			
Douglas A-20 (Havoc)	339	1,025	4,000-lb bombs
North American B-25 (Mitchell)	275	1,275	4,000-lb bombs
Martin B-26 (Marauder)	283	1,100	4,000-lb bombs
Boeing B-17 (Flying Fortress)	300	1,850	17,600-lb bombs
Consolidated B-24 (Liberator)	300	3,100	5,000-lb bombs (12,800 at short range)

CARRIER- OR LAND-BASED DIVE-BOMBERS AND TORPEDO PLANES			
Douglas SBD (Dauntless)	252	1,115	1,000-lb bombs
Grumman TBF (Avenger)	271	1,020	1 torpedo or 2,000-lb bombs

MG: Machine gun
Bomber listings give ordnance loads only.

INDEX